Teach®
Yourself

Complete German

Paul Coggle
and Heiner Schenke

For UK order enquiries: please contact Bookpoint Ltd, 130 Milton Park, Abingdon, Oxon OX14 4SB. *Telephone:* +44 (0) 1235 827720. Fax: +44 (0) 1235 400454. Lines are open 09.00–17.00, Monday to Saturday, with a 24-hour message answering service. Details about our titles and how to order are available at www.teachyourself.com

For USA order enquiries: please contact McGraw-Hill Customer Services, PO Box 545, Blacklick, OH 43004-0545, USA. *Telephone:* 1-800-722-4726. Fax: 1-614-755-5645.

For Canada order enquiries: please contact McGraw-Hill Ryerson Ltd, 300 Water St, Whitby, Ontario L1N 9B6, Canada. *Telephone:* 905 430 5000. Fax: 905 430 5020.

Long renowned as the authoritative source for self-guided learning – with more than 50 million copies sold worldwide – the *Teach Yourself* series includes over 500 titles in the fields of languages, crafts, hobbies, business, computing and education.

British Library Cataloguing in Publication Data: a catalogue record for this title is available from the British Library.

Library of Congress Catalog Card Number: on file.

First published in UK 1998 as Teach Yourself German by Hodder Education, part of Hachette UK, 338 Euston Road, London NW1 3BH.

First published in US 1998 by The McGraw-Hill Companies, Inc.

This edition published 2010.

The *Teach Yourself* name is a registered trade mark of Hodder Headline.

Copyright © 1998, 2003, 2007, 2010 Paul Coggle and Heiner Schenke.

Advisory Editor: Paul Coggle, University of Kent at Canterbury.

Typeset by Julie Martin. Illustrated by Barking Dog Art, Sally Elford, Peter Lubach.

Printed in Dubai for Hodder Education, an Hachette UK Company, 338 Euston Road, London NW1 3BH.

The publisher has used its best endeavours to ensure that the URLs for external websites referred to in this book are correct and active at the time of going to press. However, the publisher and the author have no responsibility for the websites and can make no guarantee that a site will remain live or that the content will remain relevant, decent or appropriate.

Hachette UK's policy is to use papers that are natural, renewable and recyclable products and made from wood grown in sustainable forests. The logging and manufacturing processes are expected to conform to the environmental regulations of the country of origin.

Impression number 10 9 8 7 6 5

Year 2014 2013 2012 2011

Contents

vii *Meet the authors*

viii *Only got a minute?*

x *Only got five minutes?*

xiv *Only got ten minutes?*

xxi *Introduction*

3   **1**   **Mein Name ist …** *My name is …*
Saying who you are, greeting people and saying goodbye, asking people where they come from and where they live. Language points: *I* and *you*, word order.

17   **2**   **Mir geht's gut** *I'm fine*
Asking people how they are, saying how you are, saying which cities and countries people come from. Language points: verb endings.

31   **3**   **Wie schreibt man das?** *How do you write that?*
Counting from 0 to 100, spelling out names and words, talking about us and them. Language points: yes–no questions and plural verb forms.

45   **4**   **Sprechen Sie Deutsch?** *Do you speak German?*
Saying what languages you speak and asking others what they speak, saying whether you are working or studying, saying what nationality you are. Language points: formal and informal 'you'.

57   **5**   **In der Stadt** *In town*
Talking about places in towns and cities, counting from 101 upwards. Language points: gender and articles.

69   **6**   **Arbeit und Studium** *Work and study*
Asking people about their occupation and stating yours, asking people what they are studying and where. Language points: the verb **sein** *(to be)*, expressing 'for' or 'since'.

83   **7**   **Essen und Trinken** *Food and drink*
Asking the way and ordering food and drink. Language points: the accusative case, containers and their contents.

99   **8**   **Einkaufen und Bestellen** *Shopping and ordering*
Talking about going shopping, asking for and giving prices,

ordering food and drink in a restaurant, saying what you like eating and drinking. Language points: more plural forms of nouns and word order.

115 9 Freizeit *Leisure*
Saying what people are doing, talking about leisure pursuits and stating likes and dislikes. Language points: 'irregular' verb forms and using **gern**.

129 10 Die Uhrzeit *The time*
Telling the time and talking about daily routine. Language points: separable verbs and more on word order.

143 11 Was machen wir heute? *What are we doing today?*
Talking about what there is to do in a given town, making appointments, saying what you would like to do and what you have to do, and saying why you can't do things on the date suggested. Language points: modal verbs **können** and **müssen**, use of 'in' for focusing on position.

159 12 Eine Fahrkarte nach Heidelberg, bitte *A ticket to Heidelberg, please*
Buying railway tickets and reading timetables, saying how you travel to work or university, and asking how to get somewhere. Language points: dative case after prepositions.

175 13 Was hast du am Wochenende gemacht? *What did you do at the weekend?*
Talking about what happened at the weekend and about recent events, describing purchases. Language points: the present perfect tense and adjectival endings (1).

191 14 Wir sind ins Grüne gefahren *We went into the countryside*
More about recent events, and talking about past events. Language point: more on the present perfect tense.

207 15 Wohnen in Deutschland *Living in Germany*
Talking about different kinds of housing, rooms and about making comparisons. Language points: the comparative, possessive adjectives and more on the dative.

227 16 Welches Hotel nehmen wir? *Which hotel shall we take?*
Booking a hotel room, comparing different hotels and describing the location of buildings. Language points: the superlative and more on prepositions.

243 17 Ist Mode wichtig? *Is fashion important?*

Describing items of personal appearance and saying what clothes you like wearing. Language points: adjectival endings (2) and **etwas** + adjective.

259 18 Und was kann man ihnen schenken? *And what can we give them?*
Invitations and talking about giving things to people and asking for advice. Language points: indirect objects, various uses of the dative case and adjectival endings (3).

277 19 Gesundheit *Health*
Discussing health, naming parts of the body and aches and pains. Language points: modal verbs and **wenn** + a verb at the end of a clause.

295 20 Wetter und Urlaub *Weather and holidays*
Weather conditions and past holidays. Language points: revision of the perfect tense, prepositions and the simple past tense of modal verbs.

313 21 Telefonieren und die Geschäftswelt *Telephoning and the business world*
Making and answering phone calls, and saying what belongs to whom. Language points: revision of dative pronouns and uses of the genitive case.

331 22 Stellenangebote und Lebensläufe *Job adverts and CVs*
Job adverts and writing a CV. Language points: more on the simple past tense.

349 23 Geschichte und Allgemeinwissen *History and general knowledge*
Talking about German-speaking countries and historical events. Language points: subordinate clauses (with **dass**) and the passive.

369 *Key to the exercises*
409 *Listening comprehension transcripts*
430 *Glossary of grammatical terms*
436 *List of common irregular verbs*
438 *German–English vocabulary*
452 *English–German vocabulary*
465 *Taking it further*
467 *Index to grammar*
469 *Photo credits*

Meet the authors

So you are thinking of learning German? As the authors of **Complete German**, we are very keen to help you achieve your objectives. We are both enthusiastic and experienced teachers of German and we like to think we have produced an excellent course that has been tried, tested and recently updated.

Of course, different people learn in different ways and we have tried to take this fact into account by offering a variety of language activities. You will find a lot of listening, speaking, reading and writing practice, information on how the language works plus some facts about present-day German culture and society.

Those who like to know the ins and outs of the grammar will find what they want here, but those who just want to know enough to be able to meet their basic needs are also catered for. As long as you are up for a bit of work, complete the exercise materials, and put in some practice, you will make progress.

Whether you are an adult learner with no previous knowledge of German or someone who is a 'false beginner', we hope that you will feel we are taking you carefully through the essentials to the point where you can cope on your own.

The going will sometimes be tough, but with a bit of encouragement from us and perseverance from you, you will get there!

Good luck with learning German!

Paul Coggle and Heiner Schenke

Only got a minute?

The aim of this course is above all to help you interact with German-speaking people, both socially and in various practical situations, such as giving personal information, asking for directions, ordering food and drinks and shopping. These are just a few of the situations you will be able to handle once you have completed this course. You will also learn about the structures of the German language – about how the language works, so that you can make up your own sentences to express what you want to say in German.

German is spoken as a native language by approximately 105 million people. About a further 80 million people speak it as a second or foreign language. The standard language is called **Hochdeutsch** and this is the language taught in schools. But there are also many regional variants, especially in southern Germany, Austria and Switzerland.

Here are a few basic expressions, some of which you may already know: **Ja** *Yes*, **Nein** *No*, **Bitte** *Please*, **(Vielen) Dank** *Thank you (very much)*, **Bitte schön** *You´re welcome*, **Hallo!** *Hello!*, **Auf Wiedersehen!** *Goodbye!*, **Mein Name ist (Martina/Oliver)** *My name is (Martina/Oliver)*, **Herr** *Mr*, **Frau** *Mrs/Miss*. You will also find that many everyday German words are easy to recognise, such as **Haus** *house*, **Brot** *bread*, **Fleisch** *meat, flesh*, **Hund** *dog, hound*.

5 Only got five minutes?

Speakers of German

German is the largest language group within the European Union with around 92 million native speakers in Germany, Austria, Luxemburg and parts of Belgium and Italy. German native speakers living outside the EU in Switzerland and other communities throughout the world bring the total to approximately 105 million. About a further 80 million people speak German as a second or foreign language. German has considerable importance within the EU not only because of the number of speakers it has, but also because it is, along with English and French, one of the three procedural languages of the European Commission.

German language and vocabulary

German belongs to the West Germanic group of languages and is related to Dutch and English and more distantly to the Scandinavian languages. German has also been influenced, particularly in vocabulary, by Latin, French and in more recent decades by English. Whilst certain German words have been borrowed into English – e.g. **Delicatessen, Doppelgänger, Kindergarten, Meister, Rucksack, Schadenfreude, Weltanschauung, Zeitgeist** – the number of English words borrowed into German is much larger and constantly growing. More recent additions have been **der Airbag, der Computer, crashen** (of computers), **downloaden, die E-Mail, der JobCentre, shoppen**. Some of the borrowed words have taken on a different meaning in German, e.g. **das Handy** *cell phone, mobile phone*, **der**

Oldtimer *vintage car*, **der Showmaster** *TV host*, **der Smoking** *tuxedo, dinner jacket*.

Recent borrowings from English are often referred to as **Denglisch** (**Deutsch + Englisch**). They are regarded by some German speakers as unwelcome intruders into the language and by others as a further development of the language comparable with the importations from Latin and French in the past.

German literature

From the cultural point of view there is an enormous wealth of literature in German, much of which is available in translation, but some of which – especially poetry – must be read in the original German in order to gain the full impact of the author's use of language. Two of the best-known authors born in the 18th century are Johann Wolfgang von Goethe (1749–1832) and Friedrich Schiller (1759–1805). In more recent times those best known in the English-speaking world include Franz Kafka (1883–1924), Thomas Mann (1875–1955) and Bertolt Brecht (1898–1956), as well as Erich Kästner (1899–1974), Heinrich Böll (1917–1985), Günter Grass (1927–) and Patrick Süskind (1949–).

Acquiring language skills

Whatever your reasons are for learning German, this course will help you to build up your command of German in all four of the main communicative skills areas – listening and speaking, reading and writing. To practise speaking you will ideally have a 'study buddy' or be in a class with other learners. But the other three skills can be practised on your own, using the recordings for the listening activities and the key for self-checking your answers to all the activities in listening, reading and writing.

What the course contains

The vocabulary and the grammar that we introduce in this course have been carefully chosen to take account of your needs as a beginner and the kind of things you may want to do with German. Each new situation or topic requires a special set of words and expressions and specific grammatical constructions. For instance, to say who you are you will need the expression **Mein Name ist ...** *My name is ...*, or to say what you want you will need the phrase **Ich möchte...** *I would like ....* To talk about the present and about actions you do regularly you will need to learn the present tense form of verbs. Learning the different past tense forms will allow you to say what you did or what you used to do, etc.

The course covers all the main situations you may find yourself in, including among others ordering food in a café or restaurant, hotel bookings, asking for and giving directions, shopping for food and clothes, using the phone, agreeing on dates and times for social engagements and business appointments, etc. Each unit of your *Complete German* course gives you the opportunity to learn the language needed to perform adequately in real-life situations of a similar kind. Practice and further exposure to German will allow you to transfer what you have learned to other situations that you may encounter.

Adding to your German vocabulary

Language learning involves gaining confidence in several specific areas of language, one of which is vocabulary. Recognising new German words through their similarities with English is one way of expanding your vocabulary, but there are others. One very important skill that you should try to develop is working out meanings from the context. You may well find that in the early stages of your *Complete German* course you are tempted to look up every new word you come across, either in the German–English vocabulary at the end of the book, or in your dictionary, or in an online dictionary. Although this can sometimes be useful, you should try to get used to working out the meanings of new words by studying the context in which they occur. This is in fact what you have to do in real-life situations. Of course, you may sometimes get the wrong end of the stick, so you will need to have ways of checking that you have understood correctly, especially in conversations when you are, for example, making arrangements to meet someone at a specific time and place!

Here are a few basic German words and expressions to help you get started. You may know some of them already:

Greetings: **Hallo!** *Hello!*, **Guten Tag** *Good day*, **Guten Morgen** *Good morning*, **Guten Abend** *Good evening*, **Gute Nacht** *Good night*.

Titles: **Herr** *Mr*, **Frau** *Mrs, Miss*.

Saying 'please' and 'thank you': **Bitte** *Please*, **Danke (schön)** *Thank you (very much)*.

Saying 'goodbye': **Tschüss!** *Cheers*, *'Bye!*, **Auf Wiedersehen!** *Goodbye, see you later!*

10 Only got ten minutes?

Achieving your goals in German

Whatever your communication needs are, there are certain basic language activities which you will need to engage in and handle efficiently. All the most predictable ones are covered in this book, from simple ones such as giving information about yourself, introducing yourself and others, asking for directions, and ordering food, etc., to more complex ones like talking about your work or your daily routine, using the phone, giving biographical information, etc. Being able to handle these adequately will in turn allow you to transfer what you have learned to new situations, thus expanding your capacity to communicate. The vocabulary, grammatical constructions and the many activities contained in this book are there to help you achieve this communication.

Where German is spoken

German is spoken as a native language by approximately 105 million people. About a further 80 million people speak it as a second or foreign language. German is the official language or one of the official languages in Germany, Austria, Luxemburg, Liechtenstein, Switzerland and the Südtirol area of Italy.

There are communities of German native speakers in Russia (approx. 2.9 million), Canada (over 438,000), the Südtirol (Alto Adige) region of Italy (over 290,000), the USA (around 100,000), the Walloon Region of Belgium (73,000) and Romania (45,000).

The remaining German speakers in the United States are quite often members of religious groups, such as the Amish and Mennonites. It was, you may recall, an Amish family that featured in the 1985 movie 'Witness'. The Amish, based in former times mainly in German-speaking Switzerland, began migrating to Pennsylvania in the 18th century as part of a larger migration from the Palatinate region of Germany. They were driven to migration by religious conflict, poverty, and religious persecution. Their language came to be referred to as Pennsylvania Dutch (where 'Dutch' is really 'Deutsch'). Nowadays it is primarily the Old Order Amish and Old Order Mennonites who continue to speak Pennsylvania Dutch.

GERMAN VOCABULARY

If you are a beginner in German you may be wondering how difficult German will turn out to be or how different it is from English. If you already know some German you will be aware that there are many similarities between German and English in the area of vocabulary. Many words in both languages have their origins in their shared Germanic past, for example **Apfel** *apple*, **backen** *to bake*, **Bad** *bath*, **danken** *to thank* and **Garten** *garden*. You may not always spot the link between two words straight away, as with **Zaun** *fence*. This in fact has the same origin as the English word *town*. Early settlements often had fences around them to keep out wild animals, etc. The huntsmen returning to the settlement would go back to the fenced area or to what historical linguists think was called the **tuna**.

Both English and German have borrowed words from Latin. The similarities are sometimes obvious, sometimes less so, for example Latin 'tegula' **Ziegel** *tile*, 'pirum' **Birne** *pear*, 'caseus' **Käse** *cheese*, 'planta' **Pflanze** *plant*. While the Norman invasion of England brought many Norman French words into English, German too was influenced, although to a much lesser extent, by French, e.g. **Visage**, *face*, **ordinär** *uncouth*, **frivol** *frivolous*, **Affäre** *affair*, **Restaurant** *restaurant*.

In more recent times by far the largest number of borrowings into German have been from English. The following paragraph was put together by the staff of **deutsch-online** to illustrate borrowing from

English of words ending in **-y**. (The plural forms in German are usually **-ys**, rather than **-ies**.) You don't need to understand German in order to spot the 13 loan words:

Die traurige Geschichte von drei englischen Ladys

Es waren einmal drei englische Ladys mit gleichen Hobbys. Sie sammelten alte Pennys, besuchten Derbys und Wohltätigkeitspartys, züchteten Guppys und hatten eine Schwäche für stramme Bobbys und rührselige Shantys. Es gab nur eines, vor dem sie sich zutiefst fürchteten: Rowdys, die in Cities lebten und nachts aus den Gullys krochen, um armen Babys die Teddys wegzunehmen. (From deutsch-online)

But recognising the similarity between a German word and one you already know in English or another language will not always suffice. A very useful skill that you should try to develop as you progress through the course is guessing the meanings of new words from the context in which they occur. You may feel at a loss at first but as you gain experience you may even find yourself skipping the odd new word and trying to get the gist of what a text says, just as you do in your own language sometimes.

GERMAN GRAMMAR

In terms of the grammar, you will find that there are some important differences between English and German. But in this course the main grammar points are presented in manageable portions for you. Two examples of such points are:

▶ *Gender* Words which name things such as tree, flower and book have gender in German, that is they are either masculine, feminine or neuter. For example, **Baum** *tree*, is masculine while **Blume** *flower* is feminine and **Buch** *book* is neuter. Whilst there are a few rules that help with the remembering of the genders, the best thing is to learn each word with its gender when you first encounter it. In vocabulary lists the gender is usually indicated by adding the word for 'the', e.g. **der Baum, die Blume, das Buch**.

▶ *Plurals* In general English speakers simply add an 's' for saying that there is more than one of something, e.g. one book, two books. But this rule for forming the plural does not always work, e.g. one child, two children, one woman, two women. In German adding the 's' is the exception rather than the rule and it is mainly reserved for words borrowed from other languages, e.g. **das Ticket, die Tickets**. Instead there are several different plural endings, for example adding an umlaut (2 dots) to the preceding syllable and an '-e' at the end of the word: **der Baum, die Bäume**; an '-n' to the end of the word: **die Blume, die Blumen**; an umlaut to the preceding syllable and '-er' at the end of the word: **das Buch, die Bücher**. You will fairly quickly get a feel for the correct form of the plural, especially if you learn this together with the gender.

GERMAN VERBS

German, like English, uses changes in the verb to denote the present, as in 'I play', the past, as in 'I played' and 'I have played'. These changes are referred to as tense. In German, the verb endings for each tense are in general dependent on two factors: time (past, present, etc.) and person (**ich** *I*, **du** *you*, **er/sie/es** *he/she/it*, **wir** *we*, etc.).

Many German verbs follow a fixed pattern of change and so are called regular, but some behave in a different way and are called irregular. Once you know the forms for a particular tense of a regular verb, for example the present of **spielen** *to play*, you will know how to form the present tense of hundreds of other verbs.

SAYING 'YOU' IN GERMAN

In German there are three different forms for 'you' depending on whether you are addressing someone in an informal or formal way and whether you are talking to one or more than one person (singular or plural). Generally, the informal **du** (one person) and **ihr** (more than one person) are used to address friends, family members, equals, younger people, God and animals. The formal form **Sie** (used for both one person and more than one person) is used as a sign of respect to address people one does not know, the elderly, one's superiors, etc. The use of **du** has become increasingly common among German speakers in recent times.

SPELLING AND PRONUNCIATION

German spelling is much more consistent than English. Most words are pronounced as they are spelled. Once you become familiar with the sounds of German and with German stress patterns, you should have little difficulty in reading a text in German out loud, even if you cannot fully understand its meaning.

German spelling was not fully standardized till 1901 when the **Reichsamt des Innern** *Reich Ministry of the Interior* convened the 2nd Berlin Orthography Conference. In 1902 the rulings of this conference became legally binding and were laid down in Konrad Duden's dictionary. In 1994 representatives of the Ministries of Culture and of the Interior in Austria, Switzerland and the Federal Republic of Germany agreed on a common draft for a spelling reform. After a further 13 years of discussion and resistance to the reforms, the new spelling rules became legally binding in schools in 2007. German news agencies now write their material according to the recommendations of **Duden** and **Wahrig**.

THE ALPHABET

The German alphabet, which you will find in Unit 3 of *Complete German*, uses the same 26 letters as the English alphabet, but with an additional four letters. Three of these are formed by adding a so-called Umlaut – two dots above the letters 'a', 'o' and 'u': **ä, ö, ü**. They are used in words such as **Bäcker** *baker*, **schön** *beautiful, nice* and **Übung** *exercise*. German speakers are strict about using the Umlaut and do not omit it. For writing e-mails, mobile phone (cell phone) texts and blogs it is acceptable to add an 'e' after the vowel instead of using the Umlaut: e.g. **Bäcker → Baecker**, **schön →
schoen**.

The fourth extra letter is **ß**, which is called **scharfes s** or **esszett**, and sounds like the 's' in 'miss'. This is used after a long vowel in words such as **Straße** *street* and **Fußball** *football*. After a short vowel **ss** is used: **Pass** *passport*, **Kuss** *kiss*.

Help with pronouncing the letters is given on the recording for Unit 3.

WORD STRESS

All words of more than one syllable have what is called word stress. This means that at least one of the syllables is longer and louder than the other syllables. Word stress in German often falls on the first syllable, as in **DEUTSCHland** *Germany* and **MITtagessen** *lunch*. But the word stress can appear on other syllables as well, e.g. **erLAUBen** *to allow*, **MetzgerEI** *butcher's shop*. A few words that are written the same have different stress for different meanings, e.g. **überSETZen** *to translate*, **ÜBERsetzen** *to ferry across*.

CAPITAL LETTERS

All nouns are written with a capital letter in German: **Bank** *bank*, **Haus** *house*. There have been moves to abandon this practice, but so far they have not succeeded. Some people use lower-case initials in informal writing, such as e-mails and mobile phone (cell phone) texts.

Some adjectives which are written with a capital letter in English are written with lower-case letters in German, e.g. adjectives describing nationality: **mein deutscher Freund** *my German (boy) friend*, **ein englisches Buch** *an English book*. Similarly, words denoting political and religious groups have lower-case initials. e.g. **eine sozialistische Regierung** *a Socialist government*, **ein katholisches Land** *a Catholic country*.

We hope we have managed to persuade you to have a go at learning German. It will open up a new world for you! We wish you **Viel Erfolg und viel Spaß!** *Lots of success and lots of fun!*

Introduction

Welcome to Complete German!

Is this the right course for you?

If you are an adult learner with no previous knowledge of German and studying on your own, then this is the course for you. Perhaps you are taking up German again after a break from it, or you are intending to learn with the support of a class? Again, you will find this course very well suited to your purposes.

DEVELOPING YOUR SKILLS

The language introduced in this course is centred around realistic everyday situations. The emphasis is first and foremost on using German, but we also aim to give you an idea of how the language works, so that you can create sentences of your own.

The course covers all four of the basic skills – listening and speaking, reading and writing. If you are working on your own, the recordings will be all the more important, as they will provide you with the essential opportunity to listen to German and to speak it within a controlled framework. You should therefore try to obtain a copy of the recordings if you haven't already got one.

The structure of this course

The course book contains 23 course units plus a **reference section** at the back of the book. There are also **two CDs** which you really do need to have if you are going to get maximum benefit from the course.

THE COURSE UNITS

The course units can be divided roughly into the following categories, although of course there is a certain amount of overlap from one category to another.

Statement of aims
At the beginning of each unit you will be told what you can expect to learn, in terms of a) what you will be able to do in German by the end of the unit and b) the language points that are being introduced.

Presentation of new language
This is usually in the form of text material, often supported by illustrations, or of a dialogue. Most of the dialogues are recorded

on the audio (indicated with ◀) and also printed in the book. Some assistance with vocabulary is also given. The language is presented in manageable chunks, building carefully on what you have learned in earlier units.

Practice of the new language
Practice is graded, so that activities which require mainly **recognition** come first. As you grow in confidence in manipulating the language forms, you will be encouraged to produce both in writing and in speech.

Description of language forms and grammar
Information on the forms of the language is presented in two ways: i) in digestible 'bites' within the body of the unit (**SPRACHINFO**) and ii) in the grammar section at the end of the unit.

Learning the **forms** of the language will enable you to construct your own sentences correctly. For those who are daunted by grammar, assistance is given in various ways.

Pronunciation and intonation
The best way to acquire good pronunciation and intonation is to listen to native speakers and to try to imitate them. But most people do not actually notice that certain sounds in German are pronounced differently from their English counterparts, until this is pointed out to them. For this reason we include specific advice within the course units.

Insight boxes
Here you will find tips on how to learn the language and information on various aspects of life – from the level of formality that is appropriate when you talk to strangers to how the health service works if you should fall ill.

Vocabulary
To help you monitor your own learning of vocabulary, much of the new vocabulary is presented as it occurs. At the end of the book there are also short German–English and English–German reference vocabularies.

Monitoring your progress

You will of course want to monitor your own progress. We provide a 'Test Yourself' section and a checklist at the end of every unit to help you be sure that you have mastered the main points.

The reference section

This contains:

- ▶ *a list of German irregular verbs*
- ▶ *a key to the activities*
- ▶ *transcripts of the recordings*
- ▶ *a German–English vocabulary*
- ▶ *an English–German vocabulary*

How to use this course

Make sure at the beginning of each course unit that you are clear about what you can expect to learn.

Read any background information that is provided. Then either read the text material or listen to the dialogues on the recording. With the recording try to get the gist of what is being said before you look at the printed text in the book. Then refer to the printed text and the *Key words and phrases* in order to study the dialogues in more detail.

Don't fall into the trap of thinking you have 'done that' when you have listened to the recording a couple of times and worked through the dialogues in the book. You may **recognize** what you hear and read, but you almost certainly still have some way to go before you can **produce** the language of the dialogues correctly and fluently. This is why we recommend that you keep listening to the recording at every opportunity – sitting on the train or bus, waiting at the dentist's or stuck in a traffic jam in the car, using what would otherwise be 'dead' time. Of course, you must also be internalizing what you hear and making sense of it – just playing it in the background without really paying attention is not enough!

Some of the recordings are listen-only exercises. The temptation may be to go straight to the transcriptions in the back of the book, but try not to do this. The whole point of listening exercises is to improve your listening skills. You will not do this by reading first. The transcriptions are there to help you if you get stuck.

As you work your way through the exercises, check your answers carefully in the back of the book. It is easy to overlook your own mistakes. If you have a 'study buddy' it's a good idea to check each other's answers. Most of the exercises have fixed answers, but some are a bit more open-ended, especially when we are asking you to talk about yourself. We then, in most cases, give you a model answer which you can adapt for your own purposes.

We have tried to make the grammar explanations as user-friendly as possible, since we recognize that many people find grammar daunting. But in the end, it is up to you just how much time you spend on studying and sorting out the grammar points. Some people find that they can do better by getting an ear for what sounds right, others need to know in detail how the language is put together.

Before you move on to a new unit always make sure that you know all the new words and phrases in the current unit. Trying to recall the context in which words and phrases were used may help you learn them better.

Language learning is a bit like running – you need to do it regularly for it to do any good! Ideally, you should find a 'study buddy' to work through the course with you. This way you will have someone to try out your German on. And when the going gets tough, you will have someone to chivvy you on until you reach your target.

Commonly used instructions in *Complete German*:

Hören Sie (zu)	*Listen*
Lesen Sie…	*Read…*
Schreiben Sie…	*Write…*
Spielen Sie die Rolle von…	*Play the role of…*

German in the modern world

German is spoken as a first language by approximately 110 million people who live mainly in Germany, Austria and Switzerland. But German is also spoken elsewhere – for instance in Luxemburg, Liechtenstein, the South Tyrol region of Italy and in border regions of Belgium. German-speaking communities are also to be found in Eastern Europe, particularly in Romania, in North America (e.g. the Pennsylvania Dutch) and in southern Africa (Namibia).

After English, German is the most widely spoken language within the European Union and is an important language in business and commerce, particularly in Eastern Europe.

Where can I find real German?

Don't expect to be able to understand everything you hear or read straight away. If you watch German-speaking programmes on TV or buy German magazines, you should not get discouraged when you realize how quickly native-speakers speak and how much vocabulary there is still to be learned. Just concentrate on a small extract – either a video/audio clip or a short article – and work through it till you have mastered it. In this way, you'll find that your command of German increases steadily.

We hope you enjoy working your way through *Complete German*. Try not to let yourself get discouraged. Mastering a new language does take time and perseverance and sometimes things can seem just too difficult. But then you'll come back to it another day and things will begin to make more sense again.

Mein Name ist …
My name is …

In this unit you will learn
- *how to say who you are and greet people and say goodbye*
- *how to ask people where they come from and where they live*

Language points
- *I and you*
- *word order*

Saying 'hello'

1 ICH HEISSE … *I AM CALLED …*

🔊 **CD 1, TR 2**

Listen to how these people introduce themselves.

> Guten Tag. Ich heiße Helga Kirsch.

Guten Tag. (*lit.* *) *Good day.*
Hallo. *Hello.*
Ich heiße ... (*lit.*) *I am called ...*
Mein Name ist ... *My name is ...*
*A literal translation (lit.) of the German is sometimes given to help you understand what the German actually says. But don't always think in terms of single-word translations: try to learn to use complete expressions.

QUICK VOCAB

Did you notice the different ways they give their names?

Now have a go at giving your own name in German.

Tip: Try saying the two different sentences for giving your name. You could also record your responses. Then write the sentences down.

2 WIE IST IHR NAME? *WHAT'S YOUR NAME?*

Listen to the recording. What are the two ways of asking someone's name in German?

CD 1, TR 3

- Guten Tag. Wie heißen Sie?
- Ich heiße Elisabeth Schuhmacher.
- Wie ist Ihr Name, bitte?
- Mein Name ist Paul Matthiesen.
- Und Sie? Wie heißen Sie?
- Ich heiße Bianca Schulz.
- Guten Tag. Wie ist Ihr Name, bitte?
- Mein Name ist Deichmann, Oliver Deichmann.

bitte *please*
Und Sie? *And you?*
Wie ist Ihr Name? *What is your name?*
Wie heißen Sie? *What are you called?*

VOCAB

3 EIN UNFALL *AN ACCIDENT*

◀) CD 1, TR 4

Listen to the recording and see if you can answer the questions.

a What is the name of the first person?
Is it Gertrud Gruber / Gerda Gruber / Gertrud Huber?

b Is the name of the second person
Martin Baumann / Markus Braun / Martin Braun?

c Is the third person
Boris Schulz / Boris Schwarz / Moritz Schulz?

Insight

Hearing German spoken without seeing how it is written can be quite hard when you start learning German. But give yourself a chance to understand the recording by listening to it several times. If you really find you need more help, then turn to the transcripts at the end of the book.

Greeting people

4 GUTEN MORGEN! GUTEN TAG!

Good morning! Good day!

◄) **CD 1, TR 5**

Hören Sie zu und wiederholen Sie! Listen and repeat.

Hallo!

Guten Morgen!

Guten Tag!

Guten Abend!

Gute Nacht!

Auf Wiedersehen!

Useful expressions
Hallo. *Hello.*
Guten Morgen. *Good morning.*
Guten Tag. *Good day.*
Guten Abend. *Good evening.*
Gute Nacht. *Good night.*
Auf Wiedersehen. *Goodbye.*
The greeting **Guten Tag** is used from about 10 am until 6 pm.
Note there is no German equivalent for *Good afternoon.*

5 GUTEN MORGEN, HERR SCHNEIDER!

GOOD MORNING, MR SCHNEIDER!

Which greetings or farewells go with which picture?

 a  **b**  **c**

d

1 – Gute Nacht, Frau Naumann! – Auf Wiedersehen!

2 – Auf Wiedersehen, Frau Hermann! – Auf Wiedersehen, Herr Schneider!

3 – Guten Abend, Frau Naumann! – Guten Abend!

4 – Guten Morgen, Herr Schneider! – Guten Morgen, Frau Hermann!

Insight

Germans often shake hands when they meet and when they say goodbye. They also often give only their surname when they introduce themselves. The courtesy titles **Herr** and **Frau** are used rather like *Mr* and *Mrs* … in English. **Fräulein** (Miss) is hardly used any more. Women irrespective of whether they are married or not are addressed with **Frau**.

6 GRÜSSE IM RADIO UND FERNSEHEN
GREETINGS ON RADIO AND TV

◀) CD 1, TR 6

Hören Sie zu! How many different greetings did you hear? What were they?

SPRACHINFO
All nouns begin with a capital letter in German:

> Guten Tag. Guten Morgen. Guten Abend. Gute Nacht.
> Mein Name ist Claudia.

Note that the polite forms **Sie** (you) and **Ihr** (your) also start with a capital letter.

Why is it **Guten Tag** but **Gute Nacht**? This will be dealt with a bit later!

Where do you come from?

7 ICH KOMME AUS ..., ICH WOHNE IN ...
I COME FROM ..., I LIVE IN ...

◀) CD 1, TR 7

Hören Sie zu! Listen to these people introducing themselves.

a

> **Ich heiße Danielle Bouvier. Ich komme aus Frankreich, aus Dijon. Ich wohne in Hamburg.**

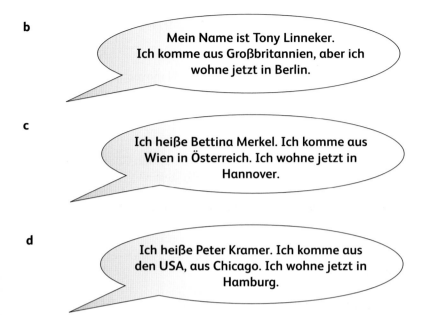

b

Mein Name ist Tony Linneker.
Ich komme aus Großbritannien, aber ich
wohne jetzt in Berlin.

c

Ich heiße Bettina Merkel. Ich komme aus
Wien in Österreich. Ich wohne jetzt in
Hannover.

d

Ich heiße Peter Kramer. Ich komme aus
den USA, aus Chicago. Ich wohne jetzt in
Hamburg.

Ich komme aus … *I come from …*
Frankreich *France*
Ich wohne in … *I live in …*
Großbritannien *Great Britain*
… aus den USA *… from the USA*
aber *but*
Wien *Vienna*
Österreich *Austria*
jetzt *now*

QUICK VOCAB

True or false?

a Danielle comes from Dijon and lives in Hamburg.
b Tony Linneker comes from Berlin, but now lives in London.
c Bettina comes from Austria and lives in Germany.
d Peter lives in Germany but comes from the USA.

8 IN DER FUSSGÄNGERZONE
IN THE PEDESTRIAN PRECINCT

Here are two interviews with visitors to Hanover. A reporter from a German radio station is finding out what their names are, where they come from and where they live.

Interview 1

Reporter	Entschuldigen Sie, bitte. Guten Tag, Radio N–4. Darf ich Ihnen ein paar Fragen stellen?
Passant	Ja, bitte.
Reporter	Wie heißen Sie?
Passant	Ich heiße Jochen Kern.
Reporter	Und woher kommen Sie?
Passant	Ich komme aus Aachen.
Reporter	Wo wohnen Sie, bitte?
Passant	Ich wohne jetzt in Bonn.
Reporter	Danke schön.

Interview 2

Reporter	Wie ist Ihr Name, bitte?
Passantin	Ich heiße Dana Frye.
Reporter	Ah. Und woher kommen Sie?
Passantin	Ich komme aus Stuttgart.
Reporter	Und wo wohnen Sie?
Passantin	Ich wohne jetzt hier in Hannover.

QUICK VOCAB

Entschuldigen Sie *excuse (me)*
Darf ich Ihnen ein paar Fragen stellen? *Can I ask you a few questions?*
ja *yes*
ein paar Fragen *a few questions*
wo? *where?*
Danke schön *thank you*
woher? *where ... from?*
Wo wohnen Sie? *Where do you live?*
Woher kommen Sie? *Where do you come from?*

Now listen to the recording again and fill in the grid below as you listen. Try not to look at the text. Note that the German for 'place of birth' is **Geburtsort** and for 'place of residence' is **Wohnort**.

Name	Geburtsort	Wohnort
Ich heiße …	Ich komme aus …	Ich wohne jetzt in …
1		
2		

9 WOHER KOMMEN SIE?
WHERE DO YOU COME FROM?

◢) **CD 1, TR 9**

How would you say what your name is, where you come from and where you live? Try answering the questions on the recording. Then write your answers down.

_____

Grammar

1 PERSONAL PRONOUNS

The personal pronouns (words for *I, you,* etc.) in German are:

Singular (one person)		Plural (more than one person)	
1 ich	*I*	**wir**	*we*
2 du	*you (informal)*	**ihr**	*you (informal)*
Sie	*you (formal)*	**Sie**	*you (formal)*
3 er, sie	*he, she*	**sie**	*they*
es, man	*it, one*		

So far you have met **ich** and **Sie** (the formal *you*). Note that **Sie** is written with a capital letter. You will learn about the others in the next few units.

In German you need to learn which endings to put on the verb for each pronoun. The endings that go with **ich** and **Sie** are given in Section 2 below.

2 VERB ENDINGS

A verb normally expresses an action or state. In this unit you have met the verbs **heißen, kommen** and **wohnen**. The form of the verb that you find in a dictionary or glossary is called the infinitive: e.g. **wohnen** (*to live*).

The infinitive can be divided into two parts: **wohn-** the *stem*, **-en** the *ending*. The endings change according to the *subject* used (i.e. **ich, Sie,** etc.).

For most verbs the endings you add with **ich** and **Sie** are:

		wohn-**en**	komm-**en**	heiß-**en**
ich	-e	wohn**e**	komm**e**	heiß**e**
Sie	-en	wohn**en**	komm**en**	heiß**en**

If you are curious about the other endings, you could have a look at the sections on verb endings in the next few units.

3 WORD ORDER

In a German sentence the verb is usually in the second position, as you can see from the examples below:

Statements:

Ich	heiße	Schmidt.
Ich	komme	aus Bonn.
Ich	wohne	in Köln.

Wh- questions: These are questions which in English start with *What?*, *Who?*, *Where?*, etc. Hence the name Wh- questions, even though the question *How?* also comes into this category. In German these question words tend to start with **W-**. As you can see, the verb is again the second element.

Wie	heißen	Sie?
Woher	kommen	Sie?
Wo	wohnen	Sie?

TESTING YOURSELF

1 **Wann sagt man was?** *When would you use the following greetings? Tick the appropriate box.*

	Guten Morgen	Guten Tag	Guten Abend	Gute Nacht
14:00		✔		
8:00				
23.00				
10.00		✔		
18.00		✔		

2 **Wo? Woher? Wie?** *Write in the missing words.*
  a ... heißen Sie?
  b ... wohnen Sie?
  c ... kommen Sie?
  d ... ist Ihr Name?

3 **-e, -en?** *Fill in the missing endings.*
  a *Ich heiß__ Simone Becker. Wie heiß__ Sie?*
  b *Ich wohn__ in Berlin. Wo wohn__ Sie?*
  c *Ich komm__ aus Großbritannien. Woher komm__ Sie?*

4 **Welche Worte fehlen?** *Which words are missing? Here is an interview from* **8 In der Fußgängerzone** *with some of the words missing. Supply the missing words.*

Reporter	a__ heißen Sie?
Passant	b__ heiße Jochen Kern.
Reporter	Und c__ kommen Sie?
Passant	Ich komme d__ Aachen.
Reporter	e__ wohnen Sie, bitte?
Passant	Ich wohne f__ in Bonn.

Now that you have completed Unit 1, can you: tick

1 say who you are? ☐

2 greet someone and say goodbye? ☐

3 ask people where they come from? ☐

4 ask people where they live? ☐

2

....

Mir geht's gut
I'm fine

In this unit you will learn
- *how to ask people how they are*
- *how to say how you are*
- *how to say which cities and countries people come from*

Language points
- *verb endings*

_____

How are you?

1 SEHR GUT ... SCHLECHT *VERY GOOD ... BAD*

Here are some words people use to say how they are feeling.

+++
sehr gut
ausgezeichnet
prima (*informal*)

+
gut

+ –
es geht

–
nicht (so) gut

– – –
schlecht
furchtbar

sehr gut *very good*
ausgezeichnet *excellent*
prima *great*
gut *good*
es geht *(it's) ok*
nicht (so) gut *not (so) good*
schlecht *bad*
furchtbar *terrible*

2 WIE GEHT ES IHNEN?
HOW ARE YOU?

◀) **CD 1, TR 10**

Now listen to these people asking each other how they are. Fill in the grid as you listen. Try to do this without looking at the printed text. You'll probably need to listen to each dialogue several times.

	ausgezeichnet	sehr gut	gut	es geht	nicht so gut	schlecht
Frau Renger			✔			
Frau Müller						
Herr Schulz						
Frau Koch						
Herr Krämer						
Herr Akdag						

Wie geht es Ihnen? *How are you? (lit. How goes it to you?)*
Und Ihnen? *And (how are) you?*
Wie geht's? *How are you? (less formal version)*
Das freut mich. *I am pleased. (lit. that pleases me)*
nicht *not*
heute *today*
na ja *oh well*

QUICK VOCAB

Insight

Learn set expressions such as **Das freut mich** as one phrase (*I am pleased*). You should not try to translate word for word all the time, even though we do sometimes give you the literal meaning of expressions the first time they occur.

3 IM BÜRO *IN THE OFFICE*

◀ **CD 1, TR 11**

Listen to these three people arriving at work. Which three of the six responses below did you hear on the recording and in what order?

a Danke, gut.
b Ach, es geht.
c Mir geht's wirklich sehr gut.
d Mir geht's heute wirklich schlecht.
e Mir geht es heute nicht so gut.
f Nicht schlecht. Und Ihnen?

Mir geht es gut. *I am fine.*
Mir geht's gut. *I'm fine.*
wirklich *really*
Das tut mir leid. *I'm sorry about that.*

4 WIE GEHT ES DIESEN LEUTEN? *HOW ARE THESE PEOPLE?*

Answer the question **Wie geht es Ihnen heute?** for each of these people in turn and give the reply suggested by the picture. Select an appropriate answer from those given on the next page.

a

Danke, mir geht's …

b

_____

c

_____

d

_____

Ach, es geht.

Mir geht es gut.

Mir geht's heute nicht so gut.

Mir geht's heute schlecht.

Danke, mir geht's wirklich sehr gut.

Danke, gut.

5 WORTSUCHE _WORD SEARCH_

How many words can you find? They have all occurred in this unit.
You should be able to find at least 15.

M	E	I	N	S	I	E	A	N	H	D	Z	G
G	E	H	T	E	S	P	R	I	M	A	S	U
A	U	S	G	E	Z	E	I	C	H	N	E	T
H	W	I	R	K	L	I	C	H	L	K	H	O
T	N	O	C	H	H	E	U	T	E	E	R	P

6 WOHER KOMMEN DIESE LEUTE?
WHERE DO THESE PEOPLE COME FROM?

◀ CD 1, TR 12

i Where do these people come from? Listen to the recording and
find out. Then read the texts.

a Rainer Görner ....   **b** Martina Schümer ....
c Susanna Vermeulen ....   **d** Michael Naumannn ....

Rainer Görner kommt aus Berlin. Aber er wohnt nicht mehr in Berlin. Er wohnt jetzt in Frankfurt am Main. Frankfurt ist in Deutschland.

Martina Schümer kommt aus Basel. Sie wohnt noch in Basel. Basel liegt nicht in Deutschland, sondern in der Schweiz.

Susanne Vermeulen kommt aus Brüssel in Belgien. Sie wohnt aber nicht mehr dort. Sie arbeitet jetzt im Hotel Lindenhof in Düsseldorf.

Michael Naumann kommt aus Leipzig. Er wohnt jetzt in Salzburg. Liegt Salzburg in der Schweiz? Nein! Es ist in Österreich und es ist sehr schön.

QUICK VOCAB

nicht mehr *no longer (lit. not more)*
am Main *on the (river) Main*
noch *still*
liegen *to lie, be*
nicht ..., sondern ... *not ..., but ...*
in der Schweiz *in (the) Switzerland*
aber *but, however*
dort *there*
arbeiten *to work*
schön *beautiful, nice*

ii Decide whether these statements are true (**richtig**) or false (**falsch**). Correct the wrong statements.

Statement Rainer Görner kommt aus Wien.
Answer Falsch. Rainer Görner kommt aus Berlin.

a Rainer Görner wohnt jetzt in Frankfurt am Main.

b Zürich liegt nicht in Deutschland, sondern in Österreich.

c Martina Schümer kommt aus Basel und wohnt noch in Basel.

d Susanne Vermeulen kommt aus Delft in den Niederlanden.

e Sie wohnt jetzt in Düsseldorf und arbeitet im Hotel Lindenhof.

f Michael Naumann kommt aus Dresden und wohnt jetzt in Linz, in Österreich.

SPRACHINFO: *Verb endings with he, she, it*
For the third person singular (he = **er**, she = **sie**, it = **es**, one = **man**) you add a -**t** to the stem of the verb:

> *er komm* -**t**
> *sie wohn* -**t**
> *es lieg* -**t**

Note: **arbeiten** (to work) is slightly different. You add -**et** rather than just -**t** to the stem so that it's easier to pronounce:

> *er arbeit* -**et.**

7 DIE LÄNDER EUROPAS *THE COUNTRIES OF EUROPE*

◀) **CD 1, TR 13**

On the recording you will hear the names of some of the countries listed on the next page. Tick off those that are mentioned.

Then listen to the recording again. Can you figure out where German speakers usually put the stress? Underline the correct part of the names of the countries that you hear.

You can check your answers in the Key.

Beispiel <u>Deutsch</u>land

Belgien	Irland	Schweden
Dänemark	Italien	die Schweiz
Deutschland	die Niederlande	Spanien
England	Österreich	die Tschechische Republik
Frankreich	Polen	die Türkei
Griechenland	Portugal	Ungarn
Großbritannien	Schottland	Wales

Note that for the great majority of countries you would just say:

*Ich komme aus Irland, Großbritannien, Deutschland etc. and
Ich wohne in Irland, Großbritannien, Deutschland etc.*

There are a few exceptions, including Switzerland, Turkey, the
Czech Republic and the Slovak Republic, the Netherlands and the
USA.

Ich komme aus der Schweiz/aus der Türkei/aus der
Tschechischen Republik/aus der Slowakischen Republik.
Ich wohne in der Schweiz/in der Türkei/in der Tschechischen
Republik/in der Slowakischen Republik.
Ich komme aus den Niederlanden/aus den USA.
Ich wohne in den Niederlanden/in den USA.

8 WIE GUT SIND SIE IN GEOGRAPHIE?
HOW GOOD ARE YOU AT GEOGRAPHY?

Which statements are true (**richtig**) and which false (**falsch**)?
Correct the wrong statements.

Statement Zürich liegt in Deutschland.
Answer Falsch. Zürich liegt nicht in Deutschland, sondern in der
Schweiz.

Statement Innsbruck liegt in Österreich.
Answer Richtig.

a Brüssel liegt in Belgien.
b Heidelberg liegt in Österreich.
c Köln liegt in den Niederlanden.
d Salzburg liegt in Österreich.
e Amsterdam liegt in Belgien.

9 BERÜHMTE LEUTE *FAMOUS PEOPLE*

Woher kommen diese Leute und wo wohnen diese Leute jetzt?
Where do these people come from and where do these people live
now?

Of course, the answers to the second part of these questions
will change from time to time. If you have more up-to-date
information, by all means write that instead.

Beispiel: Boris Becker. D / USA, D
You write Boris Becker kommt aus Deutschland. Er wohnt jetzt in
den USA und in Deutschland.

D = Deutschland, GB = Großbritannien, Ö = Österreich

a Naomi Campbell GB / USA
b Madonna GB / USA
c Karl Lagerfeld D / F
d Michael Schuhmacher D / Ö
e Arnold Schwarzenegger Ö / USA
f Claudia Schiffer D / GB

10 ROLLENSPIEL: IM HOTEL *IN THE HOTEL*

You meet Ulrike Peters in a hotel lobby and get into conversation with her. Was antworten Sie? *What do you answer?* Fill in the answers and play the part of Sheena MacDonald on the recording. Sheena comes from Edinburgh (**Edinburg, Schottland**).

CD 1, TR 14

Ulrike	Guten Tag! Mein Name ist Ulrike Peters.
Sheena	*Return the greetings and say your name.*
Ulrike	Und woher kommen Sie?
Sheena	*Say that you come from Edinburgh in Scotland. Then ask her where she lives.*
Ulrike	Ich wohne hier in München.
Sheena	*Say Munich is beautiful.*
Ulrike	Ja, München ist sehr schön. Aber Edinburg ist auch sehr schön!

Pronunciation

◀ȇ **CD 1, TR 15**

ei in German is pronounced like the English letter *i*:

> *Beispiel, heißen, Einstein, Wein*

26

ie is pronounced like the English letter *e*:

> *Dietrich, Sie, Wien (Vienna)*

How would you pronounce this sentence (which means *I drink wine in Vienna*)?

> *Ich trinke Wein in Wien.*

Grammar

1 *VERB ENDINGS*

Here is a summary of the verb endings you have met so far.

ich	komme	höre	wohne	arbeite
Sie	kommen	hören	wohnen	arbeiten
er/sie/es	kommt	hört	wohnt	arbeitet

Note that an extra **e** is slipped in between **arbeit** and the **t** ending in the **er/sie/es** form. This is to make it easier to pronounce.

2 *NEGATION*

Note that the negative **nicht** (*not*) is usually placed after the verb in German:

| **Ich wohne in London.** | *I live in London.* |
| **Anke wohnt nicht in London.** | *Anke doesn't live in London.* |

The equivalent of *not …, but …* is **nicht …, sondern** in German:

| **Wien liegt nicht in Deutschland, sondern in Österreich.** | *Vienna is not in Germany, but in Austria.* |

3 NAMES OF TOWNS AND COUNTRIES

As you saw in this unit, some place names are spelt the same in both English and German, but are pronounced differently: e.g. Berlin, Frankfurt and England.

Others are different in German from their English versions: e.g. **Köln** *Cologne*; **München** *Munich*; **Hannover** *Hanover*; **Wien** *Vienna*; **Braunschweig** *Brunswick*; **Nürnberg** *Nuremberg*.

TESTING YOURSELF

1 *Here are some extracts from* **6 Woher kommen diese Leute?**
Fill in the missing words.

Rainer Görner kommt **a**__ *Berlin,* **b**__ *er wohnt nicht mehr in
Berlin. Er wohnt* **c**__ *in Frankfurt am Main.*

Susanne Vermeulen kommt **d**__ *Brüssel in* **e**__. *Sie wohnt*
f__ *nicht mehr dort. Sie* **g**__ *jetzt im Hotel Lindenhof in
Düsseldorf.*

2 **Schreiben Sie die Fragen!** *Write out the questions. Find the
questions that these sentences would answer.*

Frage (question)   *Wie geht es Ihnen? / Wie geht's?*
Antwort (answer)   *Mir geht's gut, danke.*

a _____ ?
Ich heiße Susi Reinhardt.

b _____ ?
Ich komme aus Köln.

c _____ ?
Ich wohne jetzt in Bonn.

d _____ ?
Mir geht es heute nicht so gut.

Now that you have completed Unit 2, can you: tick
1 say how you are?   ☐
2 ask other people how they are?   ☐
3 say where people come from (country, city)?   ☐

3

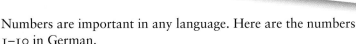

Wie schreibt man das?
How do you write that?

In this unit you will learn
- *how to count from 0 to 100*
- *how to spell names and words*
- *how to talk about us and them*

Language points
- *yes–no questions*
- *plural verb forms*

Numbers 1–10

1 EINS BIS ZEHN *ONE TO TEN*

◆) **CD 1, TR 16**

Numbers are important in any language. Here are the numbers 1–10 in German.

Hören Sie zu und wiederholen Sie! *Listen and repeat.*

1 eins	**2 zwei**	**3 drei**	**4 vier**	**5 fünf**
6 sechs	**7 sieben**	**8 acht**	**9 neun**	**10 zehn**

On the phone or the radio, **zwo** is sometimes used instead of **zwei** to distinguish it from **drei**.

Note that the word for *nil* or *zero* is **null** in German.

Listen to the recording and tick off six of these numbers as you hear them.

| 1 | 9 | 7 | 3 | 10 | 1 | 8 | 5 | 4 | 7 | 6 | 1 | 5 | 2 |

2 FUSSBALLBUNDESLIGA
FEDERAL GERMAN SOCCER LEAGUE

🔊 **CD 1, TR 17**

Hören Sie zu! Listen and fill in the results of each match.

BUNDESLIGA			
Bayern München	2	Stuttgart	2
Köln	3	Leverkusen	4
Hamburg		Dortmund	
Bochum		Hannover	
Duisburg		Mönchengladbach	
Bielefeld		Wolfsburg	
Schalke		Freiburg	
Nürnberg		Hertha Berlin	
Bremen		Frankfurt	

The alphabet

3 JOSEF LERNT DAS ALPHABET
JOSEF IS LEARNING THE ALPHABET

◀) **CD 1, TR 18**

Hören Sie zu und wiederholen Sie!

A-B-C   D-E-F   G-H-I   J-K-L   M-N-O   P-Q-R   S-T-U
V-W-X   Y-Z

Other letters used in German:

Ä Ö Ü: the two dots (**Umlaut** *umlaut*) over these letters change
the pronunciation, as you may have already noticed in words like
schön and **Übung**.

ß (**sz** or **scharfes s** *sharp s*) is used instead of a double *s* after a long
vowel or a diphthong.

Long vowels: **Straße, Fußball**
Diphthong: **heißen**
Short vowel: **passt**

Note how you pronounce the letters A, E and I in German: **A** as in
Africa; **E** as in **E**lephant; **I** as in **I**srael. Don't mix them up with the
pronunciation of the English letters R, A and E!

Bitte buchstabieren Sie das! *Please spell that!*

QV

4 WER IST DA? *WHO HAS ARRIVED?*

◀) **CD 1, TR 19**

Listen to these people checking in at a conference and tick off the
names as they arrive.

...

Baumgart, Waltraud	☐
Henning, Sebastian	☐
Hesse, Patrick	☐
Hoffmann, Silke	☐
Ludwig, Paul	☐
Schanze, Martin	☐
Schidelowskaja, Tanja	☐
Schulte, Christel	☐

...

5 WELCHE FIRMENNAMEN HÖREN SIE?
WHAT COMPANY NAMES CAN YOU HEAR?

🔊 **CD 1, TR 20**

Hören Sie zu! Listen to the radio excerpt from a stock market report. Which of the companies, whose logos appear on the next page, are mentioned?

AEG	☐	**DER**	☐
DB	☐	**MAN**	☐
BMW	☐	**DZ BANK**	☐
VW	☐	**E-ON**	☐

AEG Die Bahn

  DZ BANK

[reproduced with permission of Volkswagen AG]

6 ROLLENSPIEL: WIE SCHREIBT MAN IHREN NAMEN?
HOW DO YOU SPELL YOUR NAME?

Answer the two questions on the recording, first giving your name and then spelling your surname.

Here is what you would say if your name were Karen Franks.

	Wie ist Ihr Name?
You	Franks, Karen Franks.
	Und wie schreibt man das?
You	F-R-A-N-K-S.

CD 1, TR 21

Numbers 11–100

7 MEHR ZAHLEN *MORE NUMBERS*

🔊 **CD 1, TR 22**

Hören Sie bitte zu und wiederholen Sie!

11 elf	**14** vierzehn	**17** siebzehn
12 zwölf	**15** fünfzehn	**18** achtzehn
13 dreizehn	**16** sechzehn	**19** neunzehn
20 zwanzig	**50** fünfzig	**80** achtzig
30 dreißig	**60** sechzig	**90** neunzig
40 vierzig	**70** siebzig	**100** (ein)hundert

In German, numbers such as 24 and 48 start with the last number and work backwards (a bit like the four-and-twenty blackbirds of nursery rhyme fame).

21 einundzwanzig	**43** dreiundvierzig
32 zweiunddreißig	**54** vierundfünfzig

Numbers in German are written as one word. German speakers don't seem to mind long words, as you will discover! Please note the following spelling variations: the 's' at the end of 'eins' is dropped in **einundzwanzig, einunddreißig** etc.; **dreißig** is written with a 'ß' and not with a 'z'.

How do you think you say these numbers in German? The answers are on the recording.

99 _____   **26** _____

48 _____   **52** _____

87 _____

8 DIE LOTTOZAHLEN *THE NATIONAL LOTTERY NUMBERS*

◄» CD 1, TR 23

You will hear a recording from a German draw. Choose six numbers first and then see if you have won.

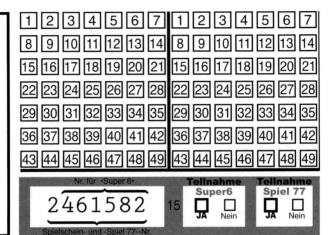

LOTTO Normal

1	2	3	4	5	6	7	1	2	3	4	5	6	7
8	9	10	11	12	13	14	8	9	10	11	12	13	14
15	16	17	18	19	20	21	15	16	17	18	19	20	21
22	23	24	25	26	27	28	22	23	24	25	26	27	28
29	30	31	32	33	34	35	29	30	31	32	33	34	35
36	37	38	39	40	41	42	36	37	38	39	40	41	42
43	44	45	46	47	48	49	43	44	45	46	47	48	49

Nr. für ·Super 6·

2 4 6 1 5 8 2   15

Spielschein- und -Spiel 77--Nr.

Teilnahme Super6 ☐ JA ☐ Nein

Teilnahme Spiel 77 ☐ JA ☐ Nein

Insight: Telefonnummern *Phone numbers*

In German you can say your phone number in single digits: 7 – 6 – 2 – 8 – 3 – 4
sieben – sechs – zwei/zwo – acht – drei – vier,
or in pairs: 76 – 28 – 34 **sechsundsiebzig – achtundzwanzig – vierunddreißig.**

This also applies to dialling codes: 0521
null – fünf – zwei/zwo – eins, or 05 – 21
null – fünf – einundzwanzig.

9 ANRUFE BEI DER AUSKUNFT
CALLING DIRECTORY ENQUIRIES

◀) **CD 1, TR 24**

Welche Namen und Telefonnummern hören Sie? What names and phone numbers do you hear on the recording?

a Name _____ Telefonnummer _____

b Name _____ Telefonnummer _____

Wie ist Ihre Telefonnummer? *What is your telephone number?*
Wie ist Ihre Handynummer? *What is your mobile number?*
Wie ist Ihre Faxnummer? *What is your fax number?*
Wie ist Ihre E-Mail-Adresse? *What is your e-mail address?*
Meine Telefonnummer, Handynummer, Faxnummer, E-Mail-Adresse ist ... *My telephone number, mobile number, fax number, e-mail-address is ...*

10 ROLLENSPIEL: TELEFONNUMMERN, HANDYNUMMERN, USW.
TELEPHONE NUMBERS, MOBILE NUMBERS, ETC.

◀) **CD 1, TR 25**

To give you some more practice in German numbers, try answering the questions on the recording.

Listen again and note down the numbers given by Jochen:

Telefon _____ Handy _____

Fax _____ E-Mail _____

Note that the @ sign in German is pronounced as in English.

SPRACHINFO: *Saying 'we', 'they'*

So far you have learned to talk about yourself (**ich**) and about a third person (**er, sie**) and to talk directly to someone (**Sie**).

What if you wanted to talk about yourself together with somebody else? In German you use **wir** (*we*). In the **wir** form the verb takes an **-en** ending.

Wir wohnen in Bonn.	*We live in Bonn.*
Wir arbeiten in Köln.	*We work in Cologne.*

To talk about two or more other people, you use **sie** (*they*). Again, the verb takes an **-en** ending.

Sie heißen Gerd und Sabine.	*They are called Gerd and Sabine.*
Sie kommen aus München.	*They come from Munich.*

11 SPRECHEN SIE FRANZÖSISCH?
DO YOU SPEAK FRENCH?

These German tourists are visiting Paris. Two couples are getting to know each other while they wait in the hotel foyer for the tour bus. Where do the two couples come from? Do they speak French? Listen to the recording and find out.

CD 1, TR 26

Jochen	Guten Morgen! Ich heiße Jochen Klempner und das ist meine Frau, Katja.
Marga	Guten Morgen! Wir heißen Marga und Peter Krumbacher. Wir kommen aus Jena. Wir arbeiten bei Carl Zeiss. Woher kommen Sie?
Katja	Wir sind aus Stuttgart. Sprechen Sie Französisch?
Peter	Nur ein wenig. Wir sprechen aber ziemlich gut Englisch. Und Sie?
Jochen	Wir sprechen kein Französisch und nur ein bisschen Englisch.

sprechen *to speak*
Französisch *French (language)*
nur ein wenig *only a little*
ziemlich *fairly*
Englisch *English (language)*
kein Englisch *no English*
ein bisschen *a bit (of)*

Richtig oder falsch? Korrigieren Sie die falschen Aussagen. *Correct the wrong statements and answer the question.*

a Jochen und Katja kommen aus Stuttgart.
b Sie sprechen ziemlich gut Französisch.
c Marga und Peter sind aus Weimar.
d Sie sprechen nur ein wenig Französisch.
e Sie sprechen kein Englisch.
f Arbeiten Marga und Peter bei Jenapharm oder bei Carl Zeiss?

Grammar

1 YES–NO QUESTIONS

Yes–no questions, as their name suggests, are those questions which require a *yes* or a *no* answer.

Statement Peter und Marga sprechen Englisch.
Question Sprechen Peter und Marga Englisch?

Statement Katja spricht kein Französisch.
Question Spricht Katja Französisch?

As you can see, yes–no questions start with a verb followed by the subject. Note that **ja** and **nein** are separated from the main part of the sentence by a comma and are not counted as an integral element of a sentence.

Yes – No Questions

1	2	
Verb	*Subject*	
Sprechen	**Sie**	Deutsch?
Wohnen	**Sie**	in Hamburg?
Kommen	**sie**	aus Berlin?

Statements

	1	2	
	Subject	*Verb*	
Ja,	**ich**	**spreche**	Deutsch.
Nein,	**ich**	**wohne**	nicht in Hamburg.
Nein,	**sie**	**kommen**	aus München.

2 VERB ENDINGS

You have now met the verb endings for most personal pronouns. Here is an overview.

Singular				*Plural*			
ich	komm**e**	sprech**e**	arbeit**e**	wir	komm**en**	sprech**en**	arbeit**en**
Sie	komm**en**	sprech**en**	arbeit**en**	Sie	komm**en**	sprech**en**	arbeit**en**
er/sie/es	komm**t**	spri**ch**t	arbeit**et**	sie	komm**en**	sprech**en**	arbeit**en**

Reminder: **arbeiten** needs an extra **e** in the **er/sie/es** form.

Note: **sprechen** has a vowel change to **spricht** in the **er/sie/es** form.

There are other verbs that behave like **sprechen**. You will be meeting more of them in Unit 9.

As you already know, the verb **sein** (*to be*) is irregular.

Singular		Plural	
ich	**bin**	wir	**sind**
Sie	**sind**	Sie	**sind**
er/sie/es	**ist**	sie	**sind**

3 *VARIOUS MEANINGS OF* **SIE**

You might think it a little confusing that the word **sie** has so many different meanings. In practice there are several ways of distinguishing between them. Firstly, the formal **Sie** (*you*) always takes a capital initial letter, secondly the ending of the verb for **sie** (*she*) is **-t** as opposed to **-en** for **sie** (*they*). Thirdly, and probably most importantly, the context nearly always makes the meaning clear.

TESTING YOURSELF

1 *Yes–no questions. You are somewhat surprised by the information given in these statements, so you query each one.*

Aussage: *Thomas und Johanna sprechen sehr gut Englisch.*
Frage: *Sprechen sie wirklich sehr gut Englisch?*
Reminder: **wirklich** *means really.*

    a *Ich heiße Brunhilde Bachmeyer-Goldhagen.*
    b *Ich komme aus Hollywood.*
    c *Thomas und Johanna wohnen in München.*
    d *Johanna arbeitet in Nürnberg.*
    e *Thomas spricht ein wenig Spanisch.*
    f *Wir kommen aus Innsbruck.*

2 **Visitenkarten:** *Here are the business cards of two people. Pretend that you are each person in turn and write as much as you can about yourself at this stage.*

a

 Delta Software GmbH

Matthias Peters
Marketing

Burchardstraße 34 20095 Hamburg
Telefon 040-300526 Fax: 040-376284
E–Mail m.peters@delta.com

b

ANTIQUITÄTEN CENTER
Marienstraße 21 44000 Münster

Dorothea Johannsen
ART DECO, ART NOUVEAU

Telefon 02 51/51 43 86
E-Mail johannsen@artdeco.de

Now that you have completed Unit 3, can you:	tick
1 spell your name in German?	☐
2 count from 0 to 100+?	☐
3 talk about us and them?	☐

4

Sprechen Sie Deutsch?
Do you speak German?

In this unit you will learn
- *how to say what languages you speak and ask others what they speak*
- *how to say whether you are working or studying*
- *how to say what nationality you are*

Language points
- *formal and informal 'you'*

I speak German

1 EIN ABENDKURS IN EINER VOLKSHOCHSCHULE
AN EVENING COURSE AT AN ADULT EDUCATION INSTITUTION

◆) **CD 1, TR 27**

Some people are introducing themselves to their fellow course members. Listen to the recording then answer the questions on the next page.

> **Dialog 1**
> Guten Abend! Mein Name ist Norbert Schicker und ich bin Deutscher.
> Ich komme aus Potsdam in der Nähe von Berlin, aber ich wohne jetzt hier in Leipzig.
> Ich spreche Deutsch und ich kann auch sehr gut Russisch. Ich bin verheiratet und ich bin seit zwei Jahren pensioniert.

Deutscher *(a) German (male)*
in der Nähe von ... *near* ...
ich kann ... *I can (speak)* ...
auch *also*
Russisch *Russian (the language)*
seit zwei Jahren *for (lit. since) two years*
Deutsche *(a) German (female)*
natürlich *of course*
Französisch *French (the language)*
verstehen *to understand*
Spanisch *Spanish (the language)*
studieren *to study*

> **Dialog 2**
> Hallo! Ich heiße Heike Berger und bin Deutsche.
> Ich bin ledig und komme aus Merseburg, in der Nähe von Leipzig.
> Ich spreche natürlich Deutsch und ein wenig Französisch. Ich verstehe auch ein bisschen Spanisch.
> Ich studiere hier in Leipzig.

Familienstand *marital status*
verheiratet *married*
ledig *single, unmarried*
geschieden *divorced*
verwitwet *widowed*
pensioniert *retired*
arbeitslos *unemployed*

46

Check if you understood what Heike and Norbert said about themselves. Write an **N** if the description fits Norbert or an **H** if it fits Heike.

N oder H?

a __ versteht ein bisschen Spanisch.
b __ ist Deutscher und kommt aus Potsdam.
c __ ist verheiratet.
d __ kann sehr gut Russisch.
e __ studiert in Leipzig.
f __ ist seit zwei Jahren pensioniert.

2 NOCH ZWEI ABENDKURSSTUDENTEN
TWO MORE EVENING CLASS STUDENTS

◀) **CD 1, TR 28**

Listen to the recording and fill in the grid as you listen.

Türke *(a) Turkish (male)*
Türkisch *Turkish (the language)*
Österreicherin *(an) Austrian (female)*

Fill in the missing details.

Name	Gür Yalezan	Susi Merkl
Nationalität (*nationality*)	Türke	
Geburtsort		
Wohnort	Taucha	Rötha
Sprachen (*languages*)		
Familienstand (*marital status*)		
Arbeit? (*work*)		
Studium? (*study*)		

In English you do not in general say 'I'm a German' or 'He's a Turk'. You prefer to say 'I'm German' or 'He's Turkish' – using the adjective rather than the noun. In German, it is normal to use the noun, but the word for 'a' is not needed:

> *Ich bin Deutscher / Deutsche.*
> *Gür ist Türke.*
> *Susi ist Österreicherin.*

Nationalities and languages

3 ICH ÜBER MICH *ABOUT ME*

Read the following text. Can you find out which languages Michael speaks?

 Michaels Home-Page – Ich über mich
Ich heiße Michael Schulmeyer und bin 23 Jahre alt.
Ich bin Österreicher und komme aus Wien.
Ich studiere auch in Wien (Fremdsprachen).
Meine Muttersprache ist Deutsch.
Ich spreche auch Englisch und Französisch.
Ich verstehe ein wenig Spanisch.
Ich lerne im Moment Japanisch.
Mehr über mich?

Hier klicken!

ich über mich *about me (lit. I about myself)*
alt *old*
Fremdsprachen *foreign languages*
meine Muttersprache *my mother tongue*
lernen *to learn*
im Moment *at the moment*

Beantworten Sie die Fragen. *Answer the questions in full sentences.*

Frage Ist Michael 23 Jahre alt?
Antwort Ja, er ist 23 Jahre alt.
Frage Kommt Michael aus Salzburg?
Antwort Nein, er kommt aus Wien.

a Ist Michael Deutscher?
b Ist er arbeitslos?
c Studiert er in Innsbruck?
d Spricht er Deutsch?
e Spricht er auch Russisch?
f Versteht er ein wenig Spanisch?
g Lernt er im Moment Türkisch?

4 NATIONALITÄTEN *NATIONALITIES*

Here are some nationalities and languages that you already know together with some new ones.

What are the two endings on the nationalities used for men? What is the main ending for female nationalities? What do almost all the languages end in? Check your answers in the Grammar section later in this unit.

♂	♀	**Sprache** (*language*)
Ich bin **Deutscher.**	Ich bin **Deutsche.**	**Deutsch**
Bernd ist **Österreicher.**	Susi ist **Österreicherin.**	**Deutsch**
Er ist **Engländer.**	Sie ist **Engländerin.**	**Englisch**
Sind Sie **Amerikaner?**	Sind Sie **Amerikanerin?**	**Englisch**
David ist **Waliser.**	Sîan ist **Waliserin.**	**Englisch/Walisisch**
Iain ist **Schotte.**	Una ist **Schottin.**	**Englisch**
Padraig ist **Ire.**	Maire ist **Irin.**	**Englisch**
Gür ist **Türke.**	Yildiz ist **Türkin.**	**Türkisch**
Jean-Claude ist **Franzose.**	Nadine ist **Französin.**	**Französisch**
Miguel ist **Spanier.**	Manuela ist **Spanierin.**	**Spanisch**
Masahide ist **Japaner.**	Kumi ist **Japanerin.**	**Japanisch**

5 WER SIND SIE? *WHO ARE YOU?*

Rachel Jenkins has written down details about herself. Write down your own details following the same pattern.

> *Mein Name ist Rachel Jenkins. Ich bin Engländerin.*
> *Ich komme aus Preston. Ich wohne jetzt in Manchester.*
> *Ich spreche Englisch und ein bisschen Deutsch.*
> *Ich bin ledig und ich arbeite hier in Manchester.*

6 ROLLENSPIEL: UND JETZT SIE! *AND NOW YOU!*

◀) **CD 1, TR 29**

Now listen to the questions on the recording and give your responses orally, using the pause button to allow yourself to speak.

SPRACHINFO: *Informal ways of saying 'you'* **(du, ihr)**
Before you move on to other topics it's important to know that in German there are formal and informal ways of saying you: **Sie** (*formal*) and **du** (*informal*) are used when addressing one person; **Sie** (*formal*) and **ihr** (*informal*) are needed when talking to more than one person. As you might expect the verb endings for **Sie, du**

and **ihr** are different. Here are some examples of all three forms, starting with the **Sie** form that you have practised already.

Sie -en	du -st	ihr -t
Wie heißen Sie?	Wie heißt du?	Wie heißt ihr?
Woher kommen Sie?	Woher kommst du?	Woher kommt ihr?
Wo wohnen Sie?	Wo wohnst du?	Wo wohnt ihr?
Sprechen Sie Deutsch?	Sprichst du Deutsch?	Sprecht ihr Deutsch?

If the stem of a verb ends in **ß**, **ss** or **z**, only **-t** is added to the stem in the **du** form: **du heißt, du tanzt**.

With **sprechen** the vowel changes to an **i** in the **du** form, just as it does in the **er** form: **du sprichst, er spricht**. See the Grammar section for a summary of the verb endings in the present.

7 DU UND SIE

Here is a dialogue between two students, Markus and Christian, meeting in a London hotel foyer. They are using the **du** form. Re-write the dialogue for two businessmen, Klaus Thomas and Gerhard Braun, meeting in the same hotel foyer. They would use the **Sie** form. Make the greeting more formal too. You can check your new version on the recording.

Markus	Hallo! Ich heiße Markus. Und wie heißt du?
Christian	Ich bin Christian. Woher kommst du?
Markus	Aus München. Kommst du auch aus München?
Christian	Nein, aus Nürnberg. Sprichst du Englisch?
Markus	Ja, ziemlich gut. Und du?
Christian	Na ja, es geht.

⌖ CD 1, TR 30

Insight: Saying 'you'

Here are a few tips for when to use the formal and informal modes of address in German:

- Use **Sie** with people you are not particularly close to. **Sie** is spelt with a capital **S** wherever it comes in the sentence. Use **Sie** to address one or more persons.

- Use **du** to a person you feel close to, and to a child or a pet; **du** is also used among young people and students; **du** can only be used to address one person.

- Use **ihr** to two or more people who you would address individually as **du**.

When you are not sure, use **Sie**.

In everyday situations where English speakers might immediately adopt first name terms, many German speakers tend to prefer a certain degree of formality. For instance, work colleagues often call each other **Herr X** or **Frau Y** and use the **Sie** form to each other even after years of working together.

Pronunciation

◆) **CD 1, TR 31**

A **w** in German is pronounced more like an English *v*. And a **v** in German is pronounced like an *f* in English.

wie?	**wo?**	**wer?**
verheiratet	**verwitwet**	**vierzig**

St and **sp** in German are pronounced as *sht* and *shp* at the beginning of a word or syllable.

Straße	studieren	verstehen
Sport	Spanisch	versprechen (to promise)

How are these words pronounced?
viel, wirklich, Sprachen, Beispiel,
Studium.

Grammar

1 NATIONALITIES AND LANGUAGES

As you will have seen in **Übung 4 Nationalitäten**, the endings on
nouns indicating nationality are:

For males		*For females*	
-er	**-e**	**-erin**	**-in**
Amerikaner	Franzose	Amerikanerin	Französin
Engländer	Türke	Engländerin	Türkin
Spanier	Grieche	Spanierin	Griechin

The main exception to this is the female version of *a German*: **eine
Deutsche.**

Most languages end in -isch: **Englisch, Französisch, Japanisch,** etc.
Again the exception is *German*: **Deutsch!**

Note that **Franzose** does not have an umlaut (¨), but **Französin** and
Französisch do.

2 SUMMARY OF VERB ENDINGS

This summary of the verb endings includes the **du** and **ihr** forms
that you have met in this unit. Note that most verbs follow the
regular pattern like **wohnen**, but some verbs, like **sprechen**, have a
vowel change in the **du** and the **er/sie/es** forms. You will meet more
of these in Unit 9. Also note that verbs whose stem ends in **t,** such

as **arbeiten**, add an extra -e in the **du** and **ihr** forms. Verbs ending with an ß, ss or z only add a -t in the **du** form: **du heißt, du tanzt**. We have included the irregular verbs **sein** *to be* and **haben** *to have* because they occur so frequently.

		wohnen	sprechen	arbeiten	sein	haben
Singular	ich	wohne	spreche	arbeite	bin	habe
	du	wohnst	sprichst	arbeitest	bist	hast
	Sie	wohnen	sprechen	arbeiten	sind	haben
	er/sie/es	wohnt	spricht	arbeitet	ist	hat
Plural	wir	wohnen	sprechen	arbeiten	sind	haben
	ihr	wohnt	sprecht	arbeitet	seid	habt
	Sie/sie	wohnen	sprechen	arbeiten	sind	haben

3 DIFFERENT WORDS FOR 'YOUR'

There are three words for 'your'. When they are used with certain nouns you have to add an **e** to them. The reason for this is that these nouns are feminine. There is more on this in the next unit.

Sie – Ihr(e)	du – dein(e)	ihr – euer/eure
Wie ist **Ihr** Name?	Wie ist **dein** Name?	Wie ist **euer** Name?
Wie ist **Ihre** Telefonnummer?	Wie ist **deine** Telefonnummer?	Wie ist **eure** Telefonnummer?

Note that an **e** is dropped from **euer** when there is an **e** at the end. Words for *your* or *my* (**mein**) are called *possessive adjectives*. For a more detailed list of possessives in German see Unit 15, Grammar 2.

4 ASKING HOW SOMEONE IS

There are three ways of asking 'How are you?' in German, depending on the context (formal, informal) and the number of people being addressed.

Sie → Ihnen	du → dir	ihr → euch
Wie geht es Ihnen?	Wie geht's dir?	Wir geht's euch?

TESTING YOURSELF

1 Rollenspiel: Machen Sie ein Interview.

🔊 **CD 1, TR 32**

Take on the role of Jürgen Krause and answer the questions on the recording.

Name	Jürgen Krause
Staatsangehörigkeit	Österreicher
Geburtsort	Wien
Wohnort	Salzburg
Sprachen	Deutsch und Englisch
Familienstand	seit drei Jahren verwitwet
Arbeit?	Ja, in Salzburg

2 Sagen Sie es anders.
Match the sentences on the left with those of similar meaning on the right.

a Wie ist dein Name?

i Woher seid ihr?

b Welche Telefonnummer habt ihr?

ii Welche Handynummer hast du?

c Woher kommt ihr?

iii Wie heißt du?

d Wie ist deine Handynummer?

iv Woher kommst du?

e Wie heißen Sie?

v Wie ist eure Telefonnummer?

f Woher bist du?

vi Wie ist Ihr Name?

3 *Sie, du und ihr. Here are some questions which you might ask a stranger in a hotel:*

   a *Wie heißen Sie?*
   b *Woher kommen Sie?*
   c *Und wo wohnen Sie jetzt?*
   d *Wie geht's Ihnen heute?*
   e *Sprechen Sie Englisch?*
   f *Sind Sie aus Hamburg?*
   g *Wie ist Ihre Handynummer?*

   i *Now re-formulate the questions as if you were a student who has just met another student in a hall of residence.*
     Beispiel *a* Wie **heißt du**?
  ii *And now re-formulate the questions yet again as if you were a young person who has just met a young couple in a hotel.*
     Beispiel *a* Wie **heißt ihr**?

Now that you have completed Unit 4, can you:	tick
1 say what language you speak?	☐
2 say whether you are working, studying, retired or unemployed?	☐
3 say what nationality people are?	☐
4 use the various forms for *you* correctly?	☐

5

In der Stadt
In town

In this unit you will learn
- *how to talk about places in towns and cities*
- *how to count from 101 upwards*

Language points
- *gender and articles*

Towns and cities

1 WAS IST DAS? *WHAT IS THAT?*

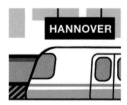

a Das ist ein Bahnhof.

Das ist **der** Bahnhof in Hannover.

b Das ist ein Flohmarkt.

Der Flohmarkt in Hannover.

c Das ist eine Bäckerei.

Die Stadtbäckerei.

d Das ist eine Kneipe.

Die Kneipe heißt ‚Das Weinloch'.

e Das ist ein Kino.

Das Abaton-Kino.

f Das ist ein Hotel.

Das Hotel Schmidt in Celle.

QUICK VOCAB

der Bahnhof *the railway station*
der Flohmarkt *the flea market*
die Bäckerei *the bakery*
die Kneipe *the pub*
das Kino *the cinema*
das Hotel *the hotel*

SPRACHINFO: *Genders of nouns*

All German nouns have a gender: they are either masculine, feminine or neuter:

	the ...	*a ...*
masculine	**der Bahnhof**	**ein Bahnhof**
feminine	**die Bäckerei**	**eine Bäckerei**
neuter	**das Kino**	**ein Kino**

In the plural the word for *the* is **die**: **die** Bahnhöfe, **die** Bäckereien, **die** Kinos. But there will be more about plural forms later in the book. If a noun is made up of two or more nouns, it is always the last noun which determines the gender:

> das *Bier* + der *Garten:* der *Biergarten*
> das *Telefon* + die *Nummer:* die *Telefonnummer*

Words like **mein** (*my*), **dein** (*your*/informal) and **Ihr** (*your*/formal) also have masculine, feminine and neuter forms. In German these endings don't depend on the person who speaks but on the gender of the noun that comes after **mein, dein** etc.

masculine **Mein** Name ist Ulrike Weber. Wie ist **Ihr** Name? (der Name)

feminine **Meine** Telefonnummer ist 774876. Wie ist **deine** Telefonnummer? (die Telefonnummer)

neuter Das ist **mein** Haus. Wo ist **dein** Haus? (das Haus)

Don't forget that the formal word for *your* takes a capital letter: Wie ist **Ihre** Telefonnummer?

Note that from this unit onwards, new nouns are usually given with their gender. You should also be able to check the gender of nouns in all good dictionaries. When you look up the gender in a dictionary, masculine nouns are usually indicated with (m), feminine nouns with (f) and neuter nouns with (nt).

2 ROLLENSPIEL: EIN STADTPLAN *TOWN MAP*

🔊 **CD 1, TR 33**

Nennen Sie die Gebäude. *Name the buildings.*

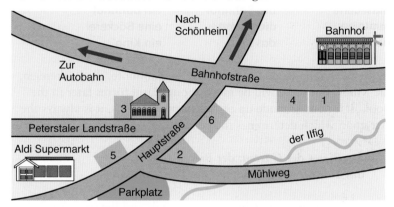

Six of the places on the map are represented by a number.

1 Kneipe – Bierstübl
2 Biergarten – Mönchbräu
3 Kirche – Jakobskirche
4 Hotel – Bahnhofshotel
5 Café – Café Krause
6 Markt – Buttermarkt

A visitor to the town wants you to tell them what these places are. Write down your answers and then check them on the recording. Make sure you have got the genders right! Also pay special attention to the pronunciation of the place names.

Then say your answers out loud and check them once more against the recording.

Beispiel Eins ist eine Kneipe. Die Kneipe heißt Bierstübl.
Zwei ist **ein** Biergarten. **Der** Biergarten …

der Biergarten *the beer garden*
die Kirche *the church*
das Café *the café*

3 WORTSPIEL *WORD GAME*

Write down the words which the pictures represent horizontally on the grid below and another word will appear vertically.

1 Bakery   **2** Station   **3** Hotel

4 Church   **5** ?   **6** Beer

4 WELCHE ENDUNGEN? *WHICH ENDINGS?*

Which endings are needed in these sentences? In some cases no ending is needed.

a Das ist ein__ Kino.
b D__ Hotel heißt Vier Jahreszeiten.
c Dort ist ein__ Bäckerei.
d Wie ist Ihr__ Name?
e Wo ist d__ Bahnhofshotel?
f Wo ist hier ein__ Café?
g Wie ist dein__ Telefonnummer?
h D__ Kneipe heißt Blauer Engel.

5 EINE POSTKARTE AUS MÜNCHEN
A POSTCARD FROM MUNICH

Lesen Sie die Postkarte und beantworten Sie dann die Fragen. *Read the postcard and answer the questions.*

München, 3. September
Hallo Jörg,
wie geht 's? Mir geht es wirklich sehr gut. Ich bin jetzt zwei Wochen in München. Die Stadt ist sehr schön, besonders das Stadtzentrum und der ‚Englische Garten'. Ich gehe auch in eine Sprachschule. Die Sprachschule heißt ‚Superlang'. Ich spreche ziemlich viel Deutsch. Das Bier in München ist sehr gut. Es heißt Weizenbier.
Bis bald
deine Tracy

An
Jörg Kümmerli
Mozartstraße 43a
A-5020 SALZBURG
Österreich

besonders *especially*
ziemlich viel *quite a lot*
bis bald *see you soon*
Weizenbier *wheat beer*

Beantworten Sie die Fragen. *Answer the questions.*

a Wo ist Tracy?
b Wie ist die Stadt?
c Was ist besonders schön?
d Wie heißt die Sprachschule?
e Spricht Tracy nur Englisch?
f Was ist auch sehr gut in München?
g Wie heißen die Artikel: **der, die** oder **das**?
    die Woche (*week*)
    … Stadtzentrum (*city centre*)
    … Garten (*garden*)
    … Sprachschule (*language school*)
    … Bier (*beer*)

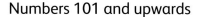

Numbers 101 and upwards

🔊 **CD 1, TR 34**

Hören Sie bitte zu und wiederholen
Sie! *Listen and repeat.*

101	(ein)hunderteins
102	(ein)hundertzwei
110	(ein)hundertzehn
111	(ein)hundertelf
120	(ein)hundertzwanzig
121	(ein)hunderteinundzwanzig
201	zweihunderteins
312	dreihundertzwölf
999	neunhundertneunundneunzig

1 000	(ein)tausend
2 843	zweitausendachthundertdreiundvierzig
10 962	zehntausendneunhundertzweiundsechzig
1 000 000	eine Million
4 000 000	vier Millionen
1 000 000 000	eine Milliarde

Note how even long numbers are written as one word in German.

6 NOTRUFE *EMERGENCY CALLS*

🔊 **CD 1, TR 35**

Say the numbers for police, fire and emergency doctor out loud. Then check your answers on the recording.

Notrufe

Polizei ... 110

Feuer ... 112

Notarzt ... 115

7 WELCHE ZAHLEN HÖREN SIE?

🔊 **CD 1, TR 36**

Listen to the six numbers on the recording and tick the ones you hear.

1	a 237	b 273	c 327
2	a 459	b 954	c 495
3	a 642	b 624	c 426
4	a 1 321	b 1 231	c 1 132
5	a 4 762	b 4 267	c 6 462
6	a 11 329	b 11 932	c 11 293

8 WIE VIELE EINWOHNER HABEN DIESE STÄDTE?
HOW MANY INHABITANTS DO THESE CITIES HAVE?

Write out in full the number of inhabitants for each city.

Beispiel Köln	986 000	neunhundertsechsundachtzigtausend

Heidelberg	143 000
Dresden	502 000
Frankfurt am Main	660 000
München	1 326 000
Hamburg	1 750 000
Berlin	3 402 000

Grammar

1 GENDER OF NOUNS AND ARTICLES

As you have seen, German nouns are either *masculine*, *feminine* or *neuter*. This is their *gender*. The words for the and a (the so-called *definite* and *indefinite articles*) have to match the gender of the nouns:

masculine	**der Bahnhof** *(the station)*	**ein Bahnhof** *(a station)*
feminine	**die Kirche** *(the church)*	**eine Kirche** *(a church)*
neuter	**das Café** *(the café)*	**ein Café** *(a café)*

If a noun is made up of more than one noun, it is the last element that determines the gender:

das Bier + der Garten	→	**der Biergarten**
das Haus + die Frau	→	**die Hausfrau**

There are a few guidelines to help you know the gender of nouns in German. As you have already seen, many 'things' are not neuter, but masculine (e.g. **der Garten, der Bahnhof**) or feminine (e.g. **die Kneipe, die Kirche**). Also, some words referring to people are neuter, such as **das Mädchen** (*girl*). However, there are some basic rules. Here are just a few of them:

masculine nouns: many nouns ending in -en: der Garten

feminine nouns: most nouns ending in **-e: die Kirche, Kneipe**
    most nouns ending in **-ei: die Bäckerei**
    all nouns ending in **-ung: die Zeitung**
    all nouns ending in **-tät: die Nationalität**

neuter nouns: most nouns ending in **-um: das Zentrum**

In general, you need to learn the noun with its definite article: **der, die** or **das** when you first meet it. If you look up the gender in a dictionary, masculine nouns are usually indicated with (m), feminine nouns with (f) and neuter nouns with (nt).

2 ENDINGS FOR POSSESSIVE ADJECTIVES

Don't forget that words like **mein** *my* and **Ihr** *your*, so-called *possessive adjectives*, need endings and follow the pattern of **ein/eine**:

masculine	**mein Name**
feminine	**meine Adresse**
neuter	**mein Haus**

For a list of possessive adjectives please see Unit 15.

TESTING YOURSELF

1 *Fill in the gaps with the correct versions of* **Ihr(e)** *or* **mein(e):**

    a *Wie ist ____ Name? – ____ Name ist Astrid.*
    b *Wie ist ____ Adresse? – ____ Adresse ist Hauptstraße 45.*
    c *Wo liegt ____ Haus? – ____ Haus liegt im Zentrum.*
    d *Wie ist ____ Telefonnummer? – ____ Telefonnummer ist
      753412.*
    e *Wie heißt ____ Mann? – ____ Mann heißt Gerhard.*

2 **Schreiben Sie Ihre erste Postkarte.** *Write your first postcard in German.*

    You just have to fill in the missing words. Choose the person you would like to write to.

    der – schön – Die – fantastisch – bald – eine – das – heißt – spreche – geht's – eine – Die

Wien, 7. Februar
Hallo _____ ,
wie _____? Mir geht es _____ .
Ich bin jetzt _____ Woche in Wien.
_____ Stadt ist sehr _____ ,
besonders _____ Zentrum und
_____ Stadtpark. Ich gehe jetzt
auch in _____ Sprachschule. _____
Sprachschule _____ ‚Eurolingua'. Ich
_____ jetzt viel Deutsch.
Was machst du?
Bis _____
♀ deine _____
♂ dein _____

An
_____
_____
_____

Now that you have completed Unit 5, can you: tick

1 name five buildings in a town with the correct articles? ☐

2 count from 100 onwards? ☐

3 give the correct articles for a few masculine, feminine and neuter nouns in this unit? ☐

4 name one typical ending each for masculine, feminine and neuter nouns? ☐

6

Arbeit und Studium
Work and study

In this unit you will learn
- *how to ask people about their occupation and state yours*
- *how to ask people what they study and where*

Language points
- *the verb* sein *(to be)*
- *plural forms of nouns*
- *'for' or 'since'*

Occupations

1 WAS SIND DIESE LEUTE VON BERUF?
WHAT DO THESE PEOPLE DO FOR A LIVING?

Welches Wort passt zu welchem Bild? *Which word from the list of professions below matches which picture on the next page?*

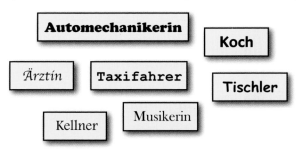

Automechanikerin

Koch

Ärztin

Taxifahrer

Tischler

Kellner

Musikerin

a Paul Meier

b Helga Neumann

c Heike Müller

d Manfred Lustig

e Kurt Leutner

f Ulrike Wagner

g Marc Straßburger

Write short descriptions of the people in the pictures.

a Das ist Paul Meier. Er ist Taxifahrer.
b Das ist Helga Neumann. Sie ist Automechanikerin.
c Das ist __. Sie ist __, etc.

SPRACHINFO: Mehr Berufe
More professions
Here is a list of common professions.
Note the different forms for males and females.

der (masculine)	**die** (feminine)	
Automechaniker	Automechaniker**in**	*car mechanic*
Friseur	Friseur**in**	*hairdresser*
Journalist	Journalist**in**	*journalist*
Kellner	Kellner**in**	*waiter/waitress*
Lehrer	Lehrer**in**	*teacher*
Maurer	Maurer**in**	*bricklayer*
Musiker	Musiker**in**	*musician*
Sekretär	Sekretär**in**	*secretary*
Student	Student**in**	*student*
Taxifahrer	Taxifahrer**in**	*taxi driver*
Tischler	Tischler**in**	*carpenter*
Verkäufer	Verkäufer**in**	*shop assistant*

Ausnahmen *Exceptions*

Arzt	**Ä**rztin	*doctor*
Bankkauf**mann**	Bankkauf**frau**	*qualified bank clerk*
K**o**ch	K**ö**chin	*chef*
Angestellt**er**	Angestellt**e**	*employee*
Kranken**pfleger**	Kranken**schwester**	*nurse*

2 SIND SIE BERUFSTÄTIG? *DO YOU HAVE A JOB?*

🔊 **CD 1, TR 37**

Jutta Sammer aus Borken lernt Ingrid Baker aus Whitstable kennen. *Jutta Sammer from Borken gets to know Ingrid Baker from Whitstable.*

Listen to the first part of the dialogue (1) and try to find answers to these two questions:

a How is it that Ingrid Baker speaks German so well?
b Why does she mention a period of 18 years?

Dialog 1

Jutta Sammer	Willkommen in Borken! Mein Name ist Jutta Sammer. Hoffentlich sprechen Sie Deutsch!
Ingrid Baker	Guten Abend! Ja, ich spreche Deutsch. Ich heiße Ingrid Baker.
Jutta Sammer	Prima! Sie sprechen ja sehr gut Deutsch. Sind Sie denn Deutsche, Frau Baker?
Ingrid Baker	Ja, aber mein Mann ist Engländer und ich wohne seit 18 Jahren in England.
Jutta Sammer	Ach so. Sind Sie berufstätig?
Ingrid Baker	Ja, ich bin Verkäuferin.

QUICK VOCAB

willkommen *welcome*
denn *(here) then*
mein Mann *my husband*
Sind Sie berufstätig? *Do you have a job?*

And now listen to the second part of the dialogue (2) and try to work out the answers to these two questions:

c Which of the women works – Jutta, Ingrid or both of them?
d Whose husband is retired – Jutta's or Ingrid's?

Wo arbeiten Sie? *Where do you work?*
der Supermarkt *supermarket*
seit wann? *since when?*
seit drei Jahren *for (lit. since) three years*
Was sind Sie von Beruf? *What job do you do? (lit. What are you by profession?)*
Er arbeitet bei … *He works for …*
Was macht Ihr Mann? *What does your husband do?*
war *was*

Now read through both dialogues again, noting the new vocabulary as you go.

Richtig oder falsch? Korrigieren Sie die falschen Aussagen.

e Ingrid Baker ist Österreicherin.
f Ingrid wohnt seit 18 Jahren in England.
g Sie ist Verkäuferin von Beruf.
h Jutta Sammer ist Bankkauffrau von Beruf.
i Herr Sammer ist seit neun Monaten pensioniert.
j Herr Baker war Journalist von Beruf.

3 JOCHEN KRENZLER AUS DRESDEN LERNT RAINER TIETMEYER AUS COVENTRY KENNEN

◀) **CD 1, TR 38**

Listen to the recording and find the correct answer.

Welche Antwort passt?

a Herr Tietmeyer ist Deutscher / Schweizer.

b Frau Tietmeyer ist Deutsche / Engländerin.

c Herr Tietmeyer wohnt seit 14 Jahren / 20 Jahren / 24 Jahren in England.

d Herr Tietmeyer ist Kellner / Tischler / Bankkaufmann von Beruf.

4 ROLLENSPIEL: BEANTWORTEN SIE DIE FRAGEN

◀) **CD 1, TR 39**

Answer the questions on the recording as if you were Frau Murphy-Heinrichs.

Here are her details:

- ▶ *Deutsche*
- ▶ *Mann ist Ire*
- ▶ *wohnt seit 17 Jahren in Münster*
- ▶ *ist Sekretärin bei Mannesmann*
- ▶ *Mann ist Taxifahrer*

5 ANAGRAMME *ANAGRAMS*

Was sind diese Leute von Beruf? *What jobs do these people do?* Unscramble the letters to spell out these jobs.

a

NREIRLEH

b

ERURAM

c

ANSTUJORIL

d

ERNISÄTERK

What are you studying?

ZWÖLF STUDIENFÄCHER
TWELVE SUBJECTS (OF STUDY)

These are some of the most commonly studied subjects at university.

Anglistik *English language and literature*
Betriebswirtschaftslehre (BWL) *management studies*
Biologie *biology*
Chemie *chemistry*
Germanistik *German language and literature*
Geschichte *history*
Informatik *computer studies*
Jura *law*
Mathematik *maths*
Medizin *medicine*
Romanistik *Romance studies*
Volkswirtschaftslehre (VWL) *economics*

Studieren means to study at a university; **lernen** is more appropriate for study at lower levels, such as in schools, further education and adult education.

6 IN DER JUGENDHERBERGE *IN THE YOUTH HOSTEL*

Nicolai lernt Karin und Anke kennen. *Nicolai gets to know Karin and Anke.* Listen to the recording and decide if the statements that follow are true or false.

Nicolai	Grüß euch! Ich heiße Nicolai. Wie heißt ihr?
Karin	Hallo! Mein Name ist Karin.
Anke	Und ich bin die Anke.
Nicolai	Und woher kommt ihr?
Anke	Wir kommen aus Gießen. Und du? Woher kommst du?
Nicolai	Aus Frankfurt. Ich studiere dort Romanistik. Studiert ihr auch?
Karin	Ja, wir studieren BWL in Marburg.
Nicolai	Und ist das interessant?
Anke	Na ja, es geht, ein bisschen langweilig.

♫ CD 1, TR 40

QUICK VOCAB

Grüß euch! *Hallo, hi (a familar greeting used to more than one person)*
na ja *(informal) oh well*
es geht *it's all right*
langweilig *boring*

Richtig oder falsch?

a Anke und Karin kommen aus Gelsenkirchen.
b Nicolai kommt aus Frankfurt.
c Nicolai studiert Germanistik.
d Anke und Karin studieren BWL.
e Sie studieren in Marburg.
f Sie finden es sehr interessant.

7 WAS STUDIEREN SIE?

◄» CD 1, TR 41

Listen to the recording and fill in the information that these students give about themselves.

Name	Paul	Daniel	Heike	Martina
Geburtsort		Hamburg		
Studienort	Bremen			
Studienfach			Informatik	

die Bildung *education*
die Ausbildung *training*

8 ICH ÜBER MICH

Write down as much information about yourself as your German
will allow. Use Vicki Farrow's model below to help you.

Ich über mich

Ich heiße Vicki Farrow. Ich komme aus Newcastle, aber ich
wohne jetzt in Peckham. Das ist in London. Meine Eltern
wohnen noch in Newcastle.

Ich bin Krankenschwester und ich arbeite in Southwark.
Ich spreche Englisch, Französisch und ein bisschen
Deutsch.

Mein Partner heißt Darren und er ist Arzt. Er arbeitet in
Battersea. Er spricht sehr gut Deutsch.

Pronunciation

◄) CD 1, TR 42

In German the use of the umlaut (¨) always changes the way a vowel (such as **a, o** or **u**) or a diphthong (such as **au**) is pronounced.

Listen to the way **a** plus an umlaut is pronounced in these words:

Engländer   Universität   berufstätig   Sekretärin
Kindergärtnerin

Listen to the way **au** plus an umlaut is pronounced:
Verkäufer   Fräulein

How would you pronounce these words?
Ärztin, Bäckerei, Dänemark, Häuser.

Check your answers on the audio.

Grammar

1 THE VERB SEIN (TO BE)

Remember that this is an irregular verb:

	Singular			Plural	
Ich	**bin**	Student.	**Wir**	**sind**	Engländer.
Du	**bist**	Sekretärin.	**Ihr**	**seid**	Amerikaner.
Sie	**sind**	verheiratet.	**Sie**	**sind**	Japaner.
Er/Sie/Es	**ist**	alt.	**Sie**	**sind**	arbeitslos.

2 SAYING 'FOR' OR 'SINCE'

In the dialogue **Sind Sie berufstätig?** in this unit there are two examples of the preposition **seit** (*for, since*):

> *Ich wohne seit 18 Jahren in England.*
> *Seit drei Jahren.*

In these examples **seit** corresponds to the English *'for'* (for 18 years, for 3 years).

The plural of Jahr ist Jahre, but when it is used with **seit** an extra **-n** is added (**drei Jahre – seit drei Jahren**).

3 PLURAL OF NOUNS

German nouns do not simply add -s to form their plurals (a book, two books). You need to learn the plural of a noun when you first meet it, along with the gender. In this unit you met:

> *Singular:* **Ich bin Student.**
> *Plural:* **Seid ihr Studenten?**

A few other types of plural are:

> *nouns which do not change:* **ein Engländer, zwei Engländer**
> *nouns – usually referring to female professions – which add*
> **-nen: eine Studentin, zwei Studentinnen**
> *nouns which add an umlaut (") and an* **-e: ein Bahnhof,**
> **zwei Bahnhöfe.** *Note that this pattern often applies to masculine nouns:* **ein Koch, zwei Köche.**

You will meet more plural forms in Unit 8.

TESTING YOURSELF

1 *Anke and Thomas meet up and ask each other a few questions. Put what they say into the correct order to make a continuous dialogue. There may be more than one solution.*

  a Anke *Bist du Student?*
  b Thomas *Hallo! Mein Name ist Thomas.*
  c Anke *Und woher kommst du?*
  d Thomas *Ja, ich studiere Chemie in Leipzig. Und du?*
  e Anke *Hallo! Ich heiße Anke. Wie heißt du?*
  f Thomas *Ich komme aus Leipzig.*
  g Anke *Ich bin auch Studentin. Ich studiere Anglistik in München.*

2 Setzen Sie ein. *Fit these words into the gaps:*
Kellnerin, Engländer, Studentin, Ire, Verkäuferin, Journalist, Schottin, Sekretärinnen, Studenten
  – *Sind Herr und Frau Brookes* **a**__?
  – *Nein, Herr Brookes kommt aus Dublin und ist* **b**__ *und Frau Brookes ist* **c**__ .
  – *Sind Doris und Walther* **d**__?
  – *Doris ist* **e**__, *aber Walther ist* **f**__ *bei der Süddeutschen Zeitung.*
  – *Sind Elke und Birgit* **g**__?
  – *Nein, Elke ist* **h**__ *bei Karstadt und Birgit ist* **i**__ .

3 Wie heißt es richtig? *Supply the correct forms of the verb* **sein**.
  a *Ich b__ Deutscher.*
  b *S____ Sie auch Deutscher?*
  c *Claudia i__ ledig und Petra i__ verheiratet.*
  d *Ich b__ nicht verheiratet.*
  e *Peter i__ Amerikaner.*
  f *B__ du auch Engländer?*
  g *S__ ihr aus Japan?*

Now that you have completed Unit 6, can you: tick
1 ask people their occupation and say your own? ☐
2 give both the male and female forms of five
occupations? ☐
3 name at least four subjects you can study at
university? ☐
4 say you have been doing something for several
years? ☐
5 use the various forms of the verb **sein**? ☐

7

....

Essen und Trinken
Food and drink

In this unit you will learn
- *how to ask the way*
- *how to order food and drink*

Language points
- *the accusative case*
- *containers and their contents*

___

Asking the way

1 GIBT ES HIER IN DER NÄHE ...?
IS THERE ... NEARBY?

◆) **CD 1, TR 43**

Look at the drawing on the next page and make yourself familiar with the way people give directions in German.

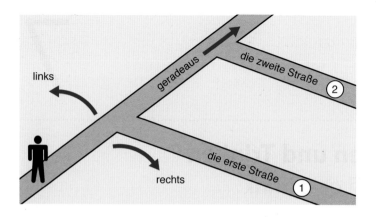

Listen to the three dialogues in which people are asking the way and find out the following information in each case:

▶ *What are they looking for?*
▶ *What directions are they given?*
▶ *How far do they need to go?*

Dialog 1
– Entschuldigen Sie bitte, gibt es hier in der Nähe eine Bank?
– Ja, gehen Sie die erste Straße links. Da ist eine Bank.
– Ist es weit?
– Nein, ungefähr fünf Minuten.
– Gut, danke. Ich brauche nämlich Geld.

Dialog 2
– Entschuldigung. Gibt es hier in der Nähe einen Supermarkt?
– Mmh. Einen Supermarkt? Na klar, gehen Sie immer geradeaus. Dort finden Sie einen ‚Plus'– Markt.
– Ist es weit?
– Nein, etwa 400 Meter.

> **Dialog 3**
> – Hallo. Entschuldigen Sie. Gibt es hier in der Nähe ein nettes Café?
> – Ja, natürlich. Das Café Hansa. Gehen Sie hier rechts um die Ecke. Es ist nicht weit. Dort ist der Kuchen ausgezeichnet.

Gibt es hier in der Nähe einen/eine/ein …? *Is there a … nearby?*
gehen *to go*
Ist es weit? *Is it far?*
ungefähr *about*
brauchen *to need*
nämlich *you see (lit. namely)*
na klar *of course*
dort *there*
finden *to find*
etwa *about*
um die Ecke *around the corner*
Es ist nicht weit. *It's not far.*
der Kuchen *cake*

Now look at the dialogues. See if you can work out when to use **einen, eine** and **ein** after **Gibt es hier in der Nähe …?**

What conclusion did you come to about **einen, eine** and **ein?** Here is the answer:

After **es gibt** the indefinite article **ein** changes to **einen** for masculine nouns only:

Gibt es hier in der Nähe   **einen Supermarkt?**
                                      einen Park?
                                      einen Biergarten?

Feminine and neuter nouns are not affected:

Gibt es hier in der Nähe   **eine Bank?**
                                      eine Kneipe?

Gibt es hier in der Nähe   **ein Café?**
                                            ein Hotel?

There's more about this later in this unit.

2 WAS FRAGEN DIE LEUTE?

Setzen Sie die fehlenden Wörter ein. *Fill in the missing words.*

a Entschuldigen Sie. Gibt es hier in der Nähe __ Bank?

b Entschuldigung. Gibt es hier in der Nähe __ __?

c Entschuldigung. Gibt es __ __ __ __ __ Park?

d Entschuldigen Sie, bitte. Gibt __ __ __ __ __ __ Biergarten?

SPRACHINFO: *The accusative case*
You have already seen how **ein** sometimes changes to einen after
Gibt es hier in der Nähe ...? Here are some more examples:

Ich	trinke	ein**en** Kaffee.
Es	gibt	ein**en** Supermarkt hier.
Sie	finden	ein**en** Biergarten dort.
Subject	*verb*	*object*

In a German sentence with a subject (e.g. **Sie,
ich, es**) and an object (e.g. **Supermarkt,
Biergarten, Kaffee**), the article for masculine
nouns **ein** changes for the object to **einen**.

In grammatical terms this structure is called the 'accusative case'.

Note that the verb **sein** is not followed by the accusative, e.g. **Das
ist ein Supermarkt.** There is more on this later. But first, here is
some practice in **Übung 3** and **4**. Remember, the change applies
only to masculine nouns, not to feminine and neuter nouns.

3 WOHIN GEHEN DIE LEUTE?

What do these people find when they follow the directions given
them? Write your answers in the gaps.

Ein Stadtplan von Gellingen

Sie stehen auf dem X.

a Gehen Sie geradeaus und dann links in die Hauptstraße. Nehmen Sie die erste Straße rechts. Das ist die Rathausstraße. Dort finden Sie rechts __ __ .

b Gehen Sie geradeaus und nehmen Sie die erste Straße rechts, die erste Straße links und gehen Sie dann rechts in die Kantstraße. Dort finden Sie links __ __ .

c Gehen Sie geradeaus und dann rechts in die Hauptstraße. Nehmen Sie die zweite Straße links und dort finden Sie links __ __ .

4 SETZEN SIE EIN

Fill in the missing articles **ein**, **eine** or **einen**.

a Entschuldigen Sie, bitte. Gibt es hier in der Nähe ___ Bank?
b Wo finde ich hier ___ Supermarkt?
c Entschuldigen Sie, bitte. Finde ich hier in der Nähe ___ Café?
d Ich brauche ___ Bier.
e Gibt es ___ Biergarten hier in der Nähe?
f Wo finde ich ___ Park hier in der Nähe, bitte?

In a café

5 WAS TRINKEN SIE, BITTE?

◄» **CD 1, TR 44**

a Read the menu and try to work out what the items mean in English. You can check your answers in the key.

SPEISEKARTE

WARME GETRÄNKE	€	EIS-SPEZIALITÄTEN	€
Tasse Kaffee	2,25	Gemischtes Eis	3,00 4,00 5,00
Cappuccino	2,75	Pfirsich Melba	4,50
Heiße Schokolade	2,80	Krokant-Becher	4,75
Schwarzer Tee (Glas)	2,25		

KUCHEN	€	ALKOHOLFREIE GETRÄNKE	€
Butterkuchen	1,75	Coca Cola	2,20
Schwarzwälder Kirschtorte	2,80	Limonade	2,10
Diverse Obstkuchen	3,00	Orangensaft	2,10
Portion Sahne	0,80	Mineralwasser	2,00

BIERE	€
König-Pilsener (0,33l)	2,50
Weizenbier (0,5l)	2,75

---

b Herr and Frau Häfner are sitting with their children in a café. What do they order? Listen to the recording, then decide whether the statements on the next page are true or false.

Vater	Oh, bin ich jetzt durstig. Ich brauche jetzt ein Bier.
Mutter	Nicht schon wieder ein Bier, Vater. Du bist zu dick.
Vater	Ach, Bier ist gesund. Hallo. Wir möchten bestellen.
Kellner	Guten Tag. Was möchten Sie, bitte?
Mutter	Ich möchte ein Mineralwasser und einen Kaffee, bitte.
Kellner	Ein Mineralwasser und einen Kaffee. Und was nehmen Sie, bitte?
Vater	Also, ich nehme ein Weizenbier. Schön kühl, bitte.
Kellner	Kein Problem. Und was bekommst du?
Junge	Ich trinke einen Orangensaft. Mit Eis.
Kellner	Und du? Was bekommst du?
Mädchen	Ich bekomme eine Limonade. Aber ohne Eis. Limonade schmeckt lecker.

QUICK VOCAB

der Vater *father*
die Mutter *mother*
der Junge *boy*
Ich bin durstig. *I am thirsty.*
zu dick *too fat*
gesund *healthy*
möchte(n) *would like*
bestellen *to order*
nehmen *to take*
kühl *cold/chilled*
bekommen *to get*
schmecken *to taste*
lecker *delicious*
mit *with*
ohne *without*

Richtig oder falsch? Korrigieren Sie die falschen Aussagen.

i Der Vater ist durstig.
ii Er möchte eine Limonade.
iii Der Vater findet, Bier ist gesund.
iv Die Mutter bestellt einen Orangensaft und einen Zitronentee.

v Der Junge bekommt eine Cola und einen Hamburger.
vi Das Mädchen findet, Limonade schmeckt lecker.

6 DIFFERENT WAYS OF ORDERING DRINKS

Did you notice that there are various expressions people can use when ordering drinks? Complete the sentences below with the correct form of the verbs **trinken, bekommen** and **nehmen**.

i *Was sagt der Kellner?*
  a *Was möchten Sie, bitte?*
  b *Was tr_____ Sie, bitte?*
  c *Was bek_____ Sie, bitte?*
  d *Was ne_____ Sie, bitte?*

ii *Was sagen Sie?*
  a *Ich möchte einen Kaffee.*
  b *Ich tr_____ einen Kaffee.*
  c *Ich bek_____ einen Kaffee.*
  d *Ich ne_____ einen Kaffee.*

7 GETRÄNKE

a Der, die oder **das?** Lesen Sie den Dialog noch einmal. Wie heißen die fehlenden Artikel? *Read the dialogue again. Can you find out the missing articles for the drinks?*

i der Tee
ii die Cola
iii ___ Mineralwasser
iv ___ Bier
v ___ Orangensaft
vi der Wein
vii ___ Kaffee
viii der Schnaps
ix der Sekt
x die Milch

b Note the names for containers in German and their plural forms.

i eine Tasse Kaffee
ii ein Glas Wasser
iii eine Flasche Wein
iv eine Dose Cola
v Paul isst einen Becher Eis.

Plurale:
i zwei Tassen Kaffee
ii drei Gläser/Glas Wasser
iii drei Flaschen Wein
iv drei Dosen Cola
v zwei Becher Eis

The German for 'pot' is **das Kännchen**.

Aufpassen! *Watch out!*
Sie bekommt **ein** Eis *aber* Sie bekommt **einen** Becher Eis (der Becher)

Ich nehme **einen** Kaffee *aber* Ich nehme **eine** Tasse Kaffee (die Tasse)

Er trinkt **einen** Weißwein *aber* Er trinkt **ein** Glas Weißwein (das Glas)

Insight: Genders

Don't feel overwhelmed by the three different genders for nouns in German. Remember that certain endings of nouns can help you to identify their gender (see Unit 5 for a few simple guidelines).

Also, nouns in the same group tend to have the same gender. For instance, most alcoholic drinks – with the exception of **das Bier** – are masculine: **der Wein, der Sekt, der Schnaps,** etc. as well as the following non-alcoholic beverages: **der Kaffee, der Cappuccino, der Espresso; der Tee; der Orangensaft, der Apfelsaft, der Zitronensaft** etc..

8 WHAT ARE THE ENDINGS?

Ergänzen Sie die Endungen. *Fill in the endings (but sometimes none is needed).*

a Ich möchte ein__ Cola, bitte.
b Ich nehme ein__ Limonade.
c Ich möchte ein__ Orangensaft.
d Marco bekommt ein__ Kaffee und ein__ Mineralwasser.
e Wir möchten ein__ Cappuccino und ein__ Tee.
f Ich nehme ein__ Glas Tee.

9 WER BEKOMMT WAS?

The Häfner family are waiting for their drinks. Here comes the waitress. Hören Sie zu! Beantworten Sie dann die Fragen.

◊ CD 1, TR 45

Kellnerin	Guten Tag! Mein Kollege hat jetzt Feierabend. Ich bin nicht ganz sicher, wer was bekommt. (zu der Mutter) Bekommen Sie den Orangensaft und das Eis?
Mutter	Nein, ich bekomme das Mineralwasser und den Kaffee. Mein Sohn bekommt den Orangensaft und das Eis.
Kellnerin	Gut! Bitte schön. (zum Mädchen) Und du? Du bekommst sicher die Limonade.
Mädchen	Ja, richtig! Die Limonade bekomme ich.
Vater	Und ich bekomme das Weizenbier.
Kellnerin	So, bitte schön.
Vater	Ach, das Bier ist zu warm!
Mutter	Und der Kaffee ist zu kalt!
Kellnerin	Oh! Entschuldigung.

Mein Kollege hat Feierabend. *My colleague has finished work.*
jetzt *now*
sicher *sure(ly)*
wer *who*
wer was bekommt *who gets what*
der Sohn *son*
zu warm, zu kalt *too warm, too cold*

Richtig oder falsch?

a Der Vater bekommt den Orangensaft.
b Die Mutter bekommt den Kaffee.
c Das Mädchen bekommt das Weizenbier.
d Das Bier ist zu kalt.

SPRACHINFO: *The accusative –* **den**
In the accusative case the definite article for masculine nouns changes as well: **der** becomes **den**. Feminine and neuter nouns are not affected. Here is a summary:

		a	the
m	Ich möchte …	**einen** Kaffee	**den** Kaffee
	Meine Freundin trinkt …	**einen** Tee	**den** Tee
f	Ich nehme …	**eine** Limo	**die** Limo
	Mein Freund bekommt …	**eine** Cola	**die** Cola
nt	Ich bekomme …	**ein** Mineralwasser	**das** Wasser
	Meine Frau bekommt …	**ein** Eis	**das** Eis

Note the change in both **ein** (to **einen**) and **der** (to **den**) in the masculine examples above.

94

Grammar

1 THE NOMINATIVE AND ACCUSATIVE CASES

In the sentence *I need a coffee*, 'I' is said to be the subject of the sentence and *'a coffee'* is said to be the object. In German the subject (often the doer of an action) has to be in the nominative case and the object has to be in the so-called accusative case. Note that the nominative case is also used after the verb **sein** (*to be*).

Cases in German are often indicated by the words in front of the relevant noun, usually articles, such as **der, die, ein, eine** etc.

As you saw earlier in this unit the articles for masculine nouns **der** and **ein** change to **den** and **einen** when used for the object of a sentence (accusative case). Note that these changes also apply to the negative form (**kein** → **keinen** *no, not a*) and the possessive adjectives (**mein** → **meinen** *my*, **Ihr** → **Ihren** *your*, etc.).

Feminine, neuter and the plural forms are the same in the nominative and accusative cases:

	Nominative	Accusative
masc. sing.	Der Kaffee schmeckt gut.	Den Kaffee nehme ich.
	Ist das ein Wein aus Chile?	Ich bekomme einen Wein.
	Mein Tee ist ganz kalt!	Du trinkst meinen Tee!
fem. sing.	Die Milch ist nur für Babys.	Wir kaufen die Milch.
	Hier liegt eine Flasche.	Er findet eine Flasche.
	Meine Cola ist lecker.	Sie bezahlt meine Cola.
neut. sing.	Das Eis kostet viel.	Ich bezahle das Eis.
	Da steht ein Bier.	Alle trinken ein Bier.
	Wo ist mein Glas?	Ihr habt mein Glas.
pl.	Die Hamburger sind hier.	Wir essen die Hamburger.
	Meine Kinder sind klein.	Mögen Sie meine Kinder?

2 CONTAINERS AND THEIR CONTENTS

When you are talking about containers and their contents, such as a cup of tea, a glass of wine, a dish of ice-cream, etc., you do not use the equivalent of the word 'of' in German:

eine Flasche Wein	*a bottle of wine*
ein Glas Mineralwasser	*a glass of mineral water*
ein Kännchen Kaffee	*a pot of coffee*
eine Tasse Tee	*a cup of tea*

TESTING YOURSELF

1 **Wie heißt es richtig?** *How well do you know your accusative endings? Sometimes no ending is needed.*

   a *Elmar ist müde. Er braucht ein__ Kaffee.*
   b *Katrin bestellt ein__ Glas Bier.*
   c *Die Kinder sind sehr durstig. Sie bestellen ein__ Orangensaft und ein__ Cola.*
   d *Bekommen Sie d__ Kaffee oder d__ Tee?*
   e *Geben Sie mir bitte d__ Orangensaft.*
   f *Ich bekomme d__ Weizenbier und mein Mann bekommt d__ Mineralwasser.*

2 **Was gehört zusammen?** *Match up the two sides. There may be more than one possibility.*

a *Er möchte einen Orangensaft*	**i** *Kaffee.*
b *Frau Müller nimmt ein Kännchen*	**ii** *sehr viele Kalorien.*
c *Limonade ist*	**iii** *Eis.*
d *Ich möchte einen Becher*	**iv** *zu dick.*
e *Ein Eis hat*	**v** *sehr durstig.*
f *Sie trinkt eine Tasse*	**vi** *Tee.*
g *Ich bin jetzt*	**vii** *mit Wodka.*
h *Du bist*	**viii** *lecker.*

3 *Rollenspiel: Bitte bestellen Sie! How would you make the following orders in German? You can check your answers on the recording. For answers* **c** *and* **d** *use the correct form of* **nehmen.**

   ◄)) **CD 1, TR 46**

   a *I'd like a coffee, please.*
   b *I'd like a mineral water and an orange juice.*
   c *I'll have a cup of tea, please.*
   d *I'll have a coke and a glass of beer.*

Now that you have completed Unit 7, can you: tick
1 ask if something is situated nearby?   ☐
2 order food and drink?   ☐
3 be sure when to use the accusative case?   ☐

8

Einkaufen und Bestellen
Shopping and ordering

In this unit you will learn
- *how to talk about going shopping*
- *how to ask for and give prices*
- *how to order food and drinks in a restaurant*
- *how to say what you like eating and drinking*

Language points
- *more plural forms of nouns*
- *word order*

Food and shopping

1 LESEN UND LERNEN

das Brot

das Müsli

der Wein

die Äpfel

der Reis

die Karotten

der Zucker

der Käse

die Tomaten

das Öl

ÖL
500ml

die Kartoffeln

der Blumenkohl

das Salz

Write down the above items and all the others you already know (including drinks) using the examples provided below as a guide. Check genders in the German – English vocabulary or in a dictionary. Note that **Lebensmittel** means *food*, **das Obst**, *fruit* and **das Gemüse**, *vegetables*.

Lebensmittel	Obst	Gemüse	Getränke
der Reis	der Apfel	die Kartoffel	der Tee
das Öl	Äpfel (pl)	Kartoffeln (pl)	das Mineralwasser

2 WIE HEISST DAS?

Note the German name for containers and quantities:

a Das ist eine Flasche Öl.
b Das ist ein Stück Käse.
c Das ist eine Dose Mais.
d Das ist eine Tüte Gummibärchen.
e Das ist eine Packung Cornflakes.

3 VERSCHIEDENE GESCHÄFTE

Was bekommt man hier? Finden Sie mindestens einen Artikel, den man hier kaufen kann. *What can you get here? Find at least one item you can buy from these shops.*

Beispiel
Das ist eine Bäckerei. Hier **kann** man Brot, Brötchen und Kuchen **kaufen**.

Note that when you use **kann** (*can*), the second verb (in this instance **kaufen**) goes to the end of the sentence.

a Das ist ein Markt. Hier kann man Obst, _____ kaufen.

b Das ist eine Fleischerei. Hier kann man _____ kaufen.

c Das ist ein Getränkemarkt. Hier kann man _____ kaufen.

d Das ist ein Supermarkt. Hier kann man zum Beispiel Käse, Brot, _____, _____ kaufen.

4 WAS STIMMT?

Finden Sie, was zusammengehört. *Find the pairs.*

a eine Dose	**i** Wein
b eine Flasche	**ii** Tomaten
c eine Packung	**iii** Salami
d eine Tüte	**iv** Bonbons
e ein Stück	**v** Cornflakes

Shopping

5 IM LADEN *AT THE SHOP*

Das ist der Laden von Herrn Denktash. Hier kann man viel kaufen: Brot und Brötchen, Butter, Käse, Obst, Gemüse, Getränke und vieles mehr.

Hören Sie zu und beantworten Sie dann die Fragen.

a Wie viele Brötchen kauft Frau Berger?
b Was kosten die Tomaten?
c Was für Wein kauft sie?
d Was kostet alles zusammen?

CD 1, TR 47

Herr Denktash	Guten Tag, Frau Berger. Was bekommen Sie, bitte?
Frau Berger	Ich möchte zehn Brötchen, bitte.
Herr Denktash	Sonst noch etwas?
Frau Berger	Was kosten die Tomaten?
Herr Denktash	Ein Kilo €1,80. Sie sind ganz frisch. Sonst noch etwas?
Frau Berger	Wie teuer ist denn der Riesling?
Herr Denktash	Der kostet €4,95.
Frau Berger	Dann nehme ich zwei Flaschen, bitte.
Herr Denktash	Ist das alles?

Frau Berger	Ja, das ist alles.
Herr Denktash	So, das macht zusammen €12,35 … €15. €2,65 zurück.
Frau Berger	Auf Wiedersehen, Herr Denktash.
Herr Denktash	Auf Wiedersehen, Frau Berger, und noch einen schönen Tag.

das Brötchen (-) *roll*
Sonst noch etwas? *Anything else?*
Ist das alles? *Is that all?*
Was kostet …? (sing.) *What does … cost?*
Was kosten …? (plural) *What do … cost?*
Wie teuer ist …? (sing.) *How much is …?*
Wie teuer sind …? (plural) *How much are …?*
Das macht (zusammen) … *That is … /That comes to …*
Was für … *What kind of …*

6 ROLLENSPIEL: WAS SAGT DER KUNDE?
WHAT DOES THE CUSTOMER SAY?

◄) **CD 1, TR 48**

Match the customer's sentences (a–f) with those of the shopkeeper (i–vi) to make a dialogue. The shopkeeper's sentences are in the right order. You can check your answers on the recording.

i *Guten Tag.*

ii *Ja, natürlich haben wir Eier. Wie viele nehmen Sie?*

iii *12 Stück. Sonst noch etwas, bitte?*

iv *Der Sekt kostet €4,75.*

v *Zwei Flaschen. Gern. Ist das alles?*

vi *Gut, das macht zusammen €10,75.*

a *12 Stück, bitte.*

b *Dann nehme ich zwei Flaschen.*

c *Guten Tag. Haben Sie Eier?*

d *Ja, das ist alles.*

e *€10,75. Bitte schön.*

f *Was kostet der Sekt?*

Insight: Neighbourhood shops

Tante-Emma-Läden were the traditional corner shops where people could buy lots of different things. As in other countries, these have steadily been replaced by other forms of shops, such as supermarkets.

In recent years, however, neighbourhood shops have seen something of a revival in certain cities. These are often owned and run by Turkish people.

SPRACHINFO: Geld/Währung *Money/currency*

Man schreibt: € 7,20. Man sagt: 7 Euro 20 *oder* 7 Euro und 20 Cent.

Man schreibt: € 6,40. Man sagt: 6 Euro 40 *oder* 6 Euro und 40 Cent.

Gewichte *Weights*

Ein Pfund = 500 Gramm, ein halbes Kilo.

The metric pound weighs slightly more than the UK or US pound.

7 ROLLENSPIEL: WAS KOSTET ...?

◀) **CD 1, TR 49**

Beantworten Sie die Fragen auf der Audioaufnahme.

On the recording you will hear questions about the prices of items. Press the pause button, formulate your answers and say them out loud. Then listen to check your answers.

Beispiel:
Audio Was kostet eine Flasche Wein?
You €4,90 (*You say it as* vier Euro neunzig)

Roggenbrot

€1,10

1 Kilo

€12,25

1 Kilo

€1,95

WEIN

€2,05

YUM
Müsli

€1,65

€0,89

Öl
500ml

€5,40

€4,90

8 RÄTSEL

Here is a puzzle involving words for groceries. Fill in the German words for the across clues and a further word will be revealed diagonally. What is **i** on the diagonal?

Horizontal – **Waagerecht**

a cheese	**d** fruit	**g** eggs
b salad	**e** tea	**h** cake
c bread	**f** tomatoes	**i** ?

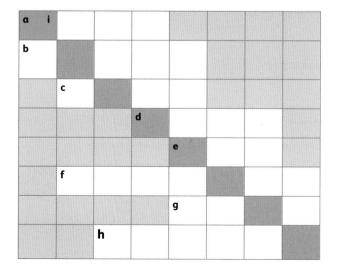

In a restaurant

Read the menu. Can you figure out what the items mean in English?

GASTSTÄTTE SCHNITZEL-RANCH

Speisekarte

Vorspeisen	€
Französische Zwiebelsuppe	3,20
Gemüsesuppe	3,00
Omelett	4,80

Salate	
Grüner Salat	2,50
Tomatensalat	3,50
Gemischter Salat	3,80

Hauptgerichte	
Pfeffersteak mit Grilltomaten und Pommes frites	13,00
Paniertes Schnitzel mit Pommes frites	10,50
Nudeln mit Tomatensoße	4,50

Nachtisch	
Gemischter Eisbecher	3,80
Obstsalat	4,50
Apfelstrudel	5,00

Alkoholfreie Getränke		Alkoholische Getränke	
Mineralwasser	1,50	Glas Rotwein	3,80
Tasse Kaffee	2,00	Glas Weißwein	3,40
Tasse Tee	1,80	Bitburger Pilsener	2,90
Coca Cola	1,70		

die Zwiebelsuppe (-n) *onion soup*
die Gemüsesuppe (-n) *vegetable soup*
das Omelett (-e or **-s)** *omelette*
der Salat (-e) *salad*
grün *green*
gemischt *mixed*
der Pfeffer *pepper*
die Grilltomate (-n) *grilled tomato*
das Schnitzel (-) *cutlet, schnitzel*
paniert *breaded*
Pommes frites (pl.) *French fries*
Nudeln (pl.) *pasta*
der Eisbecher (-) *a tub or dish of ice-cream*

SPRACHINFO: *Plural of nouns*

Starting in this unit, we give the plural forms of nouns in the vocabulary boxes: e.g. **die Tomate (-n)** means that it is **eine Tomate** singular, **zwei Tomaten** plural. The vocabularies at the end of the book also provide the plural forms of nouns.

9 SONJA AUER BESTELLT DREI GERICHTE

Sonja Auer orders three courses, but makes some effort to keep a check on her calorie intake.

Listen to the dialogue and then answer the questions.

Sonja Auer	Herr Ober! Ich möchte bestellen.
Kellner	Bitte schön. Was möchten Sie?
Sonja Auer	Als Vorspeise nehme ich eine Gemüsesuppe.
Kellner	Eine Gemüsesuppe – und als Hauptgericht?
Sonja Auer	Als Hauptgericht nehme ich das Pfeffersteak mit Grilltomaten, bitte. Ich möchte aber keine Pommes frites. Kann ich stattdessen einen gemischten Salat haben?
Kellner	Aber selbstverständlich. Und zum Trinken?
Sonja Auer	Ich nehme ein Perrier.

> *(20 Minuten später)*
> **Kellner** So? Hat es geschmeckt?
> **Sonja Auer** Danke. Sehr gut.
> **Kellner** Gut! Möchten Sie vielleicht auch etwas als Nachtisch?
> **Sonja Auer** Ja. Als Nachtisch bekomme ich einen gemischten Eisbecher – ohne Sahne. Und ich trinke auch eine Tasse Kaffee.
> *(später)*
> **Sonja Auer** Ich möchte bezahlen, bitte.
> **Kellner** Einen Moment, bitte. Das macht zusammen €23,30.

stattdessen *instead of that*
selbstverständlich *of course*
Hat es geschmeckt? *Did it taste good?*
als Nachtisch *for dessert*
die Sahne *cream*

Richtig oder falsch?

a Als Vorspeise bekommt sie eine Suppe.
b Sie isst das Pfeffersteak mit Pommes frites.
c Sie trinkt ein Glas Rotwein.
d Als Nachtisch hat sie einen Eisbecher mit Sahne.
e Zusammen macht es €29,50.

Ich möchte bestellen. *I'd like to order.*
Als Vorspeise nehme ich … *As a starter I'll take …*
Als Hauptgericht bekomme ich … *For my main course I'll have …*
Als Nachtisch/Dessert möchte ich … *For dessert I'd like …*
Ich möchte bezahlen. *I'd like to pay.*

SPRACHINFO: *Word order*
The verb in a German sentence usually has to be the second idea or component. So if the sentence starts with anything other than the subject, the verb and subject have to be swapped around.

[1]	[2]	[3]	
Ich *subject*	**nehme** *verb*	eine Gemüsesuppe.	
Als Vorspeise	**nehme** *verb*	**ich** *subject*	eine Gemüsesuppe.

10 WAS PASST ZUSAMMEN?

◄)) **CD 1, TR 51**

Put these sentences in order to create a dialogue between Frau Trübner and the waiter, starting with Frau Trübner. Listen to the recording and check your answers.

Frau Trübner

a Ja, einen Kaffee, bitte.
b Ich möchte bitte bestellen.
c Einen gemischten Eisbecher, bitte.
d Ja, sehr gut. Ich möchte jetzt bezahlen.
e Ich nehme die Nudeln mit Tomatensoße, bitte.
f Ohne, bitte.

Kellner

i Mit oder ohne Sahne?
ii Gut, als Hauptgericht die Nudeln. Und als Dessert?
iii Einen Moment. Das macht zusammen €10,30.
iv (*20 Minuten später*) Hat es geschmeckt?
v Bitte schön. Was bekommen Sie?
vi Und möchten Sie etwas zum Trinken?

11 ROLLENSPIEL: MARTIN MERLIN ISST SEHR GERN

Martin Merlin likes eating. Take his role and order for him. Write down the answers first, then listen to the recording, using the pause button so that you can say your responses out loud. Then listen to the recording to check your answers.

Martin Merlin	*Say that you would like to order.*
Kellner	Ja, was möchten Sie?
Martin Merlin	*Say that for a starter you'd like a French onion soup.*
Kellner	Eine französische Zwiebelsuppe. Und als Hauptgericht?
Martin Merlin	*Say that for your main course you'll have the schnitzel and French fries. And you'd also like a mixed salad.*
Kellner	Jawohl. Und was trinken Sie dazu?
Martin Merlin	*Say you'd like a glass of white wine. And for dessert you'll have the apple strudel.*

Kellner	Mit oder ohne Sahne?
Martin Merlin	*Say with cream, and afterwards you'd like a coffee.*

12 UND JETZT SIE!

Decide if the following dishes are normally eaten as a starter, as a main dish or as a dessert. Sometimes, of course, more than one answer is possible.

	Vorspeise	Hauptgericht	Nachtisch
Schnitzel		✔	
Eisbecher			
Obstsalat			
Zwiebelsuppe			
Nudeln			
Omelette			
Pfeffersteak			

Pronunciation

◀)) **CD 1, TR 53**

The **s** at the beginning of a word or syllable is pronounced like an English *z*:

> *Saft, Sie, sehr, Sohn*
> *gesund, lesen, Musiker, reisen*

At the end of a word or syllable the **s** is pronounced like an English *s*:

> *es, was, das, Haus*
> *Eisbecher, Reisplatte, Auskunft, arbeitslos*

How would you pronounce these words:

> *Sekt, Supermarkt, zusammen, besonders, alles, Mais?*

Grammar

1 PLURAL FORMS OF NOUNS

In Unit 6 you were introduced to a few patterns when forming
the plural in German. Here are some tips which might make it
easier for you to deal with the plural. But you have to be careful as
these are only broad guidelines, and there are many exceptions in
German. Always make sure that you learn the plural forms of new
nouns as you meet them.

1 Many feminine nouns add -n or -en:	die Tasse → die Tassen die Packung → die Packungen
2 a Many masculine nouns add an -e and very often an umlaut:	der Saft → die Säfte
b Important exceptions, where no umlaut is added, include:	der Salat → die Salate der Tag → die Tage
3 a Neuter nouns often add -e, but no umlaut:	das Geschenk → die Geschenke das Problem → die Probleme
b Another common ending is -er and an umlaut where possible:	das Glas → die Gläser
4 a Nouns ending with -chen don't change in the plural:	ein Brötchen → vier Brötchen ein Kännchen → zwei Kännchen
b Nouns ending in -er often stay the same or add an umlaut when possible:	ein Eisbecher → zwei Eisbecher eine Mutter → zwei Mütter
5 Nouns imported from English or French tend to add an -s in the plural:	ein Café → zwei Cafés ein Taxi → zwei Taxis

Note that the singular form is preferred to the plural in certain expressions of quantity:

Drei **Pfund** Äpfel, bitte.	*Three pounds of apples, please.*
250 **Gramm** Käse.	*250 grams of cheese.*
Zwei **Stück** Kuchen.	*Two pieces of cake.*
Drei **Glas** Wein.	*Three glasses of wine.*

2 WORD ORDER

As you saw earlier in this unit, the verb **können** sends the second verb to the end of the sentence:

> **Man kann *jetzt hier in Hamburg sehr gute Tomaten* kaufen.**
> **Wo können *wir hier Äpfel* bekommen?**

This also applies to **möchten**:

> **Ich möchte *bitte ein Stück Kuchen* bestellen.**
> **Wir möchten *jetzt bitte* bezahlen.**

You also learned in this unit that the main verb, i.e. the verb with the appropriate ending for the subject, is normally the second element in the sentence. This leads to the subject and verb being swapped round if the sentence starts with anything other than the subject. This swap is often referred to as subject-verb inversion.

[1]	**[2]**	**[3]**	
Als Vorspeise	**nehme**	**ich**	**eine Suppe.**
Zum Trinken	**möchten**	**wir**	**eine Flasche Wein.**
Nachher	**bekommen**	**wir**	**ein Kännchen Kaffee.**
	verb	*subject*	

TESTING YOURSELF

1 Fill the gaps with the correct form.

	Singular	Plural
a	der Apfelsaft	die _____
b	der Salat	die _____
c	die Tomate	die _____
d	die Flasche	die _____
e	die Tasse	die _____
f	die _____	die Kartoffeln
g	das Brötchen	die _____
h	das Glas	die _____
i	der _____	die Väter
j	das Restaurant	die _____
k	die Party	die _____

2 Move the item in bold type to the beginning of the sentence and make the necessary changes to the sentence structure.
   a Ich möchte **als Vorspeise** eine Gemüsesuppe.
   b Ich nehme **als Hauptgericht** das Schnitzel.
   c Wir möchten **zum Trinken** eine Flasche Mineralwasser bestellen.
   d Wir bekommen **als Dessert** den Obstsalat mit Sahne.
   e Wir trinken **nachher** eine Tasse Kaffee und eine Tasse Tee.
   f Wir möchten **jetzt** bitte bezahlen.

Now that you have completed Unit 8, can you: tick
1 name at least 8 items of food with the correct gender?   ☐
2 ask for and give prices?   ☐
3 order food and drink in a restaurant?   ☐
4 say how feminine nouns often form their plural?   ☐

9

Freizeit
Leisure

In this unit you will learn
- *how to say what people are doing*
- *how to talk about leisure pursuits*
- *how to state likes and dislikes*

Language points
- *'irregular' verb forms*
- *using* gern

What are these people doing?

1 LESEN UND LERNEN

Look at the pictures and read what the people are doing.

a Frau Thielemann kocht.

b Die Leute schwimmen im Schwimmbad.

c Frau Ihßen hört Musik. Sie hört klassische Musik.

d Sie spielen Fußball.

e Frau Copa liest eine Zeitung.

f Herr und Frau Gerber fahren nach Berlin.

g Die Leute machen ein Picknick.

h Die Leute spielen Schach. Sie spielen im Park.

2 WIE HEISSEN DIE VERBEN?

Write an appropriate verb in each of the spaces.

Fußball → spielen

a nach London → _____
b im Schwimmbad → _____
c Schach → _____
d ein Buch → _____
e Rock-Musik → _____
f Nudeln → _____ oder → _____

3 WIE HEISSEN DIE ENDUNGEN? ERGÄNZEN SIE.

Complete the verb endings.

a Ich schreib__ eine Postkarte.
b Susanne arbeit__ als Kellnerin.
c Wir les__ ein Buch.
d Robert hör__ viel Musik.
e Spiel__ du Schach?
f Trink__ ihr viel Weizenbier?

SPRACHINFO: *Verbs with a vowel change*
Some verbs in German have a change in the vowel in the **du** and **er,
sie, es** forms. Here are some of the ones you have met so far:

	lesen	essen	sprechen	nehmen	fahren
ich	lese	esse	spreche	nehme	fahre
du	liest	isst	sprichst	nimmst	fährst
er, sie, es	liest	isst	spricht	nimmt	fährt

4 ÜBEN SIE IRREGULÄRE VERBEN

Complete the sentences with the correct form of the verb in brackets.

a Er _____ sehr gut Deutsch. (sprechen)
b _____ du Englisch? (sprechen)
c Ich _____ nach Berlin. (fahren)
d Was _____ du als Vorspeise? (nehmen)
e Frau Peters _____ viel Agatha Christie. (lesen)
f Er _____ viel Nudeln. (essen)

Hobbies and leisure time

5 FRAUKE UND SANDRO LERNEN SICH IN EINER BAR KENNEN

Frauke and Sandro are getting to know each other in a bar. Listen to the dialogue and answer the questions.

CD 1, TR 54

Frauke	Hast du eigentlich ein Hobby?
Sandro	Tja, ich trainiere gern und ich schwimme auch gern. Und du?
Frauke	Ich lese gern Romane und ich fotografiere gern.
Sandro	Ach so! Und gehst du auch gern ins Kino?
Frauke	Oh ja! Ins Kino gehe ich sehr gern.
Sandro	Und isst du gern italienisch?
Frauke	Ja sicher, ich esse sehr gern Pizza.
Sandro	Gut, dann gehen wir ins Kino und nachher essen wir Pizza!

QUICK VOCAB

eigentlich *actually*
tja *well*
trainieren *to train, work out*
der Roman (-e) *novel*
fotografieren *to take photos*
sicher *sure, certain(ly)*
nachher *afterwards*

Richtig oder falsch? Korrigieren Sie die falschen Aussagen.

a Sandro trainiert gern.
b Er schwimmt auch gern.
c Frauke liest gern Zeitung.
d Sie arbeitet auch gern im Garten.
e Ins Kino geht sie nicht gern.
f Sie isst gern italienisch.

SPRACHINFO: *Using* **gern**
If you want to express in German what you do or do not like doing you use **gern** or **nicht gern**:

Ich gehe gern ins Kino.	*I like going to the cinema.*
Ich lese gern.	*I like reading.*
Ich esse gern italienisch.	*I like eating Italian food.*
Ich lese nicht gern.	*I don't like reading.*
Ich schwimme nicht gern.	*I don't like swimming.*

6 WAS IST IHR HOBBY?

◀) **CD 1, TR 55**

Eine Radio-Umfrage in Travemünde.
Hören Sie zu!

Listen to the interviews and tick the hobbies mentioned. Put a cross against those which are not mentioned.

Lesen	☐	**Golf**	☐	**Fitness**	☐
Reisen	☐	**Surfen**	☐	**Fotografieren**	☐
Fußball	☐	**Schwimmen**	☐	**Pop-Musik**	☐
Computer	☐	**Kino**	☐	**Garten**	☐
Klassische Musik	☐	**Tennis**	☐	**Segeln**	☐
Sport	☐	**Wandern**	☐	**Joggen**	☐

QUICK VOCAB

die Umfrage (-n) *survey*
der Krimi (-s) *crime story, detective story*
die Biographie (-n) *biography*
die Fotografie *photography*
die klassische Musik *classical music*
das Reisen *travelling*
das Wandern *hiking*
das Segeln *sailing*

7 BEANTWORTEN SIE DIE FRAGEN

Write out your answers to these questions.

Frage Sprechen Sie gern Deutsch?
Antwort Ja, ich spreche gern / sehr gern Deutsch.
oder Nein, ich spreche nicht gern Deutsch.

Fragen
a Lesen Sie gern Zeitung?
b Hören Sie gern Elvis Presley?
c Essen Sie gern Pizza?
d Reisen Sie gern?
e Arbeiten Sie gern im Garten?
f Trinken Sie gern Bier?
g Gehen Sie gern ins Kino?
h Kochen Sie gern?

Insight

There are many kinds of **Vereine** (*clubs*) in Germany covering a multitude of interests, from gardening to coin collecting or singing. **Gesangsvereine** (*singing clubs*) have over two million members and **Sportvereine** (*sports clubs*) manage to attract nearly ten times that figure. As in most other countries nowadays, many young people tend to be interested in 'pop' culture and clubbing.

8 WIE OFT GEHEN DIE DEUTSCHEN AUS?
HOW OFTEN DO THE GERMANS GO OUT?

◀) **CD 1, TR 56**

Lesen Sie den Artikel aus einer deutschen Zeitung und beantworten Sie dann die Fragen. *Read the following article and find out how often the four people from Berlin go out and where they go.*

Frage der Woche: Wie oft gehen Sie im Monat aus? Und wohin gehen Sie?

Statistiken zeigen es: Die Lieblingsbeschäftigung der Deutschen in ihrer Freizeit ist das Fernsehen. Doch immer mehr Deutsche gehen in den letzten Jahren auch wieder ins Kino, treiben Sport und gehen ins Restaurant. Wir haben vier Berliner gefragt, wie oft sie ausgehen und was sie dann machen.

Herr Protschnik (37, Bankangestellter)
Ich gehe viermal pro Woche ins Fitnesscenter und habe wenig Zeit, etwas anderes zu machen. Am Wochenende gehe ich manchmal ins Kino, wenn es einen interessanten Film gibt. Ich gehe aber lieber ins Restaurant, meistens einmal die Woche. Ich esse sehr gern italienisch, aber ich koche auch viel zu Hause.

* * *

Herr Schmidt (65, Rentner)
Ins Museum oder ins Theater gehe ich nie mehr. Als ich jung war, da war ich ein großer Kino-Fan. Aber jetzt sind wir Rentner und bleiben abends meistens zu Hause und sehen lieber fern. Einmal oder zweimal pro Woche gehe ich in die Kneipe. Und wir gehen jeden Tag in den Park. Dort ist es sehr schön. Und manchmal gehe ich auch noch ins Fußballstadion.

* * *

Frau de Grille (36, Architektin)

Ich gehe auch gern ins Museum, normalerweise zweimal im Monat. Hier in Berlin gibt es sehr gute Museen. Einmal im Monat gehen mein Mann und ich auch in die Oper. Wir haben ein Abonnement. Und mit den Kindern gehen wir oft ins Kindertheater. Die finden das super.

* * *

Petra Kant (24, Studentin)

Ich bin ein großer Kino-Fan und gehe mindestens einmal die Woche ins Kino. Jeden Montag ist Kino-Tag, da ist es besonders billig. Ich liebe die Filme mit Brad Pitt. Er ist sehr attraktiv. Ins Museum gehe ich sehr selten, moderne Kunst finde ich langweilig. Ich gehe lieber mit Freunden in die Disco, meistens zweimal die Woche.

QUICK VOCAB

Wie oft? *How often?*
einmal, zweimal, dreimal usw. *once, twice, three times, etc.*
einmal pro/die Woche *once per/a week*
zweimal im Monat *twice a month*
mindestens *at least*
die Lieblingsbeschäftigung (-en) *favourite activity*
Sport treiben *to do sports*
das Fitnesscenter (-) *gym*
lieber *(here) prefer*
der Rentner (-) *pensioner*
das Fußballstadion (-stadien) *football stadium*
billig *cheap*
das Abonnement (-s) *season ticket, subscription*
die Kunst *art*

Note that you can also listen to the interviews and check the pronunciation.

i Wie heißen die Antworten?

a Warum hat Herr Protschnik wenig Zeit?
b Wohin geht er lieber: ins Restaurant oder ins Kino?
c Was macht Herr Schmidt normalerweise abends?
d Wie oft geht Frau de Grille ins Museum?
e Wohin geht sie oft mit ihren Kindern?
f Wohin geht Petra Kant: in die Disco oder ins Museum?
g Wie findet sie Brad Pitt?

QUICK VOCAB

oft / häufig *often/frequently*
nie *never*
meistens *mostly*
selten *seldom*
normalerweise *normally, usually*
manchmal *sometimes*
immer *always*

ii Read the text again and see if you can find out when to use in **die**, **ins** and **in den**. Look at the gender of the nouns.

What conclusion did you come to? Here are the answers.

After **in** when movement is indicated, answering the question **wohin?** (*where to?*), the accusative case endings are needed in German:

> *Frau Norbert geht jeden Tag* in den *Stadtpark.*

> *Herr Gerber geht zu oft* in die *Kneipe.*

> *Heike geht sehr oft* ins Kino. (in das → ins)

SPRACHINFO: Wohin gehen Sie? *Where are they going to?*

When 'in' means 'towards', it is followed by the accusative case:

der		in den	Park.
			Biergarten.
die	Ich gehe …	in die	Oper.
			Kneipe.
das		ins	Kino.
			Restaurant.

9 WAS STIMMT HIER NICHT?

Wohin gehen die Leute wirklich? What is wrong with these sentences? Say where the people really go, by correcting the information given in bold, as shown in the example.

Beispiel   Frau Jörgensen findet moderne Kunst interessant und geht oft **in die Kneipe.**

Nein, sie geht nicht in die Kneipe, sie geht ins Museum.

a Peter und Heike essen gern chinesisch und gehen einmal die Woche **ins Kino.**

b Frau Schweigert hört gern klassische Musik und geht oft **ins Café.**

c Frau Müller liebt Schwarzwälder Kirschtorte. Sie geht jeden Tag **in die Oper.**

d Herr Knobl findet Fußball gut. Er geht oft **ins Restaurant.**

e Herr Radek trinkt gern Bier und geht häufig **ins Museum.**

f Gerd liebt alte Hollywood-Filme. Er geht oft **ins Fitnesscenter.**

Asking and answering questions about places you go to

FRAGEN *QUESTIONS*

Gehen Sie / Gehst du oft …	**ins Theater?**
Wie oft gehen Sie / gehst du …	**ins Restaurant?**
Gehen Sie / Gehst du gern …	**in die Kneipe? / in die Oper?**

ANTWORTEN *ANSWERS*

Ich gehe oft / manchmal / selten / nie ins Theater.
Ich gehe einmal die Woche / zweimal im Monat ins Restaurant.
Ich gehe (sehr) gern in die Kneipe.
Ich gehe nicht gern in die Oper.

Grammar

1 IRREGULAR VERBS

Earlier in this unit you saw that some verbs in German have a change of vowel in the **du** and **er, sie, es** forms: e.g. **lesen, fahren** and **sprechen**. Many more of these verbs can be found in the verb list at the end of the book.

>*Ich lese Krimis. Liest du auch Krimis?*
>*Paula fährt heute nach Frankfurt.*
>*Ich spreche Französisch. Sprichst du auch Französisch?*

As you can see, this change does not happen at all in the plural forms:

wir	lesen	essen	sprechen	nehmen	fahren
ihr	lest	esst	sprecht	nehmt	fahrt
Sie/sie	lesen	essen	sprechen	nehmen	fahren

2 GERN

The word **gern** is used together with a verb to say that you like doing something:

Ich koche gern.	*I like cooking.*
Ich spreche gern Deutsch.	*I like speaking German.*
Ich arbeite gern im Garten.	*I like working in the garden.*

To say that you do not like doing something, you simply add nicht:

| **Ich schwimme nicht gern.** | *I don't like swimming.* |
| **Ich jogge auch nicht gern.** | *I don't like jogging either.* |

There is also another way in German to express likes or dislikes using **mögen. Mögen** is irregular:

Ich mag Musik.	*Wir mögen Musik.*
Magst du Musik?	*Mögt ihr Musik?*
Mögen Sie Musik?	*Mögen Sie Musik?*
Er / Sie / Es mag Musik.	*Sie mögen Musik.*

Mögen is more often used with a noun than with a verb, e.g. **Ich mag Fußball. Ich mag Musik.**

Look at the following examples:

Ich spiele gern Fußball.	**Ich mag Fußball.**
Ich lerne gern Deutsch.	**Ich mag Deutsch.**
Ich höre gern Barockmusik.	**Ich mag Barockmusik.**

3 VERBS AND NOUNS

Most German verbs can be used as nouns:

schwimmen	*to swim*	→	**das Schwimmen**	*swimming*
joggen	*to jog*	→	**das Joggen**	*jogging*
reisen	*to travel*	→	**das Reisen**	*travelling*

As you can see, these nouns are neuter and, of course, start with a capital letter.

TESTING YOURSELF

1 *Fill in the gaps using the correct form of the verb in brackets.*

 a ____ *du gern Pizza? (essen)*
 b *Sein Hobby* ____ *Kino. (sein)*
 c ____ *du Deutsch? (sprechen)*
 d *Er* ____ *Karten. (spielen)*
 e ____ *ihr Deutsch? (sprechen)*
 f *Ich* ____ *gern. (fotografieren)*
 g *Er* ____ *Zeitung. (lesen)*
 h *Ihre Hobbys* ____ *Sport und Reisen. (sein)*

2 **Wie sagt man es anders?** *Can you say these sentences in a different way, using* **gern** *together with a suitable verb instead of* **mag/mögen?**

Beispiel *Ich mag Obst.*
     Ich esse gern Obst.

 a *Ich mag Rotwein.*
 b *Ich mag Pommes frites.*
 c *Wir mögen klassische Musik.*
 d *Wir mögen Schach.*
 e *Ich mag die Süddeutsche Zeitung.*
 f *Magst du Kaffee?*

Now that you have completed Unit 9, can you:	tick
1 talk about people's leisure pursuits and hobbies?	☐
2 say what you like and don't like doing?	☐
3 say how often you go out and where you go to?	☐
4 name three verbs in which vowel changes in the second and third person singular forms occur?	☐

10

Die Uhrzeit
The time

In this unit you will learn
* **how to tell the time**
* **how to talk about daily routines**

Language points
* **separable verbs**
* **more on word order**

The time

1 WIE VIEL UHR IST ES? *WHAT'S THE TIME?*

◀)) **CD 1, TR 57**

Listen out for the two ways in which you can ask for the time in German.

> *Entschuldigen Sie, bitte.*
> *Wie spät ist es?*

> *Zwei Uhr.*

> *Entschuldigung. Wie viel Uhr ist es, bitte?*

> *Es ist zehn vor vier.*

 Wie viel Uhr ist es, bitte? *What is the time, please?*
Wie spät ist es? *What's the time? (lit. How late is it?)*

2 DIE 12-STUNDEN-UHR *THE 12-HOUR CLOCK*

🔊 **CD 1, TR 58**

Look at the times below and listen to them on the recording.

Es ist zwei Uhr.

Es ist zehn **nach** zwei. Es ist zehn Minuten **nach** zwei.

Es ist zehn Minuten **vor** vier.

Es ist zwei Minuten **nach** neun. Es ist **kurz nach** neun.

Es ist **Viertel** nach fünf.

Es ist **Viertel** vor sieben.

Es ist **halb** zwei. (!)

Es ist **halb** fünf. (!)

Can you find the German words for: **a** *past*, **b** *before*, **c** *quarter*, **d** *half*?

3 HÖREN SIE ZU!

◄) **CD 1, TR 59**

Write in the right-hand column the order in which you hear these times on the recording:

a 4:30 _____   **c** 8:45 _____
b 8:50 _____   **d** 6:28 ____1____

4 SCHREIBEN SIE DIE UHRZEITEN
WRITE OUT THE TIMES

◄) **CD 1, TR 60**

Listen to the recording again and write out the times you hear, or work them out from the pictures. There may be more than one way of saying the time!

Beispiel: 1 *Es ist sechs Uhr achtundzwanzig.*

5 MORGENS ODER ABENDS? *A.M. OR P.M.?*

◄) **CD 1, TR 61**

Make yourself familiar with what the Germans say for a.m. and p.m. Then do the exercise below.

Es ist neun Uhr **morgens**.

Es ist ein Uhr **mittags**.

Es ist vier Uhr **nachmittags**.

Es ist sieben Uhr **abends**.

Es ist ein Uhr **nachts**.

Sagen Sie die Uhrzeit. Überprüfen Sie Ihre Antworten auf dem Audio:

1 pm 4 pm 8 pm 11 pm 9 am 6 am

6 DIE 24-STUNDEN-UHR *THE 24-HOUR CLOCK*

◀) **CD 1, TR 62**

The 24-hour clock is used for official purposes. Look at the following examples:

a 21:00 - Es ist einundzwanzig Uhr.

b 17:15 - Es ist siebzehn Uhr fünfzehn. Es ist siebzehn Uhr und fünfzehn Minuten.

c 8:30 - Es ist acht Uhr dreißig. Es ist acht Uhr und dreißig Minuten.

d 17:56 - Es ist siebzehn Uhr sechsundfünfzig. Es ist siebzehn Uhr und sechsundfünfzig Minuten.

Üben Sie die 24-Stunden-Uhr. Überprüfen Sie Ihre Antworten auf dem Audio:

13:00 15:20 7:45 18:12 23:35 4:17

7 RADIO- UND FERNSEHPROGRAMME
RADIO AND TV PROGRAMMES

◀) **CD 1, TR 63**

Listen to the excerpts from various programmes and fill in the missing times.

a Es ist _____ Uhr. Hier ist das Erste Deutsche Fernsehen mit der Tagesschau.

b Radio Bremen. Sie hörten die Nachrichten. Es ist _____. Und jetzt der Wetterbericht.

c Beim Gongschlag war es _____. Hier ist die Deutsche Welle mit den Nachrichten.

d _____. Und jetzt die Verkehrslage auf Deutschlands Straßen.

e Das war das Aachener Nachrichtenmagazin. Es ist jetzt _____ .

f RTL. Radio-Shop. Es ist _____.

SPRACHINFO: eins/ein Uhr *one o'clock*
Have you noticed the difference between **Es ist eins** and **Es ist ein Uhr?** In German when using **Uhr** (*o'clock*) after the digit one you need to drop the **s** from **eins.**

Note that **die Uhr** also means *the clock*, whereas *hour* in terms of duration is **die Stunde** in German.

_____

A typical day

8 WAS MACHT FRAU HAASE?

Read the text below and find out what Frau Haase does on a typical day (**ein typischer Tag**).

aufstehen *to get up*
dann *then*
danach *afterwards*
anfangen *to start*
anrufen *to phone*
Um Viertel nach fünf hat sie Feierabend. *She finishes work at a quarter past five.*
der Feierabend *end of work*
einkaufen *to shop*
isst sie zu Abend *she has her evening meal/dinner*
anschließend *afterwards*
abholen *to fetch, pick up*
fernsehen *to watch TV*

Es ist 7 Uhr 10. Frau Haase steht auf. Dann duscht sie und frühstückt. Normalerweise isst sie ein Brötchen und trinkt Kaffee.

Um Viertel vor acht geht sie normalerweise aus dem Haus. Sie geht ins Büro. Ihre Arbeit fängt um halb neun an.

Frau Haase arbeitet in einer Bank. Um 10 Uhr ruft sie eine Kundin an. Danach schreibt sie einen Brief. Um halb zwölf macht sie Mittagspause.

Um Viertel nach fünf hat sie Feierabend. Dann geht sie in den Supermarkt und kauft ein. Um sechs Uhr ist sie wieder zu Hause. Um Viertel nach sechs isst sie zu Abend.

Um sieben Uhr holt Frau Haase eine Freundin von der Arbeit ab. Anschließend gehen sie zusammen ins Kino und dann in die Kneipe.

Um halb elf ist sie wieder zu Hause. Sie sieht noch ein bisschen fern. Sie sieht die Nachrichten. Sie sieht aber nur selten fern. Um halb zwölf geht sie dann ins Bett.

SPRACHINFO: *Separable verbs*

Can you figure out what often happens to verbs like **aufstehen, anfangen, anrufen, einkaufen** and **fernsehen** when they are used in a German sentence? Are there similar constructions in English?

What conclusion did you come to? Here is the answer: there are a number of verbs in German which are called **trennbare Verben** (*separable verbs* in English).

The first part (prefix) separates from the main part (stem) and usually goes to the end of the sentence:

aufstehen	**Frau Haase steht auf.**	*Mrs Haase gets up.*
anfangen	**Die Arbeit fängt um 9 Uhr an.**	*Work starts at 9 o'clock.*
anrufen	**Sie ruft eine Kundin an.**	*She phones a client.*
einkaufen	**Sie kauft im Supermarkt ein.**	*She shops at the supermarket.*
fernsehen	**Sie sieht manchmal fern.**	*She sometimes watches TV.*

There are certain similarities to English phrasal verbs like *to get up*, but remember that in German **auf, an,** etc. usually have to go to the final position in the sentence.

Insight: The working day

The working day (the **Arbeitstag**) in Germany tends to start earlier than in Britain. Offices and schools, for instance, often start at 8.00 am. The earlier start means that many people finish work earlier too. **Der Feierabend** – the time when work is finished – is commonly regarded as a time to be enjoyed and not to be spent doing chores. The common way of asking someone in German what time they finish work is: **Wann hast du Feierabend?** The answer will be along the lines of: **Ich habe um vier Uhr Feierabend.**

9 WAS MACHEN DIE LEUTE?

Using the appropriate separable verb, write down what the people in the pictures are doing.

| einkaufen | *aufstehen* | fernsehen | anfangen |

Das Mädchen _____
um sieben Uhr _____.

Der Mann _____ _____ .

Die Schule _____ um acht
Uhr _____ .

Der Mann _____ im
Supermarkt _____ .

10 EIN TAG IM LEBEN VON HERRN FABIONE

🔊 **CD 1, TR 64**

Listen to Mr Fabione describing a typical day.

Autowerkstatt (¨en) *garage, car repair shop*
Schwiegermutter (¨) *mother-in-law*
passt auf die Kinder auf *looks after the children*
später *later*

Richtig oder falsch?

a Herr Fabione ist Lehrer.
b Seine Arbeit fängt um acht Uhr an.
c Mit den Kindern geht er manchmal schwimmen.
d Er bleibt oft zu Hause.

Hören Sie noch einmal zu und beantworten Sie die Fragen. *Listen again and answer the questions.*

e Wann steht Herr Fabione normalerweise auf?
f Wann hat er Feierabend?
g Sieht er viel fern?
h Wann geht er normalerweise ins Bett?

Pronunciation

🔊 **CD 1, TR 65**

Here are some nouns with their plural forms. Notice what an important difference the adding of an umlaut can make to the pronunciation and to the meaning.

Tochter *(daughter)*, **Töchter**   **Koch** *(cook)*, **Köche**
Mutter *(mother)*, **Mütter**   **Kuss** *(kiss)*, **Küsse**

What are the plural forms of these words? **Bruder** (*brother*), **Sohn** (*son*), **Buch** (*book*).

Grammar

1 SEPARABLE VERBS

In English you have verbs such as *to get up*, *to pick up* and *to come along* where the verb is made up of two parts. In German, too, there are verbs like this, but in the infinitive (the form that appears in the dictionary) the two parts are joined together: **aufstehen, anfangen, abholen**, etc. When you use these verbs, you frequently need to separate the first part (prefix) from the main part and send the prefix to the end of the sentence:

aufstehen	**Wann stehst du auf?**
	When do you get up?
anfangen	**Der Film fängt um sechs Uhr an.**
	The film starts at 6 o'clock.
abholen	**Ich hole dich um acht Uhr ab.**
	I'll pick you up at 8 o'clock.

From now on separable verbs will be shown as follows in the vocabulary lists: **an|fangen** *to start*. In good dictionaries separable verbs are usually indicated with '(sep)'.

2 WORD ORDER

As you learned earlier in Unit 8 the verb in German is usually the second element in the sentence. The first element in a sentence can be the subject, a time expression or another element; it can even be an object. The verb, however, needs to be in second place and this often means putting the subject in third place.

1	2 = verb	3	4
Ich	trinke	eine Tasse Kaffee	zum Frühstück.
Zum Frühstück	trinke	ich	eine Tasse Kaffee.
Eine Tasse Kaffee	trinke	ich	zum Frühstück.
Normalerweise	trinke	ich	eine Tasse Kaffee.

Note that **und** and **aber,** which usually connect two sentences, do not count and do not affect the word order.

	0	1	2 = verb	3	4
Ich gehe ins Café	und	danach	gehe	ich	ins Kino.
Zuerst dusche ich	und	dann	frühstücke	ich.	
Ich stehe früh auf	und	ich	lese	die Zeitung.	
Ich esse kein Fleisch,	aber	Gemüse	esse	ich	gern.
Ich treibe keinen Sport,	aber	ich	gehe	oft	ins Café.

TESTING YOURSELF

1 **Wie gut kennen Sie trennbare Verben?** *How well do you know your separable verbs? Complete the verbs with an appropriate prefix. Sometimes there might be more than one possibility.*

fern	auf	an	ein	ab	an

a ___ rufen   **d** ___ kaufen
b ___ sehen   **e** ___ fangen
c ___ stehen   **f** ___ holen

2 **Ein Tag im Leben von Herrn Reinhard. Was macht er?**

Write an account of Herr Reinhard's day. Use the 12-hour clock in this exercise.

6:30 aufstehen – 7:00 zur Arbeit fahren – 9:00 eine Kundin anrufen – 12:30 zur Bank gehen – 17:00 einkaufen – 19:00 mit Helga in die Kneipe gehen – 22:00 fernsehen

Beispiel *Um halb sieben steht er auf. Um sieben Uhr fährt er …*

3 **Und was machen Sie am Sonntag?**

*Write an account of what you do on Sundays. Use words such as **dann, danach, anschließend, normalerweise** and **meistens** to make it more fluent, but remember that the verb in German has to be the second element.*

Now that you have completed Unit 10, can you:	tick
1 ask for and tell the time?	☐
2 talk about your daily routine?	☐
3 explain what separable verbs are?	☐
4 be sure you know the correct word order in German?	☐

11

....

Was machen wir heute?
What are we doing today?

In this unit you will learn
- *how to describe/say what there is to do in a given town*
- *how to make appointments*
- *how to say what you would like to do and what you have to do*
- *say why you can't do things on the date suggested*

Language points
- *modal verbs* können *and* müssen
- *use of* in *for focusing on position*

Going out

1 WAS KANN MAN AM WOCHENENDE IN HANNOVER MACHEN?

Lesen Sie, was man am Wochenende in Hannover machen kann und beantworten Sie die Fragen. *Can you figure out what one can do on a weekend in the German town of Hanover? Read the text and do the true–false questions.*

der Höhepunkt (-e) *highlight*
die Stadtführung (-en) *guided tour (of the town)*
der Treffpunkt (-e) *meeting point*
das Abenteuer (-) *adventure*
der Samstag (-e) *Saturday*
der Sonntag (-e) *Sunday*
das Theaterstück (-e) *play*
Erwachsene *adults*

HEUTE IN HANNOVER

Die Höhepunkte fürs Wochenende

HANNOVER
MESSE

Samstag

13:00	Stadtführung durch Hannovers historische Altstadt, Treffpunkt: Touristen-Information.
15:30	Fußball: Hannover 96 – Bayern München. Bayern ist der Favorit. Keine Chance für Hannover 96?
20:00	Theater: Ein Sommernachtstraum, Klassiker von William Shakespeare, Gartentheater Herrenhausen – Vergessen Sie die Regenschirme nicht!
20:30	Konzert: Tina und die Caprifischer spielen Soul, Funk und HipHop, anschließend Disco, Tanzclub Hippodrom.

Sonntag

10:00	Fahrrad-Tour, Treffpunkt: Hauptbahnhof.
15:00	Theater: Die Abenteuer von Aladdin – Für Kinder und Erwachsene; anschließend Spiele, Eis und Bratwurst, Faust-Theater.
20:30	Konzert: Melody Makers aus Frankfurt spielen Oldies und Goldies, Bar Domingo.
21:00	Kino: Mission Possible, James Bond wieder in Action – der neue Film mit dem britischen Superagenten. Kann er die Welt retten? Colosseum.

Richtig oder falsch? Was kann man am Samstag machen?

a Man kann um 13.00 Uhr eine Stadtführung machen.

b Man kann ein Fußballspiel sehen. Hannover 96 ist der Favorit.

c Man kann ins Theater gehen. Es gibt ein Theaterstück von Goethe.

d Um 20.30 Uhr kann man ins Konzert gehen und danach kann man tanzen.

SPRACHINFO: können *to be able to*
When you use **können** with another verb, the second verb goes to the end of the sentence and is in the infinitive. When you use **können** with a separable verb (**an|fangen, an|rufen**, etc), therefore, the whole of the separable verb goes to the end:

Ich kann morgen anfangen.	*I can start tomorrow.*
Kannst du mich vom Flughafen	*Can you collect me from the*
abholen?	*airport?*

2 WAS KANN MAN AM SONNTAG IN HANNOVER MACHEN?

Lesen Sie noch einmal, was man am Sonntag machen kann und beantworten Sie die Fragen:

Beispiel Was kann man um 10 Uhr machen?
Um 10 Uhr kann man eine Fahrrad-Tour machen.

a Was für ein Theaterstück kann man sehen?
b Was kann man anschließend machen?
c Was für Musik kann man um halb neun hören?
d Was können James-Bond-Fans machen?

3 WAS KANN MAN NOCH AM WOCHENENDE MACHEN?
WHAT ELSE CAN ONE DO AT THE WEEKEND?

Try to write at least ten sentences. You will find some ideas below.

Freunde besuchen	lange schlafen
auf eine Party gehen	*zusammen kochen*
auf den Flohmarkt gehen	

Beispiele Man kann Freunde besuchen. Am Wochenende kann man auf den Flohmarkt gehen.

Außerdem kann man …

SPRACHINFO: *Going to a party etc.*
Note that if you want to say that you are going to a party or a street market, the preposition **auf** is frequently used: Ich gehe **auf** den Flohmarkt, **auf** eine Party.

4 WORTSPIEL

Finden Sie die Wörter und schreiben Sie sie waagerecht (*horizontally*). **k** ist ein neues Wort. Wie heißt es?

a Hier arbeitet man, schreibt E-Mails, telefoniert usw.
b Hier kann man einen Film sehen.
c Hier findet man meistens alte, interessante Sachen.
d Hier kann man ein Picknick machen.
e Nicht heute, nicht gestern!
f Hier kann man die Nachrichten hören.
g Hier kann man heiraten.
h Hier schläft man.
i Hier kann man ein Glas Wein trinken.
j Hier kann man Geld bekommen.
k Was kann man hier tun?

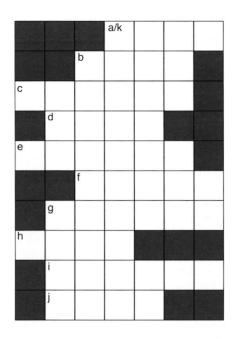

Arrangements

5 DIE WOCHENTAGE

Can you put the days in the right order?

6 KOMMST DU MIT INS KINO?
ARE YOU COMING ALONG TO THE CINEMA?

Hören Sie, was Petra und Simone sagen. Beantworten Sie dann die Fragen.

CD 1, TR 66

Petra	Hallo Simone. Na, wie geht's?
Simone	Ganz gut. Und dir?
Petra	Auch ganz gut. Simone, ich möchte nächste Woche ins Kino gehen. Es gibt einen neuen Film mit Cate Blanchett. Kommst du mit?
Simone	Ja, gern. Und wann?
Petra	Kannst du am Montag? Da ist Kino-Tag.
Simone	Tut mir leid. Am Montagabend muss ich zum Geburtstag von Birgit. Vielleicht am Mittwoch?
Petra	Am Mittwochabend muss ich meine Schwester abholen. Sie kommt aus Griechenland zurück. Geht es am Donnerstag?
Simone	Donnerstag ist gut. Wann fängt der Film an?
Petra	Um halb neun. Wann treffen wir uns?
Simone	Um acht vielleicht?
Petra	Ja, acht ist gut. Und wo treffen wir uns? Im Kino oder in der Kneipe?
Simone	Im Kino, das ist eine gute Idee. Also, dann bis Donnerstag.
Petra	Mach's gut. Bis dann.

QUICK VOCAB

der Geburtstag (-e) *birthday*
die Schwester (-n) *sister*
der Bruder (¨) *brother*
Geht es am Donnerstag? *Is Thursday all right?*
Wann treffen wir uns? *When shall we meet?*
Mach's gut. *All the best.*

Richtig oder falsch? Korrigieren Sie die falschen Sätze.

a Petra möchte einen Film mit Brad Pitt sehen.
b Am Montag muss Simone zum Geburtstag von Birgit.
c Am Mittwoch muss Petra ihren Bruder abholen.
d Sie gehen am Donnerstag ins Kino.
e Der Film fängt um halb neun an.
f Sie treffen sich um Viertel nach acht im Kino.

SPRACHINFO: *Using* **müssen, können** *must, can*
Like **können**, **müssen** sends the other verbs to the end of the sentence:

Ich muss heute arbeiten.	*I have to work today.*
Ich muss heute Nachmittag einkaufen.	*I have to do some shopping this afternoon.*

The same applies to **möchten**:

Ich möchte heute Abend ins Kino gehen.	*I'd like to go to the cinema tonight.*

See the **Grammar** section in this unit for the forms of these verbs.

Kommst du mit? *Are you coming along?*

Ein Freund fragt:

Ich möchte am Samstag ins Kino gehen. Kommst du mit?

Was können Sie sagen?

Ja ... 🙂	Nein ... 🙁
Ja, gerne.	**Tut mir leid, aber ich habe leider keine Zeit.**
Ja, ich komme gern mit.	**Ich möchte mitkommen, aber ich muss lernen.**
Ja, das ist eine gute Idee.	**Da muss ich arbeiten, einkaufen etc.**

7 EINE VOLLE WOCHE *A BUSY WEEK*

Matthias has a busy week. His friend Jörg wants to go to the cinema with him. Look at his diary below and write down what he has to do and why he can't make it this week.

Mo: 20.00 Dr. Schmidt treffen
Di: abends zum Geburtstag von Bernd gehen
Mi: bis 22.00 Uhr arbeiten ☹
Do: mit den Kollegen essen gehen
Fr: mit Tante Gisela in die Oper gehen ☹
Sa/So: nach München fahren

a Am Montag muss er um 20.00 Uhr Dr. Schmidt treffen.
b Am Dienstag muss _____
c Am Mittwoch _____
d _____
e _____
f Am Wochenende _____

SPRACHINFO: in + *movement and* **in** + *position*
In **Dialogue 6 Kommst du mit ins Kino?** you might have been puzzled by the way Petra asked Simone where they would meet: **Im Kino oder in der Kneipe?** So far you have been using **Ich gehe ins Kino** or **Er geht in die Kneipe.** How can this be explained?

In German it often makes a difference
  a if movement from one point to another is indicated (e.g. **Wir gehen ins Kino**).
or
  b if the focus is on position or location (e.g. Wir treffen uns **im Kino**).

This distinction is made after prepositions like **in**. Look at the following examples:

	Movement	**Position/location**
masc.	Er geht in den Biergarten.	Er ist im Biergarten.
fem.	Frauke geht in die Kneipe.	Sie trinkt in der Kneipe.
neut.	Heike und Peter gehen ins Restaurant.	Sie essen im Restaurant.

Note that **im** is the short form of **in dem**. There are some other prepositions that behave in the same way as **in**. You will meet these in later units. There is also more information in the **Grammar** section.

8 WAS PASST ZUSAMMEN?

Match the questions below with the most appropriate answers:

1 Wo kann man ein Guinness trinken?

    a Im Restaurant *Deutscher Michel.*

2 Wo kann man einen Film sehen?

    b Im Bett.

3 Wo kann man Englisch lernen?

    c In der *Disco Heaven.*

4 Wo kann man typisch deutsch essen?

    d Im Supermarkt.

5 Wo kann man einen Kaffee trinken?

    e Im *Lumiere-Kino.*

6 Wo kann man einkaufen?

    f In der irischen Kneipe.

7 Wo kann man tanzen?

    g Im *Café Kaffeeklatsch.*

8 Wo kann man schlafen?

    h In der Sprachschule.

9 ERGÄNZEN SIE, BITTE

Use these phrases to fill in the gaps.

in die Sprachschule   ins Café   ins Kino   **im Café**

IM RESTAURANT   in der Sprachschule   **im Kino**   INS RESTAURANT

a Ich möchte einen Film sehen. Kommst du mit _____ ?

b _____ *Müller* kann man sehr gut Kuchen essen.

c Ich möchte einen Kaffee trinken. Wir gehen _____ .

d Karsten ist Kellner _____ *Deutscher Michel.*

e Er muss Englisch lernen und geht _____ *Lingua plus.*

f Er möchte chinesisch essen und geht _____ *Shanghai.*

g _____ gibt es einen neuen Film mit Jude Law.

h _____ *Lingua plus* kann man Deutsch und andere Sprachen lernen.

10 MOVEMENT OR POSITION?

Indicate if **in** refers to movement or position in the sentences below. The first two sentences have been done for you.

a
i Gehen wir heute **ins** Kino? *(movement)*
ii Es gibt einen neuen französischen Film **im** Kino. *(position)*

b
i Sie arbeitet jeden Tag im Büro. (_____)
ii Wann gehst du ins Büro? (_____)

c
i Annett kauft meistens im Supermarkt ein. (_____)
ii Ich gehe noch schnell in den Supermarkt und hole Milch.
(_____)

d
i Kommst du mit in den Park? (_____)
ii Ja, im Park kann ich gut joggen. (_____)

e
i Treffen wir uns im Restaurant? (_____)
ii Morgen gehe ich ins Restaurant. (_____)

11 ROLLENSPIEL: KOMMST DU MIT ESSEN?

Write down your responses for this dialogue. Then play the
recording, using the pause button to enable you to say your part
out loud. You can check your answers on the recording after each
response.

Jutta	Hallo, hier ist Jutta. Wie geht's?	**◆ CD 1, TR 67**
Sie	*Return the greetings, say you are fine and ask how she is.*	
Jutta	Danke, gut. Klaus und ich möchten nächste Woche essen gehen. Wir möchten in die neue Pizzeria La Mamma gehen. Kommst du mit?	
Sie	*Say that this is a good idea and ask when.*	
Jutta	Kannst du am Dienstagabend?	
Sie	*Say you are sorry but you can't make Tuesday evening. You have to work.*	
Jutta	Und am Freitag?	
Sie	*Say you are sorry but on Friday you have to go to Cologne. Ask if Saturday evening is all right.*	

Jutta	Ja, am Samstag geht es.
Sie	*Ask what time you should meet.*
Jutta	Acht Uhr vielleicht? Und wo treffen wir uns?
Sie	*Say 8 o'clock is fine. Say you could meet in the restaurant.*
Jutta	Das ist eine gute Idee. Dann bis Samstag. Und iss nicht zu viel vorher.
Sie	*Say bye bye; until Saturday evening.*

Grammar

1 *MODAL VERBS* **KÖNNEN** *AND* **MÜSSEN**

There is a special group of verbs called modal verbs. You have met two of these already. They are **können** and **müssen**. Modal verbs behave differently from ordinary verbs. For instance, they do not take the usual endings in the **ich** and **er/sie/es** forms:

ich kann	wir können	ich muss	wir müssen
du kannst	ihr könnt	du musst	ihr müsst
Sie können	Sie können	Sie müssen	Sie müssen
er/sie/es kann	sie können	er/sie/es muss	sie müssen

Modal verbs are usually used together with another verb. This second verb goes to the end of the sentence:

Er kann sehr viel Bier trinken. *He can drink a lot of beer.*

Ich muss morgen nach Berlin fahren. *I have to go to Berlin tomorrow.*

When you use **können** or **müssen** with a separable verb, the prefix of the separable verb joins up with its stem at the end of the sentence:

Ich muss morgen früh aufstehen. *I have to get up early tomorrow.*

Möchten is formed from another modal verb **mögen** (*to like*). It too sends the second verb to the end of the sentence:

Ich möchte heute Abend ins *I would like to go to the cinema*
Kino gehen. *this evening.*

Here are the full forms of **möchten**:

ich möchte	*wir möchten*
du möchtest	*ihr möchtet*
Sie möchten	*Sie möchten*
er/sie/es möchte	*sie möchten*

2 LOCATION AND POSITION

In Unit 9 you learned how to express motion from one point to another: **Ich gehe in den Park, in die Oper, ins Kino.** In this unit you have been learning how to focus on location or position. Here is a summary of both systems:

	Movement	**Position/location**
masc.	Wir gehen **in den** Park.	Wir sitzen **im** Park.
fem.	Ich gehe **in die** Bäckerei.	Ich kaufe Brot **in der** Bäckerei.
neut.	Ich gehe heute früh **ins** Bett.	Ich lese gern **im** Bett.

The plural forms are **in die** if motion is indicated and **in den** for position: Er geht oft **in die** Parks. Er sitzt oft **in den** Parks.

Note: **ins** and **im** are abbreviations for **in das** and **in dem**. The examples under **Movement** are in the accusative case and those under **Position/location** are in what is referred to as the dative case. For more information on the dative case, see Unit 12.

There are some more prepositions which behave in this way. You have already met one of them: **auf.**

	Movement	**Position/location**
masc.	Wir gehen **auf den** Markt.	Wir treffen uns **auf dem** Markt.
fem.	Gehst du heute **auf die** Party?	Wir sehen uns dann **auf der** Party.
neut.	Wir fahren morgen **aufs** Land. *(to the countryside)*	Wir haben ein Haus **auf dem** Land. *(in the countryside)*

Aufs is an abbreviation for **auf das.**

You will meet more of these prepositions in later units.

TESTING YOURSELF

1 **Wie heißt es richtig?** *Can you put the sentences in the right order? Start with the bold word or phrase.*

   a *ein Stück von Shakespeare –* **im Theater** *– man – kann – sehen*

   b *möchte – heute – gehen – Abend – in die Kneipe –* **er**

   c *sehr gut – Tango tanzen –* **er** *– kann*

   d *kann – man –* **was** *– machen? – in London*

   e *essen gehen –* **ich** *– möchte – am Dienstag*

   f *sprechen –* **Frau Johnson** *– Deutsch – kann – sehr gut*

2 **Eine harte Woche.**
   Brigitte Mira's diary for the next few days is full of appointments that she doesn't like but which she has to keep. She has written down the things she would like to do instead.

Mo:	ins Kino gehen 🙂
	abends für das Mathe-Examen lernen ☹
Di:	Klaus treffen 🙂
	Mathe-Examen machen ☹ ☹
Mi:	lange schlafen 🙂
	morgens um 7.30 Uhr ins Fitnesscenter ☹
Do:	in die Kneipe gehen 🙂
	für Hannelore Babysitting machen ☹

Write down what she has to do and what she would like to do.

Beispiel Am Montag möchte sie ins Kino gehen, aber sie muss abends für das Mathe-Examen lernen.

Now that you have completed Unit 11, can you: tick
1 say what people can do at the weekend or
any other day?   ☐
2 make appointments?   ☐
3 say what you have to do and what you would
like to do?   ☐
4 explain when to use **in** with the accusative and
when with the dative case?   ☐

12

Eine Fahrkarte nach Heidelberg, bitte

A ticket to Heidelberg, please

In this unit you will learn
- *how to buy a ticket and read timetables*
- *how to say how you travel to work or university*
- *how to ask how you can get somewhere*

Language points
- *dative case after prepositions*

Buying a train ticket

1 AUF DEM BAHNHOF

Bernadette Klose kauft eine Fahrkarte auf dem Bahnhof. *Bernadette Klose buys a ticket at the train station.* Listen to the dialogue and see if you can figure out what the Germans say for *single ticket*, *return ticket* and *platform*.

Bernadette Klose	Ich möchte eine Fahrkarte nach Berlin, bitte.
Herr Schulze	Einfach oder hin und zurück?
Bernadette Klose	Hin und zurück, bitte. Was kostet die Fahrkarte?
Herr Schulze	Das macht €53, inklusive ICE-Zuschlag.
Bernadette Klose	Ja, gut. *(Gibt €60)* Muss ich umsteigen?
Herr Schulze	Nein, der Zug ist direkt. Hier ist Ihre Fahrkarte und € 7 zurück.
Bernadette Klose	Und wann fährt der nächste Zug?
Herr Schulze	Der nächste Zug fährt in 10 Minuten.
Bernadette Klose	Und von welchem Gleis fährt er?
Herr Schulze	Von Gleis 14.
Bernadette Klose	Vielen Dank.

Did you get the answers? They are **einfach** (*single ticket*), **hin und zurück** (*return ticket*) and **Gleis** (*platform/track*).

die Fahrkarte (-n) *ticket*
einfach *single (for bus or train fare)*
hin und zurück *return*
der Zuschlag (–¨e) *supplement*
Muss ich umsteigen? *Do I have to change? (trains, coaches, etc.)*
Von welchem Gleis fährt der Zug? *What platform (track) does the train leave from?*
Von Gleis 14. *From platform 14.*

2 BEANTWORTEN SIE DIE FRAGEN

a Wohin fährt Bernadette Klose?
b Was kostet die Fahrkarte?
c Muss sie umsteigen?
d Wann fährt der nächste Zug?
e Von welchem Gleis fährt der nächste Zug?

Ich möchte eine Fahrkarte. *I would like a ticket.*
Was kostet die Fahrkarte? *What does the ticket cost?*
Wann fährt der nächste Zug? *When does the next train go?*
Von welchem Gleis fährt der nächste Zug? *Which platform does the next train leave from?*

Insight: German railways

If you are planning to do some travelling in Germany, it might be worth studying the special fare offers available from the German rail operator **Deutsche Bahn**: there are **Sparpreise** (*concessionary fares*) for **ICE** (*Inter-City Express*) trains or other kinds of train, such as the **IC** (*Inter-City*), **EC** (*Euro-City*) or **IR** (*Inter-Regio*); with a **Guten-Abend-Ticket** it is cheaper to travel after 7.00 pm and a **Schönes-Wochenende-Ticket** offers special travel at weekends.

The **Bahncard** offers frequent rail travellers various discounts. Up-to-date information on the **Deutsche Bahn** can be found on the internet at http://www.bahn.de.

Die Bahn **DB**

Preiswert reisen am Wochenende

Mit dem Schönes-Wochenende-Ticket können bis zu fünf Personen einen ganzen Tag im Nahverkehr durch Deutschland fahren.

Das Ticket gilt samstags oder sonntags von 0.00 Uhr bis 3.00 Uhr des Folgetages für beliebig viele Fahrten.

SPRACHINFO: abfahren, ankommen *to depart, to arrive*
Two useful verbs for when a train departs or arrives somewhere are: **ab|fahren** (*to depart/to leave*) and **an|kommen** (*to arrive*). They are both separable verbs:

Wann fährt *der nächste Zug* ab? *Er* fährt *um* 15.07 *Uhr* ab.

Wann kommt *er in Heidelberg* an? *Er* kommt *um* 18 *Minuten nach vier* an.

On a timetable the prefixes **ab** and **an** are commonly used to indicate the departure and arrival of trains.

3 WANN FÄHRT DER NÄCHSTE ZUG NACH HEIDELBERG?

Study the timetable below, then answer the questions.

Hannover Hbf
→ **Heidelberg Hbf**
Fahrplanauszug – Angaben ohne Gewähr –

441 km

ab	Zug	Umsteigen	an	ab	Zug		an	Verkehrstage
1.24	D 1599						6.21	täglich
5.21	ICE 997 ✕	Frankfurt(M)	7.43	7.51	IR 2473 ⓣ		8.43	Mo - Sa 01
6.12	IR 2475						10.43	Mo - Sa 01
6.50	ICE 571 ✕						9.51	Mo - Sa 01
7.24	ICE 791 ✕	Frankfurt(M)	9.43	9.51	IR 2475 ⓣ		10.43	täglich
7.50	ICE 775 ✕	Mannheim Hbf	10.42	10.54	IC 119 ✕		11.05	täglich
8.12	IR 2477 ⓣ						12.43	täglich
8.50	ICE 573 ✕						11.51	täglich
9.23	ICE 793 ✕	Frankfurt(M)	11.43	11.51	IR 2477 ⓣ		12.43	täglich
9.50	ICE 873 ✕	Frankfurt(M)	12.01	12.06	ICE 73 ✕			täglich
		Mannheim Hbf	12.42	12.54	IC 513 ✕		13.05	
10.12	IR 2479 ⓣ	Frankfurt(M)	13.38	13.51	IR 2101 ⓣ		14.43	täglich
10.50	ICE 575 ✕						13.51	täglich
11.18	ICE 971 ✕	Frankfurt(M)	13.38	13.51	IR 2101 ⓣ		14.43	täglich 02
11.50	ICE 71 ✕	Mannheim Hbf	14.42	14.54	IC 613 ✕		15.05	täglich

Answer the questions below in relation to the following days and times:

a Wann fährt der nächste Zug nach Heidelberg, bitte?
b Muss ich umsteigen?
c Kann ich im Zug etwas zu essen bekommen?
d Und wann kommt der Zug in Heidelberg an?

- **Montag um 10.00 Uhr**
- **Dienstag um 06.00 Uhr**
- **Sonntag um 06.30 Uhr**

- **Donnerstag um 09.30 Uhr**
- **Freitag um 11.45 Uhr**

Beispiel Montag um 10.00 Uhr

a Der nächste Zug fährt um 10.12 Uhr.
b Ja, Sie müssen in Frankfurt umsteigen.
c Ja, es gibt einen Speisewagen (*dining car*).
d Er kommt um 14.43 Uhr in Heidelberg an.

4 ROLLENSPIEL: UND JETZT SIE! WAS SAGEN SIE?

Write down the answers first, then listen to the recording, using the pause button so that you can say your responses out loud. Then check your answers.

Sie	*Ask how much a ticket to Frankfurt costs.*
Verkäufer	Einfach oder hin und zurück?
Sie	*Say a single ticket.*
Verkaüfer	Das macht €42,50, inklusive ICE-Zuschlag.
Sie	*Say yes, that's OK.*
Verkäufer	Vielen Dank, hier ist Ihre Fahrkarte und €2,50 zurück.
Sie	*Ask when the next train goes to Frankfurt.*
Verkäufer	Der nächste Zug fährt in 10 Minuten.
Sie	*Ask which platform it leaves from.*
Verkäufer	Von Gleis 14.
Sie	*Ask if you have to change.*
Verkäufer	Nein, der Zug ist direkt.
Sie	*Say thank you very much.*

🎧 CD 1, TR 69

5 WELCHE ANTWORT PASST AM BESTEN?

Choose the appropriate answer for the question in each instance.

a *Kann ich eine Fahrkarte nach Freiburg bekommen?*
  i *Der nächste Zug fährt um 16.00 Uhr.*
  ii *Das macht € 37.*
  iii *Einfach oder hin und zurück?*
b *Wann fährt der nächste Zug nach Innsbruck?*
  i *Von Gleis 7.*
  ii *In 10 Minuten.*
  iii *Einfach oder hin und zurück?*
c *Von welchem Gleis fährt der Zug?*
  i *Sie müssen nicht umsteigen.*
  ii *Gleis 10.*
  iii *Es ist ein Direktzug.*
d *Was kostet die Fahrkarte?*
  i *Das macht €43.*
  ii *Sie brauchen einen Zuschlag.*
  iii *Sie können mit Ihrer Visa-Karte bezahlen.*

Getting around town

6 LESEN UND LERNEN

Wie fahren die Leute? How
do these people get where they
want to go?

Bettina fährt mit dem Fahrrad.

Herr Abramcik fährt mit dem Auto in die Stadt.

Paul fährt mit dem Zug von Hamburg nach Berlin.

Sie fahren mit dem Bus für ein Wochenende nach Paris.

Frau Schulz fährt mit der U-Bahn ins Stadtzentrum.

Sabine fährt mit der Straßenbahn.

Markus und Hans gehen zu Fuß.

Note that **Zug** and **Bus** are masculine, **U-Bahn** and **Straßenbahn** are feminine, and **Fahrrad** and **Auto** are neuter in German. Can you figure out what happens with the articles (**der, die** and **das**) when they appear after **mit**?

SPRACHINFO: *Means of transport*

To talk about means of transport in German you use the preposition **mit**. As you can see **mit** is followed by the **Dativ** (*dative*):

der Bus	**Frau Krause fährt mit dem Bus.**
die U-Bahn	**Rainer Krause fährt mit der U-Bahn.**
das Auto	**Herr Krause fährt mit dem Auto.**

Note that the dative form of the word for *the* is **dem** for masculine and neuter nouns and **der** for feminine nouns, as you already saw in Unit 11.

To say *to go on foot* in German, you use **zu Fuß gehen**: Saskia Krause geht zu Fuß.

7 WAS PASST?

Ergänzen Sie. *Complete these sentences.*

....
der – dem – dem – der – dem
....

a In Amsterdam fahren viele Leute mit _____ Fahrrad.

b Mit _____ U-Bahn ist man in sieben Minuten in der Stadt.

c In Ostberlin kann man mit _____ Straßenbahn fahren.

d Er fährt mit _____ Auto nach Österreich.

e Mit _____ Zug kostet es €60 bis nach Freiburg.

8 WIE FAHREN SIE ZUR ARBEIT? WIE LANGE DAUERT DIE FAHRT?

🔊 **CD 1 TR 70**

i Listen to these four people talking about how they get to work or to school and how long it takes them. Rearrange the items in columns 2 and 3 so that they match what is said in the recording.

Beispiel Person 1 → mit dem Fahrrad → 20 Minuten

Person	Wie fahren sie?	Wie lange brauchen sie?
Person 1	mit dem Auto	10 Minuten
Person 2	mit dem Fahrrad	50 Minuten
Person 3	geht zu Fuß	eine Stunde
Person 4	mit dem Bus und der U-Bahn	20 Minuten

ii Now read the text and answer questions a–f.

Frauke Gerhard (27, Studentin)
‚Also, ich fahre immer mit dem Fahrrad zur Universität. Das geht schnell, ist gesund und außerdem gut für die Umwelt. Von meinem Haus bis zur Uni brauche ich ungefähr 20 Minuten. Im Winter fahre ich manchmal mit dem Bus. Ich habe einen Führerschein, aber ich fahre nur selten mit dem Auto.'

Matthias Michaelis (34, Angestellter bei der Post)
‚Ich fahre meistens mit dem Bus zum Bahnhof. Dann muss ich umsteigen. Vom Bahnhof nehme ich die U-Bahn zur Arbeit. Ich habe eine Monatskarte. Bus und Bahn sind nicht so teuer und in der U-Bahn kann ich auch lesen. Die Fahrt dauert ungefähr 50 Minuten.'

Günther Pfalz (38, Elektriker)
‚Ich fahre immer mit dem Auto. Da kann ich Radio hören, im Winter ist es warm und es geht schnell. Die Verbindung mit Bus

und Bahn ist nicht gut. Da brauche ich zwei Stunden. Mit dem Auto dauert es aber nur eine Stunde.'

Andreas (14, Schüler)
,Meine Schule ist nicht weit, ich kann zu Fuß gehen. Meistens hole ich einen Freund ab und dann gehen wir zusammen. Ich brauche nur 10 Minuten. Im Winter fährt mich manchmal mein Vater mit dem Auto.'

die Umwelt *environment*
ungefähr *approximately, about*
im Winter *in winter*
der Führerschein (-) *driving licence*
um|steigen *to change (a train, bus, etc.)*
die Monatskarte (-n) *monthly ticket*
die Verbindung (-en) *connection, link*
dauern *to last*

9 BEANTWORTEN SIE DIE FRAGEN

Now answer the following questions.

Beispiel Wie fährt Frauke zur Universität? → Sie fährt mit dem Auto.

a Wie lange braucht sie bis zur Uni?
b Wie fährt Herr Michaelis zum Bahnhof?
c Was macht er in der U-Bahn?
d Was sagt Herr Pfalz über die Verbindung mit Bus und Bahn?
e Wie lange fährt er mit dem Auto zur Arbeit?
f Wie kommt Andreas normalerweise zur Schule?

SPRACHINFO: *PREPOSITIONS* **MIT, ZU, VON** *+ DATIVE*

You might have been puzzled by the different forms of **zu** and **von** in the interviews: **zum Bahnhof** but **zur Arbeit**.

Like **mit, zu** and **von** are always followed by the dative case, but it is common to abbreviate many of the forms, as you can see in the following examples:

mit, zu

der Bus, Bahnhof   Ich fahre mit *dem* Bus bis *zum* (= *zu dem*) Bahnhof.

die U-Bahn, Universität   Sie fährt mit *der* U-Bahn *zur* (= *zu der*) Universität.

das Auto, Stadion   Er fährt mit *dem* Auto *zum* (= *zu dem*) Stadion.

von

der Park   Wie komme ich *vom* (= *von dem*) Park zum Supermarkt?

die Kirche   Wie kommt man *von* der Kirche zur Post?

das Hotel   Ich möchte bitte *vom* (= *von dem*) Hotel bis zum Stadtzentrum kommen.

10 WAS FRAGEN DIE LEUTE?

Ergänzen Sie. *Complete the questions.*

a Entschuldigen Sie bitte, wie komme ich ___ Bahnhof?

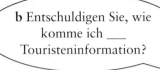

b Entschuldigen Sie, wie komme ich ___ Touristeninformation?

c Entschuldigung bitte, wie komme ich v___ Bahnhof z___ Hotel Germania?

d Entschuldigen Sie bitte, wie komme ich ___ Fußballstadion?

Grammar

PREPOSITIONS + DATIVE

In Unit 11 you saw how some prepositions are followed by the accusative case endings when motion is involved and the dative case endings when position or location is involved.

Some prepositions are followed only by the dative case endings, irrespective of whether movement or location is being talked about.

The prepositions that you have met in this category are **mit, zu** and **von.** Other prepositions that behave in the same way are:

aus *(out (of), from)*, **bei** *(with, at, in)*, **nach** *(after)*, **seit** *(since)*.

masculine	**Er fährt mit *dem* Bus.**
feminine	**Er arbeitet bei *der* Firma Bräuer.**
neuter	**Er kommt aus *dem* Haus.**

The plural form of the definite article (*the*) is **den** in the dative:

Er kommt aus *den* USA.

Note that the following contracted forms are commonly found:

> *bei dem* → *beim*   *zu dem* → *zum*
> *von dem* → *vom*   *zu der* → *zur*

The indefinite article (**ein, eine**) becomes **einem** in the masculine and neuter dative and **einer** in the feminine dative.

masculine	**Er wohnt jetzt bei *einem* Freund.**
feminine	**Wir essen heute Abend bei *einer* Freundin.**
neuter	**Er arbeitet seit *einem* Jahr in London.**

You will find many of these prepositions and endings used and practised in later units.

TESTING YOURSELF

1 Wie heißt es richtig? Verbinden Sie. *The gender is given in brackets.*

Wie komme ich	zur zum	Flughafen (m) Bahnhof (m) Gedächtniskirche (f) Café Mozart (nt) Stadtbäckerei (f) Fußballstadion (nt) Bundesstraße (f)	**?**

2 Üben Sie den Dativ: **dem** oder **der**, **zum** oder **zur**? Ergänzen Sie.

a *Peter lebt sehr gesund: Er fährt jeden Tag mit d___ Fahrrad z___ Universität.*

b *In Berlin kann man schlecht parken. Frau Braun fährt immer mit d___ U-Bahn z___ Arbeit.*

c *Herr Krause hat heute wenig Zeit und fährt mit d___ Taxi z___ Bahnhof.*

d *Mit d___ Zug ist man in drei Stunden in München.*

e *In Ostberlin kann man noch mit d___ Straßenbahn fahren.*

3 Was passt zusammen?

Put these sentences in order to create a dialogue between Herr Marktgraf and a ticket seller at the Deutsche Bahn. Start with c.

Herr Marktgraf	Verkäufer
a Vielen Dank.	**i** Von Gleis 18.
b Und von welchem Gleis fährt er?	**ii** Hier bitte. Das macht €70.

c Ich möchte eine Fahrkarte nach Köln.

iii Nein, Sie brauchen nicht umsteigen.

d Und wann fährt der nächste Zug?

iv Gern geschehen. Gute Fahrt.

e Hin und zurück.

v Einfach oder hin und zurück?

f Muss ich umsteigen?

vi In einer Viertelstunde.

Now that you have completed Unit 12, can you   tick

1 ask for and buy a train ticket? ☐

2 say how you travel to work or university? ☐

3 ask how to get to the train station, the airport and other places? ☐

4 name at least three prepositions which are followed by the dative case? ☐

13

Was hast du am Wochenende gemacht?
What did you do at the weekend?

In this unit you will learn
- *how to say what happened at the weekend*
- *how to talk about recent events*
- *how to describe purchases*

Language points
- *present perfect tense*
- *adjectival endings (1)*

Talking about the past

1 LESEN UND LERNEN

Was haben die Leute am Wochenende gemacht? Welches Bild passt? Match the sentences with the pictures which indicate what these people did at the weekend.

i Die Leute haben einen Ausflug gemacht.
ii Frau Meier hat im Krankenhaus gearbeitet.
iii Sandra hat für ihr Examen gelernt.
iv Frau Nowitzki hat auf dem Markt Blumen gekauft.

v Frau Weber hat viel fotografiert.
vi Ronni hat im Stadtpark Fußball gespielt.

VOCAB

der Ausflug (¨e) *excursion*
das Krankenhaus (¨er) *hospital*
die Blume (-n) *flower*

a

b
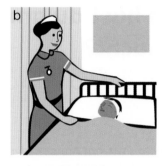

c

d

e

f

SPRACHINFO: *Present perfect tense of regular verbs*

When they talk about the past, Germans most often use the present perfect tense. The present perfect tense of regular verbs like **spielen** and **kaufen** is formed by using **haben** with what is known as the past participle. This is very similar to the present perfect tense in English:

Ich habe viel gelernt.   *I've learned a lot.*

USAGE

However, you need to know that, whereas in English the present perfect tense is usually used when an event is still connected fairly closely with the present (*I have just …*), it can also be used in German when speaking about events that have happened a long time ago:

Letztes Jahr habe ich mein   *Last year I did my exam in*
  Englisch-Examen gemacht.   *English.*
1492 hat Kolumbus Amerika   *In 1492 Columbus discovered*
  entdeckt.   *America.*

FORMATION

The present perfect tense is formed by using the appropriate form of **haben** + the past participle. To form the past participle of regular verbs you take the stem of the verb, i.e. **spiel-**, **kauf-**, add **ge-** at the beginning and **-t** at the end:

spiel·en   ge·spiel·t
kauf·en   ge·kauf·t

If the stem ends in **-t**, then an extra **-e-** is added before the **-t**:

arbeit·en   ge·arbeit·et

Regular verbs like these are sometimes called 'weak' verbs.

In German, the past participle normally goes to the end of the sentence:

Ich habe Tennis gespielt.   *I have played/played tennis.*
Ich habe ein Auto gekauft.   *I have bought/bought a car.*

POINTS TO WATCH OUT FOR:
Separable verbs put the -ge- between the prefix and the stem:
einkaufen – eingekauft.

No **ge-** is added before the verb with prefixes, such as: **be-**
(**bezahlen – bezahlt**), ent- (**entdecken – entdeckt**), ver- (**verkaufen**
– verkauft).

There is also no **ge-** added with verbs ending with -ieren (**studieren**
– studiert).

THE VERB *HABEN*
Here is a reminder of the forms of **haben** you might need when
forming the present perfect tense.:

ich habe	**wir haben**
du hast	**ihr habt**
Sie haben	**Sie haben**
er/sie/es hat	**sie haben**

Note that the past participle of **haben** is **gehabt**:

Ich habe viel Spaß gehabt.   *I have had/had a lot of fun.*

2 WIE HEISSEN DIE PARTIZIPIEN?

Write down the past participles of these verbs:

a spielen   *gespielt*   **f** kochen   _____

b tanzen   _____   **g** telefonieren   *telefoniert*

c machen   _____   **h** bezahlen   _____

d frühstücken   _____   **i** besuchen   _____

e kosten   _____   **j** einkaufen   *eingekauft*

3 WELCHES WORT PASST?

Re-use the past participles from **Übung 2** to complete these sentences:

a Der Computer hat €1500 *gekostet*.

b Sie haben in der Disco bis fünf Uhr am Morgen _____ .

c Sie hat Freunde _____ .

d Er hat im Supermarkt _____ .

e Er hat mit seiner Visa-Karte _____ .

f Letztes Wochenende hat er Nudeln mit Tomatensoße _____ .

g ‚Hast du wieder eine Stunde mit Boris in New York _____?'

SPRACHINFO: war, waren *was, were*
War and **waren** are the words most commonly used in German to say *was* or *were*:

Wo war Jochen gestern?	*Where was Jochen yesterday?*
Wir waren auf dem Markt.	*We were at the market.*

The full forms are:

ich war	**wir waren**
du warst	**ihr wart**
Sie waren	**Sie waren**
er/sie/es war	**sie waren**

4 SONNTAGMORGEN

◀) **CD 2, TR 1**

Ulrike and Angela erzählen, was sie am Samstag gemacht haben.

Hören Sie die Gespräche. Listen to the recording and decide who – **U** (for Ulrike) or **A** (for Angela) – says the following sentences, relating what they did on Saturday.

Wer sagt was?	Ulrike (U)	Angela (A)
a Am Morgen war ich in der Stadt und habe eingekauft.	U	
b Am Abend haben ich und Bernd gekocht.		A
c Wir haben viel Spaß gehabt.		
d Wir haben klassische Musik gehört.		
e Ich habe gestern Morgen einen neuen Computer gekauft.		
f Am Nachmittag habe ich Britta und Georg besucht.		
g Ich habe den ganzen Tag mit dem Computer gespielt.		
h Am Abend waren wir dann zusammen in der neuen ‚Mondschein Bar' und haben bis drei Uhr getanzt.		
i Ich habe auch im Internet gesurft.		

5 SCHREIBEN SIE, WAS DIE BEIDEN GEMACHT HABEN

Now put the sentences from Exercise 4 **Sonntagmorgen** in the right order and write a full version of what both women did. Don't forget to use the 3rd person singular (**sie**):

Am Morgen war Ulrike in der Stadt und hat eingekauft. Am Nachmittag hat sie …

6 WAS HAT BETTINA AM WOCHENENDE GEMACHT?

Here are some details about Bettina's weekend. Write out a full version of what she did on Saturday/Sunday in the morning, in the afternoon and in the evening.

Beispiel Am Samstagmorgen hat Bettina eingekauft. Danach hat sie …

Samstag		Sonntag	
10:00	einkaufen, Fotos abholen	7:30	Ausflug machen
15:00	Georg im Krankenhaus besuchen	15:30	im Garten arbeiten
19:00	Schach spielen mit Pia – Nudeln kochen	20:00	mit Christina telefonieren, für das Deutsch-Examen lernen

At the flea market

7 LESEN UND LERNEN

◀) **CD 2 TR 2**

Was haben Sie denn auf dem Flohmarkt gekauft?

Read the article from a German newspaper on the next page and find out what the four people have to say about their purchases at the flea market. Then answer the following questions.

a Was haben Renate und Bernd Schmidt gekauft?
b Wohin fährt Herr Günther diesen Sommer und was macht er gern?
c Was hat Annett gekauft und wie viel hat sie bezahlt?
d Welches Problem hat Herr Eickes?

Flohmärkte sind im Moment sehr populär. Ob alt oder jung, arm oder reich, altmodisch oder trendy – jeden Samstagmorgen gehen Tausende auf den Flohmarkt. Der Tagesanzeiger wollte wissen, was den Flohmarkt so interessant macht und was die Leute kaufen.

Wir haben letztes Wochenende vier Besucher interviewt.

Renate und Bernd Schmidt, 42, 47

‚Wir haben eine alte Platte von den Rolling Stones gekauft. Die Rolling Stones sind einfach super, unsere Lieblingsband. Mick Jagger hat eine fantastische Stimme. Wir haben die Platte zwei Jahre gesucht. €17,50 ist nicht billig, aber dafür ist die Platte einfach toll.'

Heinz Günther, 62

‚Ich habe ein interessantes Buch über Lateinamerika gekauft. Ich reise gern und möchte diesen Sommer nach Mexiko fahren. Letztes Jahr habe ich schon Peru besucht. Das Buch hat informative Texte und viele schöne Fotos.'

Annett Wunderlich, 24

‚Ich habe ein neues Hemd gekauft. Für €7,50, aus London. Im Kaufhaus zahle ich €15 oder mehr. Es sieht sehr cool aus, oder? Man kann tolle Sachen auf dem Flohmarkt finden, fast alles.'

Christine Brandt und Werner Eickes, 20, 30

‚Wir haben einen alten, mechanischen Wecker gekauft. Mein Mann hat ein großes Problem: Er kann morgens schlecht aufstehen. Ich glaube, der Wecker hier ist so laut, den muss man hören. Und wir haben nur €2,50 bezahlt.'

You can also hear their answers on the recording and check the pronunciation.

die Platte (-n) *record, vinyl*
einfach *simple, simply*
toll *fantastic, great*
die Stimme (-) *voice*
das Hemd (-en) *shirt*
das Kaufhaus (¨er) *department store*
der Wecker (-) *alarm clock*
Er kann morgens schlecht aufstehen. *He finds it difficult to get up in the morning.*
laut *loud, noisy*

8 ERGÄNZEN SIE

Use the newspaper article above to help you complete these sentences.

a Bernd und Renate sagen, Mick Jagger hat eine _____ Stimme.

b Herr Günther hat ein _____ Buch über Südamerika gekauft.

c Annett sagt, man kann _____ Sachen auf dem Flohmarkt finden.

d Frau Brandt und Herr Eickes haben einen _____, _____ Wecker gekauft.

SPRACHINFO: *Adjective endings*

Any adjective which comes between the indefinite article **ein** and a noun has to be given an ending, depending on the gender and case of the noun: e.g. when you say what someone has or buys, etc., you need the accusative case and the endings are:

masculine	**-en**	Werner hat einen mechanisch**en** Wecker gekauft.	der Wecker
feminine	**-e**	Renate kauft eine alt**e** Platte.	die Platte
neuter	**-es**	Heinz kauft ein interessant**es** Buch.	das Buch

In the plural, if there is no article, the ending is **-e** for all genders:

Auf dem Flohmarkt kauft man tolle Sachen.

For more details on adjectival endings see the **Grammar** section.

9 ÜBEN SIE ADJEKTIVENDUNGEN

Practise those adjective endings.

a Er braucht einen neu__ Computer.
b Sie hat ein toll__ Auto.
c Ich möchte eine groß__ Flasche Mineralwasser.
d Peter hat einen interessant__ Beruf.
e Hast du ein schön__ Wochenende gehabt?
f Sie haben alt__ Freunde besucht.

10 WIE HEISST DAS GEGENTEIL?

What is the opposite of these words:

teuer – neu – altmodisch – schwer – arm – groß – langweilig – ~~schlecht~~

Beispiel gut – schlecht

a klein – _____

b billig – _____

c interessant – _____

d alt – _____

e reich – _____

f leicht – _____

g modisch – _____

Insight: Flohmärkte *Fleamarkets*

Markets selling antiques and second-hand goods are very popular in Germany. The **Flohmarkt am Tiergarten**, on the **Straße des 17. Juni**, is a must-see if you are in Berlin. Look out for leaflets advertising markets in smaller towns and even in remote villages. You'll find details of big city markets in magazines like **Zitty**.

Here's a typical extract from the **Flohmarkt** section of **Zitty**. See how much you can understand. Try to guess as much as you can from the context before you look at the vocabulary given below.

Flohmarkt am Tiergarten Straße des 17. Juni,
Tel: 26 55 00 96 Sa/So 10 – 17 Uhr

Einer der meistbesuchten Flohmärkte in Berlin, der auch viele Touristen anzieht. Dementsprechend liegen die Preise etwas höher als bei anderen Locations. Doch wer ein bisschen tiefer schürft, wird auch hier ein Schnäppchen machen können. Es gibt Platten und CDs der verschiedensten Musikrichtungen, aber auch Möbel. Direkt angeschlossen ist ein Kunsthandwerkermarkt.

(Quelle: http://www.zitty.de)

anlziehen *to attract*
dementsprechend *accordingly*
liegen *to lie*
etwas höher als *somewhat higher than*
doch *however*
tief *deep*
schürfen *to dig*
das Schnäppchen (-) *bargain*
verschieden *different, varied*
die Richtung (-en) *direction, trend*
das Möbel (-) *furniture*
angeschlossen *(here) adjoining*
der Kunsthandwerkermarkt (¨e) *craft market*

Pronunciation

◆ **CD 2, TR 3**

Listen to the pronunciation of the letter l in these words.

leben	**lernen**	**ledig**	**Lehre**
helfen	**wollen**	**vielleicht**	**wirklich**
Enkel	**Onkel**	**manchmal**	**kühl**

The German l is closer to the first l in *little* as pronounced in standard British English. Try to avoid using the so-called dark l (the second l in little) in German.

How would you pronounce these words? **Schlüssel, selten, Milch**

Grammar

1 PRESENT PERFECT TENSE

The main details of **regular** or so-called **weak** verbs are given in the **SPRACHINFO** earlier in this unit. There will be more on the present perfect tense in Unit 14.

2 ADJECTIVAL ENDINGS – IN THE ACCUSATIVE

Earlier in this unit you practised the endings that are added to adjectives after the indefinite article (**ein**, etc.) in the accusative case. These endings are used not only after **ein** but also after **kein, mein, dein,** etc.

masc. acc.	-en	Gibt es hier keinen interessanten Flohmarkt?
fem. acc.	-e	Wo finde ich eine neue Lampe?
neut. acc.	-es	Hast du mein altes Hemd gesehen?

Note that in the plural the endings differ. After words like **kein**, **mein**, **dein** etc. you have to add **-en** to the adjective:

Ich habe meine alten CDs verkauft.
Ich habe keine neuen Bücher gekauft.

Otherwise the ending is **-e**:

Er hat neue Hemden gekauft.

No endings are added to the adjective if it does not occur in front of the noun:

Ist dein Hemd neu?
Dieser Flohmarkt ist wirklich sehr interessant.

TESTING YOURSELF

1 Frau Adorno arbeitet bei einer Marketingfirma. Dort gibt es immer viel zu tun. Das hat sie zum Beispiel am Dienstag gemacht. *This is what Frau Adorno did on Tuesday.*

DIENSTAG

8:30	Besprechung mit Dr. Paul
10:00	mit Frau Martini telefonieren
10:30	die Firma Schmidt + Consultants besuchen
12:45	Mittagspause machen
15:00	Briefe diktieren und Tickets für Reise nach Rom buchen
17:00	einen schönen Mantel kaufen
18:30	mit Michael Squash spielen

VOCAB

die Besprechung (-en) *meeting, discussion*
der Mantel (¨) *coat*

Was hat sie gemacht? Schreiben Sie. *Write out what she did.*

a *Um 8 Uhr 30 hat sie eine Besprechung mit Dr. Paul gehabt.*
b *Um 10 Uhr hat sie …, etc.*

2 Was wir am Samstag auf dem Flohmarkt gekauft haben.

Fill in the missing endings on the adjectives. The first three have been done for you. If you are not sure of the meanings or genders of some of these nouns, check them in the German–English vocabulary at the back of the book.

a ein alt*es* Kaffeekännchen

b einen elektrisch*en* Wecker

c eine cool*e* Sonnenbrille

d ein alt___ Radio

e eine gut___ Jacke

f ein modisch___ Hemd

g eine fantastisch___ Lampe

h einen warm___ Mantel

i eine neu___ CD

j ein alt___ Fahrrad

k ein neu___ Handy

Now that you have completed Unit 13, can you   tick

1 tell someone what you did at the weekend and talk about the recent past? ☐

2 describe purchases that you have made? ☐

3 work out what endings to use on adjectives in the accusative case? ☐

14

Wir sind ins Grüne gefahren
We went into the countryside

In this unit you will learn
- *how to talk about recent events (continued)*
- *how to talk about the more distant past*

Language points
- *more on the present perfect tense*

More about the past

1 LESEN UND LERNEN. DER AUSFLUG INS GRÜNE

A family of four decided to go on an excursion into the countryside. Here and overleaf are pictures showing what they did. Match the sentences overleaf to the pictures.

a

b

c

d

e

f

g

h

i Sie haben im Zug geschlafen.
ii Um 17.00 Uhr haben sie den Zug genommen.
iii Sie haben gut gegessen und getrunken.
iv Sie sind lange spazieren gegangen.
v Sie sind mit dem Zug gefahren.
vi Sie sind um halb sieben aufgestanden.
vii Um ein Uhr sind sie sehr müde gewesen.
viii Sie haben gesungen.

spazieren gehen *to go for a walk*
müde *tired*

QV

SPRACHINFO: *The present perfect of irregular verbs*
Irregular verbs form their past participles with a **ge-** at the beginning and an **-en**, rather than a **-t**, at the end:

geb-en	**ge-geb-en**	*(give, given)*
seh-en	**ge-seh-en**	*(see, seen)*

These verbs often change their stem, and are also called 'strong verbs':

trink-en	**ge-trunk-en**	*(drink, drunk)*
schreib-en	**ge-schrieb-en**	*(write, written)*

For a list of common irregular verbs see the end of this book.

SOME VERBS TAKE **SEIN:**
Some verbs – often indicating movement or coming and going – form their perfect tense with **sein** rather than **haben**. The most important ones that you have met so far are:

gehen	Ich **bin** gestern auf den Markt **gegangen.**
kommen	Tom **ist** erst um ein Uhr morgens nach Hause **gekommen.**
fahren	Ich **bin** im Oktober nach Italien **gefahren.**
aufstehen	Sie **ist** um halb acht **aufgestanden.**

The past participle of **sein** is quite irregular:

Ich **bin** gestern sehr müde **gewesen.** *I was very tired yesterday.*

Note that it is very common to say **Ich war ...** instead of **Ich bin ...**
gewesen.

POINTS TO WATCH OUT FOR:
- ▶ *Separable verbs put the* -ge- *where the verb separates:*
  aufstehen –aufgestanden
- ▶ *As mentioned in the previous unit, verbs beginning with* **be-,**
  ent- *or* **ver-** *do not add a* **ge-** *in the past participle. This also*
  applies to verbs beginning with **emp-** *(empfehlen – empfohlen*
  to recommend), **er-** *(erhalten – erhalten to receive) and* **zer-**
  (zerbrechen – zerbrochen to destroy).

There is an overview of the present perfect tense of both regular
and irregular verbs in the **Grammar** section of this unit.

2 WAS FEHLT? (HABEN ODER SEIN)

Fill in the correct form of either **haben** or **sein.** If you would like
to remind yourself how these verbs are formed, look at Unit 4,
Grammar 2.

Beispiel a Am Wochenende **bin** ich nach Köln gefahren.

b Er ___ in München sehr viel Bier getrunken.

c ___ Sie schon den neuen Film mit Russell Crowe gesehen?

d Am Donnerstag ___ Birgit ins Theater gegangen.

e ___ du schon einmal in Deutschland gewesen?

f Am Sonntag ___ Thomas seine Großeltern besucht.

g Gestern ___ ich einen alten Freund getroffen.

h Oh, das ___ ich vergessen.

3 EINE ANSTRENGENDE WOCHE *A TIRING WEEK*

Read the longer text below about the German pop singer Peter Wichtig. Try to get an idea of the main events first and then go back and look more closely at the details. Note that you can find most of the key words in the text in the vocabulary at the back of the book. When you've read the text, complete the two exercises on the next page.

DAS PORTRÄT:
Peter Wichtig

Peter Wichtig, 34, gelernter Elektriker, ist der Sänger der deutschen Rockband ‚Die grünen Unterhemden'. Bislang hat die Band zwei goldene Schallplatten bekommen. Im Moment bereitet er mit seiner Band eine große Tournee vor. Wir haben ihn in seinem Studio getroffen und mit ihm über das Leben eines Rockstars gesprochen und ihn gefragt: ‚Was haben Sie letzte Woche gemacht?'

‚Im Moment arbeite ich sehr viel. Ich bin praktisch kaum zu Hause gewesen. Mein Terminkalender ist total voll. Also, am Montag bin ich nach New York geflogen. Dort habe ich einige Produzenten getroffen. Am Abend war ich auf einer Party bei meinem alten Freund Robert (de Niro) und habe Kaviar gegessen und Champagner getrunken. Ich bin nur einen Tag in New York geblieben. Es war einfach zu kalt dort.

Dienstag und Mittwoch bin ich in Florida gewesen und bin im Meer geschwommen. Das war wunderbar. Außerdem habe ich einige Interviews gegeben und auch ein paar neue italienische Anzüge gekauft. Vom besten Designer natürlich. Ja, ich liebe Florida. Ich möchte mir dort gern eine Villa kaufen.

Donnerstag bin ich nach Deutschland zurückgekommen: Am Abend habe ich in einer Fernsehshow für MTV gesungen. Am Freitag habe ich wieder Interviews gegeben und bin dann nach Salzburg gefahren, wo ich ein kleines Haus habe und bin abends ins Kasino gegangen. Am Wochenende bin ich Ski gelaufen und habe den Video-Clip für meinen neuen Song gesehen. Das Lied heißt: *Ich kann dich nicht vergessen.* Sie können es bald kaufen, es ist fantastisch. Es kommt in einer Woche auf den Markt.'

Which of the verbs in the text take **sein** and which take **haben**?

gelernter Elektriker *(a) qualified electrician*
das Unterhemd (-en) *vest, undershirt*
vor|bereiten *to prepare*
der Terminkalender (-) *diary*
bleiben *to stay*
der Anzug (¨e) *suit*

Was ist hier falsch? Korrigieren Sie, bitte.

a Peter Wichtig ist nach Sibirien geflogen.

b Auf einer Party hat er Hamburger gegessen und Dosenbier getrunken.

c Er hat Robert Redford getroffen.

d In Florida ist er im Hotel-Swimming-Pool geschwommen.

e Er hat neue Socken gekauft.

f Am Freitag ist er ins Kino gegangen.

g Am Wochenende ist er im Park spazieren gegangen.

h Das neues Lied heißt: Ich habe dich vergessen.

4 WIE HEISST ES RICHTIG?

Fill in the missing information. All verbs appear in the text.

Infinitive	Past participle	Infinitive	Past participle
a *trinken*	*getrunken*	**e** *gehen*	_____
b _____	*getroffen*	**f** *fahren*	_____
c *essen*	_____	**g** _____	*geflogen*
d *sprechen*	_____	**h** _____	*geblieben*

5 MEHR ÜBER PETER WICHTIG

🔊 **CD 2, TR 4**

Peter Wichtig war beim Radio-Sender OK München und hat ein Interview gegeben. Hören Sie bitte das Interview und beantworten Sie die Fragen.

a Wie lange macht er Musik?
b Was war sein erster Hit?
c Wie viele CDs hat er gemacht?
d Wer schreibt seine Songs?
e Was macht er in seiner Freizeit?

When	What you did
Gestern	habe ich (lange/viel/im Garten) gearbeitet
	habe ich Fußball/Tennis/Golf gespielt.
	habe ich meine Eltern/Freunde besucht.
Am Montag/Am Dienstag, etc.	bin ich ins Kino/ins Theater/in die Oper/ in die Kirche gegangen.
	bin ich im Park spazieren gegangen.
Am Montagmorgen	bin ich nach Brighton/Paris gefahren.
Am Mittwochabend, etc.	habe ich ferngesehen.
Letzte Woche/Letztes Wochenende	habe ich einen langweiligen Film/eine englische Band/ein interessantes Theaterstück gesehen.

USEFUL EXPRESSIONS

Achtung!
Remember that the preposition **in** is followed by the accusative if movement is indicated, or by the dative case if the focus is more on location and position: *Ich bin* **ins** *Kino gegangen* and *Ich war* **im** *Kino*. For more details see Unit 11.

6 UND JETZT SIE!

Eine Brieffreundin in Deutschland möchte wissen, was Sie letzte Woche oder letztes Wochenende gemacht haben. Bitte schreiben Sie ihr!

You may find it helpful to refer to the **Useful expressions** above when completing this exercise.

Liebe Petra,

wie geht es dir? Ich hoffe, gut.

Also, du möchtest wissen, was ich _____ gemacht habe. Kein Problem.

Also,

_____

_____

Ich freue mich schon auf deinen nächsten Brief.

Viele Grüße

dein/deine

7 HEINRICH BÖLL: SEIN LEBENSLAUF

Here is a list of some of the main events in the life of the German author, Heinrich Böll. Write a report on his life, using the information provided.

Der Lebenslauf des deutschen Schriftstellers Heinrich Böll

1917 am 21. Dezember in Köln geboren
1924–28 besucht die Volksschule in Köln-Raderthal
1928–37 besucht das Kaiser-Wilhelm-Gymnasium in Köln
1937 macht das Abitur
1937 beginnt in Bonn eine Buchhandelslehre

1939 studiert Germanistik an der Universität Köln
1939–45 ist Soldat im Zweiten Weltkrieg
1942 heiratet Annemarie Zech
1946–49 schreibt Kurzgeschichten in Zeitschriften
1949 sein erstes Buch erscheint (*Der Zug war pünktlich*)
1949–85 schreibt viele literarische Werke
1972 bekommt den Nobelpreis für Literatur
1985 stirbt am 16. Juli in Hürtgenwald/Eifel

Most of this vocabulary you have already met elsewhere. Try to work out from the context the meaning of those words which you don't know. In order to complete Exercise 7, however, you will need to know that **heiraten** *to get married* is a regular verb whereas the following are irregular: **beginnen → begonnen, erscheinen → erschienen*, bekommen → bekommen, sterben → gestorben*.**
(The asterisk (*) means that these verbs form their past tense with **sein**.)

Beispiele Heinrich Böll ist am 21. Dezember 1917 in Köln geboren.
Von 1924 bis 1928 hat er die Volksschule in Köln-Raderthal besucht.
Von 1928 bis 1937 hat er ...

der Schriftsteller (-) *author*
der Buchhandel *book trade*
die Lehre (-n) *apprenticeship*
der Soldat (-en) *soldier*
der Weltkrieg (-e) *World War*
die Kurzgeschichte (-n) *short story*
die Zeitschrift (-en) *journal*
erscheinen* *to appear*
das Werk (-e) *work*

QUICK VOCAB

Früher und heute *Then and now*

8 LESEN UND LERNEN

Herr Huber wird 65 Jahre alt. Lesen Sie über das Leben von Herrn Huber und beantworten Sie die Fragen.

vor einem Jahr *a year ago*
vor zwei, zehn, zwanzig Jahren *two, ten, twenty years ago*
schreien *to yell, to scream*
stark rauchen *to smoke heavily*
bauen (gebaut) *to build (built)*
gesund *healthy*
Spaß am Leben *enjoyment of life*
in den Ruhestand treten *to retire (go into retirement)*
Rentner/in *male/female pensioner*
vor allem *above all*
glücklich *happy*

Vor 65 Jahren war er ein Baby und hat keine Haare gehabt. Er hat lange geschlafen, aber er hat auch oft laut geschrien.
Vor 40 Jahren hat er in München Betriebswirtschaftslehre (BWL) studiert. Damals hat er lange Haare gehabt. Er hat auch ziemlich stark geraucht und Rockmusik gehört.
Vor 30 Jahren hat er bei der Dresdner Bank gearbeitet. Zu der Zeit hat er kurze Haare gehabt. Er hat geheiratet und ein Haus gebaut. Er hat bald viel Stress gehabt und dann begonnen, zu viel zu essen und zu viel Alkohol zu trinken.
Vor 20 Jahren ist er schwer krank geworden. Er hat aufgehört zu rauchen und zu trinken. Er hat wieder Sport getrieben, ist dreimal in der Woche schwimmen gegangen und hat viel trainiert.
Vor 10 Jahren hat er graue Haare gehabt. Er war aber wieder gesund und hat viel Spaß am Leben gehabt.
Vor 5 Jahren ist er dann in den Ruhestand getreten, ist viel gereist und hat viel von der Welt gesehen. Er hat interessante Fotos gemacht und hat andere Sprachen gelernt.
Heute ist er Rentner und hat lange, weiße Haare. Er liest wieder viel, vor allem Heinrich Böll, hört manchmal Rockmusik und ist sehr glücklich.

Richtig oder falsch?

a Vor 40 Jahren hat er in Marburg Soziologie studiert.

b Damals hat er lange Haare gehabt und hat auch stark geraucht.

c Vor 30 Jahren hat er bei Siemens gearbeitet.

d Damals hat er begonnen, zu viel Alkohol zu trinken.

e Vor 10 Jahren war er sehr krank.

f Vor 10 Jahren hat er auch keinen Spaß am Leben gehabt.

g Heute arbeitet er nicht mehr und ist sehr glücklich.

SPRACHINFO: *Using* **früher**
The word **früher**, meaning *earlier*, *previously* or *in former times*, is what you use in German to say what people used to do.

> **Früher haben Klaus und Doris nur klassische Musik gehört.**
> *Klaus and Doris used to only listen to classical music.*

9 HÖREN SIE ZU! KLASSENTREFFEN

🔊 **CD 2, TR 5**

Vor 25 Jahren sind sie zusammen in die Schule gegangen und jetzt treffen sie sich und reden über die alten Zeiten.

Listen to these people comparing past times with the present, then fill in the two grids.

Was haben die Leute früher gemacht?

	Haare	Trinken	Musik	Freizeit
Bernd	_____	hat viel Cognac getrunken	_____	hat in einer Band gespielt
Dieter	hat lange Haare gehabt	_____	_____	_____

Und heute?

	Haare	Trinken	Musik	Freizeit
Bernd	_____	_____	_____	_____
Dieter	_____	_____	hört klassische Musik	_____

10 UND WAS HABEN SIE FRÜHER GEMACHT?

Now it's your turn. Write at least four sentences about what you did in the past and compare them to the present. Use the previous exercises as a guide.

_____

Grammar

PRESENT PERFECT TENSE – OVERVIEW

Remember that in German the present perfect tense is most often used when people are describing past events informally, especially when they are speaking. Here is a summary of the different forms.

Regular verbs
Regular verbs like **kaufen** and **spielen** form the present perfect tense with **haben** + past participle. These past participles normally begin with **ge-** and end in **-t** and do not change their stems:

| machen | gemacht |
| spielen | gespielt |

Irregular verbs

The past participles of verbs like **fahren, gehen, nehmen** and **schreiben** normally begin with **ge-** and end in **-en**. They often change their stems, too.

fahren	gefahren
gehen	gegangen
nehmen	genommen
schreiben	geschrieben

Some verbs take **sein**

Although most irregular verbs form the present perfect tense with **haben**, there are also some verbs which take **sein**. The most important ones are:

- ▶ *verbs indicating movement e.g. coming and going, e.g.* **fahren, fleigen, gehen, kommen**
- ▶ *verbs indicating a change of state, e.g.* **sterben** *(to die),* **wachsen** *(to grow)*
- ▶ *a few other verbs, such as* **bleiben** *(to stay)*

fahren: Daniela ist heute nach München gefahren. *Daniela went to Munich today.*

sterben: Jimmy Hendrix ist 1970 gestorben. *Jimmy Hendrix died in 1970.*

bleiben: Wir sind den ganzen Tag zu Hause geblieben. *We stayed at home all day.*

Mixed verbs

Some verbs, when forming their past participles, combine the features of both regular and irregular verbs (hence the name 'mixed verbs'). These past participles end in **-t** like weak verbs, but also change their stem like many irregular verbs.

kennen	gekannt
bringen	gebracht

Separable verbs

The past participles of separable verbs add the -ge- where the verbs separate:

aufhören	aufgehört
aufstehen	aufgestanden

Haben and sein

Haben *(to have)* and **sein** *(to be)*: these two past participles are used so frequently that they need to be listed separately:

haben	gehabt
sein	gewesen

No ge- in front

Remember that verbs beginning with **be-**, **ent-**, **emp-**, **er-**, **ver-** and **zer-** do not add ge- to their past participles:

bekommen *to get*	bekommen
entlassen *to dismiss*	entlassen
empfehlen *to recommend*	empfohlen
erhalten *to receive*	erhalten
verstehen *to understand*	verstanden
zerbrechen *to break*	zerbrochen

A list of the most common irregular verbs is given at the end of the book.

TESTING YOURSELF

1 Schreiben Sie die Sätze im Perfekt? Ergänzen Sie. *Complete the sentences with the correct past participle.*

    a *Werner Lübke ist letzten Freitag nach Zürich _____ (fliegen).*

    b *Dort hat er seine Freundin Dagmar _____ (besuchen).*

    c *Dagmar hat ihn vom Flughafen _____ (abholen).*

    d *Freitagabend sind sie ins Kino _____ (gehen).*

    e *Sie haben einen sehr guten Film _____ (sehen).*

    f *Samstag haben sie lange _____ (schlafen).*

2 *Sein* oder *haben*? **Die Geschichte geht weiter …**

    a *Erst um 10.30 Uhr ___ Werner und Dagmar aufgestanden.*

    b *Um 11 Uhr ___ sie dann gefrühstückt.*

    c *Sie ___ frische Brötchen gegessen.*

    d *Dazu ___ sie zwei Tassen Kaffee getrunken.*

    e *Und um 11.30 Uhr ___ sie dann im Stadtzentrum spazieren gegangen.*

    f *Sie ___ mehrere neue Kleidungsstücke gekauft.*

3 *Which of the past participles fits best? The first one has been done for you.*

....

empfohlen – verstanden – vergessen – ~~bezahlt~~ – erhalten – besucht

....

    a *Herr Dietrich hat mit seiner Kreditkarte bezahlt.*

    b *Entschuldigen Sie bitte, aber ich habe das nicht*

        _____ .

    c *Carola hat meinen Namen _____ .*

    d *Gestern haben wir Frau Hermann im Krankenhaus*

        _____ .

    e *Der Kellner hat uns die Gemüsesuppe _____ .*

    f *Heinrich Böll hat 1972 den Nobelpreis _____ .*

Now that you have completed Unit 14, can you   tick
1 talk about recent events?   ☐
2 say how things have changed compared with how
they used to be?   ☐
3 distinguish between regular and irregular verbs in
the present perfect tense?   ☐
4 be sure which verbs take **sein** and which take **haben**
in the present perfect tense?   ☐

15

Wohnen in Deutschland
Living in Germany

In this unit you will learn
- *how to talk about different kinds of housing*
- *how to name the various rooms in a house or flat*
- *how to make comparisons*

Language points
- *more on the dative case*
- *the comparative*
- *possessive adjectives*

Where do you live?

1 LESEN UND LERNEN

Wie heißt das? Match the German words with the pictures.

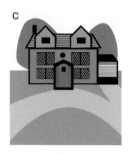

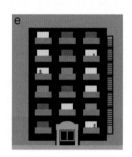

i	Hochhaus	☐
ii	Reihenhaus	☑
iii	Einfamilienhaus	☐
iv	Studentenwohnheim	☐
v	Zweifamilienhaus	☐

QUICK VOCAB

die **Wohnung (-en)** *flat*
das **Zweifamilienhaus ("er)** *semi-detached house*
das **Reihenhaus ("er)** *terraced house*
das **Einfamilienhaus ("er)** *detached house*
das **Studentenwohnheim (-e)** *student accommodation*
das **Hochhaus ("er)** *multi-storey building, tower block*
die **Altbauwohnung (-en)** *flat in an old building*
die **Wohngemeinschaft (-en)** *flat share*

2 WO WOHNEN DIE LEUTE?

◀ CD 2, TR 6

Vier Leute erzählen, wo sie wohnen. These four people are talking about where they live.

Listen to the interviews and then rearrange the items in columns 2 and 3 so that they match what is said in the text.

Wer?	Wo wohnen sie?	Wie ist es?
Person 1	in einer Wohngemeinschaft	hell und ruhig
Person 2	in einem Hochhaus	grün und ruhig
Person 3	in einem Einfamilienhaus	nicht zu teuer
Person 4	in einer Altbauwohnung	nett und interessant

Now read the texts and then answer the questions in **Übung 3**.

1 Karl Potschnik, 57, Monteur bei VW
,Ich wohne mit meiner Frau seit fünf Jahren in einem Hochhaus. Wir haben eine schöne Wohnung und einen wunderbaren Blick auf die Stadt, aber leider gibt es zu viele Graffitis. Die Miete ist nicht zu teuer, €375. Wir sind ganz zufrieden hier.'

2 Elisabeth Strutzak, 45, Angestellte bei der Post AG
,Früher haben wir im Stadt-Zentrum gewohnt, aber vor zehn Jahren haben wir das Einfamilienhaus hier gekauft. Wir haben einen großen Garten. Es ist sehr grün und ruhig hier, die Nachbarn sind nett, nur für die Kinder ist es ein bisschen weit bis zur Schule.'

3 Matthias Michaelis, 24, Jura-Student
,Ich wohne in einer Wohngemeinschaft mit drei anderen Studenten. Wir teilen die Miete und alle Nebenkosten. Manchmal gibt es natürlich Probleme, aber dann sprechen wir darüber. Ich wohne gern mit anderen Leuten zusammen. Es ist immer jemand da, mit dem man sprechen kann. Es ist nett und interessant.'

4 Jutta Heinrich, 73, Rentnerin
,Ich wohne seit fünfzig Jahren in meiner Wohnung. Die Wohnung ist sehr hell und auch ruhig. Hundert Meter von hier bin ich auch geboren. Früher habe ich mit meinem Mann und den Kindern hier gewohnt. Aber mein Mann ist vor zehn Jahren gestorben und meine Kinder sind ausgezogen, und jetzt lebe ich allein.'

hell *light, bright*
ruhig *quiet*
der Blick (-e) *view*
die Miete (-n) *rent*
zufrieden *happy, content*
der Nachbar (-n) *neighbour*
nett *nice*
teilen *to share*
die Nebenkosten (pl.) *bills*
aus|ziehen *to move out*

3 RICHTIG ODER FALSCH?

Korrigieren Sie die falschen Aussagen.

a Herr Potschnik zahlt €375 Miete und ist nicht zufrieden.

b Frau Strutzak wohnt gern in ihrem Einfamilienhaus und sagt, die Nachbarn sind sehr nett.

c Matthias findet das Leben in seiner Wohngemeinschaft interessant.

d Frau Heinrich lebt seit 73 Jahren in einer Altbauwohnung.

e Ihr Mann ist vor zehn Jahren gestorben.

SPRACHINFO: *Dative case endings*
You have already seen that some prepositions (e.g. **mit** and **zu**) are always followed by dative case endings and that others (e.g. **in** and **auf**) are followed by the dative when the focus is on position or location. In this unit you will find some more practice in using the dative case.

You know that in the dative case the endings on the definite articles change (**der** and **das** become **dem**, and **die** becomes **der**). Similar changes apply for the indefinite articles where the ending is **-em** for masculine and neuter nouns and **-er** for feminine nouns. This pattern also applies to the so-called possessive adjectives **mein, dein, sein,** etc.

masc. -(e)m	Bernd wohnt	mit ein**em** Freund	zusammen.
	Frau Krüger hat früher	mit ihr**em** Mann	hier gewohnt.
fem. -(e)r	Frau Heinrich lebt	in ein**er** Altbauwohnung.	
	Herr Thomas wohnt	mit sein**er** Freundin	zusammen.
neut. -(e)m	Jutta wohnt	in ein**em** Hochhaus.	
	Dieter Schneider lebt	mit sein**em** Kind	in Hamburg.

Note that, in the dative plural, not only the article or possessive adjective ends in **-(e)n**, but that, where possible, an **-n** is also added to the noun.

pl. -(e)n … -n	Ich wohne	mit mein**en** Freund**en**	zusammen.
	Kirsten wohnt	mit ihr**en** Kinder**n**	in Köln.
	Rainer wohnt	seit viel**en** Jahr**en**	in Spanien.

The dative can occur more than once in a sentence:

Herr Thomas wohnt mit seiner Frau und seinen zwei Kindern in einem Einfamilienhaus.

4 WIE HEISST ES RICHTIG?

Fill in the correct dative case endings.

a Frau Demitrez wohnt in ein__ Reihenhaus.
b Petra lebt seit drei Jahren in ein__ Wohngemeinschaft.
c Familie Schmidt wohnt in ein__ Hochhaus.
d Hans lebt in ein__ Studentenwohnheim.
e Lukas wohnt mit sein__ Freundin zusammen.
f Susanne lebt mit ihr__ Sohn in Berlin.
g Sie sind mit ihr__ Kinder_ in die USA gefahren.

> ## Insight: Mieten oder kaufen? *Rent or buy?*
> In Germany more people rent their homes than in most
> other European countries. Only about 45% of homes
> in the western **Länder** and about 35% in the eastern
> **Länder** are owner-occupied, although these figures are
> steadily rising. The majority of people live in apartments
> rather than individual houses, and apartments tend
> to be quite spacious, especially in older buildings, or
> **Altbauwohnungen**. Over recent decades the government
> has tried to ease the housing shortage by giving incentives
> for the provision of owner-occupied properties. Buy-to-
> rent investment schemes have also become an established
> feature of the German housing scene.

In the home

5 LESEN UND LERNEN

Look at the plan of a flat and note the words for the various
rooms.

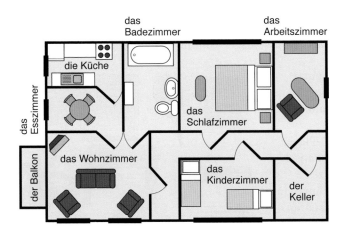

das Badezimmer

das Arbeitszimmer

die Küche

das Esszimmer

das Schlafzimmer

der Balkon

das Wohnzimmer

das Kinderzimmer

der Keller

6 WIE HEISSEN DIE ZIMMER?

a *das Schlafzimmer:* dort schläft man

b _____: ein Zimmer für Kinder

c _____: dort kocht man

d _____: dort kann man sich waschen

e _____: dort wohnt man, liest, sieht fern etc.

f _____: dort kann man im Sommer sitzen

g _____: dort kann man lernen, am Computer arbeiten

7 WOHIN KOMMEN DIE SACHEN?

Herr und Frau Wichmann are moving house. The removal men want to know where all the furniture and other items go. *Was kommt ins Wohnzimmer, ins Kinderzimmer, ins Arbeitszimmer, in die Küche, in den Keller etc.?*

Remember that **in** will need the accusative case as the focus is on movement *into* the various rooms.

Beispiele Der Computer kommt ins Arbeitszimmer.
Der Tennisschläger kommt in den Keller.

1 der Computer
2 der Tennisschläger
3 der Schrank
4 das Bett
5 der DVD-Player
6 der Küchentisch
7 die Pflanze
8 die Waschmaschine
9 der Kühlschrank
10 das Sofa
11 der Sessel
12 der Fernseher
13 das Bild
14 die Magazine
15 das Regal
16 die Bücher
17 der Topf
18 die Gummiente
19 die Teller

8 HERR UND FRAU MARTINI HABEN EINE NEUE WOHNUNG

Herr und Frau Martini haben sehr lange eine neue Wohnung
gesucht und endlich eine schöne Wohnung gefunden. Lesen Sie
ihren Brief. Beantworten Sie dann die Fragen.

Dortmund, 23. August

Liebe Imra,

danke für deinen netten Brief. Endlich, endlich haben wir eine neue Wohnung. Du weißt, wir haben fast sechs Monate gesucht. Bernd, Sven und ich sind jetzt natürlich sehr glücklich, denn endlich haben wir mehr Platz.

Es ist nämlich eine sehr große Wohnung und sie liegt relativ zentral, in der Nähe vom Stadtpark. Die Umgebung ist ruhig und sehr grün, aber leider ist es bis zum nächsten Supermarkt ein bisschen weit.

Wir haben vier Zimmer, ein Wohnzimmer, ein Schlafzimmer und ein Kinderzimmer für Sven und dann sogar ein kleines Arbeitszimmer und eine große Küche und ein Badezimmer. Die Zimmer sind groß und hell. Aber leider haben wir keinen Garten.

Die Miete ist nicht so teuer, €465, natürlich plus Nebenkosten, also plus Wasser, Strom und Gas. Das ist ziemlich günstig.

Die Verkehrsverbindungen sind sehr gut, denn bis zur U-Bahn sind es nur fünf Minuten und mit der U-Bahn brauche ich dann nur noch 10 Minuten bis zur Arbeit. Im Sommer kann ich mit dem Fahrrad zur Arbeit fahren: ein gutes Fitness-Programm.

Und wie geht es dir? Und deinem Mann und den Kindern? Hat Peter schon einen neuen Job gefunden?

Grüß alle herzlich und ich hoffe, es geht euch gut.

Deine Marlies

Beantworten Sie die folgenden Fragen:

a Wie lange haben sie gesucht?
b Wie viele Zimmer hat die Wohnung?
c Wie hoch ist die Miete?
d Wo liegt die Wohnung?
e Wie sind die Verkehrsverbindungen?

der Platz (¨e) *here: space*
die Umgebung (sing.) *surroundings (pl.)*
der Strom *electricity*
günstig *reasonable (of price), cheap*
die Verkehrsverbindungen (pl.) *transport (links)*
relativ *relatively*

9 MACHEN SIE EINE LISTE

Was für Vorteile und Nachteile hat die neue Wohnung? Make a list of five more advantages and two more disadvantages of Herr and Frau Martini's new flat.

Vorteile (+)	Nachteile (−)
Sie haben jetzt mehr Platz.	Bis zum nächsten Supermarkt ist es ein bisschen weit.
−	−
−	−
	−
	−
	−

10 WIE HEISST DAS GEGENTEIL?

~~außerhalb~~ – antik – teuer – neu – klein – laut – dunkel – interessant

a zentral – außerhalb
b groß –
c hell –
d langweilig –

e billig –
f alt –
g modern –
h ruhig –

Talking about where you live

Ich wohne / Wir wohnen …	in einem Reihenhaus, in einer Wohnung, in einem Studentenwohnheim etc.
Die Wohnung / Das Haus hat …	2/3/4 Zimmer.
Die Wohnung liegt relativ / ziemlich …	zentral, außerhalb.
Die Zimmer sind relativ / sehr …	klein, groß, laut, hell etc.
Wir haben …	viele, wenige, alte, neue, moderne, antike Möbel.
Die Umgebung ist nicht so / ziemlich …	grün, ruhig, laut.
Die Verkehrsverbindungen sind …	gut, schlecht.

11 ROLLENSPIEL: UND JETZT SIE!

◀) CD 2, TR 7

Take on the role of Marlies Martini from **Übung 8** and answer the questions below. Write down your replies first and then answer the questions on the audio. You can compare your answers with our replies on the audio.

a Wohnen Sie in einem Haus oder in einer Wohnung?
b Wie viele Zimmer hat die Wohnung?
c Wie sind die Zimmer?
d Haben Sie einen Garten?
e Ist die Miete oder die Hypothek teuer?
f Wie ist die Umgebung?
g Haben Sie gute Verkehrsverbindungen?
h Wie lange fahren Sie zur Arbeit?
i Fahren Sie mit dem Auto, mit dem Bus oder mit der U-Bahn?

Now go through the questions again, this time answer for yourself. Change **Wohnung** to **Haus** and **zur Arbeit** to **zur Universität** or in **die Stadt** as appropriate.

Town or country?

SPRACHINFO: *Making comparisons*
To make comparisons in English you simply add -er to short adjectives (e.g. *cheap*), or put **more** in front of longer ones (e.g. *interesting*):

> *This house is cheaper (than that one).*
> *This book is more interesting (than that one).*

Using adjectives in this way is called the comparative. In German normally only the -er form is used:

> *Dieses Haus ist billiger.*
> *Dieses Buch ist interessanter.*

Most adjectives of one syllable with an **a**, **o** or **u** take an umlaut:

> *Im Winter ist es hier viel kälter.*
> *Deine Wohnung ist größer.*
> *Marion ist viel jünger.*

Note that the word for *than* is **als**:

Auf dem Land ist die Luft besser als in der Stadt.

For more details see the **Grammar** section later in this unit.

12 LEBEN SIE LIEBER IN DER STADT ODER AUF DEM LAND?

Read the article below to find out what these people have to say about living in town and living in the country.

STADT ODER LAND? PRO UND CONTRA

Unsere Städte werden immer größer, lauter, hektischer. Ist es nicht besser, auf dem Land zu leben? Wir haben zwei Personen gefragt: Leben Sie lieber auf dem Land oder in der Stadt? Und warum? Was ist besser?

Manfred Teutschek, 27, Student

‚Auf dem Land wohnen? Nie wieder! Ich habe als Kind dort gelebt, es ist viel zu langweilig. Ich lebe gern in der Stadt. Das Leben ist interessanter, bunter als auf dem Land. Die Leute sind offener und man kann mehr machen. Aber manchmal ist es auch stressiger als auf dem Land, der viele Verkehr zum Beispiel und die Anonymität. Aber dann die vielen Theater, Clubs, Restaurants… Ich liebe es hier, denn es ist so kosmopolitisch.'

Esther Reimann, 45, Psychotherapeutin

‚Wir haben 15 Jahre in Berlin gelebt und sind vor einem Jahr aufs Land gezogen. Es ist viel grüner hier, die Luft ist besser, die Leute sind freundlicher. Es war die richtige Entscheidung, ich vermisse die Stadt nicht. Zum Einkaufen brauche ich jetzt länger, denn ich muss mit dem Auto fahren, aber das Leben ist so viel entspannter hier.'

auf dem Land *in the country*
bunt *colourful*
offen *here: open-minded*
kosmopolitisch *cosmopolitan*
die Luft *air*
die Entscheidung (-en) *decision*
entspannt *relaxed*

13 WAS FEHLT HIER?

Lesen Sie den Text **Stadt oder Land** noch einmal und setzen Sie die fehlenden Wörter ein.

a Herr Teutschek findet die Leute in der Stadt <u>**offener**</u> als auf dem Land.

b Das Leben in der Stadt, sagt er, ist _____ und _____ .

c Manchmal ist es aber auch _____ als auf dem Land.

d Frau Reimann sagt, auf dem Land ist die Luft _____ und die Leute sind _____ .

e Zum Einkaufen braucht sie jetzt _____ .

f Aber das Leben ist viel _____ auf dem Land.

14 SO EIN QUATSCH! WIDERSPRECHEN SIE!

Contradict these false claims.

Beispiel Birmingham ist größer als New York.
So ein Quatsch! Birmingham ist kleiner als New York.

So ein Quatsch! *What nonsense/rubbish!*

a Die Akropolis ist jünger als der Eiffelturm.

b In Deutschland ist es wärmer als in Südafrika.

c Das Essen im ‚Gourmet-Restaurant' ist schlechter als in der Mensa.

d Der Toyota Prius ist teurer als der Porsche.

e Tokio ist kleiner als Paris.

f Berlin ist langweiliger als Stuttgart.

Pronunciation

🔊 **CD 2, TR 8**

The **ch** sound in German is often difficult for English speakers who tend to close their throats and pronounce a **k**. In fact, if you keep your throat open and let the air continue to flow, you will make the right sound.

The pronunciation of **ch** depends on the kind of vowel in front of it. Listen to the recording and spot the differences.

ich	**Rechnung**	**Töchter**	**Bücher**	**Mädchen**	**Milch**
mache	**Sprache**	**einfach**	**kochen**	**Tochter**	**Buch**

When the **ch** is followed by an **s**, it is pronounced as a **k**:

Sachsen   sechs   Fuchs

How would you pronounce these words?
Nichte, Dach, Märchen, Lachs.

Grammar

1 *THE COMPARATIVE*

As you saw earlier in this unit, making comparisons in German is straightforward and is very similar to the English *cheap, cheaper* pattern:

comparative	
billig	billiger
interessant	interessanter

Most adjectives of one syllable with an **a**, **o** or **u**, like **warm** and **groß**, take an umlaut in the comparative forms:

> *Unsere alte Wohnung war groß.*
> *Unsere neue Wohnung ist größer.*

> *Hier ist es schon im April ziemlich warm.*
> *Im Mai ist es wärmer.*

A few adjectives, like **gut** and **hoch**, are irregular:

> *Ich finde, dieses Auto ist gut.*
> *Aber dieses Auto ist noch besser.*

> *Das Matterhorn ist hoch.*
> *Der Mount Everest ist aber noch höher.*

The word **noch** (*even*) is often used with the comparative to provide emphasis, as in the last two examples.

Another common word with irregular forms is **gern**:

Ich spiele gern Fußball.
I like playing football.

Aber ich spiele lieber Tennis.
But I prefer playing tennis.

Some words, like **teuer** and **dunkel** (*dark*), often lose one **e** in the comparative form:

> *In Frankfurt sind Wohnungen ziemlich teuer. In München sind sie aber teurer.*

> *Im Herbst ist es morgens dunkel. Im Winter ist es aber dunkler.*

As you saw earlier in this unit, the equivalent of the English *than* in comparisons is **als**:

> *Die Wohnungen in München sind teurer als die in Frankfurt.*

2 POSSESSIVE ADJECTIVES

Words that indicate possession or who something belongs to are called possessive adjectives. Here is an overview of the *possessive adjectives* in German:

mein *my*	mein Freund, meine Mutter	unser *our*	unser Haus, unsere Wohnung
dein *your*	dein Auto, deine Schule	euer *your*	euer Vater, eure Mutter
Ihr *your*	Ihr Buch, Ihre Frau	Ihr *your*	Ihr Hotel, Ihre Wohnung
sein *his* ihr *her* sein *its*	sein Sohn, seine Tochter ihr Vater, ihre Mutter sein Essen, seine Milch	ihr *their*	ihr Sohn, ihre Tochter

Don't forget that possessive adjectives need various endings when used in structures with the accusative or dative case. (See also next section.)

3 *THE DATIVE CASE*

Here is a summary of the uses of the dative case that you have met so far:

a after **an, auf, in** when the focus is on position or location.

> *Wir haben auf dem Markt ein interessantes Buch gekauft.*

In the next unit you will learn more prepositions of this kind.

b always after **aus, bei, mit, nach, seit, von, zu.**

> *Ich fahre immer mit dem Fahrrad zur Schule.*

Remember, the dative endings are -(e)m for masculine and neuter nouns, -(e)r for feminine and -(e)n for plural nouns (all genders). This applies to the definite article (**der**), the indefinite article (**ein**) and the possessive adjectives (**mein, dein,** etc.).

TESTING YOURSELF

1 Wie heißt der Komparativ?

   a klein – kleiner   **e** teuer – ___

   b groß – ___   **f** hoch – ___

   c alt – ___   **g** billig – ___

   d gut – ___   **h** interessant – ___

2 Wohnungstausch *Flat swap*: Eine deutsche Familie aus Hamburg möchte im Sommer einen Wohnungstausch machen. Schreiben Sie einen Brief an Frau Löschmann und beschreiben Sie Ihre Wohnung.

Frau Löschmanns Fragen:

   a *Wo liegt Ihre Wohnung? Zentral? Außerhalb?*

   b *Liegt sie ruhig oder nicht so ruhig?*

   c *Wie weit ist es bis zum Supermarkt?*

   d *Wie sind die Verkehrsverbindungen?*

   e *Wie viele Schlafzimmer hat die Wohnung?*

   f *Und wie viele Badezimmer?*

   g *Ist die Küche groß oder ziemlich klein?*

   h *Haben Sie einen Fernseher? Wenn ja, kann man auch deutsche Programme bekommen?*

   i *Haben Sie einen Garten oder einen Balkon?*

   j *Gibt es in der Nähe einen Park? Schreiben Sie mehr, wenn Sie wollen!*

Liebe Frau Löschmann,

ich danke Ihnen für Ihren Brief. Ich bin gerne bereit, Ihre Fragen zu beantworten.

Meine Wohnung liegt _____ , usw.

Mit freundlichen Grüßen

Ihr/Ihre _____

der Austausch *swap, exchange*
bereit *ready, prepared*

Now that you have completed Unit 15, can you: tick
1 talk about different types of housing and locations? ☐
2 describe your home? ☐
3 make comparisons? ☐
4 use the correct endings for the dative case? ☐

16

Welches Hotel nehmen wir?
Which hotel shall we take?

In this unit you will learn
- **how to book a hotel room**
- **how to compare different hotels**
- **how to describe the location of buildings**

Language points
- **the superlative**
- **more prepositions (+ acc./dat.)**

Booking a hotel room

1 IM HOTEL

Make yourself familiar with the German words for single room, double room, bath, shower and key.

Einzelzimmer   *Doppelzimmer*   *Bad*   *Dusche*   *Schlüssel*

Hören Sie jetzt den Dialog und beantworten Sie dann die Fragen in **Übung 2.**

Herr Oetken	Guten Tag. Haben Sie ein Zimmer frei?
Empfangsdame	Ja, ein Einzelzimmer oder ein Doppelzimmer?
Herr Oetken	Ich möchte ein Doppelzimmer für zwei Personen, bitte.
Empfangsdame	Und für wie lange?
Herr Oetken	Für zwei Nächte.
Empfangsdame	Für zwei Nächte. Von heute, Montag bis Mittwoch?
Herr Oetken	Ja. Von Montag bis Mittwoch. Meine Frau und ich möchten nämlich auf die Antiquitätenmesse gehen.
Empfangsdame	Das ist bestimmt interessant. Möchten Sie ein Zimmer mit Bad oder mit Dusche?
Herr Oetken	Mit Bad, bitte.
Empfangsdame	Da habe ich Zimmer Nr. 14 zu €77,50.
Herr Oetken	Ist das Zimmer ruhig?
Empfangsdame	Ja, das Zimmer liegt zum Park. Es ist sehr ruhig.
Herr Oetken	Gut. Dann nehme ich das Zimmer.
Empfangsdame	So. Hier ist der Schlüssel. Bitte tragen Sie sich ein.
Herr Oetken	Um wie viel Uhr gibt es Frühstück?
Empfangsdame	Zwischen sieben und zehn Uhr.
Herr Oetken	Vielen Dank.
Empfangsdame	Ich wünsche Ihnen einen angenehmen Aufenthalt.

QUICK VOCAB

die Antiquitätenmesse (-n) *antiques fair*
Das Zimmer liegt zum Park. *The room faces / looks out onto the park.*
Bitte tragen Sie sich ein. *Please fill in your details.*
zwischen *between*
Ich wünsche Ihnen einen angenehmen Aufenthalt. *I wish you a pleasant stay.*

2 RICHTIG ODER FALSCH?

Korrigieren Sie die falschen Aussagen.

a Herr Oetken nimmt ein Einzelzimmer.

b Er bleibt zwei Nächte.

c Er möchte mit seiner Sekretärin auf eine Antiquitätenmesse gehen.

d Herr Oetken nimmt ein Zimmer mit Dusche.

e Das Zimmer kostet €67,50.

f Frühstück gibt es bis 10 Uhr.

Haben Sie ein Zimmer frei? *Have you got a room?*	**UE**
Ist das Zimmer ruhig? *Is the room quiet?*	
Um wie viel Uhr gibt es Frühstück? *What time is breakfast?*	

3 WELCHE ANTWORT PASST ZU WELCHER FRAGE?

a *Haben Sie ein Zimmer frei?*

b *Haben Sie ein Doppelzimmer frei?*

c *Ein Zimmer mit Bad oder Dusche?*

d *Was kostet das Zimmer?*

e *Ist das Zimmer ruhig?*

f *Von heute bis Freitag?*

g *Wann gibt es Frühstück?*

i *Zwischen halb sieben und neun.*

ii *Ja, genau. Bis Freitag.*

iii *Ja, für wie viele Tage?*

iv *Tut mir leid, wir haben nur noch Einzelzimmer.*

v *Ein Zimmer mit Dusche.*

vi *€80, inklusive Frühstück.*

vii *Nein, leider nicht. Es liegt zur Straße.*

4 ROLLENSPIEL: UND JETZT SIE! WAS SAGT DER GAST?

Book a hotel room using the prompts in the picture. Check your answers on the recording.

3 Nächte

  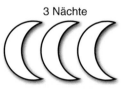

Gast	Guten Tag. Haben Sie ein **a** _____?
Empfangsdame	Ein Einzelzimmer oder ein Doppelzimmer?
Gast	**b** _____
Empfangsdame	Und für wie viele Nächte?
Gast	**c** _____
Empfangsdame	Möchten Sie ein Zimmer mit Bad oder Dusche?
Gast	**d** _____
Empfangsdame	Gut. Zimmer 14. Bitte tragen Sie sich hier ein.
Gast	**e** _____
Empfangsdame	Zwischen halb sieben und halb neun. Ich wünsche Ihnen einen angenehmen Aufenthalt.

5 IN DER TOURISTENINFORMATION

◀》 **CD 2, TR 11**

Frau Johannsen sucht ein Zimmer. Hören Sie bitte zu und beantworten Sie die Fragen.

Richtig oder falsch?

a Frau Johannsen sucht ein Zimmer für drei Tage.
b Das Hotel Offenbach liegt im Zentrum.

c Das Hotel Atlanta liegt 30 Minuten vom Zentrum entfernt.
d Die Pension Schneider kostet €57,50 pro Nacht.
e Das Hotel Atlanta ist billiger als das Hotel Offenbach.
f Sie nimmt das Zimmer im Hotel Offenbach.

6 HATTEN SIE RECHT?

Lesen Sie jetzt bitte den Dialog und überprüfen Sie Ihre Antworten.
Now check your answers by reading the dialogue.

Frau Johannsen	Guten Tag, ich suche ein Hotelzimmer für zwei Tage. Haben Sie etwas frei?
Frau Izmir	Im Moment ist es ein bisschen schwierig, einen Augenblick – ja, ich habe hier drei Hotels gefunden: das Hotel Offenbach, das Hotel Atlanta und die Pension Schneider.
Frau Johannsen	Welches Hotel liegt denn am zentralsten?
Frau Izmir	Am zentralsten liegt das Hotel Offenbach, nur fünf Minuten vom Zentrum.
Frau Johannsen	Und am weitesten?
Frau Izmir	Am weitesten entfernt ist das Hotel Atlanta, etwa eine halbe Stunde.
Frau Johannsen	Und preislich, welches Hotel ist am billigsten?
Frau Izmir	Am billigsten ist die Pension Schneider, das Einzelzimmer für €67,50. Ein Einzelzimmer im Hotel Offenbach kostet €90 und im Hotel Atlanta ist es am teuersten: €130.
Frau Johannsen	Und welches ist am komfortabelsten?
Frau Izmir	Am komfortabelsten ist das Hotel Atlanta, mit Swimming-Pool und Park. Das ist sehr schön.
Frau Johannsen	Ich glaube, ich nehme das Hotel Offenbach. Kann ich gleich bei Ihnen buchen?
Frau Izmir	Ja, kein Problem.

SPRACHINFO: *The superlative*

In English when you want to single out one item from among a group as being the cheapest or most interesting of all, you add -(e)st to a short adjective or put **most** in front of a longer one:

> *This house is the cheapest.*
> *This book is the most interesting.*

This form is called the *superlative*. In German it goes as follows:

> *Dieses Haus ist am billigsten.*
> *Dieses Buch ist am interessantesten.*

As you can see, the word **am** is added and the ending is -(e)sten. For more information on the superlative see the **Grammar** section later in this unit.

7 WELCHE INFORMATIONEN FEHLEN HIER?

Lesen Sie den Dialog in **Übung 6** noch einmal und finden Sie die fehlenden Informationen. *Read the dialogue again and fill in the missing information.*

Hotels/Pension	Zimmer	Preis für Einzelzimmer	Entfernung	Pluspunkte
Offenbach	80	_____	_____	sehr zentral, gute Bar
Atlanta	120	€ 130	_____	_____
Schneider	28	_____	20 Minuten vom Zentrum	familiäre Atmosphäre, ruhig

8 ERGÄNZEN SIE DEN SUPERLATIV

a Das Hotel Offenbach ist größer als die Pension Schneider, aber das Atlanta-Hotel ist _____ _____ .

b Das Hotel Offenbach ist billiger als das Hotel Atlanta, aber die Pension Schneider ist _____ _____ .

c Die Pension Schneider liegt zentraler als das Hotel Atlanta, aber das Hotel Offenbach liegt _____ _____ .

d Die Pension Schneider ist ruhiger als die Pension Schneider, aber das Atlanta-Hotel ist _____ _____ .

Giving directions

SPRACHINFO: *Prepositions and location*
The following prepositions can help you to express where something is situated:

in	*in (to)*	**über**	*over*
an	*at*	**unter**	*under*
auf	*on (to)*	**vor**	*in front of*
hinter	*behind*	**zwischen**	*between*
neben	*next to*		

When position or location is indicated all of the prepositions above require the dative case. They answer the question **wo?** (*where, in what location*). For more information, see **Grammar section 2** later in this unit.

QUICK VOCAB

die Bibliothek (-en) *library*
der Brunnen (-) *well, fountain*
der Parkplatz (¨ e) *parking lot*
der Imbiss (-e) *hot-dog stall, snack bar*
gegenüber *opposite (to)*

9 WO IST WAS?

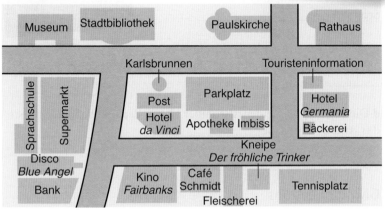

Look at the map of Greifshagen and choose the appropriate prepositions from the box to complete the following sentences.

....

~~gegenüber~~ neben gegenüber zwischen hinter neben

....

Beispiel Das Kino ist gegenüber dem Hotel da Vinci.

a Die Paulskirche ist rechts _____ der Stadtbibliothek.

b Das Museum liegt _____ der Sprachschule.

c Das Hotel Germania liegt _____ der Touristeninformation und der Bäckerei.

d Der Parkplatz liegt _____ der Apotheke.

e Das Café Schmidt ist _____ der Fleischerei.

10 WAS ANTWORTET HERR PRINZMANN?

🔊 **CD 2, TR 12**

Herr Prinzmann arbeitet in der Touristeninformation in Greifshagen. Was antwortet er auf die Fragen? Benutzen Sie den Stadtplan von **Übung 9** und finden Sie die richtige Antwort zu jeder Frage. Überprüfen Sie dann Ihre Antworten auf der Audioaufnahme.

Touristen fragen

a Wo ist denn hier das Stadtmuseum?

b Kann man hier italienisch essen?

c Gibt es in der Nähe eine öffentliche Telefonzelle?

d Wo ist denn das Rathaus?

e Wo ist denn hier ein Parkplatz?

f Gibt es hier in der Nähe ein Café?

g Ich habe gehört, es gibt hier eine tolle Disco.

Herr Prinzmann antwortet

i Direkt hier gegenüber.

ii Ja, fahren Sie geradeaus, dann die erste links, gegenüber dem 'da Vinci'.

iii Fahren Sie geradeaus, dann links und immer geradeaus. Auf der linken Seite ist die Pizzeria Mario.

iv Gehen sie links, nehmen Sie die erste Straße rechts. Es liegt zwischen der Fleischerei und dem Kino.

v Direkt hier gegenüber.

vi Ja, natürlich. Hier gegenüber, auf dem Parkplatz.

vii Gehen Sie immer geradeaus. Es ist auf der rechten Seite neben der Bibliothek.

geradeaus *straight on*
gehen Sie links/rechts *go to the left/right*
wieder links/rechts *(turn) left/right again*
auf der linken Seite *on the left-hand side*
auf der rechten Seite *on the right-hand side*
Da finden Sie … *There you'll find …*

Insight: Touristeninformation

Tourism in German-speaking countries is highly organised. Almost each town has its own **Touristeninformation** or **Fremdenverkehrsamt** and many of their services are now available online.

When using the web, type in the name of a town plus **.de** for **Deutschland**, **.at** for **Austria** or **.ch** for **Switzerland** and you will usually get straight to the town's homepage where you can find information about attractions, events and accommodation. Much of the information is also available in English.

Useful weblinks are:
http://www.germany-tourism.de/
http://www.austria.info/uk
http://www.tourismus-schweiz.ch/

Kurz nah weg
Urlaub in Deutschland

11 ROLLENSPIEL: UND JETZT SIE!

Übernehmen Sie die Rolle von Herrn Prinzmann. Schreiben Sie zuerst Ihre Antworten. Beantworten Sie dann die Fragen auf der Audioaufnahme.

Touristin	Guten Tag. Wo ist denn hier die Bibliothek?
Sie	*Go straight ahead. The library is on the right-hand side, next to the museum.*
Touristin	Und gibt es hier auch eine Post?
Sie	*Yes, of course. Go straight on and take the first street to your left. The post office is behind the fountain.*
Touristin	Gibt es hier in der Altstadt eine Apotheke?
Sie	*Yes, of course. Go to the left, then turn right. The pharmacy is between the hot-dog stall and the hotel 'da Vinci'.*
Touristin	Und haben Sie hier auch einen Supermarkt?
Sie	*Go straight on. The supermarket is opposite the museum.*
Touristin	Vielen Dank. Kann man denn hier abends auch irgendwo ein gutes Bier trinken?
Sie	*Of course. Go to the left, then left again. There you'll find a pub on the left-hand side, next to the bakery. The pub is very good.*

Grammar

1 THE SUPERLATIVE

As you already saw in Unit 15 and also in this unit, making comparisons in German and using the superlative is very similar to the English cheap, cheaper, cheapest pattern:

	Comparative	**Superlative**
billig	billig**er**	**am** billig**sten**
interessant	interessant**er**	**am** interessant**esten**

In the superlative the word **am** is added and the ending is -(e)sten.

Adjectives with an **a**, **o** or **u** which take an umlaut in the comparative form also need one in the superlative:

groß	größer	am größten
alt	älter	am ältesten
jung	jünger	am jüngsten

Here are some of the most important irregular forms:

hoch	höher	am höchsten
gut	besser	am besten
gern	lieber	am liebsten
viel	mehr	am meisten

Adjectives which lose an **e** in the comparative form, like **teuer** and **dunkel**, usually take one in the superlative:

| teuer | teurer | am **teuersten** |
| dunkel | dunkler | am **dunkelsten** |

2 PREPOSITIONS WITH THE ACCUSATIVE OR DATIVE

These prepositions, which were listed under SPRACHINFO: *Prepositions and location* earlier in the unit, need either the accusative or the dative case, depending on whether the focus is on movement or on location:

an, auf, hinter, in, neben, über, unter, vor, zwischen

Here are a few examples:

Accusative: **Wohin?** *Where to?*
Wir gehen …   an den Tisch.
auf den Marktplatz.
vor die Tür.
ins Kino.
hinter das Hotel.

Dative: **Wo?** *Where?*

Wir sitzen … am Tisch.
auf dem Marktplatz.
vor der Tür.
im Kino.
hinter dem Hotel.

Note that there are several pairs of verbs that are used to indicate movement on the one hand and location on the other. The main verbs of this kind are:

legen	*to lay, to place (in a lying position)*
liegen	*to lie, to be*
stellen	*to put, to place (in a standing position)*
stehen	*to stand, to be*
hängen	*to hang, to place (in a hanging position)*
hängen	*to hang, to be*

In English the verbs **to put** and **to be** are frequently used to cover these functions, but German generally prefers to be more precise.

Er legt das Video ins Regal. *He's putting the video onto the shelf.*

Das Video liegt im Regal. *The video is on the shelf.*

Wir stellen das Buch auf den Tisch. *We're putting the book onto the table.*

Das Buch steht auf dem Tisch. *The book is on the table.*

Susanne hängt das Picasso-Poster an die Wand. *Susanne is hanging/putting the Picasso poster onto the wall.*

Das Picasso-Poster hängt an der Wand. *The Picasso poster is (hanging) on the wall.*

TESTING YOURSELF

1 **Wo sind die Möbel jetzt?** *Do you remember Mr and Mrs Wichmann (from Unit 15) moving house? Their furniture is now where the removal men put it. Write down where the items are, following the examples:*

Das Regal haben sie neben den Fernseher gestellt. →
Das Regal steht jetzt neben dem Fernseher.

Das Picasso-Poster haben sie über das Sofa gehängt. →
Das Picasso-Poster hängt jetzt über dem Sofa.

   a *Die Waschmaschine haben sie in den Keller gestellt.*
   b *Das Foto von Oma Lisbeth haben sie ins Esszimmer gehängt.*
   c *Die CDs haben sie ins Regal gestellt.*
   d *Die Pflanze haben sie auf den Balkon gestellt.*
   e *Das Poster von Lionel Messi haben sie ins Kinderzimmer gehängt.*
   f *Das Sofa haben sie zwischen das Regal und den Tisch gestellt.*

2 **Ergänzen Sie die Komparativformen und Superlativformen.**

		Komparativ	Superlativ
a	_____	wärmer	_____
b	kalt	_____	am kältesten
c	interessant	_____	_____
d	billig	_____	_____
e	hoch	_____	_____
f	teuer	_____	_____
g	_____	lieber	_____
h	gut	_____	_____

3 Bilden Sie den Komparativ und Superlativ.

Beispiel *hoch:* *das Matterhorn, der Kilimandscharo, der Mount Everest*

Der Kilimandscharo ist höher als das Matterhorn, aber der Mount Everest ist am höchsten.

a *lang: der Rhein, der Nil, der Amazonas*
b *groß: Deutschland, Kanada, Russland*
c *alt: das Empire State Building, der Tower of London, das Colosseum*
d *hart: Silber, Gold, Granit*
e *teuer: der BMW M6, der Ferrari F430, der Maserati GranSport*

Now that you have completed Unit 16, can you: tick
1 book a hotel room?   ☐
2 compare and contrast the price and location of various hotels?   ☐
3 describe where something is located?   ☐
4 name some prepositions which need either the accusative or the dative case?   ☐

17

....

Ist Mode wichtig?
Is fashion important?

In this unit you will learn
- *how to describe items of personal appearance*
- *how to say what clothes you like wearing*

Language points
- *adjectival endings (2)*
- etwas *+ adjective*

___

Fashion

1 IST MODE WICHTIG FÜR SIE?

🔊 **CD 2, TR 14**

Listen to what these four people have to say about their attitude to fashion and decide who it is important to and who not.

a Bettina Haferkamp, 52, Lehrerin
‚Jedes Jahr gibt es etwas Neues. Dieses Jahr kurze Röcke, nächstes Jahr lange Röcke. Die Leute sollen immer etwas Neues kaufen. Ich ziehe nur an, was ich mag. Am liebsten trage ich bequeme Sachen.‘

b Johann Kurz, 38, Journalist
‚Ich finde, Mode ist ein wichtiger Ausdruck unserer Zeit. Sie zeigt, was Leute denken und fühlen. Zum Beispiel die Mode in den Fünfzigerjahren oder die Punk-Mode. Heute kann man doch anziehen, was man möchte. Das finde ich gut.'

c Boris Brecht, 28, arbeitslos, Rock-Musiker
‚Ich bin ein individueller Mensch. Schwarze Sachen finde ich am besten. Ich kaufe viel auf dem Flohmarkt oder in Secondhandshops ein. Modetrends finde ich langweilig.'

d Ulrike Maziere, 20, Kosmetikerin
‚Mode bedeutet viel für mich. Ich bin ein sportlicher Typ und trage gern schöne Sachen. Ich möchte gut aussehen. Eine modische Frisur, ein modernes Outfit – das ist sehr wichtig für mich.'

QUICK VOCAB

die Mode (-n) *fashion*
sollen *(here) are supposed to*
der Ausdruck ("e) *expression*
die Fünfzigerjahre (pl.) *the Fifties*
an|ziehen *to put on*
bedeuten *to mean*
tragen *to wear*
bequem *comfortable*
aus|sehen *to look, appear*
die Sachen *things*
die Frisur (-en) *hairstyle*

Für welche Person ist Mode wichtig (✔) und für wen ist sie unwichtig (✗)?

	✔	✗
Bettina Haferkamp	☐	☐
Johann Kurz	☐	☐
Boris Brecht	☐	☐
Ulrike Maziere	☐	☐

2 WER SAGT DAS?

Wie steht das im Text? Look at the statements in **Übung 1** again and find the expressions which convey a similar meaning.

Beispiel Ich bin sportlich. → Ich bin ein sportlicher Typ.

a Mode zeigt, was Leute denken.
b Die Leute sollen mehr Geld ausgeben.
c Schwarz finde ich am besten.
d Ich trage nur, was ich mag.
e Mode ist sehr wichtig.

SPRACHINFO: *Using* **etwas** *+ adjective*
If you want to say *something new, something cheap*, etc., you use **etwas** + adjective + **-es**:

> *etwas Neues, etwas Billiges*

Note that you need a capital letter for the word after **etwas**. The same pattern applies to **nichts** *nothing/anything*, e.g. **nichts Neues**.

3 WAS SAGEN DIE LEUTE PRO MODE UND CONTRA MODE?

List three more pros and one more con of fashion according to the four people in **Übung 1**.

Pro (+)	Contra (-)
Mode ist ein Ausdruck unserer Zeit	Die Leute sollen immer etwas Neues kaufen
–	–
–	
–	

SPRACHINFO: *Adjective endings*

So far we have dealt with the endings in the accusative after **ein, kein, dein,** etc.:

masc.	**-en**	Werner hat einen mechanisch**en** Wecker gekauft.
fem.	**-e**	Renate hat eine alt**e** Platte gekauft.
neut.	**-es**	Annett hat ein neu**es** Hemd gekauft.

This is what happens to the endings in the nominative case:

masc.	**-er**	Das ist ein billig**er** Rock.
fem.	**-e**	Das ist eine modisch**e** Frisur.
neut.	**-es**	Das ist ein modern**es** Outfit.

Remember that the nominative case is used to refer to the subject of the sentence and it is also used after the verb **sein** (*to be*). As you can see, these endings are the same as for the accusative, except for the masculine nouns.

In the plural, when there is no article, the ending on the adjective is the same for both the nominative and the accusative:

nom.	**-e**	Das sind toll**e** Sachen!
acc.	**-e**	Ihr habt toll**e** Sachen auf dem Flohmarkt gekauft.

Reminder: Endings are only required when the adjective is placed in front of a noun.

4 WIE HEISST ES RICHTIG?

Üben Sie Adjektivendungen im Nominativ.

Beispiel Die Idee ist gut. → Das ist ein**e** gut**e** Idee.

a Der Film war langweilig.
b Der Kaffee ist stark.
c Das Buch ist interessant.
d Das Problem ist schwierig.
e Der Computer ist neu.
f Die Leute sind unfreundlich.
g Das Hotel ist billig.
h Die Frage ist kompliziert.

5 FRAU MARTENS IST VERKÄUFERIN IN EINEM KAUFHAUS

◀) **CD 2, TR 15**

Was denkt sie über Mode? Hören Sie, was sie sagt. Was stimmt? *Frau Martens works in a department store. Underline what she says.*

a Sie sagt, Verkäuferin ist ein interessanter / anstrengender Beruf.

b Die Arbeit im Haushalt ist langweilig / anstrengend.

c Ihr Sohn findet Computerspiele interessant / langweilig.

d Sie findet, sie ist ein modischer / kein modischer Typ.

e Die Töchter von Frau Martens finden die Mode wichtig / unwichtig.

f Kunden sind immer freundlich / manchmal unfreundlich / oft unfreundlich.

Clothes

6 WER TRÄGT WAS?

die Farben *colours*
blau *blue*
braun *brown*
grau *grey*
grün *green*
rot *red*
schwarz *black*
weiß *white*
gelb *yellow*
dunkel *dark*
hell *light*

Make yourself familiar with the German names for clothes and colours and answer the questions below.

Richtig oder falsch? Korrigieren Sie die falschen Sätze.

a Der Mann trägt einen dunkelbraunen Anzug und eine gelbe Krawatte.

b Außerdem trägt er ein weißes Hemd, einen grauen Mantel und schwarze Schuhe.

c Die Frau trägt eine gelbe Bluse und eine dunkelbraune Jacke.

d Außerdem trägt sie einen dunkelblauen Rock, weiße Strümpfe und weiße Schuhe.

e Das Mädchen trägt eine blaue Jeans, ein weißes T-Shirt, eine rote Baseball-Mütze und weiße Turnschuhe.

f Der Junge trägt eine blaue Jeans, ein gelbes T-Shirt, eine grüne Baseball-Mütze und grüne Turnschuhe.

die Bluse (gelb)
die Jacke (braun)
der Gürtel
der Rock (braun)

das Hemd
die Krawatte (rot)
der Anzug (blau)
der Mantel (grau)
die Hose
(rot) (braun)

die Strümpfe (gelb)
die Mütze (gelb)

die Schuhe (schwarz)
(blau)
die Turnschuhe (weiß)

das T-Shirt (weiß)
(grün)
die Jeans (schwarz)
(gelb)

Hose, Jeans: Note that in English both *trousers* and *jeans* are plural, but in German **Hose** and **Jeans** are singular:

> *Ich habe heute eine neue Hose gekauft.*
> *Wo ist meine alte Jeans?*

7 LESEN UND LERNEN

Sagen Sie es eleganter! Instead of using **und** to list two items of clothing, there is a more elegant way in German to say what people are wearing, using **mit** (*with*). See in the following example how this works and how it affects the adjective:

Er trägt einen dunkelblauen Anzug mit	einem	grau**en** Mantel.
	einer	rot**en** Krawatte.
	einem	weiß**en** Hemd.
	–	schwarz**en** Schuhen.

SPRACHINFO: *Adjective endings after* **mit**

As you know, certain prepositions, like **mit** and **von**, are followed by the dative case. Here are the adjective endings you need for the dative case, after the indefinite articles.

masc.	**-en**	Werner trägt ein weißes Hemd mit einem schwarz**en** Anzug.
fem.	**-en**	Anna trägt einen braunen Rock mit einer gelb**en** Bluse.
neut.	**-en**	Florian trägt eine rote Jacke mit einem blau**en** Hemd.

In the dative plural you add -(e)n not just to the adjective, but also to the noun, if possible.

pl.	**-en**	Er trägt einen schwarzen Anzug mit schwarz**en** Schuh**en**.

If you are listing a number of items, then the preposition determines the case not only of the first item but also of the following items as well:

> *Martin trägt ein blaues Hemd mit einer dunkelblauen Hose, einem schwarzen Mantel und schwarzen Schuhen.*

As you can see, in this example all three items listed after **mit** require dative case endings.

8 WIE HEISSEN DIE ENDUNGEN?

Ergänzen Sie.

a Die Frau trägt eine gelbe Bluse mit einer dunkelbraun__ Jacke und ein__ braun__ Rock.

b Außerdem trägt sie braune Strümpfe mit braun__ Schuh__ .

c Das Mädchen trägt eine blaue Jeans mit ein__ weiß__ T-Shirt, ein__ rot__ Baseball-Mütze und weiß__ Turnschuh__ .

d Der Junge trägt eine schwarze Jeans mit ein__ grün__ T-Shirt, ein__ gelb__ Baseball-Mütze und gelb__ Turnschuh__ .

e Der Mann trägt einen dunkelblauen Anzug mit ein__ rot__ Krawatte.

f Außerdem trägt er ein weißes Hemd mit ein__ grau__ Mantel und schwarz__ Schuh__ .

9 EINLADUNG ZU EINER PARTY

Lesen Sie den Text und beantworten Sie die Fragen in **Übung 10**.

Einladung zur Bad-Taste-Party

Liebe Freunde,

wie jedes Jahr feiern wir diesen Juni wieder unsere Geburtstage mit einer großen Party. Und wie jedes Jahr haben wir auch ein besonderes Motto! Nein, dieses Mal ist es nicht Dracula (war das letztes Jahr nicht fantastisch? All der Tomaten-Ketchup und der viele Knoblauch?).

Das Motto für dieses Jahr heißt: Bad-Taste. Wer kein Englisch kann: das bedeutet ‚schlechter Geschmack'.

Also: holt die alten Hemden, Blusen, Röcke, Sonnenbrillen aus dem Schrank. Je hässlicher, schrecklicher, älter – desto besser.

Und wir haben auch einen tollen Preis für die Person, die am schlechtesten, am hässlichsten aussieht.

Also – seid kreativ!

Und natürlich gibt es wie immer auch tolle Musik zum Tanzen.

Also, bis zum 24.

Jutta und Christian

PS: Bringt etwas zum Trinken mit! Dosen-Bier von Aldi, Lambrusco, Liebfraumilch?

Einladung (-en) *invitation*
der Knoblauch *garlic*
feiern *to celebrate*
hässlich *ugly*
je ... desto *the more ... the more*

10 RICHTIG ODER FALSCH?

Wie heißen die richtigen Antworten?

a Jutta und Christian machen jeden Monat eine Party.
b Das Motto für die letzte Party war Dracula.
c ‚Bad taste' heißt auf Deutsch ‚schlechter Geschmack'.
d Die Person, die am schönsten aussieht, bekommt einen Preis.
e Die Gäste bringen etwas zum Essen mit.

11 WAS PASST AM BESTEN? ERGÄNZEN SIE.

....

Röcke   Mantel   Sachen   Anzug   Hemd

....

a Im Büro tragen viele Männer einen _____.
b Wenn es kalt ist, trägt man meistens einen _____ .
c Eine Frau trägt eine Bluse, ein Mann trägt ein _____.
d Zu Hause trägt man oft bequeme _____.
e Viele Frauen tragen jetzt lieber Hosen als _____.

12 WAS FÜR KLEIDUNG TRAGEN DIE LEUTE?

◀) CD 2, TR 16

Richard Naumann stellt die Fragen. Hören Sie zu und ergänzen Sie die Tabelle.

	bei der Arbeit	zu Hause	was sie gern tragen	was sie nicht gern tragen
Mareike Brauer				
Günther Scholz				

What I wear when

Bei der Arbeit …	trage ich meistens einen Rock mit einer Bluse, einen Anzug, ein weißes Hemd etc.
Bei der Arbeit muss ich …	eine grüne / blaue Uniform tragen.
An der Universität …	trage ich gern eine Jeans mit einem weißen Hemd / einem dunklen Pullover.
Zu Hause …	trage ich am liebsten bequeme Kleidung.
Ich mag …	helle, dunkle Farben, bequeme Kleidung.
Ich trage nicht gern …	Jeans, Röcke, Blusen, Krawatten etc.

13 ROLLENSPIEL: UND JETZT SIE! IM KAUFHAUS

You are in a department store and are looking for a jacket. A salesman helps you. Prepare your responses, using the English prompts to guide you. Then, using the recording, play your role in German.

CD 2, TR 17

Verkäufer	Guten Tag. Wie kann ich Ihnen helfen?
Sie	*Return his greeting and say that you are looking for a new jacket.*
Verkäufer	So, eine neue Jacke suchen Sie? Und welche Farbe? Schwarz? Grau?
Sie	*Say you'd like a grey jacket – for a party.*
Verkäufer	So, bitte schön. Hier haben wir graue Jacken.
Sie	*Say you're looking for something fashionable.*
Verkäufer	Tja, wenn es um Mode geht – dann haben wir hier Jacken von Armani und Versace.
Sie	*Say fine, but Italian jackets are very expensive.*
Verkäufer	Ja, das stimmt. Aber die Qualität ist auch sehr gut.
Sie	*Agree with him and say that it is also a very fashionable party in New York.*
Verkäufer	Dann nehmen Sie doch am besten eine Jacke von Armani.

Pronunciation

🔊 **CD 2, TR 18**

At the end of a word the letter **g** in German is pronounced more like an English *k*:

Tag   Ausflug   Anzug   mag

At the end of a word **ig** is pronounced like **ich**:

billig   ruhig   zwanzig   langweilig   Honig

As soon as the **g** is no longer at the end of the word or syllable it is pronounced as a **g**:

Tage   Ausflüge   Anzüge   mögen

How would you pronounce these words?
sag, sagen, fünfzig, ledig.

Grammar

1 ETWAS, WAS / ALLES, WAS

The equivalents to *something that* and *everything that* in German are **etwas, was** and **alles, was:**

Gibt es etwas, was Sie nicht gerne anziehen?	*Is there something that you don't like wearing?*
Ich trage alles, was bequem ist.	*I wear everything that is comfortable.*

Sometimes you can leave out the word *that* in English – *Is there something you don't like wearing?* In German you always have to keep the word **was**.

Note that there is a comma before the word **was**.

2 ADJECTIVE ENDINGS AFTER THE INDEFINITE ARTICLE

Here is a summary of the adjective endings that you have met in recent units.

	Nominative	Accusative	Dative
masc.	Das ist ein teuer**er** Mantel.	Er hat einen teur**en** Mantel.	... mit einem teur**en** Mantel.
fem.	Das ist eine gut**e** Idee.	Ich habe eine gut**e** Idee.	... mit einer gut**en** Idee.
neut.	Ist das ein neu**es** Hemd?	Hast du ein neu**es** Hemd?	... mit einem neu**en** Hemd.
pl.	Das sind toll**e** Sachen.	Ihr habt toll**e** Sachen.	... mit toll**en** Sachen.

Note that all these endings apply when the adjective follows the indefinite article (**ein, eine,** etc.), **kein** or the possessive adjectives (**mein, dein, Ihr,** etc.).

In the nominative and accusative plural the endings are **-en** if a possessive adjective (**mein, dein** etc.) or the negative **kein** precedes the adjective:

Das sind meine neuen CDs.
Habt ihr keine neuen CDs gekauft?

More on the endings if the adjectives follow the definite articles (**der, die, das,** etc.) in the next unit.

TESTING YOURSELF

1 Endungen. Ergänzen Sie, bitte.

a **Verkäuferin** *Ich arbeite in ein__ groß__ Kaufhaus in München. Bei d__ Arbeit trage ich ein__ schwarz__ Rock und ein__ weiß__ Bluse. I__ Winter trage ich zu mein__ schwarz__ Rock auch ein__ schwarz__ Jacke.*

b **Student** *Im Moment arbeite ich bei Burger King und muss ein__ hässlich__ Uniform tragen. An d__ Uni trage ich aber immer ein__ blau__ Levi-Jeans mit ein__ modisch__ T-Shirt. Mir gefallen am besten amerikanisch__ oder britisch__ T-Shirts. Alt__ Sachen vo__ Flohmarkt gefallen mir manchmal auch.*

2 Beantworten Sie die Fragen. *Write out your answers to these questions.*

a *Was tragen Sie normalerweise bei der Arbeit / an der Universität?*

Beispiel a *Bei der Arbeit trage ich normalerweise eine Jeans und ein weißes Hemd.*

b *Was tragen Sie am liebsten zu Hause?*
c *Was tragen Sie gern, was tragen Sie nicht gern?*
d *Haben Sie eine Lieblingsfarbe?*
e *Ist Mode wichtig für Sie?*
f *Sie gehen zu einer Bad-Taste-Party. Was ziehen Sie an?*

Now that you have completed Unit 17, can you:	tick
1 talk about clothing and give your opinion on fashion?	☐
2 say what clothes you wear for work and for relaxing ?	☐
3 use the correct endings for adjectives after the indefinite articles?	☐

18

Und was kann man ihnen schenken?

And what can we give them?

In this unit you will learn
- *how to read invitations to various events*
- *how to say what is given to whom*
- *how to ask for help and advice*

Language points
- *indirect objects*
- *various uses of the dative case*
- *adjectival endings (3)*

Invitations and presents

1 EINLADUNGEN *INVITATIONS*

Lesen Sie die Einladungen auf der nächsten Seite und finden Sie die deutschen Wörter für *birthday party*, *wedding*, *barbecue*, *house-warming party*.

Susanne Fröhlich *Michael Hartmann*

Wir heiraten am Samstag, dem 8. Mai, um 14.30 Uhr in
der Elisabethkirche, Marburg.

Zu unserer Hochzeit laden wir Sie herzlichst ein.

Ahornweg 31
35043 Marburg

Hauptstraße 48
35683 Dillenburg

 **Peter wird nächsten Samstag**

8

Jahre alt.

**Das möchten wir natürlich feiern – mit
einer ganz tollen Geburtstagsparty,
mit Kuchen und vielen Spielen.**

Wir fangen um 15.00 Uhr an. Bringt auch eure Eltern mit.

Die Adresse: Familie Schäfer, Am Bergkampe 4

Lange haben wir gesucht und endlich unser ‚Schloss' gefunden.
Darum möchten wir euch, liebe Bärbel, lieber Georg, zu unserer

HAUSEINWEIHUNGSFEIER
am 30. November, um 20.00 Uhr einladen.

Unsere neue Adresse: 90482 Nürnberg,
Waldstraße 25.
Unsere neue Telefonnummer: 378459

Viele Grüße
Uschi und Matthias
Hasenberg

Mareike und Jörg Schwichter
Krummer Weg 12
24939 Flensburg
Tel. 55 32 17

Liebe Susanne, lieber Gerd,

bevor der Winter kommt, möchten wir noch einmal eine Grill-Party in unserem Garten machen.

Der Termin: der letzte Samstag im Monat, der 27. September, ab 19.00 Uhr.

Könnt ihr kommen?

Natürlich gibt es nicht nur Fleisch, sondern wir haben auch Essen für Vegetarier.

Bringt doch bitte einen Salat mit. Alles andere haben wir.

Alles Gute

eure Schwichters

P.S. Wie war es denn in Spanien? Habt ihr viel Spaß gehabt?

QUICK VOCAB

heiraten *to marry*
ein|laden *to invite*
feiern *to celebrate*
das Schloss (¨er) *castle*
die Feier (-n) *celebration*
der Vegetarier (-)/-in (-innen) *vegetarian*

2 RICHTIG ODER FALSCH?

Korrigieren Sie die falschen Aussagen.

a Susanne und Michael heiraten am 28. Mai in Marbach.

b Familie Schäfer feiert nächsten Samstag Peters achten Geburtstag.

c Uschi und Matthias haben ihren idealen Garten gefunden.

d Susanne und Gerd wollen in ihrem Haus eine Bad-Taste-Party machen.

e Vegetarier müssen ihr Essen mitbringen.

Insight: Feiern *Celebrating*

Special occasions are generally celebrated with enthusiasm in Germany. Families make great efforts to get together for birthdays; some people travel long distances to be present.

Weihnachten, *Christmas,* is celebrated in the traditional way. Presents are usually exchanged on Christmas Eve. Christmas markets throughout Germany provide seasonal decorations, food and drink. The **Christkindlmarkt** in Nuremberg is perhaps the most famous of these markets.

Silvester, *New Year's Eve,* is celebrated with fireworks and **Sekt** (a champagne-like fizzy wine). New Year's Day is a public holiday in Germany – some people need this in order to get over their **Kater** (*hangover*).

The period before Lent is celebrated in Germany – especially in the Catholic areas – as **Karneval** (in the **Rheinland**), **Fastnacht** (around **Mainz**) and **Fasching** (in Bavaria). People disguise themselves in fancy-dress costumes. The world-famous carnival procession in Cologne is well worth seeing.

---

3 UND WAS KANN MAN SCHENKEN?

Read how giving something to someone is expressed in German. Can you find out what case is needed and what the equivalents of **ihr, ihm** and **ihnen** are in English?

Er schenkt eine Flasche Kognak. Er schenkt *dem* Mann eine Flasche Kognak. Er schenkt *ihm* eine Flasche Kognak.

Sie bringt Blumen mit. Sie bringt *der* Frau Blumen mit. Sie bringt *ihr* Blumen mit.

Sie schenken einen Luftballon. Sie schenken *dem* Kind einen Luftballon. Sie schenken *ihm* einen Luftballon.

Sie haben ein Poster mitgebracht. Sie haben *den* Leuten ein Poster mitgebracht. Sie schenken *ihnen* ein Poster.

Did you figure out the answers? **ihm** means *(to) him, it*; **ihr** means *(to) her* and **ihnen** here is equivalent to the English *(to) them*. The case needed is the dative. You can find out more about these structures in the **SPRACHINFO** below.

SPRACHINFO
DIRECT AND INDIRECT OBJECTS
You already know that the dative case is used after certain prepositions. It is also used to indicate *to whom* something is being given or done. This part of the sentence is often referred to as the *indirect object*.

We now need to distinguish between *direct* and *indirect* objects. In the sentence:

Frau Semmelbein schenkt ihrem Sohn einen Hund.

einen Hund is said to be the *direct object* of the verb **schenken** because it is directly associated with the act of giving, and **ihrem Sohn** is said to be the *indirect object* because it indicates *to whom* the object was given.

The direct object or the indirect object can also come in first place:

Einen Hund schenkt Frau Semmelbein ihrem Sohn.
Ihrem Sohn schenkt Frau Semmelbein einen Hund.

The basic meaning of these sentences remains the same; there is merely a change of emphasis. Note that in these examples the verb stays in the same place: as second element in the sentence.

INDIRECT OBJECT PRONOUNS
Words like **ihm** *(to) him* and **ihr** *(to) her* are called *indirect object pronouns*.

*Wir schenken **ihm** eine CD.*   We're giving **him** a CD.
*Wir schenken **ihr** ein Buch.*   We're giving **her** a book.

You have actually met some of these pronouns before in expressions such as

*Wie geht es **Ihnen**?*   Lit. How is it going **to you**?
*Danke, **mir** geht's gut.*   Lit. **To me** it goes well.

For a full list of these pronouns, see the **Grammar** section.

4 IHR, IHM ODER IHNEN?

Setzen Sie die fehlenden Wörter ein.

a Lena hat Geburtstag. Marcus schenkt ___ eine CD.

b Frank macht eine Party. Susi bringt ___ eine Flasche Sekt mit.

c Steffi und Caroline haben Hunger. Ihre Mutter kauft ___ Pommes frites.

d Svenja fährt nach Österreich. Ihr Bruder gibt ___ einen guten Reiseführer.

e Christina und Robert heiraten. Herr Standke schenkt ___ ein schönes Bild.

f Herr Fabian wird 65. Seine Kollegen haben ___ eine Geburtagskarte geschrieben.

5 WAS BRINGEN WIR DER FAMILIE MIT?

◄) **CD 2, TR 19**

Saskia und ihre Schwester Sys waren für drei Wochen in New York. Morgen fahren sie nach Deutschland zurück. Große Panik: sie müssen noch Geschenke für ihre Familie kaufen!

Hören Sie zu: Was schenken sie ihrer Mutter, ihrem Vater, der Großmutter, Tante Heide und Onkel Georg? Warum?

Die Geschenke: eine Schallplatte von Frank Sinatra, ein U-Bahn-Plan, ein Bademantel, Turnschuhe, eine Baseball-Mütze.

Wem?	Was bringen sie mit?	Warum?
Mutter	Sie bringen ihr eine Platte von Frank Sinatra mit.	Sie ist ein großer Fan von Sinatra.
Vater	Sie bringen ihm …	_____ ?
Oma	_____ ?	_____ ?
Tante Heidi	_____ ?	_____ ?
Onkel Georg	_____ ?	_____ ?

aufregend *exciting*
sammeln *to collect*
der Bademantel (¨) *bathrobe*

Shopping for gifts

Note these useful expressions with the dative

Können Sie mir helfen?	*Can you help me?*
Könnten Sie mir etwas empfehlen?	*Could you recommend me something?*
Gefällt Ihnen / dir das T-Shirt?	*Do you like the T-shirt?*
Gefallen Ihnen / dir die Hemden?	*Do you like the shirts?*
Können Sie mir sagen, wie spät es ist?	*Can you tell me what the time is?*
Wie geht es Ihnen / dir?	*How are you?*

USEFUL PHRASES WITH THE DATIVE

The dative case is also used after certain verbs (like **helfen**, **gefallen**):

Sie hilft **der Frau.** → Sie hilft **ihr.**
Das Auto gefällt **dem Mann.** → Das Auto gefällt **ihm.**

Furthermore, it occurs in some expressions, where often the meaning of *to* is expressed:

Können Sie mir sagen, wie spät es ist?	*Can you say to me (i.e. tell me) …?*
Können Sie mir etwas empfehlen?	*Can you recommend something to me?*

6 WAS PASST ZUSAMMEN?

Welche Antwort passt zu welcher Frage?

a	Können Sie mir helfen?	**1**	Es gefällt mir nicht. Es ist zu teuer.
b	Gefällt Ihnen das Hotel?	**2**	Ihm geht es nicht so gut.
c	Können Sie mir ein Buch für meine Tochter empfehlen?	**3**	Sie gefallen mir nicht. Sie sind schrecklich.
d	Gefällt dir Berlin?	**4**	Natürlich helfe ich Ihnen.
e	Wie geht es Frau Hansen?	**5**	Das kann ich Ihnen sagen, fünf nach vier.
f	Können Sie mir sagen, wie spät es ist?	**6**	Ja, es ist eine tolle Stadt.
g	Wie geht es Sven?	**7**	Ihr geht es wieder besser.
h	Gefallen dir die Bilder?	**8**	Ich empfehle Ihnen ‚Winnie Puuh'.

7 IM GESCHÄFT ‚ALLES FÜR DIE FRAU'

Hören Sie sich den Dialog an und beantworten Sie die Fragen.

a Wem möchte Herr Kern etwas schenken?
b Wie teuer sind die Parfüms?
c Warum nimmt er keine Tasche?
d Gefällt ihm der weiße Schal *(scarf)*?
e Welchen Schal nimmt er?

CD 2, TR 20

Herr Kern	Guten Tag. Können Sie mir helfen?
Verkäuferin	Ja, natürlich.
Herr Kern	Ich suche ein Geschenk für meine Frau. Können Sie mir etwas empfehlen?
Verkäuferin	Hier haben wir zum Beispiel das neue Parfüm von L'Oreal ‚Ägyptischer Mond' oder das bezaubernde ‚Ninette'. Beide kosten nur €49,99.
Herr Kern	Mmh, Parfüm … das ist immer schwierig. Was gibt es denn sonst noch?
Verkäuferin	Nun, wir haben hier zum Beispiel diese wunderbaren Damen-Taschen im Angebot.
Herr Kern	Sie meinen die braunen Taschen hier?
Verkäuferin	Gefallen sie Ihnen?
Herr Kern	Nun ja, die kleine Tasche hier ist schön, aber meine Frau hat schon eine.
Verkäuferin	Wie ist es denn mit einem Schal? Diese hier sind alle aus echter Seide. Beste Qualität.
Herr Kern	Der weiße Schal gefällt mir nicht. Der sieht ein bisschen zu altmodisch aus. Aber der rote hier gefällt mir. Und der blaue ist auch sehr schön.
Verkäuferin	Nun, welche Haarfarbe hat denn Ihre Frau?
Herr Kern	Blond.
Verkäuferin	Dann nehmen Sie lieber den blauen Schal. Das sieht besser aus.
Herr Kern	Wenn Sie meinen. Vielen Dank für Ihre Hilfe.
Verkäuferin	Gern geschehen. Bitte zahlen Sie da drüben an der Kasse.

wem *(to) whom*
der Schal (-s) *scarf*
bezaubernd *enchanting*
die Tasche (-n) *bag*
die Seide (no pl.) *silk*
die Kasse (-n) *cash desk*

SPRACHINFO

ADJECTIVE ENDINGS AFTER THE DEFINITE ARTICLE

You might have realized that in this dialogue there are a number of adjective endings after definite articles (**der, die, das**) and that these are different from the pattern you met in the previous unit. Once you have mastered the endings after **ein** and **kein**, these new endings will perhaps seem less challenging.

In the nominative singular all adjectives take an -e, regardless of their gender:

> *Der rote Schal ist schön. (masc.)*
> *Die kleine Tasche gefällt mir. (fem.)*
> *Das neue Buch ist fantastisch. (neut.)*

In the accusative singular all feminine and neuter forms take an -e, and the masculine -en:

> *Ich kaufe den roten Schal. (masc.)*
> *Ich möchte die braune Tasche. (fem.)*
> *Ich lese das neue Buch von Follett. (neut.)*

All forms in the dative take -en, as do all plural forms. For more examples see the **Grammar** section later in this unit.

8 ADJEKTIVENDUNGEN

Find the correct endings for the following adjectives. All the sentences use the definite article and are in the nominative case.

a Die grün__ Jacke ist toll.

b Der rot __Schal sieht sehr gut aus.
c Der neu__ Film mit George Clooney ist ein bisschen langweilig.
d Das schwarz__ Hemd sieht sehr trendy aus.
e Das kalt__ Bier hat gut geschmeckt.
f Die neu__ Songs von Moby sind fantastisch.

9 ORDNEN SIE BITTE ZU

◀) **CD 2, TR 21**

Here is a conversation between a salesperson and a customer.
Match the customer's sentences 1–8 to those of the salesperson
(a–h). Be careful – sentences a–h are in the correct order, but
the customer's sentences need re-arranging. You can check your
answers on the recording or in the key.

	Verkäufer		Kunde
a	Kann ich Ihnen helfen?	**1**	Ja, das gelbe gefällt mir. Das ist besser.
b	Ja, wie alt ist er denn?	**2**	Auf Wiedersehen.
c	Gefällt Ihnen das blaue T- Shirt?	**3**	Und was kostet es?
d	Gefällt Ihnen das gelbe hier besser?	**4**	Ja, gerne. Ich suche ein T- Shirt für meinen Enkelsohn.
e	Na, das ist schön.	**5**	Gut, das nehme ich dann.
f	€12,50.	**6**	Vorne links. Vielen Dank.
g	Ja, bitte zahlen Sie an der Kasse. Da vorne links.	**7**	Mmh, das ist ein bisschen langweilig. Haben Sie nicht etwas Modernes?
h	Auf Wiedersehen.	**8**	Acht Jahre. Können Sie mir etwas empfehlen?

10 ROLLENSPIEL: UND JETZT SIE! IN DER BUCHHANDLUNG

Sie suchen ein Buch über New York. Ein Verkäufer hilft Ihnen.
Bereiten Sie Ihre Antworten vor und spielen Sie dann die Rolle auf
der Audioaufnahme.

Verkäufer	Guten Tag.
Sie	*Return his greetings and ask if he can help you.*
Verkäufer	Ja, natürlich. Was kann ich denn für Sie tun?
Sie	*Say you are looking for a book about New York. Could he recommend something?*
Verkäufer	Ja, hier haben wir zum Beispiel den neuen Reiseführer von Merian. Sehen Sie einmal. Gefällt er Ihnen?
Sie	*Say no. You don't like it.*
Verkäufer	Hier ist das neue New York Buch von Hans Fischer.
Sie	*Say you like that one. Ask how much it costs.*
Verkäufer	€12,40.
Sie	*Say you'll take that book. Ask if they've got the new book by Dan Brown.*
Verkäufer	Ja, natürlich. Ich hole es Ihnen.
Sie	*Say thank you and ask where the cash desk is.*
Verkäufer	Gern geschehen. Die ist gleich hier vorne. Auf Wiedersehen.

Grammar

1 *THE DATIVE CASE*

Here is a summary of the three main uses of the dative case:

▶ *After certain prepositions*
   a *after an, auf, hinter, in, neben, über, unter, vor, zwischen when the focus is on position or location.*

   Wir haben auf dem Markt ein interessantes Buch gekauft.

b *always after **aus, bei, mit, nach, seit, von, zu.***

*Ich fahre immer mit **dem** Fahrrad **zur** Schule.*

▶ *To indicate to whom something is being given, done, etc. In other words to indicate the indirect object.*

*Ich schenke **meinem** Freund einen neuen CD-Spieler zum Geburtstag.*

▶ *Verbs such as **helfen, empfehlen** and **gefallen** are used with the dative.*

*Kann ich **Ihnen** helfen? Können Sie **mir** etwas empfehlen? Hat es **dir** gefallen?*

2 ADJECTIVE ENDINGS AFTER THE DEFINITE ARTICLE

Here is a summary of the adjective endings after the definite article:

Nominative	
masc.	Der neu**e** Film mit de Niro ist sehr gut.
fem.	Die neu**e** CD von Jennifer Lopez ist fantastisch.
neut.	Ist das neu**e** Buch von Dan Brown wirklich gut?
pl.	Die neu**en** Modelle von BMW sind sehr modern.
Accusative	
masc.	Hast du den neu**en** Film mit de Niro gesehen?
fem.	Hast du schon die neu**e** CD von Jennifer Lopez gehört?
neut.	Hast du das neu**e** Buch von Dan Brown gelesen?
pl.	Hast du schon die neu**en** Modelle von BMW gesehen?

Dative

masc.	In dem neu**en** Film spielt auch Kate Winslet.
fem.	Er hat mit der alt**en** Band von Herbie Hancock gespielt.
neut.	In dem neu**en** Buch gibt es ein Happy-End.
pl.	Er ist mit den neu**en** Modellen von BMW gefahren.

3 PERSONAL PRONOUNS IN THE DATIVE

Here is an overview of the personal pronouns in the dative case:

Singular

ich →	mir	**Mir** geht's gut.
du →	dir	Wie geht's **dir**?
Sie →	Ihnen	Hoffentlich geht's **Ihnen** morgen besser.
er (masc.) →	ihm	**Ihm** geht's heute nicht so gut.
sie (fem.) →	ihr	**Ihr** geht's jetzt viel besser.
es (neut.) →	ihm	**Ihm** (dem Kind) geht's leider nicht so gut.

Plural

wir →	uns	**Uns** geht's sehr gut.
ihr →	euch	Wie geht's **euch**?
Sie →	Ihnen	Wir wünschen **Ihnen** allen eine gute Reise.
sie →	ihnen	**Ihnen** geht's wirklich sehr gut.

TESTING YOURSELF

1 **Was kann man den Personen schenken?** *Write down what one could give these people as a present. Choose an appropriate gift from the list or find one yourself.*

- *eine Flasche Wein*
- *ein Computerspiel*
- *ein Buch über Indien*
- *eine CD von Maria Callas*
- *Turnschuhe*
- *ein Buch über Blumen und Pflanzen*

   a *Herr Koch, 65, liebt klassische Musik.*
   b *Gisela Anders, 25, geht gern ins Kino, findet Indien toll.*
   c *Gerd Schmücke, 40, ist ein großer Fußballfan, joggt viel.*
   d *Heinz und Martha Schmidt, 53 und 50, essen und trinken gern.*
   e *Heide, 12, liest gern, mag die Natur.*
   f *Peter, 12, arbeitet viel am Computer.*

Beispiele
   a *Man kann ihm eine CD von Maria Callas schenken.*
   b *Man kann ihr _____ .*

2 **Wer bekommt was?** *Markus is giving up his student flat to study in the US and has decided to give some of his things to friends or relatives. Fill in the missing adjective endings.*

   a *Den teur__ CD-Spieler schenkt er seinem Freund Tim.*
   b *Er gibt die schwarz__ Katze seiner Oma.*
   c *Das interessant__ Buch über Afrika schenkt er seinem Onkel.*
   d *Seiner Freundin Susi gibt er den neu__ Computer.*

e *Das alt__ Handy gibt er seiner Schwester.*
f *Die toll__ Fußballbilder schenkt er seinem Freund Lukas.*
g *Die alt__ CDs verkauft er auf dem Flohmarkt.*

Now that you have completed Unit 18, can you: tick
1 say what to give people and why? ☐
2 ask for help and recommendations? ☐
3 name three ways in which the dative case is used? ☐
4 use the correct adjective endings with the definite
article? ☐

19

Gesundheit
Health

In this unit you will learn
- *how to discuss health*
- *how to name parts of the body*
- *how to report on aches and pains*

Language points
- *modal verbs*
- wenn *+ verb at end of clause*

Healthy living

1 WAS IST GESUND? WAS IST UNGESUND?

Ordnen Sie zu. *Decide what you consider to be healthy and unhealthy.*

viele Hamburger essen • regelmäßig joggen • Salat essen • fernsehen und Kartoffelchips essen • zweimal in der Woche schwimmen gehen • ein Glas Rotwein pro Tag trinken • Fahrrad fahren • jeden Tag vier Flaschen Bier trinken • fünf Stunden ohne Pause vor dem Computer sitzen • lange spazieren gehen

gesund	ungesund
• regelmäßig joggen	• viele Hamburger essen
• _____	• _____
• _____	• _____
• _____	• _____
• _____	
• _____	

SPRACHINFO

USING WENN (*WHEN/IF*)

If you now wanted to say that you think it is healthy if one
runs regularly or you think it is unhealthy if one eats too many
hamburgers, you would form sentences with **wenn** in German:

> *Ich denke, es ist gesund, wenn man regelmäßig joggt.*
> *Ich finde, es ist ungesund, wenn man viele Hamburger isst.*

Note that the verb is in the last position in clauses starting with
wenn.

> *Ich denke, es ist gesund, <u>wenn</u> man lange spazieren <u>geht</u>.*

A comma is usually needed in order to separate the **wenn** clause
from the rest of the sentence.

2 ÜBEN SIE

Using the same pattern as the examples in the SPRACHINFO,
write down six more sentences saying what you think is healthy or
unhealthy. Use the ideas from **Übung 1**.

Beispiel *Ich finde, es ist gesund, wenn man Salate isst.*

3 IST ES GUT, WENN MAN SCHNAPS TRINKT?

Schreiben Sie Ihre Meinung. *Answer the questions and write down what you personally think. Of course, opinions may differ on the answers!*

Beispiel Ist es gesund, wenn man 12 Stunden pro Tag vor dem Computer sitzt? Nein, es ist nicht gesund, wenn man 12 Stunden pro Tag vor dem Computer sitzt.

a Ist es gut, wenn man manchmal einen Schnaps trinkt?

b Ist es schlecht, wenn man zu viel Fernsehen sieht?

c Ist man altmodisch, wenn man keine Jeans trägt?

d Ist es ungesund, wenn man jeden Tag fünf Tassen Kaffee trinkt?

e Ist es gesund, wenn man viermal pro Woche ins Fitnesscenter geht?

4 TUN SIE GENUG FÜR IHRE GESUNDHEIT?

◀) **CD 2, TR 23**

Vier Leute erzählen, ob sie genug für Ihre Gesundheit tun. Lesen Sie die folgenden Texte und beantworten Sie dann die Fragen.

Gabriela Tomascek, 21, Designerin
‚Ich treibe viel Sport, spiele Fußball, Handball, ein bisschen Tennis. Ich rauche nicht, trinke sehr wenig Alkohol. Außerdem esse ich gesund, viel Salat und Obst. Ja, ich denke ich tue genug. Ich fühle mich sehr fit und bin nur selten krank. Nächstes Jahr will ich vielleicht einen Fitnessurlaub machen.'

Michael Warnke, 45, Computer-Programmierer
‚Ich habe Probleme mit dem Herz und meinem Gewicht. Der Arzt sagt, ich darf nicht mehr rauchen und soll auch weniger Fett essen.

Außerdem soll ich auch mehr Sport treiben, denn ich sitze den ganzen Tag am Computer. Im Moment jogge ich abends, aber am Wochenende will ich auch mehr mit dem Rad fahren.'

Marianne Feuermann, 49, Bankkauffrau
,Ich habe im Moment Rückenprobleme und soll viel schwimmen gehen. Meistens schwimme ich vier- bis fünfmal pro Woche. Früher habe ich oft Volleyball gespielt. Meine Ärztin hat mir gesagt, ich darf nicht mehr Volleyball spielen. Ich darf leider auch nicht mehr Ski fahren. Ich hoffe, es geht mir bald wieder besser, denn ich treibe sehr gern Sport und will wieder aktiver leben.'

Egbert Schmidt-Tizian, 53, Verkäufer
,Meine Frau ist eine Sport-Fanatikerin. Im Sommer Windsurfen und Tauchen im Roten Meer, im Winter Ski fahren in den Alpen und ich muss immer mit. Mein Arzt hat schon gesagt, ich soll nicht mehr so viel Sport machen, denn das ist nicht gut für mich. Ich glaube, ich tue zu viel im Moment. Ich will mehr relaxen. Ich brauche mehr Freizeit.'

Sport treiben *to do sports*
krank *ill, sick*
das Gewicht (-e) *weight*
das Fett *fat*
der Rücken (-) *back*
das Tauchen *diving*

a Wer joggt abends?
b Wer möchte mehr relaxen?
c Wer hat früher Volleyball gespielt?
d Wer lebt sehr gesund?
e Wer treibt viel Sport?
f Wer darf nicht mehr Ski fahren?

Note that you can also listen to the interviews and check the pronunciation.

SPRACHINFO
MODAL VERBS

In Unit 11 you met the modal verbs **können** and **müssen**. Here are some more verbs of this kind:

wollen (*to want to, to plan to*)

> **Ich will nächstes Jahr in die Schweiz fahren.**
> *I want to go to Switzerland next year.*

dürfen (*may/to be allowed to*)

> **Darf ich noch Volleyball spielen?**
> *Am I still allowed to play volleyball?*

> **Ich darf nicht mehr rauchen.**
> *I'm not allowed to smoke any more.*

sollen (*should/ought to*)

> **Mein Arzt sagt, ich soll weniger Fett essen.**
> *My doctor says I should eat less fat.*

Like **können** and **müssen**, these other modal verbs are quite irregular. To check the right forms, look at the **Grammar** section later in this unit, where you can also revise **können** and **müssen**.

5 WIE GEHT ES DEN PERSONEN?

Lesen Sie die Texte noch einmal und finden Sie die fehlenden Informationen.

	Was tun sie im Moment?	Was dürfen sie nicht tun?	Was sollen sie tun?	Was wollen sie tun?
Gabriela	_____	X	X	will vielleicht einen Fitnessurlaub machen
Michael	_____	darf nicht mehr rauchen	_____	_____
Marianne	geht vier- bis fünfmal in der Woche schwimmen	_____	_____	_____
Egbert	_____	X	soll nicht mehr so viel Sport machen	_____

6 WAS GEHÖRT ZUSAMMEN?

Verbinden Sie die Satzteile.

darf nicht mehr Ski fahren.

Gabriela Tomascek   will mehr Freizeit haben.
Michael Warnke   fühlt sich sehr fit.
Marianne Feuermann → soll mehr Sport treiben.
Egbert Schmidt-Tizian   darf nicht mehr rauchen.

soll weniger Sport treiben.

7 SOLLEN, WOLLEN, DÜRFEN

Was passt am besten? Complete the sentences with the most suitable modal verb.

a Herr Kaspar ist zu dick. Die Ärztin sagt, er ___ weniger essen.

b Frau Meier liebt Italien. Sie ___ nächstes Jahr nach Neapel fahren.

c Peter ist morgens immer müde. Seine Mutter sagt, er ___ früher ins Bett gehen.

d Beate Sabowski hat Herzprobleme. Der Arzt sagt, sie ___ nicht mehr rauchen.

e Kinder unter 16 Jahren ___ den Film nicht sehen.

f Man ___ nicht zu viel Kaffee trinken.

g Im Sommer fahre ich nach Argentinien. Vorher ___ ich ein wenig Spanisch lernen.

Aches and pains

8 KÖRPERTEILE

Note the German words for various parts of the body.

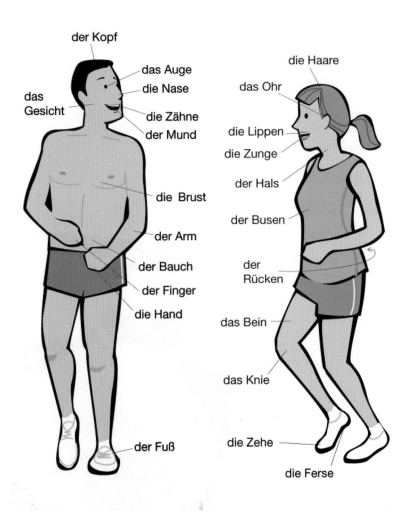

der Kopf

das Auge

die Nase

das Gesicht

die Zähne

der Mund

die Haare

das Ohr

die Lippen

die Zunge

der Hals

die Brust

der Arm

der Busen

der Bauch

der Finger

die Hand

der Rücken

das Bein

das Knie

der Fuß

die Zehe

die Ferse

9 WAS TUT HIER WEH?

Welche Sätze passen zu welchem Bild? Ordnen Sie bitte zu. *Match the sentences 1–8 with the pictures a–h.*

a
b
c
d
e
f
g
h

1 Die Augen tun weh. Sie hat 10 Stunden am Computer gearbeitet.
2 Sein Rücken tut weh. Er hat im Garten gearbeitet.
3 Der Hals tut weh. Er ist dick.
4 Sie hat eine Grippe: Kopfschmerzen und Fieber.

5 Der Zahn tut weh. Er muss zum Zahnarzt.
6 Er ist topfit. Er hat keine Schmerzen.
7 Ihr Arm tut weh. Sie hat zu viel Tennis gespielt.
8 Ihr Kopf tut weh. Sie hat zu viel Wein getrunken. Sie hat einen Kater.

wehltun *to hurt, ache*
Mein Kopf tut weh. *My head hurts / aches.*
Meine Augen tun weh. *My eyes are aching / hurt.*
die Grippe *flu*
der Schmerz (-en) *pain*
Kopfschmerzen *headache*
der Kater (-) *hangover*

Wie kann man es anders sagen?
Note the two ways you can talk about aches and pains in German:

Mein Zahn tut weh.	→	*Ich habe Zahnschmerzen.*
Sein Rücken tut weh.	→	*Er hat Rückenschmerzen.*
Ihr Hals tut weh.	→	*Sie hat Halsschmerzen.*
Meine Ohren tun weh.	→	*Ich habe Ohrenschmerzen.*

10 BEIM ARZT

Frau Philipp ist bei ihrer Ärztin. Hören Sie zu and beantworten Sie die Fragen.

Dr. Scior	Guten Tag, Frau Philipp, was kann ich für Sie tun? Was fehlt Ihnen?
Frau Philipp	Frau Scior, ich habe ziemlich starke Rückenschmerzen.
Dr. Scior	Oh, das tut mir leid. Wie lange haben Sie die Schmerzen denn schon?
Frau Philipp	Fast vier Wochen, aber es wird immer schlimmer.
Dr. Scior	Arbeiten Sie denn viel am Schreibtisch?
Frau Philipp	Ja, wir haben ein neues Computersystem, und jetzt arbeite ich fast die ganze Zeit am Computer.

Dr. Scior	Kann ich bitte einmal sehen ... Also, der Rücken ist sehr verspannt. Treiben Sie denn Sport?
Frau Philipp	Nicht sehr viel. Im Moment spiele ich nur ein bisschen Volleyball.
Dr. Scior	Also Frau Philipp, ich glaube, es ist nichts Schlimmes. Ich verschreibe Ihnen 10 Massagen und auch etwas gegen die Schmerzen. Und Sie dürfen in den nächsten Wochen nicht Volleyball spielen, gehen Sie lieber zum Schwimmen.
Frau Philipp	Kann ich denn sonst noch etwas tun?
Dr. Scior	Ja, Sie müssen bei der Arbeit bequem sitzen und der Schreibtisch muss die richtige Höhe haben. Das ist sehr wichtig.
Frau Philipp	Gut, vielen Dank.
Dr. Scior	Gern geschehen. Und gute Besserung, Frau Philipp.

Was fehlt Ihnen? *What's the matter with you?*
verspannt *seized up, in spasm*
nichts Schlimmes *here: nothing serious*
verschreiben *to prescribe*
Gern geschehen. *You're welcome.*
Gute Besserung! *Get well (soon)!*

Richtig oder falsch? Was ist richtig?

a Frau Philipp hat Rückenschmerzen.
b Die Schmerzen hat sie schon seit sechs Wochen.
c Sie arbeitet viel am Computer.
d Die Ärztin verschreibt ihr 10 Massagen.
e Frau Philipp darf nicht mehr schwimmen.
f Die Ärztin sagt, es ist sehr gefährlich.

Here are a few useful expressions for talking about what kind of pains you have and how long you have had them; also for asking what you have to do and what you can and can't do.

Ich habe ...	Magenschmerzen, Kopfschmerzen etc.
Ich habe die Schmerzen ...	seit zwei Tagen, seit einer Woche, seit einem Monat etc.
Kann ich / Darf ich ...	zur Arbeit gehen, aus dem Haus gehen ... etc.?
Muss ich ...	im Bett bleiben, ins Krankenhaus ... etc.?
Wie oft muss ich ...	die Tabletten / die Tropfen nehmen ... etc.?
Was kann ich / darf ich / darf ich nicht /soll ich ...	essen, trinken, machen ... etc.?

Insight: German health care

In Britain you go to a GP first for almost any complaint and then get referred on to a specialist if necessary. In Germany you tend to choose a doctor appropriate for a given condition. You simply take along a **Krankenversichertenkarte** (*health insurance card*) and get the doctor to sign a form. You also pay a small fee every three months. Your **Krankenkasse** (*health insurance fund*) then makes a payment on your behalf.

The **Allgemeine Ortskrankenkassen** (AOK) provide statutory health care for large numbers of people who are not insured privately or with their firm's insurance scheme.

As a UK resident travelling to German-speaking countries you are insured for most emergency treatments if you take your EHIC (European Health Insurance Card) with you. US residents should obtain adequate health insurance before commencing their journey.

11 ROLLENSPIEL: UND JETZT SIE!

Spielen Sie die Rolle der Patientin / des Patienten. Überprüfen Sie Ihre Antworten auf der Audioaufnahme.

CD 2, TR 25

Dr. Amm	Guten Tag. Wie kann ich Ihnen helfen? Was fehlt Ihnen?
Patient/in	*Say that you've got quite bad throat pains.*
Dr. Amm	Oh, das tut mir leid. Wie lange haben Sie die Schmerzen denn schon?
Patient/in	*Tell him for about three days and that it's getting worse.*
Dr. Amm	Was sind Sie von Beruf, wenn ich fragen darf?
Patient/in	*Say that you're a teacher.*
Dr. Amm	Ach so! Lehrer haben oft Probleme mit dem Hals. In der Klasse müssen Sie oft zu viel sprechen, das ist nicht gut für den Hals.
Patient/in	*Say yes, but what should you do?*
Dr. Amm	Also, ich verschreibe Ihnen Tabletten. Essen Sie auch viel Eis und trinken Sie viel Wasser. Fahren Sie bald in Urlaub?
Patient/in	*Say yes, next week you're flying to Florida.*
Dr. Amm	Gut, dann müssen Sie versuchen, ein bisschen zu relaxen. Und Sie dürfen nicht zu viel sprechen!
Patient/in	*Say, all right and thanks very much.*
Dr. Amm	Gern geschehen. Und gute Besserung.

Pronunciation

◄）CD 2, TR 26

At the end of a word or syllable the letter **b** in German is pronounced more like an English **p**:

gib   hab   Urlaub   halb   abholen   Obst

When the **b** is no longer at the end of the word or syllable it is pronounced as an English *b*:

geben   *haben*   *Urlaube*   *halbe*

How would you pronounce these words?
ob, Ober, Herbst, schreibt, schreiben.

Grammar

1 MODAL VERBS

You have now met all the main modal verbs. Here is a grid showing their present tense forms.

	dürfen	können	müssen	wollen	sollen
	may	*can*	*must*	*want (to)*	*should*
ich	darf	kann	muss	will	soll
du	darfst	kannst	musst	willst	sollst
Sie	dürfen	können	müssen	wollen	sollen
er/sie/es	darf	kann	muss	will	soll
wir	dürfen	können	müssen	wollen	sollen
ihr	dürft	könnt	müsst	wollt	sollt
Sie	dürfen	können	müssen	wollen	sollen
sie	dürfen	können	müssen	wollen	sollen

Note that with modal verbs the **ich** and **er/sie/es** forms are the same. They therefore do not have the endings (-e for **ich** and -t for **er/sie/es**) that are used with most other verbs in the present tense.

Modal verbs are occasionally used on their own:

Ich kann sehr gut Englisch.   *I can speak English very well.*
Wir wollen morgen nach München.   *We want to go to Munich tomorrow.*

But they nearly always need a second verb and this is sent to the end of the sentence or clause:

Hier	darf	man leider nicht	parken.
Jetzt	müssen	wir nach Hause	gehen.
Wir	wollen	morgen nach Berlin	fliegen.
	(*modal*)		(*second verb*)

Note: If you want to say *can't* or *mustn't* in German, you often use dürfen + nicht/kein, e.g.

| **Hier dürfen Sie nicht parken.** | *You can't park here.* |
| **Du darfst keinen Alkohol trinken.** | *You mustn't drink any alcohol.* |

2 USING WENN

As you saw earlier in this unit, **wenn** can mean *if* or *when* and it sends the verb to the end of the **wenn**-clause:

Mir gefällt es,   **wenn** *die Sonne* **scheint.**
             wenn *es im Winter* **schneit.**
             wenn *es im Herbst windig*
             ist.

Note that when you put **wenn** at the beginning of a sentence, the second clause of the sentence starts with a verb:

Wenn *es morgen Nachmittag* **regnet,** *gehe ich ins Kino.*

Wenn *ich nicht zu viel Arbeit* **habe, kann** *ich ins Café gehen.*
Wenn *meine Freundin mitkommen* **kann, möchte** *ich nach Wien fahren.*

The **wenn** clause needs a comma either at the beginning or at the end, as in the examples given above.

TESTING YOURSELF

1 Ergänzen Sie, bitte.

    a *Mein Arzt sagt, ich __soll__ mehr schwimmen gehen. (sollen)*
    b *Was _____ ich machen? (sollen)*
    c *Nächsten Monat _____ er mit einem Tanzkurs anfangen. (wollen)*
    d *Stefan und Andrea _____ im Sommer heiraten. (wollen)*
    e *_____ du eigentlich wieder Volleyball spielen? (dürfen)*
    f *Hier _____ man nicht rauchen. (dürfen)*
    g *Kinder unter 16 Jahren _____ den Film nicht sehen. (dürfen)*

2 *Join the pairs of sentences together, using* **wenn**.

    Beispiel *Du willst länger schlafen? Dann musst du früher ins Bett gehen.* → **Wenn** *du länger schlafen willst, musst du früher ins Bett gehen.*

    a *Du möchtest Englisch lernen? Dann musst du in eine Sprachschule gehen.*
    b *Bodo möchte ein altes Buch über Deutschland finden? Dann muss er auf dem Flohmarkt suchen.*
    c *Ihr wollt nächste Woche nach New York fliegen? Dann müsst ihr bald eure Tickets buchen.*
    d *Florian möchte am Wochenende zu Heikes Party gehen? Dann muss er nett zu ihr sein.*
    e *Marcus möchte ein Jahr in Madrid arbeiten? Dann muss er ja Spanisch lernen.*
    f *Sie haben kein Geld und keine Kreditkarte? Dann müssen Sie mit einem Scheck bezahlen.*

Now that you have completed Unit 19, can you: tick
1 say what you consider to be healthy and unhealthy? ☐
2 name parts of the body? ☐
3 say what aches and pains you have? ☐
4 use modal verbs correctly? ☐

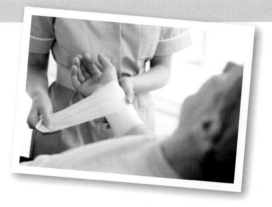

20

Wetter und Urlaub
Weather and holidays

In this unit you will learn
- *how to report on weather conditions*
- *how to talk about past holidays*

Language points
- *revision of the present perfect tense*
- *prepositions*
- *the simple past tense of the modal verbs*

Weather

1 DIE VIER JAHRESZEITEN *THE FOUR SEASONS*

der Frühling   der Sommer   der Herbst   der Winter

2 WIE IST DAS WETTER?

Read these descriptions of weather conditions. Note the past tense forms of the verbs in the sentences in italics.

Die Sonne. Heute scheint die Sonne.
Gestern hat die Sonne geschienen.

Der Regen. Im Moment regnet es.
Letzten Herbst hat es viel geregnet.

Der Schnee. Jetzt schneit es.
Im Winter hat es viel geschneit.

Der Wind. Es ist heute windig.
Im Herbst war es windig.

Der Nebel. Es ist morgens oft neblig.
In London war es früher sehr neblig.

Die Temperatur. Hier beträgt die Temperatur 24 Grad.
Die Temperatur hat 10 Grad betragen.

3 WAS FÜR WETTER HATTEN DIE LEUTE IM URLAUB?

◄) CD 2, TR 27

Hören Sie die folgenden zwei Interviews. Wo waren die Leute im Urlaub? In welcher Jahreszeit waren sie dort? Wie hoch waren die Temperaturen? Wie war das Wetter: Hat es geregnet? Hat die Sonne geschienen? Hat es geschneit?

	Wo sie waren	Jahreszeit	Temperaturen	Wetter
Bärbel Specht				
Jutta Weiß				

4 DAS WETTER IN EUROPA

Talking about the weather

In Madrid ist es …   **heiter, wolkig, bedeckt.**
In Madrid it's …   *fine, cloudy, overcast.*
In London gibt es …   **Schauer, Gewitter, Schnee, Regen, Nebel.**
In London there is / are … showers, thunderstorms, snow, rain, fog.

Sehen Sie sich die Wetterkarte auf der nächsten Seite an und beantworten Sie die Fragen.

a Wo ist es wärmer: in London oder in München?

b Wie hoch sind die Temperaturen in Dublin?

c Regnet es in Berlin?

d Regnet es in Wien?

e Wo gibt es in Europa Gewitter?

f Wie ist das Wetter in Kairo?

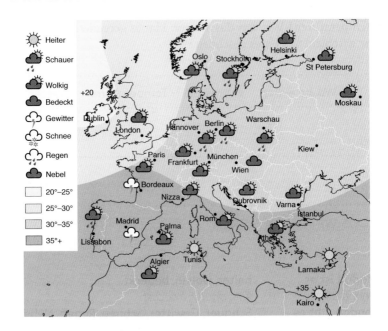

5 DER WETTERBERICHT IM RADIO

🔊 **CD 2, TR 28**

Hören Sie zu. Welche Antwort stimmt?

a Nachts sind es 6 / 16 Grad.

b Tagsüber sind es im Südosten 21 / 22 / 23 Grad.

c Montag gibt es im Norden und Osten Wolken und Regen / Wolken, aber keinen Regen.

d Dienstag gibt es in ganz Deutschland Sonne / Schauer.

e Am Mittwoch ist es schlechter / besser.

ablkühlen *to cool down*
übrig *remaining*
das Gebiet (-e) *area, region*
die Aussicht (-en) *prospect, outlook*

Holidays

6 WO WAREN SIE DIESES JAHR IM URLAUB?

◀) **CD 2, TR 29**

Vier Leute erzählen, wo sie im Urlaub waren und was sie gemacht haben. Hören Sie zu und beantworten Sie dann die Fragen.

a Was hat Wolfgang Schmidt abends gemacht?

b Konnte er nur spanisches Bier kaufen?

c Wie oft machen Sieglinde und Renate Bosch einen Skiurlaub?

d Wohin wollen sie nächstes Jahr im Urlaub fahren?

e Was für Wetter hatten Gerlinde Wagner und ihr Mann in Travemünde?

f Wollen sie nächstes Jahr wieder nach Travemünde fahren?

g Hat Peter Kemper schon einen Job gefunden?

h Was hat er vor zwei Jahren gemacht?

Wolfgang Schmidt, 47

‚Ich bin auf Mallorca gewesen, ein richtiger Strandurlaub. Ich habe tagsüber lange in der Sonne gelegen und bin ein bisschen geschwommen. Abends habe ich gut gegessen und bin manchmal in die Hotel-Bar gegangen. Man konnte auch richtiges deutsches Bier kaufen. Wie zu Hause. Das hat mir gut gefallen. Nächstes Jahr möchte ich wiederkommen.'

Sieglinde Bosch, 42

‚Im Winter machen meine Schwester und ich jedes Jahr einen Skiurlaub und fahren in die Berge. Dieses Jahr waren wir in Kitzbühel, in Österreich, fantastisch. Der Schnee war gut, die Pisten ausgezeichnet. Wir sind jeden Tag mehrere Stunden Ski gelaufen. Nach dem Urlaub haben wir uns total fit gefühlt. Nächstes Jahr wollen wir vielleicht mal in die Schweiz fahren.'

Gerlinde Wagner, 64

‚Dieses Jahr sind mein Mann und ich an die Ostsee gefahren, nach Travemünde. Das Wetter war eine Katastrophe. Wir hatten meistens Regen. Außerdem war es sehr kalt und wir konnten nur selten schwimmen gehen. Und teuer war es auch. Nein, nie wieder an die Ostsee. Nächstes Jahr fliegen wir lieber in den Süden, nach Spanien oder Griechenland.'

Peter Kemper, 25

‚Dieses Jahr habe ich keinen Urlaub gemacht. Ich habe gerade mein Studium beendet und suche jetzt einen Job. Das ist nicht einfach im Moment. Ich hoffe, nächstes Jahr habe ich mehr Geld. Dann würde ich gerne nach New York fliegen. Das ist mein Traum. Ich liebe große Städte. Am liebsten mache ich Städtereisen. Vor zwei Jahren bin ich nach Mexiko-City geflogen.'

der Strandurlaub (-e) *beach holiday*
liegen *to lie (in the sun, etc.)*
wiederlkommen *to come again/back*
der Berg (-e) *mountain*
die Ostsee *the Baltic*
beenden *to finish*
der Traum (¨e) *dream*

7 WAS PASST AM BESTEN?

Match the words and phrases (a–g) with the most appropriate verbs from the second column.

Beispiel in der Nordsee → schwimmen

a *mit dem Flugzeug*	*schwimmen*
b *auf den Berg*	*laufen*
c *zu Fuß*	*fliegen*
d *mit dem Auto*	*spazieren gehen*
e *im Meer*	*steigen*
f *Ski*	*gehen*
g *im Park*	*fahren*

Remember when talking about past events in German you usually have to use the present perfect tense form, using either **haben** or **sein** plus the past participle of the verb (**gemacht, gefahren,** etc.). Did you notice that in **Übung 6** many of the verbs indicate movement (**schwimmen, gehen, laufen,** etc.) and therefore take **sein**? Furthermore, there are also quite a few irregular verbs which usually show a vowel change in the past participle (e.g. **schwimmen** → **geschwommen**).

If you would like to remind yourself about the perfect tense, you could go back and have another look at Units 13 and 14.

8 WIE HEISST DAS IM PERFEKT?

Ergänzen Sie die folgenden Sätze mit den Verben aus **Übung 7.**

Beispiel Familie Grothe **ist** mit dem Auto nach Frankreich
gefahren.

a Er ___ zu Fuß nach Hause _____ .
b Petra und Ulrike ___ jeden Tag vier Stunden im Meer _____ .
c Frau Müller ___ fast jeden Tag Ski _____ .
d Seppl Dreier ___ auf den Mount Everest _____ .
e Diesmal ___ ich mit der Lufthansa nach London _____ .
f Annette ___ viel mit dem Fahrrad _____ .
g Er ___ im Stadtpark spazieren _____ .

SPRACHINFO

PREPOSITIONS AND PLACES

What prepositions do you use in German in connection with
places? These examples provide you with an overview of which
prepositions to use and when. Note that, as in English, a different
preposition is often used depending on whether *you are going
somewhere* or if *you are somewhere* (e.g. 'I am going *to* Berlin' and
'I am *in* Berlin').

Städte	Ich fahre **nach** Berlin.	Ich bin **in** Berlin.
Länder	Sie fährt **nach** Frankreich. Aber: Sie fährt **in** die Schweiz / **in** die Türkei. Sie fährt **in** die USA.	Sie ist **in** Frankreich. Aber: Sie ist **in** der Schweiz / **in** der Türkei. Sie ist **in** den USA.
Land	Sie sind **aufs** Land gefahren.	Sie waren **auf** dem Land.
Insel	Sie sind **nach** Mallorca geflogen.	Sie waren **auf** Mallorca.
Meere	Er fährt **ans** Meer / **an** die Ostsee / **an** den Atlantik.	Er ist **am** Meer / **an** der Ostsee / **am** Atlantik.

Berge	Sie fahren **in** die Berge.	Sie sind **in** den Bergen.
	Sie steigen **auf** den Berg.	Sie sind **auf** dem Berg.

Remember that prepositions such as **in, auf** and **an** require the accusative case forms when movement is indicated (**Sie fährt in** *die* **Schweiz**), and the dative forms when the focus is on position (**Sie ist in** *der* **Schweiz**).

Insight: German holidays

Many Germans nowadays are entitled to six weeks' paid holiday a year. They also enjoy numerous public holidays (**Feiertage**), most of which are religious in origin. The total number of **Feiertage** differs from **Land** to **Land**, but it tends to be among the highest in Europe. German reunification is celebrated on 3 October with the **Tag der deutschen Einheit** (*day of German unity*).

9 EIN AUFREGENDER URLAUB

An old friend wants to know what you did on your holiday. Rewrite the following story by adapting it to the first person singular (**ich**). Start each sentence with an item in bold type.

> *Sie waren* **letztes Jahr** *in Heidelberg im Urlaub. Sie haben* **dort** *in einer Jugendherberge gewohnt. Sie sind* **abends** *in eine Karaoke-Kneipe gegangen. Sie haben* **in der Kneipe** *ein Lied von Elvis Presley gesungen. Ein Produzent hat Sie* **dort** *gehört. Ihre Stimme hat* **ihm** *sehr gut gefallen. Sie sind* **am nächsten Tag** *mit ihm nach Berlin geflogen. Sie haben* **in einem Studio** *eine neue CD gemacht. Sie sind* 10 Tage **in** *Berlin geblieben. Sie haben* **dann** *im Fernsehen und im Radio gesungen. Sie wollen* **nächstes Jahr** *in Las Vegas singen.*

Beispiel **Letztes Jahr** war ich in Heidelberg im Urlaub.
         Dort habe ich..., etc.

10 UND WIE WAR DEIN URLAUB?

Hören Sie, was Susanne im Urlaub gemacht hat. Sind die Aussagen
richtig oder falsch?

a Ihr Urlaub war wunderbar.
b Die ersten Tage konnte sie nicht Ski fahren.
c Dann hat es sehr viel geschneit.
d Sie ist gegen einen anderen Skifahrer gefahren.
e Sie musste eine Woche im Krankenhaus bleiben.
f Jetzt geht es ihr wieder besser.

CD 2, TR 30

Peter	Hallo Susanne. Na, wie war dein Skiurlaub?
Susanne	Ach, Peter. Eine einzige Katastrophe.
Peter	Wieso, was ist denn passiert?
Susanne	Ach, die ersten Tage hatten wir viel zu wenig Schnee. Deshalb konnten wir überhaupt nicht Ski fahren.
Peter	Oh, das ist ja ärgerlich. Und dann?
Susanne	Dann hat es so viel geschneit, dann durften wir zwei Tage nicht auf die Piste. Der Schnee war zu hoch.
Peter	Und dann?
Susanne	Dann konnten wir fahren, es war ideales Wetter. Aber weißt du, was mir passiert ist? Ich wollte einen neuen Hang ausprobieren, aber er war zu schnell für mich. Tja, und dann bin ich gegen einen Baum gefahren.
Peter	Gegen einen Baum? Wie schrecklich. Und musstest du ins Krankenhaus?
Susanne	Ja. Meine Beine haben mir wehgetan, aber es war nichts Schlimmes. Ich musste nur drei Tage im Krankenhaus bleiben. Aber Ski fahren durfte ich dann nicht mehr. Ich konnte nur noch spazieren gehen.
Peter	Das tut mir leid. Und wie geht es dir jetzt?
Susanne	Jetzt geht es mir wieder gut. Aber nächstes Jahr, weißt du, da fahre ich im Winter lieber nach Teneriffa.

einzig (here) complete, absolute
überhaupt nicht not at all
deshalb therefore, so
ärgerlich annoying
der Hang (¨e) slope
aus|probieren to try out
gegen + acc. against
der Baum (¨e) tree

SPRACHINFO

THE SIMPLE PAST TENSE OF <u>HABEN</u>, <u>SEIN</u>, AND MODAL VERBS

You have learned that Germans normally use the present perfect tense when talking about past events. However, you may have noticed that in the last dialogue and in **Übung 6 war / waren** were used to mean *was / were*:

> *Das Wetter* **war** *eine Katastrophe.*
> *Der Schnee* **war** *gut.*
> *Dieses Jahr* **waren** *wir in Kitzbühel.*

War / waren are the *simple past tense* forms of the verb **sein**.

The simple past tense forms of the verb **haben – hatte / hatten –** are also often used when referring to the past. Examples from this unit are:

> *Die ersten Tage* **hatten** *wir viel zu wenig Schnee.*
> *Wir* **hatten** *meistens Regen.*

Modal verbs too are often found in the simple past tense:

können

> *Dann* **konnten** *wir fahren.*
> *Man* **konnte** *auch richtiges deutsches Bier kaufen.*
> *Wir* **konnten** *nur selten schwimmen gehen.*

müssen

> *Ich musste nur drei Tage im Krankenhaus bleiben.*
> *Er musste nach Köln fahren.*

dürfen

> *Aber Ski fahren durfte ich dann nicht mehr.*
> *Dann durften wir zwei Tage nicht mehr auf die Piste.*

For an overview of these forms see the **Grammar** section.

11 ROLLENSPIEL: UND JETZT SIE! WIE WAR IHR URLAUB?

Sie kommen aus dem Urlaub zurück. Ein Kollege fragt Sie, wie Ihr Urlaub war. Bereiten Sie Ihre Antworten vor und beantworten Sie dann die Fragen auf der Audioaufnahme.

◀ CD 2, TR 31

Kollege	Ach, da sind Sie wieder! Und wie war Ihr Urlaub?
Sie	*Tell him an absolute catastrophe.*
Kollege	Wieso, was ist denn passiert?
Sie	*Say that the first three days you had rain. So you couldn't therefore go for walks.*
Kollege	Oh, das ist ja ärgerlich. Und dann?
Sie	*Say that a friend and you drove into a tree with the car.*
Kollege	Gegen einen Baum? Wie schrecklich. Und mussten Sie ins Krankenhaus?
Sie	*Say yes, your legs hurt, but it was nothing bad.*
Kollege	Und wie lange mussten Sie im Krankenhaus bleiben?
Sie	*Say only two days, but you then had to go home.*
Kollege	Das tut mir leid. Und wie geht es Ihnen jetzt?
Sie	*Say that you're OK again now.*

12 TREND: KURZTRIP STATT STRANDURLAUB

Die Deutschen machen oft Urlaub. Aber häufig fahren sie nur für ein paar Tage weg. Wohin fahren sie dann? Lesen Sie bitte den Text und beantworten Sie dann die Fragen.

Von je 100 Befragten, die in den letzten Jahren eine 2- bis 4tägige Städtereise unternommen haben, wählten als Reiseziel:

Paris	19
Berlin	17
München	12
Wien	10
Hamburg	10
London	10
Prag	8
Rom	6
Dresden	6
Amsterdam	5
Venedig	4
Köln	3
Budapest	2
Florenz	2
Kopenhagen	2
Istanbul	2

Trend: Kurztrip statt Strandurlaub

Lieber häufiger im Jahr für einige Tage wegfahren, als im Urlaub drei Wochen lang an einem Ferienort bleiben. 22 Millionen Deutsche finden Kurztrips (vor allem Städtereisen mit dem Bus) spannender als eine große Reise. Das Ergebnis einer Tourismus-Analyse vom letzten Jahr zeigt auch: Absoluter Renner bei den Zielen für Wochenend-Trips ist immer noch Paris. Dann folgen Berlin, München, Wien und Hamburg.

der Ferienort (-e) *holiday resort*
das Ergebnis (-se) *result*
absoluter Renner *here: top seller*

VOCAB

Richtig oder falsch?

a Immer mehr Deutsche machen kurze Urlaube.
b 22 Millionen finden lange Urlaube besser.
c Die meisten Kurztrips sind mit dem Bus.
d Die meisten Städtereisenden fahren nach Paris.
e Es fahren mehr Leute nach Amsterdam als nach London.

Grammar

1 *SIMPLE PAST TENSE:* SEIN, HABEN, *MODAL VERBS*

As you saw earlier in this unit, even in speaking, the simple past tense forms are sometimes used instead of the present perfect tense forms. This applies especially to **sein** and **haben** and to the modal verbs.

Sein and haben

Here are the simple past tense forms of **sein** and **haben**, together with their present perfect tense forms. There is really little or no difference in meaning between the two forms:

Ich war letzten Sommer in Österreich.
Ich bin letzten Sommer in Österreich gewesen.
I was in Austria last summer.

Peter hatte diesen Sommer kein Geld.
Peter hat diesen Sommer kein Geld gehabt.
Peter had no money this summer.

	sein		haben	
	simple past	present perfect	simple past	present perfect
ich	war	bin gewesen	hatte	habe gehabt
du	warst	bist gewesen	hattest	hast gehabt
Sie	waren	sind gewesen	hatten	haben gehabt
er / sie / es	war	ist gewesen	hatte	hat gehabt
wir	waren	sind gewesen	hatten	haben gehabt
ihr	wart	seid gewesen	hattet	habt gehabt
Sie	waren	sind gewesen	hatten	haben gehabt
sie	waren	sind gewesen	hatten	haben gehabt

Modal verbs

Modal verbs, too, are often used in the simple past tense. Here are the simple past tense forms of the modal verbs. For their meanings see the examples given beneath the grid.

	dürfen	**können**	**müssen**	**sollen**	**wollen**
ich	durfte	konnte	musste	sollte	wollte
du	durftest	konntest	musstest	solltest	wolltest
Sie	durften	konnten	mussten	sollten	wollten
er / sie / es	durfte	konnte	musste	sollte	wollte
wir	durften	konnten	mussten	sollten	wollten
ihr	durftet	konntet	musstet	solltet	wolltet
Sie	durften	konnten	mussten	sollten	wollten
sie	durften	konnten	mussten	sollten	wollten

Note that the umlaut found in the infinitive forms of **dürfen**, **müssen** and **können** is not found in the simple past tense forms.

Here are some examples of the modal verbs being used in the simple past tense:

dürfen

> past tense meaning: *was / were allowed to*
> *Als Kind **durfte** ich nur eine Stunde pro Tag fernsehen.*
> *As a child I **was allowed to** watch TV for only one hour a day.*

können

> past tense meaning: *could, was / were able to*
> *Im Winter **konnten** wir Ski laufen.*
> *In winter we **were able** to go skiing.*

müssen

> past tense meaning: *had to*
> Bernd **musste** gestern um 6 Uhr aufstehen.
> Bernd **had to** get up at 6 o'clock yesterday.

sollen

> past tense meaning: *was / were supposed to*
> Ich **sollte** heute meine Eltern besuchen.
> I **was supposed** to visit my parents today.

wollen

> past tense meaning: *wanted to*
> Hans und Inge **wollten** ins Kino mitkommen.
> Hans and Inge **wanted** to come to the cinema with us.

You will learn more about the simple past tense in Unit 22.

TESTING YOURSELF

1 Welche Präpositionen fehlen?

München, am 3. September

Liebe Inga,

na, wie geht's? Dieses Jahr sind wir nicht _____ Indien geflogen oder _____ die Berge gefahren. Nein, wir haben Urlaub _____ der Ostsee gemacht, _____ der Insel Rügen. Rügen liegt im Nordosten Deutschlands. Das Wetter war gut, wir sind viel _____ Meer geschwommen. Außerdem haben wir einen Ausflug _____ Berlin gemacht. Dort war es natürlich auch sehr interessant. So viel hat sich verändert. Wir sind _____ Pergamonmuseum gegangen und waren auch _____ Museum für Deutsche Geschichte.

Wie ist deine neue Wohnung? Ich hoffe, es geht dir gut.

Bis bald und grüß alle!

Deine Martina

2 Setzen Sie die Modalverben in die richtige Form.

    a *Eigentlich ___ (wollen) ich gestern Abend ins Kino gehen, aber ich ___ (müssen) lange arbeiten.*

    b *Im Hotel ___ (können) wir noch nach Mitternacht etwas zu trinken bekommen.*

    c *Frau Schmidt ___ (sollen) schon letzte Woche zum Arzt gehen, aber leider ___ (können) sie nicht.*

    d *Früher ___ (dürfen) man in unserer Straße parken.*

    e *___ (müssen) Sie früher in der Schule Latein lernen?*

Now that you have completed Unit 20, can you: tick

1 report on present and past weather conditions? ☐

2 use the correct preposition with places and place names? ☐

3 talk about holidays that you have been on? ☐

4 use the simple past tense for certain verbs? ☐

21

Telefonieren und die Geschäftswelt

Telephoning and the business world

In this unit you will learn
- *how to make and answer phone calls*
- *how to say what belongs to whom*

Language points
- *revision of dative pronouns*
- *various uses of the genitive case*

Making telephone calls

1 LESEN UND LERNEN

Was kann man sagen?

a Sie sprechen direkt mit der Person:

b Sie möchten mit einer anderen Person sprechen:

Bist du es? *Is that you?*
am Apparat *on the phone, speaking*
Ich hole sie. *I'll fetch her.*
verbinden *to connect, to put through*

2 FORMELL ODER INFORMELL?

Welche Fragen und Begrüßungen sind formell, welche informell?
Machen Sie eine Liste.

Informell	Formell
– Hallo, Bernd, bist du es?	– Guten Tag, Herr Preiß.
–	–
	–
	–

SPRACHINFO

WEAK NOUNS

You will have noticed that the word **Herr** has an **n** at the end in
some of the examples. This is because **Herr** belongs to a group of
nouns (called *weak nouns*) that add -(e)n in the accusative and
dative cases:

Das ist Herr Schmidt.   *Nominative*
Kennen Sie Herr**n** Schmidt schon?   *Accusative*
Ich möchte mit Herr**n** Schmidt sprechen.   *Dative*

Other nouns that belong to this group include: **der Mensch, der Name, der Student:**

Bitte sagen Sie Ihren Name**n**.   *Accusative*
Können Sie diesem Student**en** helfen?   *Dative*

3 TELEFONANRUFE

🔊 **CD 2, TR 32**

In welchen Dialogen (**1, 2** or **3**) sagen die Leute die Sätze? Hören Sie bitte zu und kreuzen Sie an.

Die Leitung ist besetzt. *The line is busy / engaged.*
die Geschäftsreise (-n) *business trip*
zurücklrufen *to call back*
eine Nachricht hinterlassen *to leave a message*
jemandem etwas ausrichten *to give a message to someone*

	1	2	3
Sie ist beim Zahnarzt.	☐	☒	☐
Die Leitung ist besetzt.	☐	☐	☐
Er ist auf Geschäftsreise.	☐	☐	☐
Soll sie zurückrufen?	☐	☐	☐
Wollen Sie warten?	☒	☐	☐
Wollen Sie eine Nachricht hinterlassen?	☐	☐	☐
Er möchte mich morgen zurückrufen.	☐	☐	☐
Ich bin zu Hause.	☐	☐	☐
Ich rufe später noch mal an.	☐	☐	☐

Hören Sie die Dialoge noch einmal.

a Was macht Frau Dr. Martens gerade? (Dialog 1)

b Wo ist Sandy und wann kommt sie wieder nach Hause? (Dialog 2)

c Wo ist Peter Fink und wann ist er wieder im Büro? (Dialog 3)

d Was möchte Corinna ihm geben? (Dialog 3)

4 FRAGE UND ANTWORT

Was passt zusammen?

a Ist Corinna da?

b Können Sie Herrn Grün etwas ausrichten?

1 Natürlich kann ich ihm etwas ausrichten.

2 Einen Moment. Ich verbinde.

c	Spreche ich mit Frau Kemper?	**3**	Tut mir leid, sie ist nicht zu Hause.
d	Können Sie Julia sagen, ich habe angerufen?	**4**	Natürlich bin ich es.
e	Kann ich bitte mit Herrn Martin sprechen?	**5**	Ja, hier ist Kemper am Apparat.
f	Bist du es, Renate?	**6**	Natürlich kann ich ihr das sagen.

5 ERINNERN SIE SICH?

Heißt es **ihr, ihm** oder **ihnen**? Setzen Sie das richtige Pronomen ein. Wollen Sie die Formen wiederholen? Dann gehen Sie zu **Lektion 18**.

> **Beispiel** *Soll ich* Frau Martini *etwas sagen?* → *Soll ich* ihr *etwas sagen?*

a Ich sage es Herrn Lobinger. → Ich sage es ___.

b Ich richte es meinem Sohn aus. → Ich richte es ___ aus.

c Soll ich Susi und Tim eine Nachricht hinterlassen? → Soll ich ___ eine Nachricht hinterlassen?

d Soll ich Frau Martens etwas ausrichten? → Soll ich ___ etwas ausrichten?

e Sag Mutti bitte, ich bin um 5 Uhr da. → Sag ___ bitte, ich bin um 5 Uhr da.

Können Sie die Sätze ins Englische übersetzen?

6 ANRUFBEANTWORTER

🔊 **CD 2, TR 33**

Hören Sie den Anrufbeantworter von Familie Schweighofer. Welche Wörter fehlen?

Guten Tag. ___ ist der telefonische Anrufbeantworter von Evelyn und Michael Schweighofer. Wir sind im Moment ___ nicht da. Sie können uns aber gerne nach dem Pfeifton eine ___ hinterlassen. Bitte sagen Sie uns Ihren ___ und Ihre ___ und wir ___ Sie dann so schnell wie möglich ___.

7 WORTSPIEL

Setzen Sie die fehlenden Wörter ein.
In der Mitte erscheint dann (fast) ein zwölftes Wort. Was ist es?

1 Guten Morgen. Schwarz am _____ .
2 Sagen Sie bitte, er soll _____ .
3 Sprechen Sie bitte nach dem _____ .
4 Ja, Herr Gruber ist in seinem Büro. Ich _____ .
5 Es tut mir leid. Aber diese Nummer ist _____ .
6 Möchten Sie eine Nachricht _____ ?
7 Freye, Firma Braun, _____ 314.
8 Die _____ ist besetzt. Ich versuche es später noch einmal.
9 Darf ich bitte eine _____ hinterlassen?
10 Bitte sagen Sie uns Ihren _____ und Ihre Telefonnummer.
11 Möchten Sie ihr etwas _____ ?

Insight: Telephone etiquette

German speakers often answer the phone by saying their surname: **Schmidt** or **Schmidt am Apparat**. Using **du** or first names on the phone to someone you do not know is considered inappropriate. At the end of a telephone conversation people usually say **Auf Wiederhören**, instead of **Auf Wiedersehen**.

As in most countries nowadays, the use of **Handys** (*mobile phones/cell phones*) is widespread. Sending an SMS or text message is **simsen** in German: **Ich hab' ihr gesimst** *I texted her*.

At the office

8 DER ERSTE TAG IN DER NEUEN FIRMA
THE FIRST DAY IN THE NEW COMPANY

QUICK VOCAB

der Raum (¨e) *room, space*
der Texter (-) *copy-writer*
die Sekretärin (-nen) *secretary*
daneben *next to that*
der Grafiker (-) *graphic artist*
der Chef (-s) / die Chefin (-nen) *head, boss*

Frau Paul hat heute ihren ersten Tag in der Werbefirma ‚Pleinmann'. Herr Riha zeigt ihr die Firma. Lesen Sie, was er sagt und finden Sie heraus, wer in welchem Büro arbeitet. Schreiben Sie die Nummer der Büros auf.

Beispiel Hier vorne rechts ist der Raum des Designers, Bernd Buck. Er hat in New York studiert. – Büro Nr. 6

a Daneben ist das Büro der Texter, Michaela und Günther. Beide sind fantastisch, manchmal ein bisschen temperamentvoll. Büro Nr. ___

b Hier vorne links ist das Büro der Sekretärin, Frau Schüller. Sie ist wirklich sehr nett. Büro Nr. ___

c Daneben ist das Büro des Grafikers, Herrn Meier-Martinez. Büro Nr. ___

d Und ganz hinten links ist das Büro des Managers, Guido Kafka. Ein sehr intelligenter Mensch. Büro Nr. ___

e Gegenüber ist das Zimmer der Chefin, Frau Conrad. Büro Nr. ___

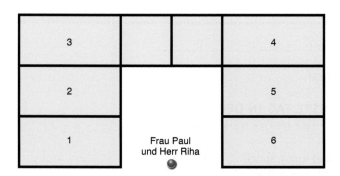

THE GENITIVE CASE

You might have realised that in **Übung 8** a new structure is used. It is the fourth and last of the cases in German, the so-called **genitive** case. You have probably already worked out from the examples that the genitive indicates some kind of possession or ownership. The definite article in the genitive can be roughly translated as *of the*. So, **das Büro der Sekretärin** is *the office of the secretary* – in other words, *the secretary's office*. Here is an overview of the genitive case using the definite article.

masc.	Hier rechts ist der Raum **des** Designer**s**.	der Designer
fem.	Hier vorne links ist das Büro **der** Sekretärin.	die Sekretärin
neut.	Herr Kafka ist der Manager **des** Büro**s**.	das Büro
pl.	Daneben ist das Büro **der** Texter.	die Texter

Note that with masculine and neuter nouns the definite article is **des** and the noun also adds an -(e)s. With feminine and plural nouns the definite article is **der** and no additional endings are required.

9 AM ABEND VERSUCHT SICH FRAU PAUL ZU ERINNERN

When she gets home, Frau Paul tries hard to remember the layout of the office. How did she do?

Richtig oder falsch? Korrigieren Sie die falschen Aussagen.

Beispiel: Vorne rechts war das Büro der Sekretärin. Nein, vorne rechts war das Büro des Designers.

a Links vorne war das Büro des Designers.

b Daneben war das Büro des Grafikers, Meier-Martinez.

c Auf der rechten Seite in der Mitte war das Zimmer der Chefin, Frau Conrad.

d Und ganz hinter rechts war der Raum des Managers, Guido Kafka.

e Ganz hinten links war dann das Zimmer der Texter, Michaela und Günther.

10 ERGÄNZEN SIE

Remember that masculine and neuter nouns will need an -(e)s and feminine nouns will not. Some of the nouns therefore don't require endings.

Beispiel Der Name **der** Firma ist Inter-Design.

a Ich habe den Namen d__ Designerin__ vergessen.
b Die Telefonnummer d__ Kundin__ ist 45 76 98.
c Die Rechnung d__ Hotel__ war astronomisch.
d Die Reparatur d__ Computer__ hat drei Wochen gedauert.
e Mir gefällt die Farbe d__ neuen Firmenauto__ nicht.
f Die Anzahl d__ Leute__ ohne Arbeit beträgt über vier Millionen.

Expressions with the genitive

am Anfang der Woche *at the beginning of the week*
Mitte der Woche *in the middle of the week*
am Ende des Monats *at the end of the month*
wegen einer Geschäftsreise *because of a business trip*
trotz der Party *in spite of the party*

Note that **wegen** (*because of*) and **trotz** (*despite*) are both prepositions. They are both followed by the genitive case.

11 EIN GESPRÄCH ZWISCHEN FRAU MUTH UND HERRN SCHNEIDER

Frau Muth and Herr Schneider are trying to rearrange an appointment over the phone.
Hören Sie zu. Sind die Aussagen richtig oder falsch?

a Frau Muth hat im Moment viel zu tun.

b Herr Schneider hat am Anfang der Woche einen Termin mit ihr.

c Er fährt auf Urlaub in die USA.

d Am Donnerstag nächster Woche hat Frau Muth eine Launch-Party.

e Sie machen einen Termin für Ende der Woche, für Freitag.

Lesen Sie dann den Text und überprüfen Sie Ihre Antworten.

Herr Schneider	Guten Tag, Frau Muth. Hier ist Konrad Schneider von der Firma B.A.T.-Grafiks.
Frau Muth	Ja, Herr Schneider. Wie geht es Ihnen?
Herr Schneider	Danke, ganz gut. Und Ihnen?
Frau Muth	Sehr gut. Danke. Im Moment haben wir sehr viel Arbeit, wegen der Messe im Februar.
Herr Schneider	Frau Muth, wir haben am Ende der Woche einen Termin. Es tut mir leid, aber ich muss ihn wegen einer dringenden Geschäftsreise in die USA absagen.
Frau Muth	Ja, natürlich. Das ist kein Problem. Sollen wir gleich einen neuen Termin ausmachen?
Herr Schneider	Ja, gerne. Ich hole meinen Terminkalender.
Frau Muth	Passt es Ihnen denn Anfang der nächsten Woche?

CD 2, TR 34

Herr Schneider	Am Anfang der Woche habe ich schon einige Termine. Besser ist es Mitte der Woche oder am Ende. Vielleicht am Donnerstag.
Frau Muth	Donnerstagvormittag ist es schlecht, wegen einer Launch-Party für unser neues Produkt. Aber am Nachmittag, da geht es. Um 14.00 Uhr?
Herr Schneider	Das passt mir gut. Aber sind Sie sicher, trotz der Party am Vormittag?
Frau Muth	Kein Problem, Herr Schneider. Und wenn Sie Zeit haben, kommen Sie doch ein bisschen früher.

die Messe (-n) *trade fair*
dringend *urgent*
ab|sagen *to cancel (an arrangement)*
einen Termin ausmachen *to make an appointment*
Passt es Ihnen …? *Does it suit you …?*
Das passt mir gut. *It suits me very well.*

12 ROLLENSPIEL: UND JETZT SIE!

Sie müssen einen Termin mit Frau Conrad von der Werbeagentur Pleinmann absagen. Schreiben Sie zuerst Ihre Antworten auf und benutzen Sie dann die Audioaufnahme.

Frau Schüller	Werbeagentur Pleinmann. Guten Tag.
Sie	*Say good day and that you would like to talk to Frau Conrad.*
Frau Schüller	Ja, einen Moment bitte. Ich verbinde.
Sie	*Say thank you very much.*
Frau Conrad	Conrad. Guten Tag.
Sie	*Say your name. Tell Frau Conrad that you have an appointment for the beginning of the week.*
Frau Conrad	Ja, das stimmt. Ja, am Montag, um 15.00 Uhr.
Sie	*Say that you are very sorry, but you have to cancel the appointment.*

Frau Conrad	Nun, das ist kein Problem. Wollen Sie gleich einen neuen Termin ausmachen?
Sie	*Say yes and ask if the end of the week suits her.*
Frau Conrad	Ja, das passt mir gut. Sagen wir Freitagmorgen, um 10.00 Uhr?
Sie	*Say you don't have any appointments for Friday morning. That suits you well. Say goodbye.*

Pronunciation

◀) **CD 2, TR 36**

In German the letter **a** is pronounced long in some words and short in others. Listen first to words that contain a short **a** and then to words that contain a long **a**:

an	machen	was	Dank	man
nach	Name	war	haben	sagen

You will probably find that you develop a feel for whether **a** should be long or short in a given word. How would you pronounce these words – all of which you have met in the course?
Hand, Nase, das, Grad, Tante, Hamburg.

Grammar

1 GENITIVE CASE

The genitive case is used (a) to indicate possession or ownership and (b) after certain prepositions.

Earlier in this unit you met the genitive forms of the definite article: **das Büro des Managers, die Telefonnummer der Kundin**, etc.

You also need to know the genitive forms of the indefinite article. Fortunately, the pattern is very similar to the one you already know. It is -(e)s for masculine and neuter nouns and -er for feminine nouns. The same pattern also applies to the possessive adjectives (**mein, dein, Ihr**, etc.) and to **kein**.

masc.	ein**es**	Was ist die Rolle ein**es** Mann**es** in der heutigen Welt?
	mein**es**	Das ist das Haus mein**es** Lehrer**s**.
fem.	ein**er**	Herr Breitling ist Manager ein**er** Firma in München.
	mein**er**	Das ist der Computer mein**er** Kollegin.
neut.	ein**es**	Das Leben ein**es** Kind**es** kann manchmal schwierig sein.
	mein**es**	Die Nebenkosten mein**es** Zimmer**s** sind sehr günstig.
plural	------	
	mein**er**	Darf ich die Mutter mein**er** Kinder vorstellen?

As you can see from the examples, nouns of one syllable (like **Mann** and **Kind**) tend to add -es in the genitive and not just -s:

die Rolle eines Mannes
das Leben eines Kindes

2 ADJECTIVE ENDINGS IN THE GENITIVE

The adjective endings in the genitive case after the definite and indefinite article and possessive adjectives are -**en** for all genders and the plural.

Die Mutter meines neuen Freundes.	*The mother of my new (boy)friend.*
Der Vater seiner neuen Freundin.	*The father of his new girlfriend.*

| Das Büro unserer neu*en* | The office of our new |
| Kollegen. | colleagues. |

3 PREPOSITIONS + GENITIVE

In this unit you met two prepositions that require the genitive:
wegen (*because of*) and **trotz** (*despite, in spite of*).

Here are some more of the most commonly used prepositions +
genitive followed by a few examples:

(an)statt	*instead of*
exklusive	*exclusive of*
außerhalb	*outside of*
bezüglich	*concerning, with regard to*
inklusive	*inclusive of*
innerhalb	*inside of*
während	*during*

Bezüglich Ihres letzten Briefes	*Concerning your last letter*
Inklusive aller Nebenkosten	*Inclusive of all extra costs*
Innerhalb unseres kleinen Zimmers	*Inside our small room*
Während ihres langen Lebens	*During her long life*

TESTING YOURSELF

1 Ordnen Sie bitte zu. Herr Kunz möchte mit Frau Nadolny sprechen. Was sagt Herr Kunz? *Herr Kunz wants to talk to Frau Nadolny. His role needs rearranging, but the role of the person at the other end of the line is in the correct order.*

Sekretärin

a *Firma Möllemann. Guten Tag!*

b *Es tut mir leid, Frau Nadolny ist gerade in einem Meeting.*

c *Das ist schwer zu sagen. Möchten Sie eine Nachricht hinterlassen?*

d *Natürlich. Was soll ich ihr ausrichten?*

e *Gut. Hat sie Ihre Nummer?*

f *Das ist vielleicht eine gute Idee.*

g *Und wie lange sind Sie heute im Büro?*

h *Ich richte es ihr aus, Herr Kunz. Vielen Dank und auf Wiederhören.*

Herr Kunz

1 *Guten Tag, Kunz. Ich möchte gern mit Frau Nadolny sprechen.*

2 *Wenn das möglich ist, gerne.*

3 *Können Sie ihr sagen, sie möchte mich bitte zurückrufen.*

4 *Auf Wiederhören.*

5 *Herr Kunz, Firma Bötticher, Anschluss 212.*

6 *Wie lange geht das Meeting denn?*

7 *Ich bin bis 16.00 Uhr an meinem Schreibtisch.*

8 *Ich denke schon, aber ich kann sie Ihnen noch mal geben.*

2 **Sagen Sie es anders.** *Practise the genitive case by re-writing the following sentences.*

Beispiel *Die Schwester von meinem neuen Freund ist sehr arrogant.*
Die Schwester meines neuen Freundes ist sehr arrogant.

a *Der Computer von meiner Kollegin ist fantastisch.*
b *Das Auto von meinem Bruder fährt sehr schnell.*
c *Die Firma von meinem alten Schulfreund war letztes Jahr sehr erfolgreich.*
d *Die Kollegen von meinem Mann sind alle schrecklich langweilig.*
e *Die Managerin von der exquisiten Boutique ‚La dame'* *kommt aus Krefeld.*
f *Das Büro von unserem neuen Designer ist sehr schick.*
g *Der Laptop von meinem Sohn hat €500 gekostet.*
h *Die Ehepartner von meinen Kollegen sind alle furchtbar nett.*

Now that you have completed Unit 21, can you:	tick
1 initiate and answer phone calls?	☐
2 say what belongs to whom?	☐
3 use the genitive case appropriately and correctly?	☐

22

Stellenangebote und Lebensläufe
Job adverts and CVs

In this unit you will learn
- *how to read job adverts*
- *how to write a CV*

Language points
- *more on the simple past tense*

Job applications

1 LESEN UND LERNEN

Here are five job adverts (**Stellenangebote**). Without looking at all the details, can you find out what kind of jobs are on offer?

A

> Student / Studentin für Bürotätigkeit 2–3 Tage pro Woche für unsere PR-Agentur gesucht. Sie müssen journalistisches Talent, sowie Büroerfahrung, PC- und Englischkenntnisse haben. Bewerbungen an: mail@joestpr.de oder anrufen bei Unternehmensberatung Joest Tel.: 08806/92300

B

Musiker-Eltern (Bayerische
Staatsoper) suchen engagierte
Kinderfrau, die zeitlich flexibel,
2–3 Vormittage und 2–3 Abende,
Nähe Westpark, 2 Kinder, ab
Mai betreut. Der Junge ist
Diabetiker und braucht eine
besondere Betreuung.
Tel.: 089/54379004
Fr. Heidt

C

Wegen einer plötzlichen
Vakanz sucht das
MALLORCA MAGAZIN, die
deutsche Wochenzeitung
auf Mallorca, möglichst
per sofort versierten
LOKALREDAKTEUR
mit perfekten
Spanischkenntnissen
und mehrjähriger
Berufserfahrung
(andere Bewerbungen
zwecklos). Eilangebote
an: MALLORCA MAGAZIN,
Redaktionsdirektion,
Apartado de Correos
304, E- 07012 Palma
de Mallorca, Fax:
003471/714533

D

Suche lebenslustigen Koch,
ab April, für Café-Restaurant
in Prenzlau/Brandenburg, der
feine Fisch- und vegetarische
Gerichte mit Hingabe kocht.
Bewerbung bitte unter
Chiffre: ZS2073098 an SZ

E

Wir suchen zum sofortigen Eintritt rüstigen Rentner / Frührentner, auch
weiblich, als Nachtportier. Arbeitszeit nach Vereinbarung.
Bewerbungen bitte an: Hotel Mayer, Augsburger Str. 45, 82110
München-Germering. Tel.: 089/844071

Here are the answers:

a Office work for student (in a PR agency); **b** a child minder; **c** a
magazine editor; **d** a cook; **e** a night porter.

2 WELCHES STELLENANGEBOT IST ES?

Lesen Sie die folgenden Sätze und finden Sie heraus, welcher Satz
zu welchem Stellenangebot passt.

Beispiel Man sucht jemanden ab April. Er muss Spaß am Leben haben. D

a Wenn Sie diesen Job nehmen, müssen Sie nachts arbeiten. ___

b Hier arbeiten Sie für ein deutschsprachiges Magazin, aber Sie müssen auch Spanisch sprechen. ___

c Bei diesem Job müssen Sie zwei Kinder betreuen. Die Eltern spielen bei der Bayerischen Staatsoper. ___

d Wenn Sie vegetarisch kochen können, gefällt Ihnen vielleicht dieser Job. ___

e Wenn Sie in einem südlichen europäischen Land arbeiten wollen, passt Ihnen vielleicht dieser Job. ___

f Wenn Sie Englisch sprechen, mit einem Computer arbeiten können und Studentin sind, passt Ihnen dieser Teilzeitjob. ___

die Kenntnis (-se) *knowledge, skill(s)*
die Erfahrung (-en) *experience*
die Bewerbung (-en) *application*
engagiert *committed*
betreuen *to look after, to care for*
versiert *well versed*
der Redakteur (-) / die -in (nen) *editor*
zwecklos *pointless*
lebenslustig *full of the joys of life*
die Hingabe *devotion, dedication*
sofort *immediately*
der Eintritt (-e) *entrance, start*
rüstig *sprightly*
der Frührentner (-) / die -rentnerin (nen) *someone who has taken early retirement*
der Teilzeitjob (-s) *part-time job*

QUICK VOCAB

3 ORDNEN SIE ZU

Wie heißen die Sätze auf Englisch?

a Er braucht eine besondere Betreuung.

You have to have office experience.

b Arbeitszeit nach Vereinbarung.

Because of a sudden vacancy.

c Sie müssen Büroerfahrung haben.

To start immediately.

d Andere Bewerbungen zwecklos.

He needs special care.

e Zum sofortigen Eintritt.

Other applications (are) pointless.

f Wegen einer plötzlichen Vakanz.

Working hours by agreement.

4 WER BEWIRBT SICH UM WELCHE STELLE?

Who is applying for which job? Match these people with the most suitable job in the advertisements in **Übung 1** above.

a Bernd Schulte, 63, ist noch sehr fit. Er möchte einen Teilzeitjob haben und vielleicht nachts arbeiten.

b Bettina Hartmann, 24, ist Studentin und muss nebenbei Geld verdienen. Sie spricht sehr gut Englisch und hat schon in verschiedenen Büros gearbeitet.

c Martina Wustermann, 35, hat jahrelang bei Lokalzeitungen als Redakteurin gearbeitet. Sie spricht mehrere Fremdsprachen (Englisch, Französisch, Spanisch) und möchte jetzt im Ausland arbeiten.

d Jochen Kinsky, 25, hat gerade eine Kochlehre beendet. Er ist Vegetarier und möchte für ein Restaurant in der Nähe von Berlin arbeiten.

e Silke Zehnder, 28, interessiert sich für Kinder. Sie möchte einen Teilzeitjob, der ihr Zeit für ihre Hobbys lässt. Sie geht auch gern mal ins Konzert.

CVs

5 *LEBENSLAUF I: PETER FRANKENTHAL*

Lesen Sie die den Lebenslauf von Peter Frankenthal.

der Werdegang (¨e) *development, career*
die Grundschule (-n) *primary school*
der Realschulabschluss (¨e) *roughly equivalent to GCSE in the UK*
die Lehre (-n) *apprenticeship*
der Bankkaufmann (¨er) *qualified bank clerk*
der Filialleiter (-) / die -in (nen) *branch manager*
fließend *fluent*

Richtig oder falsch? Korrigieren Sie die falschen Aussagen.

a Herr Frankenthal ist ledig.

b Er ist in Frankfurt geboren.

c In Frankfurt hat er auch seinen Realschulabschluss gemacht.

d Nach der Schule hat er gleich eine Lehre gemacht.

e Seinen ersten Job hatte er bei der Commerzbank.

f Von 1999 bis 2008 hat er wieder in Frankfurt gearbeitet.

g Seit 2008 ist er Filialleiter.

Insight: Lebensläufe CVs

The tabular format illustrated in Peter Frankenthal's CV is very widely used in Germany. It is common practice in German CVs to include the school you went to and the qualifications you gained.

The school system in Germany varies from **Land** to **Land**, but in general all pupils go to the **Grundschule** when they are about six, and then four years later, according to their attainment / abilities, transfer to one of various types of schools, where they do different courses and attend for different lengths of time: the **Hauptschule**, a bit like the British Secondary Modern School, where courses lead to the **Hauptschulabschluss**; the **Realschule**, leading to the **Realschulabschluss**, a bit like the GCSE qualifications in Britain; and the **Gymnasium** or grammar school, leading to the **Abitur**, which is roughly comparable to A-Levels in the UK or the High School Diploma in the US.

In some **Länder** all three types of secondary school are combined under one roof in what is known as the **Gesamtschule** (comprehensive school).

6 LESEN UND LERNEN

Der Werdegang Peter Frankenthals. This time Peter has written out in full the details of his career. Read through his CV and underline all the verbs which you think are in the past tense. Don't worry if you find this difficult – you can check your answers on the next page.

Ich bin am 29. Juli 1976 in Frankfurt am Main geboren.
Von 1982 bis 1986 ging ich in die Grundschule in Frankfurt.
Danach wechselte ich auf die Schiller-Schule in Offenbach.
1992 machte ich dort den Realschulabschluss.

Von 1992 bis 1995 machte ich eine Bank-Lehre bei der
Dresdner Bank in Offenbach. Anschließend bekam ich eine
feste Stellung als Bankkaufmann bei der gleichen Bank, wo
ich dann bis 1999 arbeitete.

1999 wechselte ich auf die Commerzbank in Frankfurt, wo
ich bis 2008 als Bankkaufmann tätig war. Von 1999 bis 2008
besuchte ich auch Sprachkurse in Englisch und Französisch.

Seit 2008 bin ich Filialleiter bei der Commerzbank in Mainz-
Süd.

7 VERBEN

Here are the simple past tense verbs that you might have
underlined in Peter's CV. Can you figure out what the infinitive of
these verbs might be?

Beispiel ging ← gehen

a wechselte ← _____
b machte   ← _____
c bekam   ← _____
d arbeitete ← _____
e war   ← _____
f besuchte ← _____

In the **SPRACHINFO** you will learn more about these forms.

SPRACHINFO
THE SIMPLE PAST TENSE

Most of the verbs in **Übung 6** are in the simple past form. This form is commonly used in German when people *write* about the past, whereas the present perfect tense is used more for the *spoken* language.

In Unit 20 you met the simple past tense forms of **sein, haben** and of **modal verbs,** which can be used in both the spoken and the written language.

Here is an overview of how you form the simple past tense:

- ▶ *regular verbs (such as* **machen** → **machte, besuchen** → **besuchte***) add a* **-t** *plus the relevant ending to their stem (see table below).*
- ▶ *irregular verbs (such as* **gehen** → **ging, bekommen** → **bekam***) usually change either their vowel or sometimes their whole stem and don't add endings in the* **ich** *and* **er/sie/es** *form.*

	regular verbs		irregular verbs	
	mach-en	besuch-en	geh-en	bekomm-en
ich	mach**te**	besuch**te**	ging	bekam
du	mach**test**	besuch**test**	ging**st**	bekam**st**
Sie	mach**ten**	besuch**ten**	ging**en**	bekam**en**
er/sie/es	mach**te**	besuch**te**	ging	bekam
wir	mach**ten**	besuch**ten**	ging**en**	bekam**en**
ihr	mach**tet**	besuch**tet**	ging**t**	bekam**t**
Sie/sie	mach**ten**	besuch**ten**	ging**en**	bekam**en**

For more information about the simple past tense, see the **Grammar** section.

8 LEBENSLAUF (II): CLAUDIA SCHULTE

◀) **CD 2, TR 37**

Claudia Schulte, von Beruf Journalistin, erzählt über ihr Leben.
Hören Sie zu und versuchen Sie die Fragen zu beantworten:

a In welchem Jahr ist sie geboren?
b Was machte sie nach der Schule?
c Wann machte sie ihr Praktikum?
d Wo studierte sie?
e Wie lange arbeitete sie bei der *Tageszeitung*?
f Seit wann arbeitet sie beim *Spiegel*?

Lesen Sie jetzt den Lebenslauf von Claudia Schulte. Hatten Sie
recht?

LEBENSLAUF

Name:	Claudia Schulte
geboren:	1.6.1978 in Bremen
Nationalität:	deutsch
Familienstand:	ledig
Wohnort:	Hamburg

Werdegang

1984–1988	Grundschule in Bremen
1998–1997	Heinrich-Heine-Gymnasium in Bremen Abschluss: Abitur
1997–1998	Reisen durch Asien
1998–1999	Praktikum bei der Hamburger Zeitung
1999–2004	Studium der Journalistik an der Universität Hamburg Abschluss: M.A. phil.
2004–2007	Journalistin bei der Tageszeitung in Berlin
seit 2007	Journalistin bei Der Spiegel in Hamburg

Besondere Kenntnisse
Englisch, Spanisch und Französisch fließend

9 FRAU SCHULTE SCHREIBT IHREN LEBENSLAUF

Helfen Sie ihr. Setzen Sie die fehlenden Wörter ein.

....

**arbeitete   ging   machte   studierte   wechselte
reiste   machte   zog   machte**

....

Ich bin am 1. Juni 1978 in Bremen geboren. Von 1984 bis 1988 _____ ich in die Grundschule in Bremen. Danach _____ ich auf das Heinrich-Heine-Gymnasium. 1997 _____ ich mein Abitur. Nach der Schule _____ ich durch Asien.

Von 1998 bis 1999 _____ ich ein Praktikum bei der *Hamburger Zeitung*.

Anschließend _____ ich Journalistik an der Universität Hamburg und 2004 _____ ich meinen Abschluss.

Nach dem Studium _____ ich von 2004 bis 2007 bei der *Tageszeitung* in Berlin.

2007 _____ ich wieder nach Hamburg und ich arbeite seitdem beim Nachrichtenmagazin *Der Spiegel*.

10 UND IHR LEBENSLAUF?

Schreiben Sie einen tabellarischen Lebenslauf wie Herr Frankenthal oder Frau Schulte (**Übung 5** and **8**).

Schreiben Sie dann einen Lebenslauf wie Frau Schulte (**Übung 9**).

Grammar

1 SAYING THE YEARS IN GERMAN

Here are a few examples of how you say the years in German:

> 1820 *achtzehnhundertzwanzig*
> 1976 *neunzehnhundertsechsundsiebzig*
> 2008 *zweitausend(und)acht*

Note that Germans usually don't use the preposition **in** when referring to years: **Peter ist 1989 geboren.** You could say **im Jahre** but this is normally only used in a formal context: **Im Jahre 1786 ist Goethe nach Italien gereist.**

2 ZAHLEN (WIEDERHOLUNG)

Numbers can be difficult to understand and produce, particularly when they are said quickly. Here is a reminder of a few points about German numbers.

- ▶ *The numbers 21–99 are 'back-to-front' compared with English numbers: 21 **einundzwanzig**, 37 **siebenunddreißig**, 98 **achtundneunzig***
- ▶ *The numbers 101–120 tend not to have an **und** to link them together: 101 **hunderteins**, 111 **hundertelf**, 120 **hundertzwanzig***

▶ *All numbers up to one million are written all as one word:*
  2 843 *zweitausendachthundertdreiundvierzig*
  10 962 *zehntausendneunhundertzweiundsechzig*

▶ *Numbers after a million are written as follows:*
  4 800 543 *vier Millionen achthunderttausendfünfhundert-*
  dreiundvierzig

Note that a comma is used in German where a decimal point
would be used in English:

  81,5 *Millionen. Say: einundachtzig Komma fünf Millionen*

3 SIMPLE PAST TENSE

In the **SPRACHINFO** earlier in this unit, you learned about the
various forms of the simple past tense. There are, however, still a
couple of points to note.

▶ **Regular verbs:** *when the stem of an infinitive ends in a* -d, -t *or*
  -gn, *an extra* -e- *is needed before the endings are added:*
  antworten → ich antwortete
  reden → ich redete
  begegnen (to meet) → ich begegnete

▶ **Irregular verbs:** *an extra* -e- *is needed to 'oil the works' in the*
  du *and* ihr *forms when the* ich *form ends in a* -t *or a* -d:
  raten (to advise) → ich riet, du rietest, ihr rietet
  finden → ich fand, du fandest, ihr fandet

Note that a number of verbs – so-called mixed verbs – change their
vowel, but have the -t endings like the regular verbs, e.g. **bringen** →
brachte which is rather like the English *bring → brought.*

Here is a reminder of how regular and irregular verbs form their simple past tense:

Regular verbs spielen		Irregular verbs gehen	
ich spielte	**-te**	ich ging	**-**
du spieltest	**-test**	du gingst	**-(e)st**
Sie spielten	**-ten**	Sie gingen	**-en**
er, sie, es spielte	**-te**	er, sie, es ging	**-**
wir spielten	**-ten**	wir gingen	**-en**
ihr spieltet	**-tet**	ihr gingt	**-(e)t**
Sie spielten	**-ten**	Sie gingen	**-en**
sie spielten	**-ten**	sie gingen	**-en**

Usage: you already know that the simple past tense is more often found in the written language than in the spoken language. This is because written language tends to be more formal than spoken language and the simple past tense does have a more formal flavour to it. A chatty letter to a friend, for instance, might well be written in the perfect tense which would be better suited to the less formal language.

Generally speaking, the simple past tense is mainly used in narrative fiction and non-fiction and in newspaper reporting. You will for instance find that German fairy tales, such as those of the Brothers Grimm, are all in the past simple.

But bear in mind that these are general rules. You will certainly find examples that seem to contradict what we have said here. For instance, the first sentence in newspaper reports is usually in the perfect tense, the rest is then in the simple past. Furthermore, it is sometimes claimed that the simple past tense is used in the ordinary spoken language more frequently in Northern Germany than it is in the South.

Tip: For regular verbs it is fairly easy to predict the forms. The best way to learn the irregular verb forms is probably to work with verb lists which you can find in any good dictionary and at the end of this book.

Try to learn the most commonly used verbs by heart and practise them as much as you can – you will soon find that you are much more confident when you are dealing with the simple past tense.

TESTING YOURSELF

1 *Here is an adapted extract from the fairy tale* **Schneewittchen** *(Snow White). Complete the story by using the appropriate verb from the box.*

....

| ging | trank | war | dachte | schlief | sah |
| blieb | standen | gab | war | aß | legte | stand |

....

Da **a** _____ *das Mädchen ein kleines Häuschen und*
b _____ *hinein. In dem Haus* **c** _____ *alles klein: da*
d _____ *ein Tisch mit sieben kleinen Tellern (plates).*
Außerdem **e** _____ *es sieben Messer (knives) und Gabeln*
(forks) und sieben Becher. An der Wand **f** _____ *sieben*
Betten. Schneewittchen **g** _____ *von jedem Teller ein wenig*
Gemüse und Brot und **h** _____ *aus jedem Becher einen*
Tropfen Wein. Dann **i** _____ *es sich in ein Bett. Es*
j _____ *im Bett liegen,* **k** _____ *an den lieben Gott und*
l _____ *ein.*

2 **Das Leben von Heinrich Böll.**

Schreiben Sie einen Lebenslauf des Schriftstellers Heinrich Böll. *Look back at* **Unit 14, Übung 7,** *and use the information given to write a report of the famous German author in the past simple. For some irregular verbs you might need to look up the correct forms in the list at the end of the book. Note that you need to make no changes to the first sentence:*

a *1917 ist Heinrich Böll am 21. Dezember in Köln geboren.*
b *Von 1924 bis 1928 besuchte er die Volksschule Köln-Raderthal.*

Now that you have completed Unit 22, can you: | tick

1 read and understand job adverts? ☐

2 write a basic CV in German in tabular format? ☐

3 form the past simple tense of regular and irregular verbs? ☐

23

Geschichte und Allgemeinwissen
History and general knowledge

In this unit you will learn
- *how to talk about German-speaking countries*
- *how to talk about historical events*

Language points
- *subordinate clauses (with* dass*)*
- *passive*

Deutschland, Österreich und die Schweiz

1 LESEN UND LERNEN

Ein Reporter fragt Leute über Deutschland, Österreich und die Schweiz. Lesen Sie die Interviews. Was passiert mit den Verben (**hat, kommt, liegt**), wenn die Leute **dass** benutzen?

QUICK VOCAB

meinen *to think, to mean*
glauben *to believe*
denken *to think*
keine Ahnung *no idea*

SPRACHINFO

USING **DASS** (*THAT*)

The word **dass** can be useful when you want to introduce an opinion in German. It is very similar to *that* in English, except that

dass sends the verb to the end of the sentence or clause, something you probably figured out yourself from the sentences in **Übung 1**:

> *Ich denke,* **dass** *St. Moritz in der Schweiz* liegt.

When you use **dass** with the perfect tense, the **haben** or **sein** verb goes right at the end:

> *Ich glaube,* **dass** *Frau Schulte in Hamburg studiert* hat.

Note that the **dass** part of the sentence starts with a comma.

You can leave out the word **dass** if you want to. The verb then comes earlier in the sentence:

> *Ich denke, St. Moritz* liegt *in der Schweiz.*

> *Ich glaube, Frau Schulte* hat *in Hamburg studiert.*

> *Ich glaube, Frau Schulte* ist *nach dem Abitur durch Asien gereist.*

2 ÜBEN SIE

Sagen Sie es anders und benutzen Sie **dass**.

Beispiel *Ich denke, viele Touristen fahren nach Heidelberg.* →
Ich denke, **dass** *viele Touristen nach Heidelberg* fahren.

a Ich meine, Frankfurt ist das Finanzzentrum von Deutschland.
b Ich glaube, es gibt in Wien viele alte Kaffeehäuser.
c Ich denke, München ist eine sehr schöne Stadt.
d Ich glaube, die Schweizer haben viel Humor.
e Ich denke, die Deutschen trinken viel Bier.
f Ich meine, Deutschland ist ein sehr interessantes Land.

3 HABEN SIE ES GEWUSST?

Können Sie die folgenden Fragen beantworten? Before you read the text, try to answer the following questions using **dass** and the verbs from the previous exercises – **meinen, denken, glauben**. If you are absolutely sure, you can say **Ich bin sicher, dass ...** If you don't have any idea, use **Keine Ahnung** *no idea*.

> **Beispiel** *Welches ist die größte Stadt in Deutschland?*

> → *Ich bin sicher, dass Berlin die größte Stadt in Deutschland ist.*

> → *Ich glaube, dass Berlin die größte Stadt in Deutschland ist.*

> → *Keine Ahnung.*

Now go through all the questions saying the answers out loud, so that you get the feel of the verb coming at the end of the **dass** clause.

a Welches Land ist größer: Österreich oder die Schweiz?
b Wie heißt die Hauptstadt der Schweiz?
c Wie viele offizielle Sprachen gibt es in der Schweiz?
d Wie viele Städte kennen Sie in Österreich?
e Wer ist in Salzburg geboren?
f Wie viele Einwohner hat die Bundesrepublik Deutschland?
g Wie heißt die Hauptstadt von Deutschland?
h Welche Stadt ist größer: Hamburg oder München?
i In welcher Stadt findet das Oktoberfest statt?
j Welche Stadt in Deutschland ist am multikulturellsten?

Lesen Sie jetzt den Lesetext 'Deutschland, Österreich und die Schweiz' und überprüfen Sie Ihre Antworten. Versuchen Sie, die Vokabeln aus dem Kontext zu verstehen.

Deutschland, Österreich und die Schweiz

Deutschland, Österreich und die Schweiz – das sind die drei Länder, wo man Deutsch als Muttersprache spricht. Aber es gibt auch noch einige andere Regionen, wo die Leute Deutsch sprechen, zum Beispiel in Belgien an der Grenze mit Deutschland, in Luxemburg, im Fürstentum Liechtenstein und in Südtirol, Italien. Deutschsprachige Minderheiten findet man auch in Kanada, den USA, Rumänien, und sogar in Namibia! Insgesamt sprechen etwa 110 Millionen Deutsch als Muttersprache.

Von den drei Ländern ist die Schweiz das kleinste. Sie umfasst 41 293 km^2 und hat 7,5 Millionen Einwohner. Die Hauptstadt ist Bern, nicht Zürich, aber Zürich ist die größte Stadt mit 367 000 Einwohnern. Interessant ist, dass man in der Schweiz vier Sprachen spricht: Deutsch, Französisch, Italienisch und Räteromanisch. Bekannt ist die Schweiz für ihre Uhren, Arzneimittel und für die Berge – ideal für einen Wanderurlaub im Sommer und einen Skiurlaub im Winter.

Österreich ist etwa doppelt so groß wie die Schweiz. Österreich hat 8,3 Millionen Einwohner und eine Fläche von 83 853 km^2. Die Hauptstadt ist Wien, mit 2,1 Millionen Einwohnern und Sehenswürdigkeiten wie das Schloss Schönbrunn, die Hofburg oder das Sigmund-Freud-Haus. Andere Städte in Österreich sind Linz, Graz, Innsbruck und Salzburg. Salzburg ist die Geburtsstadt von Wolfgang Amadeus Mozart und viele Leute besuchen die Stadt im Sommer. Sehr beliebt sind die Mozart-Kugeln, eine Süßigkeit aus Marzipan.

Seit der Wiedervereinigung 1990 umfasst die Bundesrepublik Deutschland ingesamt 356 974 km^2 und hat 82,4 Millionen Einwohner. Seit dem 3. Oktober 1990 ist Berlin die neue Hauptstadt. Davor war es Bonn für die Bundesrepublik und Ost-Berlin für die ehemalige DDR (Deutsche Demokratische Republik).

Berlin ist auch die größte Stadt in Deutschland, jetzt mit 3,6 Millionen Einwohnern.

Nach Berlin ist Hamburg die zweitgrößte Stadt mit 1,75 Millionen Einwohnern vor München mit 1,33 Millionen. München ist aber von allen Städten am beliebtesten. Die meisten Deutschen wollen hier leben, denn das Wetter ist meistens schön im Sommer und im Winter sind die Alpen nicht weit. Vielleicht gehen aber auch viele Leute gern in die Biergärten oder aufs Oktoberfest.

Deutschland ist aber auch schon längst eine multikulturelle Gesellschaft: hier leben insgesamt 7,28 Millionen Ausländer, die meisten aus der Türkei (rund 2 Millionen), aber auch Menschen aus dem früheren Jugoslawien, Griechenland, Spanien, Italien, Irland und aus der ehemaligen Sowjetunion. Unter den Ausländern gibt es auch Asylanten aus Ländern wie Afghanistan, Sri Lanka, dem Irak, dem Iran usw. Prozentual hat Frankfurt am Main mit 27 Prozent die meisten Ausländer und ist am multikulturellsten.

4 FAKTEN ÜBER DEUTSCHLAND, ÖSTERREICH UND DIE SCHWEIZ

die Muttersprache (-n) *mother tongue*
die Grenze (-n) *border*
das Fürstentum (¨er) *principality*
die Minderheit (-en) *minority*
insgesamt *in total*
umfassen *to comprise*
die Fläche (-n) *area*
km² = der Quadratkilometer (-) *square metre*
bekannt *famous, well known*
das Arzneimittel (-) *medicine*
die Sehenswürdigkeit (-en) *sight (worth seeing)*
beliebt *popular*
die Wiedervereinigung *reunification*
ehemalig *former*
die Gesellschaft (-en) *society*
der Ausländer (-) *foreigner*
der Asylant (-en) *asylum-seeker*

Ordnen Sie zu! Put the following features into the correct column in the chart below.

- **Wiedervereinigung**
- **Mozart-Kugeln**
- **Uhren**
- **82,4 Millionen Einwohner**
- **Oktoberfest**
- **vier Sprachen**
- **neue Hauptstadt**
- **7,28 Millionen Einwohner**
- **Sigmund-Freud-Haus**
- **Biergärten**
- **Arzneimittel**
- **Schloss Schönbrunn**
- **viele Leute aus der Türkei**
- **8,3 Millionen Einwohner**
- **multikulturelle Gesellschaft**
- **etwa doppelt so groß wie die Schweiz**

Schweiz	Österreich	Deutschland
Uhren	Sigmund-Freud-Haus	Wiedervereinigung
_____	_____	_____
_____	_____	_____
_____	_____	_____
_____	_____	_____
_____	_____	_____

5 FINDEN SIE DIE ZAHLEN

Beispiel Fläche der Bundesrepublik Deutschland: 356 974 km²

a Fläche von Österreich: ___
b Fläche der Schweiz: ___
c Einwohnerzahl von Deutschland: ___
d Einwohnerzahl von Österreich: ___
e Einwohnerzahl der Schweiz: ___
f Deutsche Wiedervereinigung: ___
g Seit wann Berlin Hauptstadt ist: ___
h Ausländeranteil in Frankfurt: ___%

History

6 DIE GESCHICHTE DEUTSCHLANDS NACH 1945

1945 wird der 2. Weltkrieg beendet. Deutschland wird in vier Zonen geteilt.

1949 wird in den drei Westzonen die Bundesrepublik Deutschland gegründet. In der Ostzone wird die Deutsche Demokratische Republik gegründet.

1961 wird die Berliner Mauer gebaut.

1989 wird die innerdeutsche Grenze und die Berliner Mauer geöffnet.

1990 wird Deutschland offiziell wiedervereinigt. Berlin wird als neue Hauptstadt gewählt.

2005 wird Angela Merkel als erste Frau zur Bundeskanzlerin gewählt.

der Weltkrieg (-e) *World War*
teilen *to divide*
gründen *to establish, to found*
die Berliner Mauer *Berlin Wall*
bauen *to build*
die innerdeutsche Grenze *the border between the two Germanies*
wiedervereinigt *reunited*
wählen *elected, chosen*
Bundeskanzler(-)/-in (-nen) *Federal Chancellor*

SPRACHINFO

THE PASSIVE VOICE

There are usually two ways of looking at an action. The sentence *The cat ate the mouse* is said to be in the *active voice*, whereas *The mouse was eaten by the cat* is in the *passive voice*.

In **6 Die Geschichte Deutschlands nach 1945** above, there are several examples of the present passive. For instance:

> 1945 *wird der 2. Weltkrieg beendet.*
> *Deutschland wird in vier Zonen geteilt.*

How many more examples can you spot? You should be able to find seven more.

The passive is also frequently used in the past, for instance to talk about historical events and inventions.

In German the passive is constructed by using the verb **werden** together with the *past participle* of the main verb.

Present passive
1945 **wird** Deutschland in vier Zonen **geteilt**. *In 1945 Germany **is divided** into four zones.*

Simple past passive
Am 13. August 1961 **wurde** die Berliner Mauer **gebaut**. *On 13 August 1961 the Berlin Wall **was built**.*

Present perfect passive
1990 **ist** Berlin wieder als Hauptstadt **gewählt worden**. *In 1990 Berlin **was** again **chosen** as the capital city.*

7 WAS PASSIERTE AUSSERDEM IN DER WELT?

Benutzen Sie das Passiv und schreiben Sie die Sätze **a-f** um.

Beispiele 1949 Mehrere westliche Staaten gründeten die NATO →
1949 **wurde** die NATO von mehreren westlichen Staaten **gegründet**.
1963 ermordete man John F. Kennedy →
1963 **wurde** John F. Kennedy **ermordet**.

a 1969 betrat zum ersten Mal ein Mensch den Mond. →

b 1981 ermordete man John Lennon. →

c 1990 entließ man Nelson Mandela nach 27 Jahren aus der Haft. →

d 2002 führte man in Europa den Euro als neue Währung ein. →

e 2005 zerstörte Hurrikan Katrina New Orleans. →

f 2009 wählte man Barack Obama zum Präsidenten der USA. →

Versuchen Sie, die Wörter aus dem Kontext zu verstehen. Wenn Sie Hilfe brauchen, hier ist eine Liste!

ermorden *to murder, to assassinate*
betreten *here: to walk on*
der Mond *the moon*
entlassen *to release*
die Haft *detention, custody*
ein|führen *to introduce*
die Währung (-en) *currency*
zerstören *to destroy*
erweitern *to expand*
das Mitgliedsland (¨er) *member country*

SPRACHINFO
THE GENITIVE IN USE

It is quite common in German to use genitive constructions when referring to historical events:

die Gründung der Bundesrepublik	*the foundation of the Federal Republic*
der Bau der Mauer	*the building of the Wall*
die Wiedervereinigung Deutschlands	*the reunification of Germany*

8 TESTEN SIE IHR ALLGEMEINWISSEN

Wissen Sie die Antworten? Create appropriate sentences from these components and put your general knowledge to the test.

Beispiel *Die Dampfmaschine wurde von James Watt erfunden.*

a	Die neunte Symphonie		James Watt	geschrieben
b	Die Fußballweltmeisterschaft		Alexander Fleming	gesungen
	1966		Ludwig van	gemalt
c	Die Dampfmaschine	wurde	Beethoven	komponiert
d	‚Hamlet‘	von	England	erfunden
e	‚Guernica‘		Helen Mirren	gespielt
f	Das Penizillin		Pablo Picasso	gewonnen
g	‚Waterloo‘		William Shakespeare	entdeckt
h	Die Queen		Abba	

malen *to paint*
entdecken *to discover*
erfinden *to invent*

VOCAB

9 EIN RADIOPROGRAMM

◀) **CD 2, TR 38**

Hören Sie das folgende Radioprogramm über Johann Wolfgang von Goethe und beantworten Sie die Fragen.

berühmt *famous*
übersetzen *to translate*
die Leiden *sorrows*
benennen *to name*
veröffentlichen *to publish*
die Seele (-n) *soul*
der Teufel (-) *devil*

QUICK VOCAB

i Richtig oder falsch? Korrigieren Sie die falschen Aussagen.

a Goethe wurde 1747 in Weimar geboren.

b Er studierte in Leipzig und Straßburg.

c Mit seiner Novelle ‚Die Leiden des jungen Werther' wurde er in Europa bekannt.

d 1780 ging er nach Weimar.

e 1786 reiste er für zwei Jahren nach Italien und Griechenland.

f ‚Faust' ist eines seiner wichtigsten Werke.

g Das Goethe-Institut wurde nach seinem Sohn benannt.

ii Hören Sie die Audioaufnahme noch einmal an und ergänzen Sie dann die Sätze.

a Johann Wolfgang von Goethe wurde… .

b Er studierte … .

c In ganz Europa berühmt wurde er durch … .

c 1775 ging er … .

e 1786 reiste Goethe … .

f 1808 erschien … .

g Ein Philosoph verkauft seine Seele … .

h 1832 starb er … .

i Seine Werke wurden … .

j Das Goethe-Institut wurde … .

10 ROLLENSPIEL: UND JETZT SIE!

Now you can show off your knowledge in this TV quiz show!
Schreiben Sie zuerst Ihre Antworten und beantworten Sie dann die
Fragen auf der Audioaufnahme.

🎧 CD 2, TR 39

Frage	Wissen Sie denn, wie viele offizielle Sprachen in der Schweiz gesprochen werden?
Sie	*Say yes … and say how many languages are spoken in Switzerland.*
Frage	Wann wurde die Bundesrepublik Deutschland gegründet?
Sie	*Say the Federal Republic of Germany was founded in … .*
Frage	Und in welchem Jahr wurde die Berliner Mauer gebaut?
Sie	*Say the Berlin Wall was built in … .*
Frage	Ausgezeichnet. Aber an welchem Tag wurde Deutschland offiziell wiedervereinigt?
Sie	*Say when Germany was reunited.*
Frage	Aber wissen Sie auch, von wem ‚Faust' geschrieben wurde?
Sie	*Say who 'Faust' was written by.*
Frage	Phänomenal! Aber Sie wissen bestimmt nicht, in welchem Jahr es veröffentlicht wurde.
Sie	*Say, of course, and say when it was published.*
Frage	Unglaublich! Aber wissen Sie auch, welche Institution nach Goethe benannt wurde?
Sie	*Say, of course. The Goethe-Institut was named after him.*

Pronunciation

At the end of a word or syllable the letter **d** in German is pronounced more like an English **t:**

> *Abend, Freund, Geld, Fahrrad, Land*
> *abendlich, Freundschaft, Geldschein, Radfahrer, Landschaft*

When the **d** is no longer at the end of the word or syllable it is pronounced as an English **d:**

> *Abende, Freunde, Gelder, Fahrräder, Länder*

How would you pronounce these words?
Lied, Lieder, Bad, Bäder, Hund, Hunde.

Grammar

1 *DASS*

In this unit you have learned that **dass** can be used to introduce thoughts and opinions. It can also be used to report what someone has said:

Er hat gesagt, dass Schwarzenegger aus Österreich kommt.　　*He said, that Schwarzenegger comes from Austria.*

Dass can also be used to give an indirect command:

Bitte sag ihm, dass er mich anrufen soll.　　*Please tell him to phone me (Lit. that he should phone me).*

Don't forget that the verb in the **dass** part of the sentences is in the final position:

Ich denke, dass *Hamburg in Deutschland* liegt.

When you use **dass** with the present perfect tense or with a modal verb, **haben** or **sein** or the modal verb goes to the very end:

Sie sagt, dass sie bei VW gearbeitet **hat.**
Er sagt, dass er mehr Sport treiben **will.**

2 CONJUNCTIONS

Words like *that, when, because, although* which join two sentences or clauses together are known as conjunctions:

I am learning German. I often go to Germany. →
I am learning German because I often go to Germany.

In German **dass** and **wenn** are examples of conjunctions that change the word order, i.e. the verb is sent to the end of the sentence. Other examples are **weil** (*because*) and **obwohl** (*although*):

Ich lerne Deutsch, weil *ich oft nach Deutschland* fahre.

Ich fahre oft nach Italien, obwohl *ich kein Wort Italienisch* spreche.

3 THE PASSIVE VOICE

As you saw earlier in this unit, most actions can be expressed either in the active voice or in the passive voice:

Alexander Fleming endeckte 1928 das Penizillin.
Das Penizillin wurde 1928 von Alexander Fleming endeckt.

Both sentences have more or less the same meaning, but it is possible in most passive sentences to omit the agent, the initiator of the action:

Das Penizillin wurde 1928 entdeckt.

This structure therefore lends itself particularly well to:

a scientific and technical processes:

Die Lösung wird in einem Reagenzglas geheizt.	*The solution is heated in a test tube.*
Die Bremsen werden in der Werkstatt geprüft.	*The brakes are tested in the workshop.*

b historical events:

Die Bundesrepublik Deutschland wurde 1949 gegründet.

Here is an overview of how you form the passive in the present tense, the simple past tense and the present perfect tense:

▶ *Present tense –* **werden** *(present tense) + past participle of main verb:*

Der Text *wird* in unserem Büro *übersetzt*.	*The text is being translated in our office.*
In der Schweiz *werden* vier Sprachen *gesprochen*.	*In Switzerland four languages are spoken.*

As a reference here are all present tense forms of **werden**:

ich werde	*wir werden*
du wirst	*ihr werdet*
Sie werden	*Sie werden*
er / sie / es wird	*sie werden*

▶ *Simple past tense* – **wurden** *(simple past)* + *past participle of main verb:*

Die Berliner Mauer *wurde*   *The Berlin Wall was built in 1961.*
1961 *gebaut*.

Wann *wurden* diese Bücher   *When were these books written?*
***geschrieben*?**

As a reference here are all simple past forms of **werden:**

ich wurde	*wir wurden*
du wurdest	*ihr wurdet*
Sie wurden	*Sie wurden*
er / sie / es wurde	*sie wurden*

▶ *Present perfect tense* – **worden** + *past participle:*

Die D-Mark *ist* 1948 *eingeführt*   *The D-Mark was introduced in*
***worden*.**   *1948.*

Nach dem 2. Weltkrieg *sind*   *After the Second World War many*
viele neue Wohnungen   *new dwellings were built.*
***gebaut worden*.**

Note that when **werden** is not used in a passive structure it can mean to become:

Er möchte Rennfahrer werden.   *He wants to become a racing driver.*

TESTING YOURSELF

1 Warum lernen die Leute Deutsch? Benutzen Sie *weil*. Nicht vergessen – das Verb geht ans Ende.

Beispiel Sharon – ihr Partner kommt aus Zürich. → Sharon lernt Deutsch, weil ihr Partner aus Zürich kommt.

a *Paul – er fährt oft geschäftlich nach Frankfurt. → Paul lernt Deutsch, weil er _____.*

b *Susanna – sie liebt die Musik von Mozart → Susanna lernt Deutsch, weil _____ .*

c *Richard – er lernt gern Sprachen. → Richard lernt Deutsch, weil _____ .*

d *Carlo – es ist gut für seine Karriere. → _____ .*

e *Myriam – sie findet die deutsche Sprache sehr schön. →*
_____ .

f *Deborah – sie mag Berlin → _____ .*

Und Sie? Warum lernen Sie Deutsch? Schreiben Sie.

2 Deutschland, Österreich und die Schweiz. Ergänzen Sie den Text.

Bekannt   Hauptstadt   Regionen   Städte
~~Muttersprache~~   Arzneimittel   Gesellschaft
Einwohner   Wiedervereinigung   Sehenswürdigkeiten
Ausländer   Ländern

In Deutschland, Österreich und der deutschsprachigen Schweiz spricht man Deutsch als **a** *Muttersprache.*

Man spricht Deutsch aber auch in anderen **b** *_____, zum Beispiel in Südtirol, Italien.*

Von den drei c _____ ist die Schweiz am kleinsten. Die
d _____ *ist Bern.* **e** _____ *ist die Schweiz für ihre Berge,*
Uhren und **f** _____.

Österreich hat 8,3 Millionen **g** _____ . *Die Hauptstadt*
ist Wien. Dort gibt es viele **h** _____, *wie zum Beispiel das*
Schloss Schönbrunn oder die Hofburg.

Seit der **i** _____1989 ist Berlin die Hauptstadt von*
Deutschland. Bekannte **j** _____ *in Deutschland sind auch*
Hamburg, München und Frankfurt.

In Deutschland leben sehr viele **k** _____. *Deutschland ist*
schon lange eine multikulturelle **l** _____.

3 **Was können Sie über Ihr Land sagen?** *Schreiben Sie, wie groß*
Ihr Land ist, wie viele Einwohner es hat, wie die Hauptstadt
heißt, was für Sehenswürdigkeiten es gibt etc. Zur Hilfe lesen
Sie noch einmal den Text ,Deutschland, Österreich und die
Schweiz' oben. Sehen Sie auch **Übung 2** *oben.*

Now that you have completed Unit 23, can you: tick
1 talk about German-speaking countries and cities?   ☐
2 say something about your own country?   ☐
3 express events in both the active and the passive
voices?   ☐
4 use **dass** and **weil** to express an opinion?   ☐

Congratulations on finishing *Complete German*!
We hope you have enjoyed working your way through
the course. We are always keen to receive feedback from
people who have used our course, so why not contact
us and let us know your reactions? We'll be particularly
pleased to receive your praise, but we should also like to
know if you think things could be improved. We always
welcome comments and suggestions and we do our best
to incorporate constructive suggestions into later editions.

You can contact us through the publishers at: Teach
Yourself Books, Hodder Headline Ltd, 338 Euston Road,
London NW1 3BH.

We hope you will want to build on your knowledge of
German and have made a few suggestions to help you do
this in the section entitled Taking it further, towards the
end of the book.

Alles Gute!

Heiner Schenke & Paul Coggle

Key to the exercises

Saying hello
2 a Wie heißen Sie? What are you called? b Wie ist Ihr Name? What is your name? 3 a Gertrud Gruber; b Martin Braun; c Boris Schwarz.

Greeting people
5 a 3; b 1; c 4; d 2.

6 Six greetings. Guten Abend; Guten Morgen (x2); Gute Nacht (x2); Guten Tag.

Where do you come from?
7 a True; b False; c True; d True.

8

Name	Geburtsort	Wohnort
Ich heiße…	Ich komme aus…	Ich wohne jetzt in…
Jochen Kern	Aachen	Bonn
Dana Frye	Stuttgart	Hannover

9 Sample answer: Ich heiße… Ich komme aus Manchester. Ich wohne jetzt in London.

1

	Guten Morgen	Guten Tag	Guten Abend	Gute Nacht
14:00		✔		
8:00	✔			
23.00				✔
10.00		✔		
18.00		✔	✔	

2 a Wie; b Wo; c Woher; d Wie. 3 a Ich heiße Simone Becker. Wie
heißen Sie? b Ich wohne in Berlin. Wo wohnen Sie? c Ich komme
aus Großbritannien. Woher kommen Sie? 4 a Wie; b Ich; c woher;
d aus; e Wo; f jetzt.

UNIT 2

How are you?

2

	ausgezeichnet	sehr gut	gut	es geht	nicht so gut	schlecht
Frau Renger			✔			
Frau Müller		✔				
Herr Schulz						
Frau Koch		✔				
Herr Krämer	✔					
Herr Akdag		✔				

3 e, c, b. 4 a Danke, mir geht's wirklich sehr gut. b Mir geht's heute
schlecht./Mir geht's heute nicht so gut. c Ach, es geht. d Nicht so
gut./Mir geht's schlecht. 5 ein, mein, in, sie, geht, es, prima, aus,
ausgezeichnet, ich, wirklich, wir, noch, heute, er, nicht, danke, sehr,
gut. Did you find any others? Let us know if you did!

Where do you come from?

6 i a Rainer Görner comes from Berlin in Germany. b Martina
Schümer comes from Basel in Switzerland. c Susanne Vermeulen
comes from Brussels in Belgium. d Michael Naumann comes from
Leipzig (in Germany). ii a richtig b falsch; Zürich liegt nicht in
Österreich, sondern in der Schweiz. c richtig d falsch; Susanne
Vermeulen kommt nicht aus Delft in den Niederlanden, sondern
aus Brüssel in Belgien. e richtig f falsch; Michael Naumann kommt
nicht aus Dresden, sondern aus Leipzig. Er wohnt jetzt nicht in
Linz, sondern in Salzburg, Österrreich.

7 BELgien; DÄNemark; DEUTSCHland; GroßbriTANNien;
IRland; ITALien; SPANien; die TürkEI. The first syllable is most
often stressed. GroßbriTANNien, ITALien and die TürkEI do not
fit into this category.

8 a richtig; b falsch; Heidelberg liegt nicht in Österreich, sondern
in Deutschland. c falsch; Köln liegt nicht in den Niederlanden,
sondern in Deutschland. d richtig; e falsch; Amsterdam liegt nicht
in Belgien, sondern in den Niederlanden.

9 These are some of the possible answers.

a Naomi Campbell kommt aus Großbritannien und wohnt jetzt
in den USA. b Madonna kommt aus den USA und wohnt jetzt
in Großbritannien und in den USA. c Karl Lagerfeld kommt
aus Deutschland, aber wohnt jetzt in Frankreich. d Michael
Schuhmacher kommt aus Deutschland. Er wohnt jetzt in
Österreich. Er arbeitet in Deutschland, in Italien, in Großbritannien
... e Arnold Schwarzenegger kommt aus Österreich und wohnt
jetzt in den USA. f Claudia Schiffer kommt aus Deutschland, aber
wohnt jetzt in Großbritannien.

10 Sheena Guten Tag! Ich heiße Sheena McDonald. Sheena Ich
komme aus Edinburg in Schottland. Und Sie? Wo wohnen Sie?
Sheena München ist schön.

1 a aus; b aber; c jetzt; d aus; e Belgien; f aber; g arbeitet. 2 a Wie
heißen Sie? b Woher kommen Sie? c Wo wohnen Sie jetzt? d Wie
geht es Ihnen heute?

UNIT 3

Numbers 1–10
1 9, 3, 8, 4, 6, 2. 2 Hamburg–Dortmund: 2 zu 1; Bochum–
Hannover: 6 zu 0; Duisburg–Mönchengladbach: 4 zu 2; Bielefeld–
Wolfsburg: 1 zu 3; Schalke–Freiburg: 0 zu 2; Nürnberg–Hertha
Berlin: 3 zu 0; Bremen–Frankfurt: 1 zu 0.

The Alphabet
4 Baumgart, Waltraud ✔ 1; Henning, Sebastian; Hesse, Patrick
✔ 3; Hoffmann, Silke; Ludwig, Paul; Schanze, Martin ✔ 2;
Schidelowskaja, Tanja ✔ 4; Schulte, Christel.
5 AEG, BMW, DB, DZ Bank, VW

Numbers 11–100
7 99 neunundneunzig; 48 achtundvierzig; 87 siebenundachtzig; 26
sechsundzwanzig; 52 zweiundfünfzig 8 Winning numbers Lotto:
6 8 14 23 26 46, Bonus number: 22. 9 a Schulz 040 - 30 07 51;
b Marhenke 040 - 73 45 92. 10 Telefon 0711-23 38 41; Handy
01734 06 02 94; Fax 07 11 24 89 02; E-Mail jkrause@yahoo.at

Wir, sie
11 The two couples come from Jena and Stuttgart respectively.
Jochen and Katja speak no French. Marga and Peter speak only
a little French. a richtig; b falsch; Sie sprechen kein Französisch.
c falsch; Marga und Peter sind aus Jena. d richtig; e falsch; Sie
sprechen ziemlich gut Englisch. f Sie arbeiten bei Carl Zeiss.

Testing yourself
1 a Heißen Sie wirklich Brunhilde Bachmeyer-Goldhagen? b
Kommen Sie wirklich aus Hollywood? c Wohnen Thomas und
Johanna wirklich in München? d Arbeitet Johanna wirklich in
Nürnberg? e Spricht Thomas wirklich ein wenig Spanisch?

f Kommen Sie wirklich aus Innsbruck?

2 Visitenkarte A Ich heiße Matthias Peters. Ich wohne in Hamburg. Meine Telefonnummer ist 040-300526. Meine Faxnummer ist 040-376284. Meine E-Mail-Adresse ist m.peters@delta.com

Visitenkarte B Ich heiße Dorothea Johannsen. Ich wohne in Münster. Meine Telefonnummer ist 0251 - 514386. Meine E-Mail-Adresse ist johannsen@artdeco.de

UNIT 4

I speak German
1 a H; b N; c N; d N; e H; f N. Seven differences.

2 Noch zwei Abendkursstudenten

Name	Gür Yalezan	Susi Merkl
Nationalität	Türke	Österreicherin
Geburtsort	Berlin	Innsbruck
Wohnort	Taucha	Rötha
Sprachen	Türkisch, Deutsch, Englisch	Deutsch, Englisch, Spanisch
Familienstand	ledig	verheiratet
Arbeit? Studium?	studiert in Leipzig	arbeitet in Leipzig

Nationalities and languages
3 Michael speaks German, English and French. He understands a bit of Spanish and is learning Japanese. a Nein, er ist Österreicher. b Nein, er ist Student. / Nein, er studiert. c Nein, er studiert in Wien. d Ja, er spricht Deutsch. / Ja, Deutsch ist seine Muttersprache. e Nein, er spricht Englisch und Französisch. f Ja, er versteht ein wenig Spanisch. g Nein, er lernt im Moment Japanisch.

4 Nationalities used for men end in -er or -e. Most of the female versions of nationalities end in -in. Most languages end in -isch. 6 Mein Name ist ... . Ich komme aus ... . Ich wohne jetzt in ... . Ja, ich bin Amerikaner / Amerikanerin. / Nein, ich bin ... / ... . Ja, meine Muttersprache ist Englisch. / Nein, meine Muttersprache ist

… . Ja, ich verstehe ein bisschen Deutsch. Ja, ich bin verheiratet. /
Nein, ich bin ledig / geschieden / verwitwet. Ja, ich studiere. / Nein,
ich arbeite. / Nein, ich bin arbeitslos.

Du und Sie

7 Klaus: Guten Tag! Ich heiße Klaus Thomas. Wie heißen Sie?
Gerhard: Ich bin Gerhard Braun. Woher kommen Sie? Klaus:
Aus München. Kommen Sie auch aus München? Gerhard: Nein,
aus Nürnberg. Sprechen Sie Englisch? Klaus: Ja, ziemlich gut. Und
Sie? Gerhard: Na ja, es geht.

Testing yourself

1 Jürgen Krause: Ich heiße Jürgen Krause. Nein, ich bin
Österreicher. Ich komme aus Wien. Ich wohne jetzt in Salzburg.
Ich spreche Deutsch und Englisch. Nein, ich bin seit drei Jahren
verwitwet. Ja, ich arbeite in Salzburg.

2 a iii; b v; c i; d ii; e vi; f iv. 3 i a Wie heißt du? b Woher
kommst du? c Und wo wohnst du jetzt? d Wie geht's dir heute?
e Sprichst du Englisch? f Bist du aus Hamburg? g Wie ist deine
Handynummer?

ii a Wie heißt ihr? b Woher kommt ihr? c Und wo wohnt ihr jetzt?
d Wie geht's euch heute? e Sprecht ihr Englisch? f Seid ihr aus
Hamburg? g Wie ist eure Handynummer?

UNIT 5

Towns and cities

2 Rollenspiel 1 Eins ist eine Kneipe. Die Kneipe heißt *Bierstübl*. 2
Zwei ist ein Biergarten. Der Biergarten heißt *Mönchbräu*. 3 Drei
ist eine Kirche. Die Kirche heißt *Jakobskirche*. 4 Vier ist ein Hotel.
Das Hotel heißt *Bahnhofshotel*. 5 Fünf ist ein Café. Das Café heißt
Café Krause. 6 Sechs ist ein Markt. Der Markt heißt *Buttermarkt*.

3

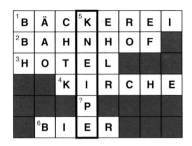

¹B	Ä	C	⁵K	E	R	E	I
²B	A	H	N	H	O	F	
³H	O	T	E	L			
		⁴K	I	R	C	H	E
		?P					
	⁶B	I	E	R			

4 a ein Kino b Das Hotel c eine Bäckerei d Ihr Name e das Bahnhofshotel f ein Café g deine Telefonnummer h Die Kneipe

5 a Sie ist in München. b Die Stadt ist sehr schön. c Das Stadtzentrum und der ‚Englische Garten' sind besonders schön. d Die Sprachschule heißt ‚Superlang'. e Nein, sie spricht ziemlich viel Deutsch. f Das Bier ist auch sehr gut in München. g die Woche, das Stadtzentrum, der Garten, die Sprachschule, das Bier

Numbers 101 and upwards
7 1 b; 2 c; 3 a; 4 c; 5 b; 6 a.

8

Heidelberg	143 000	(ein)hundertdreiundvierzigtausend
Dresden	502 000	fünfhundertzweitausend
Frankfurt am Main	660 000	sechshundertsechzigtausend
München	1 326 000	eine Million dreihundert-sechsundzwanzigtausend
Hamburg	1 750 000	eine Million siebenhundert-fünfzigtausend
Berlin	3 402 000	drei Millionen vierhundert(und)-zweitausend

Testing yourself
1 a Ihr, Mein; b Ihre, Meine; c Ihr, Mein; d Ihre, Meine; e Ihr, Mein. 2 geht's; fantastisch; eine; Die; schön; das; der; eine; Die; heißt; spreche; bald.

UNIT 6

Occupations

1 a Das ist Peter Meier. Er ist Taxifahrer. b Das ist Helga Neumann. Sie ist Automechanikerin. c Das ist Heike Müller. Sie ist Musikerin. d Das ist Manfred Lustig. Er ist Tischler. e Das ist Kurt Leutner. Er ist Kellner. f Das ist Ulrike Wagner. Sie ist Ärztin. g Das ist Marc Straßburger. Er ist Koch.

2 a She is German. b That's how long she has lived in England. c They both work. d Ingrid's husband. e falsch; Ingrid ist Deutsche. f richtig g richtig h falsch; Jutta ist Krankenschwester. i falsch; Herr Sammer ist Mechaniker bei Opel. j richtig

3 a Deutscher; b Engländerin; c 24 Jahren; d Tischler von Beruf.

4 Gudrun's responses: Ja, ich bin Deutsche. Nein, er ist Ire. Ich wohne seit 17 Jahren in Münster. Ja, ich bin Sekretärin bei Mannesmann. Er ist Taxifahrer.

5 a Lehrerin; b Maurer; c Journalist; d Sekretärin.

What are you studying?

6 a falsch; Sie kommen aus Gießen. b richtig c falsch; Er studiert Romanistik. d richtig e richtig f falsch; Sie finden es ein bisschen langweilig.

7 **Name**	Paul	Daniel	Heike	Martina
Geburtsort	Bremen	Hamburg	Düsseldorf	Köln
Studienort	Bremen	Bremen	Aachen	Aachen
Studienfach	Germanistik	Anglistik	Informatik	Mathematik

Testing yourself

1 e b c f a d g. 2 a Engländer; b Ire; c Schottin; d Studenten; e Studentin; f Journalist; g Sekretärinnen; h Verkäuferin; i Kellnerin. 3 a bin; b Sind; c ist, ist; d bin; e ist; f Bist; g Seid

Asking the way
1 Dialog 1 This woman is looking for a bank. She is told to take the first street on the left. It's about 5 minutes' walk.

Dialog 2 This woman is looking for a supermarket. She is told to keep going straight ahead. It's about 400 metres.

Dialog 3 This man is looking for a nice café. He is told to go around the corner to the right. It's not far away.

2 a eine; b ein Café; c hier in der Nähe einen; d es hier in der Nähe einen. 3 a ein Restaurant; b ein Kino; c einen Supermarkt.
4 a eine; b einen; c ein; d ein; e einen; f einen.

In a café

5

MENU			
HOT DRINKS	**€**	**ICE-CREAM SPECIALITIES**	**€**
Cup of coffee	2,25	Assorted ices	3,00,
Cappuccino	2,75		4,00, 5,00
Hot chocolate	2,80	Peach Melba	4,50
Black tea	2,25	Praliné cup	4,75
CAKES		**NON-ALCOHOLIC DRINKS**	
Butter cake	1,75	Coca Cola	2,20
Black Forest gateau	2,80	Lemonade	2,10
Various fruit flans	3,00	Orange juice	2,10
Portion of cream	0,80	Mineral water	2,00
	BEERS		
	König Pils (0,33l)	2,50	
	Wheat beer (0,5l)	2,75	

i richtig; ii falsch; Er möchte ein Bier. iii richtig. iv falsch; Sie bestellt ein Mineralwasser und einen Kaffee. v falsch; Er bekommt einen Orangensaft. vi richtig. 6 b trinken, trinke; c bekommen, bekomme; d nehmen, nehme. 7 a iii das; iv das; v der; vii der. 8 a ein; b eine; c einen; d einen, ein; e einen, einen; f ein. 9 a falsch; b richtig; c falsch; d falsch.

Testing yourself
1 a -en; b -; c -en, -e; d den, den; e den; f das, das. 2 a vii; b i / vi; c viii; d iii; e ii; f vi/i; g v; h iv. 3 a Ich möchte einen Kaffee, bitte. b Ich möchte ein Mineralwasser und einen Orangensaft. c Ich nehme eine Tasse Tee, bitte. d Ich nehme eine Cola und ein Glas Bier.

UNIT 8

Food and shopping
1 Here are some items you might have listed. We have also included some words that might be new for you; can you guess what they mean?

Lebensmittel	Obst	Gemüse	Getränke
das Brot	der Apfel	der Blumenkohl	das Bier
das Brötchen	Äpfel (pl)	die Karotte	die Cola
das Ei	die Banane	Karotten (pl)	der Kaffee
das Fleisch	Bananen (pl)	die Kartoffel	die Limonade
das Müsli	die Orange	Kartoffeln (pl)	die Milch
das Öl	Orangen (pl)	der Pilz	das Mineralwasser
der Reis		Pilze (pl)	der Orangensaft
das Salz		der Salat	der Schnaps
das Würstchen			der Sekt
der Zucker			der Tee
			der Tomatensaft
			das Wasser
			der Wein
			der Wodka

3 These are just some of the possibilities: a Gemüse und Käse; b Fleisch; c Bier, Wein und Orangensaft; d Tee, Kaffee und Zucker. 4 a Tomaten; b Wein; c Cornflakes; d Bonbons; e Salami. 5 a Sie kauft zehn Brötchen. b Ein Kilo kostet €1,80. c Sie kauft den

Riesling. d Alles zusammen kostet €12,35. 6 i c ii a iii f iv b v d vi e.

8

^a ⁱK	Ä	S	E				
^bS	A	L	A	T			
	^cB	R	O	T			
			^dO	B	S	T	
				^eT	E	E	
	^fT	O	M	A	T	E	N
				^gE	I	E	R
		^hK	U	C	H	E	N

In a restaurant

9 a richtig; b falsch; c falsch; d falsch; e falsch. 10 b – v; e – ii; c – i; f – vi; a – iv; d – iii. 11 Ich möchte bitte bestellen./Als Vorspeise möchte ich eine französische Zwiebelsuppe./Als Hauptgericht nehme ich das Schnitzel mit Pommes frites. Und ich möchte auch einen gemischten Salat./Ich möchte ein Glas Weißwein. Und als Nachtisch (als Dessert) nehme ich den Apfelstrudel./Mit Sahne. Und nachher möchte ich einen Kaffee.

	Vorspeise	Hauptgericht	Nachtisch
Schnitzel		✔	
Eisbecher			✔
Obstsalat			✔
Zwiebelsuppe	✔		
Nudeln	✔	✔	
Omelette	✔	✔	
Pfeffersteak		✔	

Testing yourself
1 a die Apfelsäfte b die Salate c die Tomaten d die Flaschen e die Tassen f die Kartoffel g die Brötchen h die Gläser i der Vater j die Restaurants k die Partys

2 a Als Vorspeise möchte ich eine Gemüsesuppe. b Als Hauptgericht nehme ich das Schnitzel. c Zum Trinken möchten wir eine Flasche Mineralwasser bestellen. d Als Dessert bekommen wir den Obstsalat mit Sahne. e Nachher trinken wir eine Tasse Kaffee und eine Tasse Tee. f Jetzt möchten wir bitte bezahlen.

UNIT 9

What are these people doing?
2 a fahren / fliegen; b schwimmen; c spielen; d lesen; e hören / spielen; f kochen / essen. 3 a schreibe; b arbeitet; c lesen; d hört; e Spielst; f Trinkt 4 a spricht; b Sprichst; c fahre; d nimmst; e liest; f isst

Hobbies and leisure time
5 a richtig; b richtig; c falsch; Sie liest gern Romane. d falsch; Sie fotografiert auch gern. e falsch; Ins Kino geht sie sehr gern. f richtig.

6

Lesen	☑	Golf	☒	Fitness	☑
Reisen	☒	Surfen	☒	Fotografieren	☒
Fußball	☒	Schwimmen	☑	Pop-Musik	☒
Computer	☒	Kino	☑	Garten	☑
Klassische Musik	☒	Tennis	☒	Segeln	☒
Sport	☒	Wandern	☑	Joggen	☒

7 Some possible answers:

a Ja, ich lese gern Zeitung. / Nein, ich lese nicht gern Zeitung.

b Ja, ich höre gern Elvis Presley. / Nein ich höre nicht gern Elvis Presley. / Ja, Elvis Presley höre ich gern. / Nein, Elvis Presley höre ich nicht gern.

c Ja, ich esse gern Pizza. / Nein, ich esse nicht gern Pizza. / Ja, Pizza esse ich gern. / Nein, Pizza esse ich nicht gern.

d Ja, ich reise gern. / Nein, ich reise nicht gern.

e Ja, ich arbeite gern im Garten. / Nein, ich arbeite nicht gern im Garten. / Ja, im Garten arbeite ich gern. / Nein, im Garten arbeite ich nicht gern.

f Ja, ich trinke gern Bier. / Nein, ich trinke nicht gern Bier. / Ja, Bier trinke ich gern. / Nein, Bier trinke ich nicht gern.

g Ja, ich gehe gern ins Kino. / Nein, ich gehe nicht gern ins Kino. / Ja, ins Kino gehe ich gern. / Nein, ins Kino gehe ich nicht gern.

h Ja, ich koche gern. / Nein, ich koche nicht gern.

8 i a Er geht viermal pro Woche ins Fitnesscenter. b Er geht lieber ins Restaurant. c Er bleibt zu Hause und sieht fern. d Sie geht normalerweise zweimal im Monat ins Museum. e Mit ihren Kindern (und mit ihrem Mann) geht sie oft ins Kindertheater. f Sie geht meistens zweimal die Woche in die Disco. Ins Museum geht sie

sehr selten. g Sie findet Brad Pitt sehr attraktiv.

9 a Nein, sie gehen nicht ins Kino, sie gehen ins Restaurant.
b Nein, sie geht nicht ins Café, sie geht ins Konzert/in die Oper.
c Nein, sie geht nicht in die Oper, sie geht ins Café.
d Nein, er geht nicht ins Restaurant, er geht ins Fußballstadion.
e Nein, er geht nicht ins Museum, er geht in die Kneipe. f Nein, er
geht nicht ins Fitnesscenter, er geht ins Kino. There may be other
possibilities.

Testing yourself
1 a Isst; b ist; c Sprichst; d spielt; e Sprecht; f fotografiere; g liest;
h sind.

2 a Ich trinke gern Rotwein. b Ich esse gern Pommes frites. c Wir
hören gern klassische Musik. d Wir spielen gern Schach. e Ich lese
gern *die Süddeutsche Zeitung*. f Trinkst du gern Kaffee?

UNIT 10

The time
2 a nach; b vor; c Viertel; d halb. 3 a 4.30–3; b 8.50–2; c 8.45–4;
d 6.28–1. 4 a Es ist halb fünf. b Es ist zehn vor neun. c Es ist
Viertel vor neun. d Es ist kurz vor halb sieben./Es ist 28 Minuten
nach sechs. 5 a Es ist ein Uhr mittags. b Es ist vier Uhr nachmittags.
c Es ist acht Uhr abends. d Es ist elf Uhr abends. e Es ist neun Uhr
morgens. f Es ist sechs Uhr morgens. 6 a Es ist dreizehn Uhr.
b Es ist fünfzehn Uhr zwanzig. c Es ist sieben Uhr fünfundvierzig.
d Es ist achtzehn Uhr zwölf. e Es ist dreiundzwanzig Uhr
fünfunddreißig. f Es ist vier Uhr siebzehn. 7 a 20.00 b 14.30
c 13.00 d 7.57 e 15.44 f 17.03.

A typical day
9 a Das Mädchen steht um sieben Uhr auf. b Der Mann sieht
fern. c Die Schule fängt um acht Uhr an. d Der Mann kauft im
Supermarkt ein.

10 a falsch; b richtig; c falsch; d richtig. e Er steht gegen halb

sieben auf. f Feierabend ist gegen vier. g Nein, er sieht nicht viel
fern. h Meistens um halb 12.

Testing yourself

1 a an; b fern; c auf; d ein; e an; f ab. 2 Um halb sieben steht er
auf. Um sieben Uhr fährt er zur Arbeit. Um neun Uhr ruft er eine
Kundin an. Um halb eins geht er zur Bank. Um fünf Uhr kauft er
ein. Um sieben Uhr geht er mit Helga in die Kneipe. Um zehn Uhr
sieht er fern.

UNIT 11

Going out

1 a richtig; b falsch; c falsch; d richtig. 2 a Man kann ein
Theaterstück für Kinder und Erwachsene (Die Abenteuer von
Aladdin) sehen. b Man kann anschließend spielen, Eis und
Bratwurst essen. c Um halb neun kann man Oldies und Goldies
hören. d Sie können ‚Mission Possible' sehen.

4

			a/k			
			B	**Ü**	**R**	**O**
		b **K**	**I**	**N**	**O**	
c **M**	**U**	**S**	**E**	**U**	**M**	
	d **P**	**A**	**R**	**K**		
e **M**	**O**	**R**	**G**	**E**	**N**	
		f **R**	**A**	**D**	**I**	**O**
	g **K**	**I**	**R**	**C**	**H**	**E**
h **B**	**E**	**T**	**T**			
	i **K**	**N**	**E**	**I**	**P**	**E**
	j **B**	**A**	**N**	**K**		

Arrangements
5 Sonntag, Montag, Dienstag, Mittwoch, Donnerstag, Freitag,
Samstag / Sonnabend.

6 a falsch; Sie möchte einen Film mit Cate Blanchett sehen.
b richtig; c falsch; Am Mittwochabend muss Petra ihre Schwester
abholen. d richtig; e richtig; f falsch; Sie treffen sich um acht.
7 a Am Montag muss er um 20.00 Uhr Dr. Schmidt treffen.
b Am Dienstag muss er abends zum Geburtstag von Bernd gehen.
c Am Mittwoch muss er bis 22 Uhr arbeiten. d Am Donnerstag
muss er mit den Kollegen essen gehen. e Am Freitag muss er mit
Tante Gisela in die Oper gehen. f Am Wochenende muss er nach
München fahren. 8 1f; 2e; 3h; 4a; 5g; 6d; 7c; 8b. 9 a ins Kino;
b Im Café; c ins Café; d im Restaurant; e in die Sprachschule; f ins
Restaurant; g Im Kino; h In der Sprachschule. 10 a i movement;
ii position; b i position; ii movement; c i position; ii movement;
d i movement; ii position; e i position; ii movement.

11 There may be other possibilities:

Hallo, Jutta. Mir geht's gut. Und dir?

Ja, das ist eine gute Idee. Wann denn?

Tut mir leid. Dienstagabend kann ich nicht. Da muss ich arbeiten.

Tut mir leid. Am Freitag muss ich nach Köln fahren. Geht es
Samstagabend?

Wann treffen wir uns?

Acht Uhr ist gut. Wir können uns im Restaurant treffen.

Tschüss, bis Samstagabend.

1 a Im Theater kann man ein Stück von Shakespeare sehen.
b Er möchte heute Abend in die Kneipe gehen. c Er kann sehr gut
Tango tanzen. d Was kann man in London machen? e Ich möchte
am Dienstag essen gehen. f Frau Johnson kann sehr gut Deutsch
sprechen.

2 Am Dienstag möchte sie Klaus treffen, aber sie muss das Mathe-
Examen machen. Am Mittwoch möchte sie lange schlafen, aber
sie muss morgens um 7.30 Uhr ins Fitnesscenter. Am Donnerstag
möchte sie in die Kneipe gehen, aber sie muss für Hannelore
Babysitting machen.

UNIT 12

Buying a train ticket

1 Einfach (single ticket); hin und zurück (return ticket); Gleis
(platform). 2 a Sie fährt nach Berlin. b Sie kostet €53. c Nein, der
Zug ist direkt. d Er fährt in 10 Minuten. e Er fährt von Gleis 14.
3 Dienstag um 6.00 Uhr – a Der nächste Zug fährt um 6.12 Uhr.
b Nein, Sie müssen nicht umsteigen. c Nein, leider gibt es keinen
Speisewagen. d Er kommt um 10.43 Uhr in Heidelberg an. Sonntag
um 06.30 Uhr – a Der nächste Zug fährt um 7.24 Uhr. b Ja, Sie
müssen in Frankfurt umsteigen. c Ja, es gibt einen Speisewagen.
d Er kommt auch um 10.43 Uhr in Heidelberg an. Donnerstag
um 9.30 Uhr – a Der nächste Zug fährt um 9.50 Uhr. b Ja, Sie
müssen in Frankfurt und Mannheim umsteigen. c Ja, es gibt einen
Speisewagen. d Er kommt um 13.05 Uhr in Heidelberg an. Freitag
um 11.45 Uhr – a Der nächste Zug fährt um 11.50 Uhr. b Ja, Sie
müssen in Mannheim umsteigen. c Ja, es gibt einen Speisewagen.
d Er kommt um 15.05 Uhr in Heidelberg an.

4 Was kostet eine Fahrkarte nach Frankfurt?/Einfach./Ja, gut./
Wann fährt der nächste Zug nach Frankfurt?/Und von welchem
Gleis fährt er?/Muss ich umsteigen?/Vielen Dank.
5 a iii Einfach oder hin und zurück? b ii In 10 Minuten. c ii Gleis
10. d i Das macht €43.

Getting around town
7 a dem; b der; c der; d dem; e dem

8

Person	Wie fahren sie?	Wie lange brauchen sie?
Person 1	mit dem Fahrrad	20 Minuten
Person 2	mit dem Bus und der U-Bahn	50 Minuten
Person 3	mit dem Auto	eine Stunde
Person 4	geht zu Fuß	10 Minuten

9 a Sie braucht ungefähr 20 Minuten. b Er fährt meistens mit dem
Bus zum Bahnhof. c In der U-Bahn liest er. / Er liest in der U-Bahn.
d Sie ist nicht gut. / Die Verbindung mit Bus und Bahn ist nicht gut.
e Er fährt eine Stunde. f Er geht meistens zu Fuß. 10 a zum; b zur;
c vom, zum; d zum.

Testing yourself
1 Wie komme ich zum Flughafen, Bahnhof, Café Mozart,
Fußballstadion? Wie komme ich zur Gedächtniskirche,
Stadtbäckerei, Bundesstraße? 2 a dem, zur; b der, zur; c dem, zum;
d dem; e der. 3 c v; e ii; d vi; b i; f iii; a iv.

UNIT 13

Talking about the past
1 a iv; b ii; c vi; d iii; e i; f v. 2 b getanzt; c gemacht; d gefrühstückt;
e gekostet; f gekocht; h bezahlt; i besucht. 3 b getanzt; c besucht;
d eingekauft; e bezahlt; f gekocht; g telefoniert.

4 Wer sagt was? a U b A c U d A e A f U g A h U i A

5 One possible version:

Am Morgen war Ulrike in der Stadt und hat eingekauft. Am
Nachmittag hat sie Britta und Georg besucht. Am Abend waren sie
dann zusammen in der neuen ‚Mondschein-Bar' und haben bis drei
Uhr getanzt. Sie haben viel Spaß gehabt.

Angela hat gestern Morgen einen neuen Computer gekauft. Der Computer hat €900 gekostet. Sie hat dann den ganzen Tag mit dem Computer gespielt. Sie hat auch im Internet gesurft. Am Abend war sie ein bisschen müde. Sie hat mit Bernd gekocht und noch ein bisschen klassische Musik gehört.

6 One possible version:

Am Samstagmorgen war Bettina in der Stadt und hat eingekauft. Danach hat sie Fotos abgeholt. Am Nachmittag hat sie dann ihren Freund Georg im Krankenhaus besucht. Am Abend hat sie mit Pia Schach gespielt. Sie hat Nudeln gekocht.

Am Sonntagmorgen hat Bettina einen Ausflug gemacht. Danach hat sie um halb vier im Garten gearbeitet. Am Abend hat sie mit Christina telefoniert und für das Deutsch-Examen gelernt.

At the flea market
7 a Sie haben eine alte Platte von den Rolling Stones gekauft. b Er fährt diesen Sommer nach Mexiko. Er reist gern. c Sie hat ein neues Hemd gekauft. Sie hat €7,50 bezahlt. d Er kann morgens schlecht aufstehen.

8 a fantastische; b interessantes; c tolle; d alten, mechanischen.

9 a neuen; b tolles; c große; d interessanten; e schönes; f alte
10 a groß; b teuer; c langweilig; d neu; e arm; f schwer; g altmodisch.

Testing yourself
1 Possible answers

Um 10 Uhr hat sie mit Frau Martini telefoniert. Danach hat sie die Firma Schmidt + Consultants besucht. Um 12.45 Uhr hat sie Mittagspause gemacht. Am Nachmittag hat sie Briefe diktiert und Tickets für die Reise nach Rom gebucht. Um 17 Uhr hat sie einen schönen Mantel gekauft. Um 18.30 Uhr hat sie mit Michael Squash gespielt.

2 d -es; e -e; f -es; g -e; h -en; i -e; j -es; k -es.

UNIT 14

More about the past

1 a vi; b v; c iv; d vii; e iii; f viii; g ii; h i. 2 b hat; c Haben; d ist; e Bist; f hat; g habe; f habe. 3 a Er ist nach New York geflogen. b Auf einer Party hat er Kaviar gegessen und Champagner getrunken. c Er hat Robert de Niro getroffen. d In Florida ist er im Meer geschwommen. e Er hat neue italienische Anzüge gekauft. f Am Freitag ist er ins Kasino gegangen. g Am Wochenende ist er Ski gelaufen. h Das neues Lied heißt: Ich kann dich nicht vergessen. 4 a getrunken; b treffen; c gegessen; d gesprochen; e gegangen; f gefahren; g fliegen; h bleiben. haben: trinken, treffen, essen, sprechen. sein: gehen, fahren, fliegen, bleiben. 5 a Seit 10 Jahren genau. b Um acht Uhr aus dem Bett, das finde ich nicht nett. c Insgesamt 10. d Er komponiert die Musik selber und schreibt auch die Texte. e Im Winter fährt er gern Ski. Im Sommer surft er oder spielt Tennis. Er geht auch auf viele Partys und sieht viele Freunde. 7 a Von 1928 bis 1937 hat er das Kaiser-Wilhelm-Gymnasium in Köln besucht. b 1937 hat er das Abitur gemacht. c 1937 hat er auch in Bonn eine Buchhandlungslehre begonnen. d 1939 hat er an der Universität Köln Germanistik studiert. e Von 1939 bis 1945 ist er Soldat im Zweiten Weltkrieg gewesen. f 1942 hat er Annemarie Zech geheiratet. g Von 1946–1949 hat er Kurzgeschichten in Zeitschriften geschrieben. h 1949 ist sein erstes Buch (*Der Zug war pünktlich*) erschienen. i Von 1949 bis 1985 hat er viele literarische Werke geschrieben. j 1972 hat er den Nobelpreis für Literatur bekommen. k 1985 ist er am 16. Juli in Hürtgenwald/Eifel gestorben.

Then and now

8 a falsch; b richtig; c falsch; d richtig; e falsch; f falsch; g richtig.

9

Früher	Haare	Trinken	Musik	Freizeit
Bernd	hat lange Haare gehabt	hat viel Cognac getrunken	hat Elvis Presley gehört	hat in einer Band gespielt
Dieter	hat lange Haare gehabt	hat Rum und Cola getrunken	hat viel Eric Clapton gehört	hat viel Fußball gespielt

Heute	Haare	Trinken	Musik	Freizeit
Bernd	hat immer noch lange Haare	trinkt Wasser, Tee, Orangensaft	hört viel Jazz-Musik	reist viel
Dieter	hat keine Haare mehr	trinkt gern französischen Wein	hört klassische Musik	spielt Tennis

Testing yourself
1 a geflogen; b besucht; c abgeholt; d gegangen; e gesehen;
f geschlafen. 2 a sind; b haben; c haben; d haben; e sind;
f haben. 3 b verstanden; c vergessen; d besucht; e empfohlen;
f erhalten.

UNIT 15

Where do you live?
1 i e; ii a; iii c; iv d; v b.

2 Wer?   Wo wohnen sie?   Wie ist es?
  Person 1   in einem Hochhaus   nicht zu teuer
  Person 2   in einem Einfamilienhaus   grün und ruhig
  Person 3   in einer Wohngemeinschaft   nett und interessant
  Person 4   in einer Altbauwohnung   hell und ruhig

3 a falsch. Er zahlt €375 Miete und er ist ganz zufrieden.
b richtig; c richtig; d falsch. Sie wohnt seit 50 Jahren in einer
Altbauwohnung. e richtig.

4 a -em; b -er; c -em; d -em; e -er; f -em; g -en -n.

In the home

6 a das Schlafzimmer; b das Kinderzimmer; c die Küche;
d das Badezimmer; e das Wohnzimmer; f der Balkon; g das
Arbeitszimmer.

7 The conventional answers are as follows. Perhaps you have other
ideas! Der Schrank kommt ins Wohnzimmer. Das Bett kommt
ins Schlafzimmer. Der DVD-Player kommt ins Wohnzimmer.
Der Küchentisch kommt in die Küche. Die Pflanze kommt ins
Wohnzimmer. Die Waschmaschine kommt in den Keller. Das
Sofa kommt ins Wohnzimmer. Die Teller kommen in die Küche.
Der Sessel kommt ins Wohnzimmer. Der Kühlschrank kommt
in die Küche. Der Fernseher kommt ins Wohnzimmer. Das Bild
kommt auch ins Wohnzimmer. Die Magazine kommen auch ins
Wohnzimmer. Das Regal kommt ins Arbeitszimmer. Die Bücher
kommen auch ins Arbeitszimmer. Der Topf kommt in die Küche.
Die Gummiente kommt ins Badezimmer.

8 a Fast sechs Monate; b Vier Zimmer, plus Küche und Bad;
c €465, + Nebenkosten; d Relativ zentral, in der Nähe vom
Stadtpark; e Sie sind sehr gut.

Vorteile (+)	Nachteile (−)
Sie haben jetzt mehr Platz. Es ist eine sehr große Wohnung.	Bis zum nächsten Supermarkt ist es ein bisschen weit.
Die Wohnung liegt relativ zentral, in der Nähe vom Stadtpark.	Das Arbeitszimmer ist sehr klein.
Die Umgebung ist ruhig und sehr grün.	Leider hat die Wohnung keinen Garten.
Die Zimmer sind groß und hell.	
Die Miete ist nicht so teuer, €465.	
Die Verkehrsverbindungen sind sehr gut.	

10 a außerhalb; b klein; c dunkel; d interessant; e teuer; f neu; g antik; h laut. 11 a Wir wohnen in einer Wohnung. b Die Wohnung hat vier Zimmer, plus Küche und Bad. c Die Zimmer sind groß und hell. d Nein, wir haben leider keinen Garten. e Die Miete ist nicht so teuer, €465, plus Nebenkosten. f Die Umgebung ist ruhig und sehr grün. g Die Verkehrsverbindungen sind sehr gut. h Ich fahre nur 10 Minuten zur Arbeit. i Ich fahre mit der U-Bahn. Im Sommer kann ich mit dem Fahrrad fahren.

Town or country?

13 b interessanter, bunter; c stressiger; d besser, freundlicher; e länger; f entspannter. 14 a So ein Quatsch! Der Eiffelturm ist jünger als die Akropolis. b So ein Quatsch! In Deutschland ist es kälter als in Südafrika. c So ein Quatsch! Das Essen im ,Gourmet-Restaurant' ist besser als in der Mensa. d So ein Quatsch! Der Toyota Prius ist billiger als der Porsche. e So ein Quatsch! Tokio ist größer als Paris. f So ein Quatsch! Berlin ist interessanter als Stuttgart.

Testing yourself

1 b größer; c älter; d besser; e teurer; f höher; g billiger; h interessanter.

2 One possible answer

Liebe Frau Löschmann,

ich danke Ihnen für Ihren Brief vom 13. Mai. Ich bin gerne bereit, Ihre Fragen zu beantworten.

Die Wohnung liegt sehr zentral — nur zwei Minuten bis zur Hauptstraße, aber sie liegt auch sehr ruhig, in der Nähe vom Stadtpark. Die Verkehrsverbindungen sind sehr gut — nur fünfzehn Minuten bis zum Hauptbahnhof und fünf Minuten bis zur Bushaltestelle.

Die Wohnung hat drei Schlafzimmer und zwei Badezimmer. Die Küche ist sehr groß, da kann man auch essen. Wir haben zwei Fernseher und einen DVD-Player. Man kann Satelliten-programme, also auch deutsche Programme bekommen.

Wir haben einen großen, schönen Garten. Dort kann man im Sommer auch essen.

Mit freundlichen Grüßen

Ihr Peter Smith

UNIT 16

Booking a hotel room

2 a falsch; Er nimmt ein Doppelzimmer. b richtig; c falsch; Er möchte mit seiner Frau auf eine Antiquitätenmesse gehen. d falsch; Er nimmt ein Zimmer mit Bad. e falsch; Das Zimmer kostet €77,50. f richtig.

3 a iii; b iv; c v; d vi; e vii; f ii; g i. **4** a Guten Tag. Haben Sie ein Zimmer frei? b Ein Einzelzimmer, bitte. c Für drei Nächte. d Mit Dusche, bitte. e Um wie viel Uhr gibt es Frühstück? **5** a falsch; Sie sucht ein Zimmer für zwei Tage. b richtig; c richtig; d falsch; Es kostet €67,50. e falsch; Das Hotel Atlanta ist teurer als das Hotel Offenbach. f richtig.

Hotels/ Pension	Zimmer	Preis für Einzelzimmer	Entfernung	Pluspunkte
Offenbach	80	€90	5 Minuten vom Zentrum	sehr zentral, gute Bar
Atlanta	120	€130	30 Minuten (eine halbe Stunde) vom Zentrum	Swimming-Pool und Park
Schneider	28	€67,50	20 Minuten vom Zentrum	familiäre Atmosphäre, ruhig

8 a am größten; b am billigsten; c am zentralsten; d am ruhigsten

9 a Die Paulskirche ist rechts neben der Stadtbibliothek. b Das Museum liegt gegenüber der Sprachschule. c Das Hotel *Germania* liegt zwischen der Touristeninformation und der Bäckerei. d Der Parkplatz liegt hinter der Apotheke. e Das Café Schmidt ist neben der Fleischerei.

Testing yourself

1 a Die Waschmaschine steht jetzt im Keller. b Das Foto von Oma Lisbeth hängt jetzt im Esszimmer. c Die CDs stehen jetzt im Regal. d Die Pflanze steht jetzt auf dem Balkon. e Das Poster von Lionel Messi hängt jetzt im Kinderzimmer. f Das Sofa steht jetzt zwischen dem Regal und dem Tisch.

2 a warm, am wärmsten; b kälter; c interessanter, am interessantesten; d billiger, am billigsten; e höher, am höchsten; f teurer, am teuersten; g gern, am liebsten; h besser, am besten

3 a Der Nil ist länger als der Rhein, aber der Amazonas ist am längsten. b Kanada ist größer als Deutschland, aber Russland ist am größten. c Der Tower of London ist älter als das Empire State Building, aber das Colosseum ist am ältesten. d Gold ist härter als

Silber, aber Granit ist am härtesten. e Der Ferrari F430 ist teurer als
der BMW M6, aber der Maserati GranSport ist am teuersten.

UNIT 17

Fashion
1 Ist Mode wichtig (✔) oder unwichtig (✗)?

	✔	✗
Bettina Haferkamp	☐	☒
Johann Kurz	☑	☐
Boris Brecht	☐	☒
Ulrike Maziere	☑	☐

2 a Sie zeigt, was Leute denken und fühlen. b Die Leute sollen
immer etwas Neues kaufen. c Schwarze Sachen finde ich am besten.
d Ich ziehe nur an, was ich mag. e Mode ist ein wichtiger Ausdruck
unserer Zeit./ Mode bedeutet viel für mich.

3

pro (+)	contra (−)
Sie zeigt, was Leute denken und fühlen.	Modetrends finde ich langweilig.
Mode bedeutet viel für mich.	
Eine modische Frisur, ein modernes Outfit – das ist sehr wichtig für mich.	

4 a Das war ein langweiliger Film. b Das ist ein starker Kaffee.
c Das ist ein interessantes Buch. d Das ist ein schwieriges Problem.
e Das ist ein neuer Computer. f Das sind unfreundliche Leute.
g Das ist ein billiges Hotel. h Das ist eine komplizierte Frage.

5 a Sie sagt, Verkäuferin ist ein interessanter Beruf. b Die Arbeit
im Haushalt ist anstrengend. c Ihr Sohn findet Computerspiele
interessant. d Sie findet, sie ist kein modischer Typ. e Die Töchter
von Frau Martens finden Mode wichtig. f Kunden sind manchmal
unfreundlich.

Clothes

6 a falsch; Der Mann trägt einen blauen Anzug und eine rote Krawatte. b richtig; c richtig; d falsch; Außerdem trägt sie einen braunen Rock, gelbe Strümpfe und braune Schuhe. e richtig. f falsch; Der Junge trägt eine schwarze Jeans, ein grünes T-Shirt, eine gelbe Baseball-Mütze und gelbe Turnschuhe. 8 a -en, -em, -en. b -en, -en. c -em, -en, -er, -en, -en, -en. d -em, -en, -er, -en, -en, -en. e -er, -en. f -em, -en, -en, -en. 10 a falsch, Jutta und Christian machen jedes Jahr eine Party. b richtig; c richtig; d falsch, Die Person, die am schlechtesten, am hässlichsten aussieht, bekommt einen Preis. e falsch; Die Gäste bringen etwas zum Trinken mit. 11 a Anzug; b Mantel; c Hemd; d Sachen; e Röcke.

12

	bei der Arbeit	zu Hause	was sie gern tragen	was sie nicht gern tragen
Mareike Brauer	eine bequeme Hose, eine Bluse, einen Pulli	eine Hose, oft eine Jeans, T-Shirt, Pullover	bequeme Sachen; alles, was bequem ist	Röcke
Günther Scholz	einen Anzug, ein weißes Hemd, eine Krawatte	ein sportliches Hemd oder ein Poloshirt	sportliche Kleidung, elegante Kleidung	bunte Kleidung, rote Hemden, Hawaii-Hemden, bunte Hosen usw.

13 Guten Tag. Ich suche eine neue Jacke. /Eine graue Jacke, für eine Party. /Ich suche etwas Modisches. /Ja, gut, aber italienische Jacken sind sehr teuer. /Ja, das stimmt und das ist auch eine sehr modische Party in New York.

Testing yourself

1 a Verkäuferin Ich arbeite in einem großen Kaufhaus in München. Bei der Arbeit trage ich einen schwarzen Rock und eine weiße

Bluse. Im Winter trage ich zu meinem schwarzen Rock auch eine schwarze Jacke. b Student Im Moment arbeite ich bei Burger King und muss eine hässliche Uniform tragen. An der Uni trage ich aber immer eine blaue Levi-Jeans mit einem modischen T-Shirt. Mir gefallen am besten amerikanische oder britische T-Shirts. Alte Sachen vom Flohmarkt gefallen mir manchmal auch.

2 b Zu Hause trage ich am liebsten bequeme Kleidung. c Ich trage gern modische und bunte Sachen. Ich trage nicht so gern dunkle Kleidung. d Meine Lieblingsfarbe ist blau. e Ja, Mode ist ziemlich wichtig für mich. f Zu einer Bad-Taste-Party ziehe ich eine gelbe Bluse mit einer grünen Hose und einer roten Jacke an.

UNIT 18

Invitations and presents
1 die Geburtstagsparty, die Hochzeit, die Grill-Party, die Hauseinweihungsfeier. 2 a falsch; Susanne und Michael heiraten am 8. Mai in Marbach. b richtig; c falsch; Uschi und Matthias haben ihr ‚Schloss' gefunden. d falsch; Mareike und Jörg wollen in ihrem Haus eine Grill-Party machen. e falsch; Sie haben auch Essen für Vegetarier.

4 a ihr; b ihm; c ihnen; d ihr; e ihnen; f ihm.

5

Wem?	Was bringen sie mit?	Warum?
Vater	Sie bringen ihm eine Baseball-Mütze von den New York Yankees mit.	Er sieht gern Baseball-Spiele im Fernsehen.
Oma	Sie bringen ihr einen neuen Bademantel mit.	Sie hat gesagt, sie möchte einen neuen Bademantel.
Tante Heidi	Sie bringen ihr Turnschuhe von Nike mit.	Nike-Turnschuhe sind in Amerika viel billiger als in Europa.
Onkel Georg	Sie bringen ihm einen U-Bahn-Plan von New York mit.	Er sammelt U-Bahn-Pläne.

Shopping for gifts

6 a 4; b 1; c 8; d 6; e 7; f 5; g 2; h 3. 7 a Er möchte seiner Frau etwas schenken. / Seiner Frau möchte er etwas schenken. b Beide kosten €49,99. c Seine Frau hat schon eine. d Nein, er gefällt ihm nicht. e Er nimmt den blauen Schal. 8 a -e; b -e; c -e; d -e; e -e; f -en. 9 a 4; b 8; c 7; d 1; e 3; f 5; g 6; h 2. 10 Guten Tag. Können Sie mir helfen?/Ich suche ein Buch über New York. Können Sie mir etwas empfehlen?/Nein. Er gefällt mir nicht./Das gefällt mir. Wie viel kostet es?/Das Buch nehme ich. Haben Sie das neue Buch von Dan Brown?/Danke schön, und wo ist die Kasse, bitte?

Testing yourself

1 a Man kann ihm eine CD von Maria Callas schenken. b Man kann ihr ein Buch über Indien schenken. c Man kann ihm Turnschuhe schenken. d Man kann ihnen eine Flasche Wein schenken. e Man kann ihr ein Buch über Blumen und Pflanzen schenken. f Man kann ihm ein Computerspiel schenken.

2 a -en; b -e; c -e; d -en; e -e; f -en g -en

UNIT 19

Healthy living

1

gesund	ungesund
• Salat essen	• fernsehen und Kartoffelchips essen
• zweimal in der Woche schwimmen gehen	• jeden Tag vier Flaschen Bier trinken
• ein Glas Rotwein pro Tag trinken	• fünf Stunden ohne Pause vor dem Computer sitzen
• Fahrrad fahren	
• lange spazieren gehen	

2 Possible answers

Es ist gesund, wenn man Salat isst.

Ich finde es ungesund, wenn man fernsieht und Kartoffelchips isst.

Es ist gesund, wenn man zweimal in der Woche schwimmen geht.

Ich finde es ungesund, wenn man jeden Tag vier Flaschen Bier trinkt.

Ich finde es aber gesund, wenn man ein Glas Rotwein pro Tag trinkt.

Es ist ungesund, wenn man fünf Stunden ohne Pause vor dem Computer sitzt.

Es ist gesund, wenn man Rad fährt und auch wenn man lange spazieren geht.

3 Possible answers

a Ja, es ist gut, wenn man manchmal (aber nicht zu oft!) einen Schnaps trinkt.

b Ja, es ist schlecht, wenn man zu viel Fernsehen sieht.

c Ja, man ist eigentlich ein bisschen altmodisch, wenn man keine Jeans trägt.

d Nein, es ist nicht ungesund, wenn man jeden Tag fünf Tassen Kaffee trinkt. (Aber es ist auch nicht besonders gesund!)

e Ja, es ist gesund, wenn man viermal pro Woche ins Fitnesscenter geht.

4 a Wer joggt abends? MW; b Wer möchte mehr relaxen? ES-T; c Wer hat früher Volleyball gespielt? MF; d Wer lebt sehr gesund? GT; e Wer treibt viel Sport? GT; f Wer darf nicht mehr Ski fahren? MF

5

	Was tun sie im Moment?	Was dürfen sie nicht tun?	Was sollen sie tun?	Was wollen sie tun?
Gabriela	treibt viel Sport, spielt Fußball, Handball, ein bisschen Tennis; raucht nicht, trinkt sehr wenig Alkohol; isst gesund	X	X	will vielleicht einen Fitnessurlaub machen
Michael	joggt abends	darf nicht mehr rauchen	soll weniger Fett essen; soll mehr Sport treiben	will am Wochenende mehr mit dem Rad fahren
Marianne	geht vier- bis fünfmal in der Woche schwimmen	darf nicht mehr Volleyball spielen; darf auch nicht mehr Ski fahren	soll viel schwimmen gehen	will wieder aktiver leben
Egbert	geht Windsurfen und Tauchen; geht auch Ski fahren	X	soll nicht mehr so viel Sport machen	will mehr relaxen

6 Gabriela Tomascek   →   fühlt sich sehr fit.
   Michael Warnek   →   darf nicht mehr rauchen.
                               soll mehr Sport treiben.
   Marianne Feuermann   →   darf nicht mehr Ski fahren.
   Egbert Schmidt-Tizian   →   soll weniger Sport treiben.
                               will mehr Freizeit haben.

7 a Herr Kaspar ist zu dick. Die Ärztin sagt, er soll weniger essen.
b Frau Meier liebt Italien. Sie will nächstes Jahr nach Neapel
fahren. c Peter ist morgens immer müde. Seine Mutter sagt, er soll

früher ins Bett gehen. d Beate Sabowski hat Herzprobleme. Der Arzt sagt, sie darf nicht mehr rauchen. e Kinder unter 16 Jahren dürfen den Film nicht sehen. f Man soll nicht zu viel Kaffee trinken. g Im Sommer fahre ich nach Argentinien. Vorher will ich ein wenig Spanisch lernen. 9 a 8; b 3; c 2; d 1; e 5; f 7; g 4; h 6. 10 a richtig; b falsch; Die Schmerzen hat sie seit fast vier Wochen. c richtig; d richtig; e falsch; Sie darf nicht Volleyball spielen. Sie soll lieber zum Schwimmen gehen. f falsch; Sie sagt, es ist sehr wichtig. 11 Ich habe ziemlich starke Halsschmerzen./Etwa drei Tage und es wird immer schlimmer./Ich bin Lehrer(in)./Ja, aber was soll ich tun?/Ja, nächste Woche fliege ich nach Florida./Gut und vielen Dank.

Testing yourself
1 a soll; b soll; c will; d wollen; e Darfst; f darf; g dürfen

2 a Wenn du Englisch lernen möchtest, musst du in eine Sprachschule gehen. b Wenn Bodo ein altes Buch über Deutschland finden möchte, muss er auf dem Flohmarkt suchen. c Wenn ihr nächste Woche nach New York fliegen wollt, müsst ihr bald eure Tickets buchen. d Wenn Florian am Wochenende zu Heikes Party gehen möchte, muss er nett zu ihr sein. e Wenn Marcus ein Jahr in Madrid arbeiten möchte, muss er Spanisch lernen. f Wenn Sie kein Geld und keine Kreditkarte haben, müssen Sie mit einem Scheck bezahlen.

UNIT 20

Weather
3

	wo sie waren	Jahreszeit	Temperaturen	Wetter
Bärbel Sprecht	auf Kreta	Frühling	um 28 Grad	Ideal. Kein Regen. Jeden Tag Sonne und ein leichter Wind.
Jutta Weiß	Australien	Dezember (Sommer in Australien)	über 35 Grad	Sonne. Manchmal ein Gewitter.

4 a In München ist es wärmer. b 20 Grad Celsius. c Ja, es gibt
Schauer. d Nein. In Wien scheint die Sonne und es ist bedeckt.
e In Spanien gibt es Gewitter. f In Kairo scheint die Sonne. Die
Temperatur beträgt 35 Grad. 5 a Nachts sind es 6 Grad. b 23
Grad. c Wolken und Regen. d Schauer. e besser.

Holidays
6 a Er hat abends gut gegessen und ist manchmal in die Hotel-Bar
gegangen. b Nein, er konnte auch richtiges deutsches Bier kaufen.
c Sie machen jedes Jahr im Winter einen Skiurlaub. d Nächstes
Jahr wollen sie vielleicht mal in die Schweiz fahren. e Das Wetter
war eine Katastrophe. Sie hatten meistens Regen. Außerdem war es
sehr kalt. f Nein, nächstes Jahr fliegen sie lieber in den Süden, nach
Spanien oder Griechenland. g Nein, er sucht jetzt einen Job. h Vor
zwei Jahren ist er nach Mexiko-City geflogen.

7 a mit dem Flugzeug fliegen; b auf den Berg steigen; c zu Fuß
gehen; d mit dem Auto fahren; e im Meer schwimmen; f Ski laufen;
g im Park spazieren gehen.

8 a Er ist zu Fuß nach Hause gegangen. b Petra und Ulrike sind
jeden Tag vier Stunden im Meer geschwommen. c Frau Müller ist
fast jeden Tag Ski gelaufen / gefahren. d Seppl Dreier ist auf den
Mount Everest gestiegen. e Diesmal bin ich mit der Lufthansa nach
London geflogen. f Annette ist viel mit dem Fahrrad gefahren. g Er
ist im Stadtpark spazieren gegangen.

9 ‚Letztes Jahr war ich in Heidelberg im Urlaub. Dort habe ich in
einer Jugendherberge gewohnt. Abends bin ich in eine Karaoke-
Kneipe gegangen. In der Kneipe habe ich ein Lied von Elvis Presley
gesungen. Dort hat mich ein Produzent gehört. Ihm hat meine
Stimme sehr gut gefallen. Am nächsten Tag bin ich mit ihm nach
Berlin geflogen. In einem Studio habe ich eine neue CD gemacht. In
Berlin bin ich 10 Tage geblieben. Dann habe ich im Fernsehen und
im Radio gesungen. Nächstes Jahr will ich in Las Vegas singen.'

10 a falsch; b richtig; c richtig; d falsch; e falsch; f richtig.

11 Eine einzige Katastrophe./Die ersten drei Tage hatten wir Regen. Deshalb konnten wir nicht spazieren gehen./Ein Freund und ich sind mit dem Wagen gegen einen Baum gefahren./Ja, meine Beine haben mir wehgetan, aber es war nichts Schlimmes./Nur zwei Tage, aber dann musste ich wieder nach Hause fahren./Jetzt geht es mir wieder gut.

12 a richtig b falsch; 22 Millionen Deutsche finden kurze Urlaube besser. c richtig d richtig e falsch; Es fahren mehr Leute nach London als nach Amsterdam.

Testing yourself
1 Na, wie geht's? Dieses Jahr sind wir nicht **nach** Indien geflogen oder **in** die Berge gefahren. Nein, wir haben Urlaub **an** der Ostsee gemacht, **auf** der Insel Rügen. Rügen liegt im Nordosten Deutschlands. Das Wetter war gut, wir sind viel **im** Meer geschwommen. Außerdem haben wir einen Ausflug **nach** Berlin gemacht. Dort war es natürlich auch sehr interessant. So viel hat sich verändert. Wir sind **ins** Pergamonmuseum gegangen und waren auch **im** Museum für Deutsche Geschichte.

2 a wollte, musste; b konnten; c sollte, konnte; d durfte; e Mussten.

UNIT 21

Making telephone calls
2

informell	formell
– Hallo, Bernd, bist du es? – Ist Inga da?	– Guten Tag, Herr Preiß. Hier spricht Frau Weber. – Spreche ich mit Frau Schmidt? – Ich möchte mit Herrn Klaus sprechen. – Kann ich bitte mit Frau Groß sprechen?

3

	1	2	3
Sie ist beim Zahnarzt.	☐	☒	☐
Die Leitung ist besetzt.	☒	☐	☐
Er ist auf Geschäftsreise.	☐	☐	☒
Soll sie zurückrufen?	☐	☒	☐
Wollen Sie warten?	☒	☐	☐
Wollen Sie eine Nachricht hinterlassen?	☐	☐	☒
Er möchte mich morgen zurückrufen.	☐	☐	☒
Ich bin zu Hause.	☐	☒	☐
Ich rufe später noch mal an.	☒	☐	☐

a Sie telefoniert. b Sie ist beim Zahnarzt und kommt in einer Stunde wieder nach Hause. c Er ist auf Geschäftsreise (in Wien) und ist wahrscheinlich morgen wieder im Büro. d Sie möchte ihm ein (fantastisches) Geschenk geben. 4 a 3; b 1; c 5: d 6; e 2; f 4. 5 a Ich sage es ihm. (I'll tell him.) b Ich richte es ihm aus. (I'll pass the message on to him.) c Soll ich ihnen eine Nachricht hinterlassen? (Should I leave them a message?) d Soll ich ihr etwas ausrichten? (Should I pass on a message to her?) e Sag ihr bitte, ich bin um fünf Uhr da. (Tell her, please, I'll be there at 5 o'clock.) 6 Guten Tag. **Hier** ist der telefonische Anrufbeantworter von Evelyn und Michael Schweighofer. Wir sind im Moment **leider** nicht da. Sie können uns aber gerne nach dem Pfeifton eine **Nachricht** hinterlassen. Bitte sagen Sie uns Ihren **Namen** und Ihre **Telefonnummer** und wir **rufen** Sie dann so schnell wie möglich **zurück**.

7

8 a 5; b 1; c 2; d 3; e 4. 9 a Nein, links vorne war das Büro der Sekretärin, Frau Schüller. b richtig. c Nein, auf der rechten Seite in der Mitte war das Zimmer der Texter, Michaela und Günther; d Und ganz hinter rechts war der Raum der Chefin, Frau Conrad. e Ganz hinten links war dann das Zimmer des Managers, Guido Kafka. 10 a Ich habe den Namen der Designerin vergessen. b Die Telefonnummer der Kundin ist 45 76 98. c Die Rechnung des Hotels war astronomisch. d Die Reparatur des Computers hat drei Wochen gedauert. e Mir gefällt die Farbe des neuen Firmenautos nicht. f Die Anzahl der Leute ohne Arbeit beträgt über vier Millionen.

11 a richtig; b falsch; Herr Schneider hat am Ende der Woche einen
Termin mit ihr; c falsch; Er fährt auf Geschäftsreise in die USA;
d richtig; e falsch; Sie machen einen Termin für Donnerstag um
14.00 Uhr.

12 Guten Tag, ich möchte gern mit Frau Conrad sprechen./Vielen
Dank./Hier spricht ... . Ich habe einen Termin für Anfang der
Woche./Es tut mir sehr leid, aber ich muss den Termin absagen./
Ja. Passt es Ihnen am Ende der Woche?/Ich habe keine Termine für
Freitagmorgen. Das passt mir gut. Auf Wiederhören.

Testing yourself
1 a 1; b 6; c 2; d 3; e 8; f 5; g 7; h 4.

2 a Der Computer meiner Kollegin ist fantastisch. b Das Auto
meines Bruders fährt sehr schnell. c Die Firma meines alten
Schulfreundes war letztes Jahr sehr erfolgreich. d Die Kollegen
meines Mannes sind alle schrecklich langweilig. e Die Managerin
der exquisiten Boutique ‚La dame‘ kommt aus Krefeld. f Das Büro
unseres neuen Designers ist sehr schick. g Der Laptop meines
Sohnes hat €500 gekostet. h Die Ehepartner meiner Kollegen sind
alle furchtbar nett.

UNIT 22

Job applications
2 a E; b C; c B; d D; e C; f A. 3 a He needs special care; b Working
hours by agreement; c You have to have office experience; d Other
applications are pointless; e To start immediately; f Because of a
sudden vacancy. 4 a E; b A; c C; d D; e B.

CVs
5 a falsch; Herr Frankenthal ist verheiratet. b richtig; c falsch; Er
hat in Offenbach seinen Realschulabschluss gemacht. d richtig;
e falsch; Seinen ersten Job hatte er bei der Dresdner Bank. f richtig;
g richtig. 7 a wechseln; b machen; c bekommen; d arbeiten; f sein;

g besuchen. 8 a 1978. b Sie ist durch Asien gereist. c 1998–99.
d An der Universität Hamburg. e Drei Jahre. f Seit 2007.

9 Ich bin am 1. Juni 1978 in Bremen geboren. Von 1984 bis 1988
ging ich in die Grundschule in Bremen. Danach **wechselte** ich auf
das Heinrich-Heine-Gymnasium. 1997 **machte** ich mein Abitur.
Nach der Schule **reiste** ich durch Asien.
Von 1998 bis 1999 **machte** ich ein Praktikum bei der *Hamburger
Zeitung.*
Anschließend **studierte** ich Journalistik an der Universität Hamburg
und 2004 **machte** ich meinen Abschluss.
Nach dem Studium **arbeitete** ich von 2004 bis 2007 bei der
Tageszeitung in Berlin.
2007 **zog** ich wieder nach Hamburg und arbeitete beim
Nachrichtenmagazin *Der Spiegel.*

Testing yourself
1 a sah; b ging; c war; d stand; e gab; f standen; g aß; h trank;
i legte; j blieb; k dachte; l schlief. 2 Das Leben von Heinrich Böll
c Von 1928 bis 1937 besuchte er das Kaiser-Wilhelm-Gymnasium
in Köln. d 1937 machte er das Abitur. e 1937 begann er in Bonn
eine Buchhandelslehre. f 1939 studierte er an der Universität Köln
Germanistik. g Von 1939 bis 1945 war er Soldat im Zweiten
Weltkrieg. h 1942 heiratete er Annemarie Zech. i Von 1946 bis
1949 schrieb er Kurzgeschichten in Zeitschriften. j 1949 erschien
sein erstes Buch *Der Zug war pünktlich.* k Von 1949 bis 1985
schrieb er viele literarische Werke. l 1972 bekam er den Nobelpreis
für Literatur. m 1985 starb er am 16. Juli in Hürtgenwald / Eifel.

UNIT 23

Deutschland, Österreich und die Schweiz
2 a Ich meine, dass Frankfurt das Finanzzentrum von Deutschland
ist. b Ich glaube, dass es in Wien viele alte Kaffeehäuser gibt.
c Ich denke, dass München eine sehr schöne Stadt ist. d Ich glaube,
dass die Schweizer viel Humor haben. e Ich denke, dass die
Deutschen viel Bier trinken. f Ich meine, dass Deutschland ein sehr
interessantes Land ist.

3 Possible answers

a Ich glaube, dass Österreich größer als die Schweiz ist. b Ich bin sicher, dass die Hauptstadt von der Schweiz Bern heißt. c Ich glaube, dass es vier offizielle Sprachen in der Schweiz gibt. d Ich glaube, dass ich nur Innsbruck, Salzburg und Wien kenne. e Ich bin sicher, dass Mozart in Salzburg geboren ist. f Ich glaube, dass die Bundesrepublik Deutschland mehr als 80 Millionen Einwohner hat. g Ich bin sicher, dass die Hauptstadt der Bundesrepublik Berlin ist. h Keine Ahnung! i Ich glaube, dass das Oktoberfest in München stattfindet. j Ich bin sicher, dass Frankfurt am multikulturellsten ist.

4	Schweiz	Österreich	Deutschland
	Arzneimittel	Mozart-Kugeln	82,4 Millionen
	vier Sprachen	Schloss Schönbrunn	Einwohner
	7,5 Millionen	etwa doppelt so groß	Biergärten
	Einwohner	wie die Schweiz	Oktoberfest
		8,3 Millionen	viele Leute aus der
		Einwohner	Türkei
			neue Hauptstadt
			multikulturelle
			Gesellschaft

5 a 83 853 km². b 41 293 km². c 82,4 Millionen. d 8,3 Millionen. e 7,5 Millionen Einwohner. f 1990. g 3.10.1990. h 29,1%.

History

7 1969 wurde der Mond zum ersten Mal von einem Menschen betreten. 1981 wurde John Lennon ermordet. 1990 wurde Nelson Mandela nach 27 Jahren aus der Haft entlassen. 2002 wurde in Europa der Euro als neue Währung eingeführt. 2005 wurde New Orleans vom Hurrikan Katrina zerstört. 2009 wurde Barack Obama zum Präsidenten der USA gewählt.

8 a Die neunte Symphonie wurde von Ludwig van Beethoven komponiert. b Die Fußballweltmeisterschaft 1966 wurde von England gewonnen. c Die Dampfmaschine wurde von James Watt erfunden. d ‚Hamlet' wurde von William Shakespeare geschrieben.

e ‚Guernica' wurde von Pablo Picasso gemalt. f Das Penizillin wurde von Alexander Fleming entdeckt. g ‚Waterloo' wurde von Abba gesungen. h Die Queen wurde von Helen Mirren gespielt.

9 i a falsch; b richtig; c richtig; d falsch; e falsch; f richtig; g falsch. ii a (am 28. August) 1749 in Frankfurt am Main geboren. b Jura. c Seine Novelle ‚Die Leiden des jungen Werther.' d an den Hof von Weimar. e nach Italien. f ‚Faust'. g an den Teufel. h in Weimar. i in fast alle Sprachen übersetzt. j nach ihm benannt.

10 Ja, in der Schweiz werden vier Sprachen gesprochen./Die Bundesrepublik Deutschland wurde 1949 gegründet./Die Berliner Mauer wurde 1961 gebaut./Deutschland wurde am 3. Oktober 1990 wiedervereinigt./‚Faust' wurde von Johann Wolfgang von Goethe geschrieben./Natürlich. Es wurde 1808 veröffentlicht./ Natürlich. Das Goethe-Institut wurde nach ihm benannt.

Testing yourself

1 a …, weil er oft geschäftlich nach Frankfurt fährt. b …, weil sie die Musik von Mozart liebt. c …, weil er gern Sprachen lernt. d …, weil es gut für seine Karriere ist. e …, weil sie die deutsche Sprache sehr schön findet. f … weil sie Berlin mag. 2 a Muttersprache; b Regionen; c Ländern; d Hauptstadt; e Bekannt; f Arzneimittel; g Einwohner; h Sehenswürdigkeiten; i Wiedervereinigung; j Städte; k Ausländer; l Gesellschaft.

Listening comprehension transcripts

UNIT 1: SAYING HELLO

3 Ein Unfall

Polizist	Wie heißen Sie, bitte?
Frau Gruber	Ich heiße Gertrud Gruber.
Polizist	Gruber, Gertrud … Und Sie? Wie ist Ihr Name?
Herr Braun	Mein Name ist Braun, Martin Braun.
Polizist	Braun, Martin … Und Sie? Wie heißen Sie?
Herr Schwarz	Ich heiße Boris Schwarz.
Polizist	Schwarz, Boris …

UNIT 1: GREETING PEOPLE

6 Grüße im Radio und Fernsehen
- Guten Abend, verehrte Zuschauer…
- Radio Bayern. Guten Morgen, liebe Zuhörer…
- Hallo, schön' guten Morgen…
- Gute Nacht, liebe Zuhörer…
- Guten Tag. Hier ist die Tagesschau…
- Unser Programm geht jetzt zu Ende. Wir wünschen Ihnen eine gute Nacht.

UNIT 1: ROLLENSPIEL: WHERE DO YOU COME FROM?

9 Woher kommen Sie?
Wie heißen Sie?
Woher kommen Sie?
Und wo wohnen Sie jetzt?

3 Im Büro

Frau Bachmann	Guten Tag, Frau Huber!
Frau Huber	Tag, Frau Bachmann! Und wie geht's Ihnen?
Frau Bachmann	Na ja … Mir geht es heute nicht so gut.
Frau Huber	Das tut mir aber leid.
Frau Bachmann	Und Ihnen? Wie geht's Ihnen denn?
Frau Huber	Mir geht's wirklich sehr gut… Oh, da kommt Herr Dietz!
Bachmann u. Huber	Tag, Herr Dietz!
Herr Dietz	Tag, Frau Huber! Tag, Frau Bachmann!
Frau Huber	Und wie geht's heute?
Herr Dietz	Ach, es geht.

UNIT 3: NUMBERS 1–10

2 Fußballbundesliga
Die weiteren Ergebnisse vom 33. Spieltag:
Hamburg–Dortmund: 2 zu 1
Bochum–Hannover: 6 zu 0
Duisburg–Mönchengladbach: 4 zu 2
Bielefeld–Wolfsburg: 1 zu 3
Schalke–Freiburg: 0 zu 2
Nürnberg–Hertha Berlin: 3 zu 0
Bremen–Frankfurt: 1 zu 0

4 Wer ist da?
– Guten Tag! Wie heißen Sie, bitte?
– Baumgart, Waltraud.
– Wie schreibt man das?
– B-A-U-M-G-A-R-T.
– Ja, gut. Sie stehen auf der Liste.
– Guten Tag! Mein Name ist Schanze, Martin Schanze.
– Und wie buchstabiert man Schanze?

- S-C-H-A-N-Z-E.
- Ja, Sie sind auch auf der Liste.
- Hallo! Mein Name ist Hesse, H-E-S-S-E.
- Danke. Ja, hier ist Ihr Name.
- Und ich heiße Schidelowskaja S-C-H-I-D-E...
- Ist schon gut! Sie sind auch dabei, Frau Schidelowskaja!

5 Welche Firmennamen hören Sie?
Und nun der Bericht von der Börse aus Frankfurt. Ein guter Tag für die AEG, plus 9 Punkte. Von der Autoindustrie ist Positives zu vermelden: BMW legte um 3 Prozent zu und auch VW meldet ein leichtes Plus. Dagegen ein schlechter Tag für die Banken: Deutsche Bank minus 5 Prozent und die DZ Bank minus 7. Nichts Neues von der Bahn: die DB meldete plus minus 0.

UNIT 3: NUMBERS 11–100

8 Die Lottozahlen
Die Lottozahlen: 6 8 14 23 26 46, und die Zusatzzahl: 22.

9 Anrufe bei der Auskunft

Kunde	Guten Tag. Ich hätte gern die Telefonnummer von Berta Schulz in Hamburg.
Frauenstimme	Schulz? Wie schreibt man das, bitte?
Kunde	S-C-H-U-L-Z.
Frauenstimme	Vorname Berta?
Kunde	Ja, richtig.
Computerstimme	Die Nummer ist 040-30 07 51.
Kunde	Hallo. Ich brauche die Nummer von Günter Marhenke hier in Hamburg.
Frauenstimme	Marhenke? Wie buchstabiert man das?
Kunde	M-A-R-H-E-N-K-E.
Frauenstimme	Können Sie das wiederholen?
Kunde	Ja, kein Problem: M-A-R-H-E-N-K-E.
Computerstimme	Die Nummer ist 040-73 45 92.

10 Rollenspiel: Telefonnummern, Handynummern, usw.

Welche Telefonnummer haben Sie?

Wie ist Ihre Handynummer?

Wie ist Ihre Faxnummer?

Wie ist Ihre E-Mail-Adresse?

Here is how Jochen replies:

> **Jochen** Meine Telefonnummer ist null – sieben – elf –
> dreiundzwanzig – achtunddreißig – einundvierzig.
> Meine Handynummer ist 01734 06 02 94. Meine
> Faxnummer ist null – sieben – elf – vierundzwanzig –
> neunundachtzig – null – zwo. Meine E-Mail-Adresse ist
> jkrause@yahoo.at

UNIT 4: I SPEAK GERMAN

2 Noch zwei Abendkursstudenten

Dialog 1

> **Gür** Hallo! Mein Name ist Gür Yalezan. Ich bin Türke und
> komme aus Berlin. Ich wohne jetzt in der Nähe von
> Leipzig, in Taucha. Ich spreche Türkisch, Deutsch und
> ziemlich gut Englisch. Ich bin ledig und studiere in
> Leipzig.

Dialog 2

> **Susi** Ich heiße Susi Merkl – das buchstabiert man S-U-S-I
> und M-E-R-K-L – und bin Österreicherin. Ich komme aus
> Innsbruck, wohne aber jetzt in Rötha, hier in der Nähe
> von Leipzig. Ich spreche Deutsch und Englisch und ich
> verstehe ein bisschen Spanisch. Ich bin seit vier Jahren
> verheiratet und arbeite zur Zeit hier in Leipzig.

UNIT 4: NATIONALITIES AND LANGUAGES

6 Und jetzt Sie!
Wie ist Ihr Name?
Woher kommen Sie?
Wo wohnen Sie jetzt?
Sind Sie Amerikaner oder Amerikanerin?
Ist Ihre Muttersprache Englisch?
Verstehen Sie ein bisschen Deutsch?
Sind Sie verheiratet?
Studieren Sie?

UNIT 4: TESTING YOURSELF

1 Rollenspiel

Interviewer	Wie heißen Sie?
Jürgen	Ich heiße Jürgen Krause.
Interviewer	Sind Sie Deutscher?
Jürgen	Nein, ich bin Österreicher.
Interviewer	Woher kommen Sie?
Jürgen	Ich komme aus Wien.
Interviewer	Und wo wohnen Sie jetzt?
Jürgen	Ich wohne jetzt in Salzburg.
Interviewer	Was sprechen Sie?
Jürgen	Ich spreche Deutsch und Englisch.
Interviewer	Sind Sie verheiratet?
Jürgen	Nein, ich bin seit drei Jahren verwitwet.
Interviewer	Arbeiten Sie?
Jürgen	Ja, ich arbeite in Salzburg.

UNIT 6: OCCUPATIONS

3 Jochen Krenzler aus Dresden lernt Rainer Tietmeyer aus Coventry kennen

Jochen	Willkommen in Dresden! Mein Name ist Jochen Krenzler. Können Sie vielleicht Deutsch?
Rainer	Guten Tag! Ja, ich spreche Deutsch. Ich heiße Rainer Tietmeyer.
Jochen	Das ist ja großartig! Sind Sie denn Deutscher?
Rainer	Ja, aber meine Frau ist Engländerin und ich wohne seit 24 Jahren in England.
Jochen	Ach so. Und was sind Sie von Beruf?
Rainer	Ich bin Tischler.

4 Beantworten Sie die Fragen

Interviewer	Sind Sie Deutsche?
Gudrun	Ja, ich bin Deutsche.
Interviewer	Ist Ihr Mann auch Deutscher?
Gudrun	Nein, er ist Ire.
Interviewer	Und wo wohnen Sie?
Gudrun	Ich wohne seit 17 Jahren in Münster.
Interviewer	Sind Sie berufstätig?
Gudrun	Ja, ich bin Sekretärin bei Mannesmann.
Interviewer	Und was ist Ihr Mann von Beruf?
Gudrun	Er ist Taxifahrer.

UNIT 6: WHAT ARE YOU STUDYING?

7 Was studieren sie?

Heike	Hallo! Ich heiße Heike und das ist Martina. Wie heißt ihr?
Paul	Hallo! Ich heiße Paul und komme aus Bremen.
Daniel	Grüß euch! Ich bin der Daniel und komme aus Hamburg. Und woher kommt ihr?

Heike	Ich komme aus Düsseldorf und Martina kommt aus Köln. Seid ihr Studenten?
Paul	Ja, wir studieren in Bremen. Ich studiere Germanistik.
Daniel	Und ich Anglistik. Ihr seid wohl auch Studenten?
Heike	Ja, in Aachen. Ich studiere Informatik und Martina studiert Mathematik.

UNIT 8: SHOPPING

7 Rollenspiel: Was kostet …?
- Was kostet eine Flasche Wein?
- 4 Euro 90.

Und jetzt Sie!
- Was kostet ein Roggenbrot?
- 1 Euro 10.
- Und wie teuer ist eine Flasche Olivenöl?
- 5 Euro 40.
- Was kostet eine Dose Tomaten?
- 89 Cent.
- Und eine Packung Müsli?
- 1 Euro 65.
- Und was kosten die Äpfel?
- 1 Kilo 2 Euro 5.
- Und wie teuer ist der Emmenthaler Käse?
- 1 Kilo 12 Euro 25.
- Und was kostet ein Blumenkohl?
- 1 Euro 95.

6 Was ist Ihr Hobby?
Interview 1

Reporter	Guten Tag. Wir sind vom Radio und machen eine Umfrage. Was ist Ihr Hobby, bitte?
Touristin	Mein Hobby? Also, mein Hobby ist mein Garten. Und ich wandere gern.

Interview 2

Reporter	Entschuldigen Sie, bitte. Haben Sie ein Hobby?
Tourist	Ein Hobby? Ja, ich schwimme gern, ich gehe gern ins Kino und ich lese gern.
Reporter	Lesen Sie gern Krimis?
Tourist	Nein, ich lese nicht gern Krimis. Ich lese gern Romane und Biographien.

UNIT 10: THE TIME

3 & 4 Schreiben Sie die Uhrzeiten
Dialog 1

Female voice	Mmh. Das riecht ja lecker. Ist das Essen fertig?
Male voice	Es dauert noch einen kleinen Moment, Schatz. Wie spät ist es denn?
Female voice	Genau 6 Uhr 28.

Dialog 2

Female voice	Richard, aufstehen! Es ist schon zehn vor neun!
Male voice	Was? Zehn vor neun? Nein, das glaube ich nicht.
Female voice	Doch. Doch. Aufstehen.

Dialog 3

> **Female voice** Anke, weißt du wie spät es ist?
> **Female voice** Ja, es ist halb fünf.

Dialog 4

> **Male voice 1** Entschuldigung, wie viel Uhr ist es, bitte?
> **Male voice 2** Äh, Viertel vor neun.
> **Male voice 1** Vielen Dank.
> **Male voice 2** Gern geschehen.

5 Morgens oder abends?

Es ist ein Uhr mittags. / Es ist vier Uhr nachmittags. / Es ist acht Uhr abends. / Es ist elf Uhr abends. / Es ist neun Uhr morgens. / Es ist sechs Uhr morgens.

6 Die 24-Stunden-Uhr

Es ist dreizehn Uhr. / Es ist fünfzehn Uhr zwanzig. / Es ist sieben Uhr fünfundvierzig. / Es ist achtzehn Uhr zwölf. / Es ist dreiundzwanzig Uhr fünfunddreißig. / Es ist vier Uhr siebzehn.

10 Ein Tag im Leben von Herrn Fabione

> **Renate** Herr Fabione, Sie arbeiten als Automechaniker in einer Autowerkstatt. Wie sieht denn ein typischer Tag bei Ihnen aus?
> **Harr Fabione** Nun, normalerweise stehe ich früh auf, so gegen halb sieben Uhr. Oft kaufe ich morgens frische Brötchen und frühstücke mit meiner Frau und den Kindern.
> **Renate** Wann fängt denn Ihre Arbeit an?
> **Herr Fabione** Um acht Uhr.
> **Renate** Wie lange arbeiten Sie denn?

Herr Fabione	Bis 16 Uhr.
Renate	Und haben Sie eine Pause?
Herr Fabione	Nun, Mittagspause machen wir um 12 Uhr.
Renate	So, Feierabend ist so gegen vier. Was machen Sie denn dann?
Herr Fabione	Tja, ich fahre nach Hause und spiele oft mit den Kindern. Manchmal gehen wir in den Park oder spielen Fußball.
Renate	Und wann essen Sie zu Abend?
Herr Fabione	Meistens um halb sieben. Danach bringen wir dann die Kinder ins Bett.
Renate	Bleiben Sie zu Hause oder gehen Sie oft aus?
Herr Fabione	Oft bleiben wir zu Hause. Wir sehen nicht viel fern, wir lesen viel und meine Frau und ich lernen im Moment auch zusammen Spanisch. Manchmal kommt meine Schwiegermutter als Babysitterin und passt auf die Kinder auf. Dann gehen meine Frau und ich aus, ins Kino oder ins Restaurant oder wir besuchen Freunde.
Renate	Und wann gehen Sie normalerweise ins Bett?
Herr Fabione	Meistens um halb 12, manchmal erst später.

UNIT 13: TALKING ABOUT THE PAST

4 Sonntagmorgen

Angela	Hallo, Ulrike. Na, wie geht's?
Ulrike	Ganz gut, ich bin noch ein bisschen müde.
Angela	Oh, habe ich dich geweckt?
Ulrike	Nein, nein, ich habe gerade gefrühstückt.
Angela	Gerade gefrühstückt? Was hast du denn gestern gemacht?
Ulrike	Am Morgen war ich in der Stadt und habe eingekauft. Am Nachmittag habe ich Britta und Georg besucht. Am Abend waren wir dann zusammen in der neuen ‚Mondschein-Bar‘ und haben bis drei Uhr getanzt. Wir haben viel Spaß gehabt. Und du?

Angela	Ich habe gestern Morgen einen neuen Computer gekauft und, na ja, dann den ganzen Tag mit dem Computer gespielt.
Ulrike	Hast du auch im Internet gesurft?
Angela	Genau, das war schon interessant.
Ulrike	Und wie viel hast du für den Computer bezahlt?
Angela	€900. Er hat €100 weniger gekostet.
Ulrike	Und was habt ihr am Abend gemacht?
Angela	Bernd und ich haben gekocht und dann noch ein bisschen klassische Musik gehört. Ganz romantisch; wie früher, weißt du. Was machst du denn heute, Ulrike?
Ulrike	Tja, ich weiß noch nicht so genau. Vielleicht können wir ja…

UNIT 14: MORE ABOUT THE PAST

5 Mehr über Peter Wichtig

Moderator	Herr Wichtig, vielen Dank, dass Sie heute zu uns ins Studio kommen konnten. Ich weiß, Sie sind sehr busy im Moment.
Peter Wichtig	Ja, das stimmt. Wir bereiten eine neue Tournee vor und wir haben gerade eine neue CD auf dem Markt.
Moderator	Ja, bevor wir Ihren neuen Song spielen, Herr Wichtig, ein paar Fragen zu Ihrer Person. Wie lange machen Sie denn schon Musik?
Peter Wichtig	Seit 10 Jahren genau. Auch meinen ersten Hit habe ich genau vor 10 Jahren geschrieben: ‚Um acht Uhr aus dem Bett, das finde ich nicht nett.' Wir haben 400.000 CDs verkauft.
Moderator	Und wie viele CDs haben Sie insgesamt gemacht?
Peter Wichtig	Insgesamt 10. Jedes Jahr eine, das ist nicht schlecht, oder?
Moderator	Schreiben Sie alle Lieder selber?

Peter Wichtig	Ja, ich komponiere die Musik und schreibe auch die Texte, klar.
Moderator	Sie sind ein Allround-Mensch, Herr Wichtig, schreiben und komponieren, geben viele Interviews, gehen zweimal im Jahr auf Tournee, haben Sie denn überhaupt Freizeit?
Peter Wichtig	Wenig, wenig.
Moderator	Und wenn, was machen Sie dann?
Peter Wichtig	Im Winter fahre ich gern Ski. Und im Sommer, nun ich surfe, spiele Tennis – ich bin ein guter Freund von Boris. Und dann die vielen Partys, New York, Berlin, Nairobi, Los Angeles, Monte Carlo… Und die vielen Freunde, die ich sehen muß: Robert de Niro, Michelle Pfeiffer, meinen Kollegen Mick Jagger, Claudia Schiffer, Franz Beckenbauer…
Moderator	Äh, Herr Wichtig, ich muss Sie leider unterbrechen, aber wir müssen im Programm weitermachen. Hier ist also die neueste Single von Peter Wichtig: ‚Dich kann man vergessen‘ – aah, pardon: ‚Ich kann dich nicht vergessen‘. Puh.

UNIT 14: THEN AND NOW

9 Hören Sie zu! Klassentreffen

Bernd	Hallo, Dieter, na, 25 Jahre ist das her. Kaum zu glauben.
Dieter	Tja, 25 Jahre, und du hast immer noch so lange Haare wie früher, Bernd. Fantastisch. Ich dagegen, na, kein Haar mehr, schon seit 5 Jahren und dabei hatte ich früher auch so schöne, lange Haare.
Bernd	Na komm, Dieter, charmant wie Yul Brynner. Sag mal, trinkst du denn immer noch so gern Rum und Cola wie früher?
Dieter	Cola und Rum, oh, das ist lange her. Nein, ich trinke

	jetzt sehr gern Wein, französischen Wein. Aber sag mal Bernd, du trinkst Mineralwasser? Früher hast du doch immer viel Cognac getrunken, das war doch dein Lieblingsgetränk.
Bernd	Ja, das stimmt. Aber, na ja, mein Arzt hat gesagt, ich soll mit dem Alkohol aufhören. Und jetzt trinke ich eben mehr Wasser, Tee, Orangensaft, weißt du. Hörst du eigentlich immer noch so gern Blues-Musik, du hast doch damals alle Platten von Eric Clapton gehabt, oder?
Dieter	Ja, das ist lange her. Am meisten höre ich jetzt klassische Musik, vor allem Beethoven. Und du, immer noch der Elvis-Fan?
Bernd	Elvis forever, haha. Nein, Rock'n Roll höre ich nicht mehr. Ich höre viel Jazz-Musik.
Dieter	Und machst du noch selber Musik? Du hast doch früher in einer Band gespielt?
Bernd	Nein, das ist lange vorbei. Wenn ich Zeit habe, reise ich. Letzten Monat war ich erst für eine Woche in Moskau. Du warst doch früher ein guter Fußballspieler?
Dieter	Tja, das stimmt, aber im Moment spiele ich nur noch Tennis, ich bereite mich auf Wimbledon vor, haha. Guck mal, da drüben ist Gerd.
Bernd	Hallo, Gerd, na, wie geht es …

UNIT 15: IN THE HOME

11 Rollenspiel: Und jetzt Sie!

Moderator	Wohnen Sie in einem Haus oder in einer Wohnung?
Frau Martini	Wir wohnen in einer Wohnung.
Moderator	Wie viele Zimmer hat die Wohnung?
Frau Martini	Die Wohnung hat vier Zimmer, plus Küche und Bad.
Moderator	Wie sind die Zimmer?

Frau Martini	Die Zimmer sind groß und hell.
Moderator	Haben Sie einen Garten?
Frau Martini	Nein, wir haben leider keinen Garten.
Moderator	Ist die Miete oder die Hypothek teuer?
Frau Martini	Die Miete ist nicht so teuer, 465 Euro, plus Nebenkosten.
Moderator	Wie ist die Umgebung?
Frau Martini	Die Umgebung ist ruhig und sehr grün.
Moderator	Haben Sie gute Verkehrsverbindungen?
Frau Martini	Ja, die Verkehrsverbindungen sind sehr gut.
Moderator	Wie lange fahren Sie zur Arbeit?
Frau Martini	Ich fahre nur 10 Minuten zur Arbeit.
Moderator	Fahren Sie mit dem Auto, mit dem Bus oder mit der U-Bahn?
Frau Martini	Ich fahre mit der U-Bahn. Im Sommer kann ich mit dem Fahrrad fahren.

UNIT 17: FASHION

5 Frau Martens ist Verkäuferin in einem Kaufhaus.

Interviewer	... Und Sie Frau Martens. Sind Sie berufstätig?
Frau Martens	Ja, ich bin Verkäuferin in der Kaufhalle hier in Hanau. Ich arbeite seit sieben Jahren dort und finde meinen Beruf eigentlich ganz interessant.
Interviewer	Interessant, aber sicher auch anstrengend?
Frau Martens	Ich arbeite nur halbtags, von acht Uhr bis um 12.30 Uhr. Meine Arbeit ist also nicht besonders anstrengend. Doch wenn meine Kinder um eins nach Hause kommen – dann wird's anstrengend! Und wenn mein Sohn im Fernsehen ein neues Computerspiel sieht – dann muss er das unbedingt haben! Die eine Tochter möchte neue Schuhe von Bruno Magli, die andere eine neue Jeans-Jacke von Calvin Klein.
Interviewer	Und für Sie? Ist Mode auch für Sie wichtig?

Frau Martens	Ich persönlich finde Mode uninteressant. Ich ziehe nur an, was ich mag.
Interviewer	Und wie sind im Allgemeinen die Kunden?
Frau Martens	Wir haben meistens ganz nette Kunden. Nur selten sind sie unfreundlich. Also, ich versuche dann immer, besonders freundlich zu sein.

UNIT 17: CLOTHES

12 Was für Kleidung tragen die Leute?
Dialog 1

Richard	Was tragen Sie denn normalerweise für Kleidung bei der Arbeit?
Mareike	Ich arbeite in einem Büro und die Atmosphäre ist sehr relaxed. Normalerweise trage ich eine bequeme Hose, meistens mit einer Bluse, wenn es kälter ist, mit einem Pulli.
Richard	Und zu Hause?
Mareike	Eigentlich dasselbe. Eine Hose, oft auch eine Jeans – bei der Arbeit trage ich kaum Jeans – T-Shirt, Pullover. Ich mag bequeme Sachen. Eigentlich trage ich alles, was bequem ist. Was ich aber nicht mag sind Röcke. Röcke ziehe ich fast überhaupt nicht an.

Dialog 2

Richard	Herr Scholz, was tragen Sie denn normalerweise bei der Arbeit?
Günther	Bei der Arbeit trage ich immer einen Anzug, meistens einen dunkelblauen. Dazu ein weißes Hemd und eine Krawatte.
Richard	Und zu Hause?
Günther	Zu Hause, nun, etwas Bequemeres, ein sportliches Hemd oder ein Poloshirt.

| Richard | Gibt es etwas, was Sie nicht gerne anziehen? |
| Günther | Nun, wie gesagt, ich trage sehr gern sportliche Kleidung in meiner Freizeit, ich spiele auch Golf und Tennis, ich mag elegante Kleidung, was ich nicht mag ist bunte Kleidung, rote Hemden, Hawaii-Hemden, bunte Hosen und solche Sachen. |

UNIT 18: INVITATIONS AND PRESENTS

5 Was bringen wir der Familie mit?

Saskia	Was für ein Stress, jetzt müssen wir auch noch nach den Geschenken suchen. Wir haben mal wieder bis zum letzten Tag gewartet.
Sys	Na ja, das ist ja nichts Neues. Aber was kaufen wir bloß?
Saskia	Wie wäre es mit einer Platte von Frank Sinatra für Mutti?
Sys	Gute Idee! Mutti war immer ein großer Fan von ihm.
Saskia	Und Vati? Was bringen wir ihm mit? Das ist doch schwierig, oder?
Sys	Vati sieht gern Baseball-Spiele im Fernsehen. Kaufen wir ihm doch einfach eine Baseball-Mütze von den New York Yankees.
Saskia	Toll! Vati mit einer Baseball-Mütze – das möchte ich sehen!
Sys	Und Oma hat gesagt, sie möchte einen neuen Bademantel.
Saskia	Gut, dann schenken wir ihr einen Bademantel. Hoffentlich ist er aber nicht zu teuer.
Sys	Oh, Tante Heidi müssen wir Turnschuhe von Nike kaufen. Nike-Turnschuhe sind in Amerika viel billiger als in Europa.
Saskia	Und Onkel Georg sammelt U-Bahn-Pläne. Ihm können wir einen U-Bahn-Plan von New York mitbringen.
Sys	Das wär's also. Gehen wir schnell einkaufen. Und vergiss nicht, deine Kreditkarte mitzunehmen!

3 Was für Wetter hatten die Leute im Urlaub?

Bärbel Specht Wir waren diesen Frühling auf Kreta. Das war fantastisch. Ich war einmal im Sommer dort, oh, das war nicht auszuhalten: über 40 Grad. Aber diesmal: meistens so um 28 Grad. Ideal. Und auch kein Regen. Jeden Tag Sonne und ein leichter Wind. Zum Windsurfen war das wirklich toll. Das kann ich nur jedem empfehlen. Kreta im Frühling: Das ist ein Erlebnis.

Jutta Weiss Mein Traum war es immer, einmal nach Australien zu fahren und eine alte Schulfreundin von mir dort zu besuchen. Und letzten Dezember hat es endlich geklappt, da hatte ich Zeit und auch genug Geld. In Deutschland war Winter, minus 12 Grad, alle haben hier gefroren, und als ich in Sydney ankam, da war dort Sommer: über 35 Grad. Und Weihnachten haben wir im T-Shirt gefeiert, die machen dort Straßenpartys, unglaublich. Drei Wochen nur Sonne, nur manchmal hat es ein Gewitter gegeben. Aber – ganz ehrlich – mir war das manchmal einfach zu heiß.

5 Der Wetterbericht im Radio

Nun die Wettervorhersage für Sonntag, den 25. Mai. Nachts kühlt es bis auf 6 Grad ab. Tagsüber im Südosten 23, in den übrigen Gebieten 13 bis 20 Grad Celsius. Die weiteren Aussichten: Montag im Norden und Osten Wolken und Regen. Dienstag in ganz Deutschland Schauer. Am Mittwoch ab und zu sonnige Abschnitte, und nur noch im Osten Schauer.

3 Telefonanrufe
Dialog 1

Receptionist	Berchtesmeier und Company. Guten Tag. Was kann ich für Sie tun?
Herr Giesecke	Guten Tag. Giesecke von der Firma Krönke, Maschinenbau. Könnte ich bitte mit Frau Dr. Martens sprechen?
Receptionist	Einen Moment bitte, ich verbinde… (Pause) Herr Giescke, es tut mir leid, aber Frau Dr. Martens telefoniert gerade. Die Leitung ist besetzt. Wollen Sie warten?
Herr Giesecke	Äh, Giesecke, mit e, nicht Giescke.
Receptionist	Oh. Entschuldigung, Herr Giesecke.
Herr Giesecke	Wie lange kann es denn dauern?
Receptionist	Ja, das ist schwer zu sagen. Soll ich Frau Dr. Martens vielleicht etwas ausrichten? Oder soll sie Sie zurückrufen?
Herr Giesecke	Nein, nein, nein. Das ist nicht nötig. Ich rufe später noch mal an. Auf Wiederhören.
Receptionist	Auf Wiederhören, Herr Giescke… äh (Pause). Puh.

Dialog 2

Nadine möchte ihre Freundin, Sandy, sprechen. Hören Sie zu.

Nadine	Hallo, Frau Stoll, hier ist Nadine. Ist die Sandy da?
Frau Stoll	Hallo, Nadine. Na, wie geht's dir?
Nadine	Ganz gut, danke.
Frau Stoll	Das ist ja schön, Nadine. Aber leider ist die Sandy im Augenblick nicht da.
Nadine	Oh, das ist schade. Wo ist sie denn?
Frau Stoll	Sie ist gerade beim Zahnarzt.
Nadine	Oh, nein. Wann kommt sie denn wieder?

Frau Stoll	Ich denke, so in einer Stunde. Soll sie dich dann zurückrufen?
Nadine	Ja, das wäre toll. Ich bin zu Hause.
Frau Stoll	Gut, ich sage es ihr. Und grüß deine Familie.
Nadine	Klar, das mache ich.
Frau Stoll	Tschüss, Nadine.
Nadine	Tschüss, Frau Stoll.

Dialog 3

Corinna	Hallo Peterle, bist du's?
Herr Schulz	Äh, meinen Sie Herrn Fink? Der ist im Moment nicht da, der ist auf Geschäftsreise.
Corinna	Oh, äh, das wusste ich gar nicht.
Herr Schulz	Ja, er musste für drei Tage nach Wien.
Corinna	Wann kommt er denn wieder?
Herr Schulz	Wahrscheinlich morgen. Wollen Sie vielleicht eine Nachricht hinterlassen?
Corinna	Wenn das geht, ja, gerne.
Herr Schulz	Natürlich. Kein Problem.
Corinna	Können Sie ihm sagen, Corinna hat angerufen und er soll mich morgen zurückrufen. Ich habe ein fantastisches Geschenk für ihn.
Herr Schulz	Gut. Das sage ich ihm.
Corinna	Vielen Dank. Auf Wiederhören.
Herr Schulz	Auf Wiederhören.

UNIT 22: CVS

8 Lebenslauf II

Frau Schulte Mein Name ist Claudia Schulte und im Moment lebe und arbeite ich in Hamburg. Geboren bin ich aber 1978 in Bremen, wo ich dann auch zur Schule gegangen bin und zwar zunächst von 1984 bis 1988 auf die Grundschule und danach aufs Heinrich-Heine-Gymnasium. Nach dem Abitur 1997 war ich dann nicht so sicher, was ich eigentlich machen sollte und habe dann ein bisschen gejobbt, um genug Geld zu haben und bin dann für ein Jahr durch Asien gereist. Das war eine wichtige Erfahrung für mich.

Als ich dann nach Deutschland zurückgekommen bin, habe ich mit etwas Glück eine Praktikumsstelle bei der *Hamburger Zeitung* gefunden und dort für zwei Jahre, von 1998 bis 1999 als Praktikantin gearbeitet.

Nach den zwei Jahren Praxis habe ich dann ein Studium an der Universität Hamburg angefangen und von 1999 bis 2004 studiert, nebenbei natürlich für verschiedene Zeitungen geschrieben.

Nach dem Studium habe ich gleich eine Stelle bei der *Tageszeitung* in Berlin gefunden und dort drei Jahre – von 2004 bis 2007 – gearbeitet.

Seit 2007 arbeite ich beim *Spiegel*, wieder in Hamburg – das ist natürlich ein Traum für jeden Journalisten.

UNIT 23: DEUTSCHLAND, ÖSTERREICH UND DIE SCHWEIZ

9 Ein Radioprogramm

Johann Wolfgang von Goethe gilt heute über 175 Jahre nach seinem Tod als einer der universalen Repräsentanten europäischer Kultur. Geboren am 28.8.1749 in Frankfurt am Main, erhielt er als Kind Privatunterricht und ging dann auf die Universitäten von Leipzig und Straßburg, wo er Jura studierte. Beinflusst wurde er durch einen anderen bekannten Schriftsteller, Johann Gottfried Herder, der ihn dazu bewegte, zu schreiben.

Berühmt wurde Goethe 1774 durch seine Novelle ,Die Leiden des jungen Werther', die ihn über Nacht in ganz Europa bekannt machte.

1775 ging Goethe an den Hof von Weimar, wo er in den Staatsdienst eintrat und auch politisch tätig wurde. Weiterhin schrieb er Theaterstücke und andere Werke.

1786 reiste er für zwei Jahre nach Italien und wurde stark vom Klassizismus beeinflusst. Zurück in Weimar begann er eine sehr produktive Zeit: Er veröffentlichte Bücher über naturwissenschaftliche Themen und schrieb einige seiner bekanntesten Werke. 1808 erschien dann sein wohl bekanntestes Theaterstück ‚Faust‘, in dem ein Wissenschaftler und Philosoph seine Seele an den Teufel verkauft. Bis zu seinem Tod 1832 in Weimar blieb Goethe ein äußerst produktiver Schriftsteller, dessen Werke in fast alle Sprachen übersetzt wurden. Das Goethe-Institut, das Kulturinstitut Deutschlands, ist nach ihm benannt.

Glossary of grammatical terms

The glossary covers the most important grammar terminology used in this book. qv (quod vide) means 'which see', i.e. please see the entry for this word.

Adjectives Adjectives are used to provide more information about nouns. In English they remain unchanged whether they stand on their own after a verb, such as *to be* or *to seem* (The car is *new.*) or whether they appear in front of a noun (The *new* car wasn't cheap.). In German the adjective does not change after a verb, such as **sein** or **scheinen** (**Das Auto ist neu.**), but endings *are* needed on adjectives that come in front of a noun (**Das *neue* Auto war nicht billig.**).

Adverbs Just as adjectives provide more information about nouns, so adverbs tend to provide more information about verbs: Wayne ran *quickly* down the stairs. But adverbs can also provide more information about adjectives: I was *completely* exhausted. In English adverbs often (but not always) end in *-ly*. In German adverbs often have the same form as adjectives: **Deine Arbeit ist *gut.*** Your work is *good*. **Du hast das sehr *gut* gemacht.** You did that very *well*.

Articles There are two main types of articles: *definite* and *indefinite*. In English the definite article is *the*. In German there are three definite articles: **der, die** and **das**, referring to the three different genders in German. The term indefinite article is given to the words *a* and *an*. In German the indefinite articles are **ein, eine**, etc. (See also **Gender.**)

Auxiliary verbs Auxiliary verbs are used as a support to the main verb, e.g. I *am* working; he *has* gone. The most important auxiliary verbs in German are **haben, sein** and **werden**. These are used in the formation of the present perfect tense (qv) and of the passive (qv): **Ich *habe* gerade einen sehr guten Film gesehen**. I *have* just seen a good film. **Die neue Schule *wurde* 1998 gebaut**. The new school *was* built in 1998. (See also **Modal verbs.**)

Cases There are four cases in German: the *nominative*, the *accusative*, the *genitive* and the *dative*. Cases are used in German to express relationships between the various parts of the sentence. Here is a short summary:

Nominative: this is the term used for the case that indicates the *subject* (qv) of the sentence:

Der *Mann* kauft einen Computer. The *man* buys a computer.

Accusative: this is the term used for the case that indicates the direct object (*object* qv) of the sentence:

Der Mann kauft *einen Computer*. The man buys a *computer*.

Dative: this is the term used for the case that indicates the indirect object (*object* qv) of the sentence:

Wir haben den Computer   We gave the computer *to my*
   meinem Bruder gegeben.   *brother.*

Genitive: this is the term used for the case that indicates possession:

Das ist der Computer *meines* That's *my brother's* computer.
   Bruders.

Note that *prepositions* (qv) in German are followed by the accusative, dative or genitive case.

Comparative When we make comparisons, we need the comparative form of the *adjective* (qv). In English this usually means adding *-er* to the adjective or putting *more* in front of it:

This shirt is cheap<u>er</u> than that one. This blouse is <u>more </u>expensive than that one.

Making comparisons in German follows the first example and adds **-er** to the adjective:

Dieses Hemd ist *billiger* als das da. Diese Bluse ist *teurer* als die da.

(See also **Superlative**.)

Conjunctions Conjunctions are words such as *and*, *but*, *when*, *if*, *unless*, *while* and *although*. They link words, clauses or sentences together: Bread *and* butter. **Brot *und* Butter.** He comes from Berlin *but* now lives in London. **Er kommt aus Berlin, *aber* lebt jetzt in London.**

In German a distinction is made between *co-ordinating conjunctions* and *subordinating conjunctions*. Co-ordinating conjunctions such as **und** *and*, **aber** *but* and **oder** *or* simply join two main clauses together and do not affect the word order: **Anna kommt aus München** *und* **ist 21 Jahre alt**. Anna comes from Munich *and* is 21 years old.

Subordinating conjunctions include such words as **wenn** *when, if*, **weil** *because*, **obwohl** *although* and **seitdem** *since* and send the verb to the end of the clause: **Er kann nicht kommen,** *weil* **er krank** *ist*. He can't come, *because* he is ill.

Demonstratives Words such as *this, that, these, those* are called demonstratives or *demonstrative adjectives*: *This* book is interesting. *Dieses* **Buch ist interessant.** *These* exercises are very difficult. *Diese* **Übungen sind sehr schwer.**

In German **dieser** (masculine), **diese** (feminine & plural), **dieses** (neuter) are the most commonly used demonstratives.

Gender In English gender is usually linked to male and female persons or animals, so for example we refer to a man as *he* and to a woman as *she*. Objects and beings of an indeterminate or no sex are referred to as having neuter gender. For instance, we refer to a table as *it*.

In German nouns have a gender irrespective of sex. For instance, the gender of the word for *girl* (**das Mädchen**) is neuter. In German there are three genders, *masculine, feminine* and *neuter*: **der Tisch** *the table*, **die Lampe** *the lamp*, **das Haus** *the house*.

Imperative The imperative is the form of the verb used to give orders or commands: *Help me*, please.

In German there are three main forms of the imperative, because of the various forms of address. *Helfen* **Sie mir, bitte!** (**Sie** form); *Hilf* **mir, bitte!** (**du** form); *Helft* **mir, bitte!** (**ihr** form).

Infinitive The infinitive is the basic form of the verb. This is the form that you will find entered in the dictionary. In English the infinitive is usually accompanied by the word *to*, e.g. *to go, to play*. In German the dictionary entry for the infinitive usually ends in **-en**: **gehen** *to go*, **spielen** *to play*, **machen** *to do*, etc.

Irregular verbs see **Verbs**

Modal verbs Verbs which express concepts such as permission, obligation, possibility, etc. (*can*, *must*, *may*) are referred to as modal verbs. Verbs in this category cannot in general stand on their own and therefore also fall under the general heading of *auxiliary verbs* (qv). Modal verbs in German include **wollen** *to want to*, **können** *to be able to*, **dürfen** *to be allowed to*.

Nouns Nouns are words like *house* **Haus**, *bread* **Brot** and *beauty* **Schönheit**. They are often called 'naming words'. A useful test of a noun is whether you can put *the* in front of it: e.g. *the house, the bread*. Nouns in German have one of three *genders* (qv) and take a capital letter.

Object The term object expresses the 'receiving end' relationship between a noun and a verb. Look at the following sentence: The dog bit the postman. **Der Hund biss den Postboten**. The postman is said to be the object of the sentence, as he is at the receiving end of the action. (See also **Subject.**)

Sentences such as: 'My mother gave my wife an expensive ring' have both a *direct object* (an expensive ring) and an *indirect object* (my wife).

In German the direct object requires the *accusative case* and the indirect object the *dative case*: **Meine Mutter gab *meiner Frau*** (dative) ***einen teuren Ring*** (accusative).

Passive voice Most actions can be viewed in two different ways: 1 The dog bit the postman. *active voice*
2 The postman was bitten by the dog. *passive voice*
In German you will also find both the active and passive voice. The passive is normally formed with the verb **werden** rather than with the verb **sein:**
1 Der Hund biss den Postboten.
2 Der Postbote *wurde* vom Hund gebissen.

Personal pronouns Personal pronouns refer to persons. In German they are: **ich** *I*; **du** *you* (informal singular); **Sie** *you* (formal singular); **er**, **sie**, **es** *he*, *she*, *it*; **wir** *we*; **ihr** *you* (informal plural); **Sie** *you* (formal plural); **sie** *they*. (See also **Pronouns.**)

Plural see **Singular**

Possessives Words such as **mein** *my*, **Ihr** *your* (formal),

dein *your* (informal), **ihr** *her*, **sein** *his* are given the term possessives or *possessive adjectives*, because they indicate who something belongs to.

Prepositions Words like **in** *in*, **auf** *on*, **zwischen** *between*, **für** *for* are called prepositions. Prepositions often tell us about the position of something. They are normally followed by a noun or a pronoun: **a** This present is *for* you. **b** *Despite* the weather I'm going to walk. **c** Your book is *on* the table.
In German prepositions require the use of a *case* (qv), such as the accusative, genitive or dative: **a Dieses Geschenk ist** *für* **dich.** (accusative) **b** *Trotz des Wetters* **gehe ich zu Fuß.** (genitive neuter) **c Dein Buch liegt** *auf dem* **Tisch.** (dative masculine)

Pronouns Pronouns fulfil a similar function to nouns and often stand in the place of nouns mentioned earlier. The *lamp* (noun) is modern. *It* (pronoun) is ugly. **Die** *Lampe* **ist modern.** *Sie* **ist hässlich.** Note that in German the pronoun has to be the same gender as the noun which it stands for (*die Lampe* → *sie*).

Singular and plural The terms singular and plural are used to make the contrast between 'one' and 'more than one': **Hund/Hunde** *dog/dogs*; **Buch/Bücher** *book/books*, **Hut/Hüte** *hat/hats*.
Most plural forms in English are formed by adding an -s, but not all: *child/children, woman/women, mouse/mice*. There are many different plural forms in German. Here are just three: **Kind/Kind***er*, **Frau/Frau***en*, **Maus/M***äu***se**.
Some nouns do not normally have plurals and are said to be *uncountable*: **das Obst** *fruit*.

Subject The term subject expresses a relationship between a noun and a verb. Look at the sentence 'The dog bit the postman'. Here the dog is said to be the subject of the verb *to bite*, because it is the dog that is doing the biting.
In German the subject of the sentence needs to be in the *nominative case*: **Der Hund biss den Postboten.**

Superlative The superlative is used for the most extreme version of a comparison: **a** This shirt is the *cheapest*. **b** This blouse is the *most* expensive of all.

The superlative in German follows a similar pattern:
a **Dieses Hemd ist** *am billigsten.* b **Diese Bluse ist die** *teuerste* **von allen.**

(See also **Comparative**.)

Tense Most languages use changes in the verb form to indicate an aspect of time. These changes in the verb are traditionally referred to as tense, and the tenses may be *present*, *past* or *future*. Tenses are often reinforced with expressions of time:

Present: *Today* I am staying at home. *Heute* **bleibe ich zu Hause.**

Past: *Yesterday* I went to London. *Gestern* **bin ich nach London gefahren.** / *Gestern* **fuhr ich nach London.**

Future: *Tomorrow* I'll be flying to Berlin. *Morgen* **werde ich nach Berlin fliegen.**

The German tenses dealt with in this book are the present, the simple past and the present perfect tense.

Verbs Verbs often communicate actions, states and sensations. So, for instance, the verb *to play* **spielen** expresses an action, the verb *to exist* **existieren** expresses a state and the verb *to see* **sehen** expresses a sensation. A verb may also be defined by its role in the sentence or clause and usually has a *subject* (qv). It may also have an *object* (qv).

Verbs in German can be *regular* (often called *weak verbs*), or *irregular* (also often referred to as *strong verbs*). The forms of irregular verbs need to be learned. A list of the most common irregular verbs is provided on the next page.

Abbreviations

The following abbreviations are used in this book:

QV *Quick vocab*
UE *Useful expressions*

List of common irregular verbs

*These verbs normally form their present perfect tense with **sein**.

Infinitive	Simple past tense (er/sie/es form)	Past participle	Vowel changes: present tense er/sie/es form
anlfangen to start, begin	fing an	angefangen	fängt an
anlrufen to call up	rief an	angerufen	
auflstehen to get up	stand auf	aufgestanden*	
beginnen to begin	begann	begonnen	
bleiben to stay	blieb	geblieben*	
bringen to bring	brachte	gebracht	
denken to think	dachte	gedacht	
einlladen to invite	lud ein	eingeladen	lädt ein
empfehlen to recommend	empfahl	empfohlen	empfiehlt
essen to eat	aß	gegessen	isst
fahren to go (by vehicle)	fuhr	gefahren*	fährt
finden to find	fand	gefunden	
fliegen to fly	flog	geflogen*	
geben to give	gab	gegeben	gibt
gefallen to be pleasing	gefiel	gefallen	gefällt
haben to have	hatte	gehabt	
halten to hold; to stop	hielt	gehalten	hält
heißen to be called	hieß	geheißen	
helfen to help	half	geholfen	hilft
kennen to know, be acquainted with	kannte	gekannt	
laufen to run	lief	gelaufen*	läuft
lesen to read	las	gelesen	liest
nehmen to take	nahm	genommen	nimmt
raten to advise; to guess	riet	geraten	rät
schlafen to sleep	schlief	geschlafen	schläft
schreiben to write	schrieb	geschrieben	
schwimmen to swim	schwamm	geschwommen*	
sehen to see	sah	gesehen	sieht
sein to be	war	gewesen*	ist
singen to sing	sang	gesungen	

sitzen *to sit*	**saß**	**gesessen**	
sprechen *to speak*	**sprach**	**gesprochen**	**spricht**
tragen *to carry; to wear*	**trug**	**getragen**	**trägt**
treffen *to meet*	**traf**	**getroffen**	**trifft**
trinken *to drink*	**trank**	**getrunken**	
tun *to do*	**tat**	**getan**	
um|steigen *to change (transport)*	**stieg um**	**umgestiegen***	
verbinden *to connect, put through*	**verband**	**verbunden**	
vergessen *to forget*	**vergaß**	**vergessen**	**vergisst**
verlassen *to leave*	**verließ**	**verlassen**	**verlässt**
verlieren *to lose*	**verlor**	**verloren**	
verstehen *to understand*	**verstand**	**verstanden**	
waschen *to wash*	**wusch**	**gewaschen**	**wäscht**
werden *to become*	**wurde**	**geworden***	**wird**
wissen *to know (a fact)*	**wusste**	**gewusst**	**weiß**
ziehen *to go, move; to pull, draw*	**zog**	**gezogen***	

German-English vocabulary

This reference vocabulary is intended to help you recall and use the most important words that you have met during the course. It is not intended to be comprehensive.

* indicates this verb or its root form is in the verb list on the preceding page and is irregular.

| indicates that a verb is separable (e.g. an|rufen).

NB: With professions, nationalities etc., the feminine version is usually given in an abbreviated form, e.g. der Mechaniker (-) /die -in. The feminine versions of professions which end in **-in** form their plural with **-nen**, e.g. die Mechanikerin, die Mechanikerinnen.

der Abend (-e) *evening*
abends *in the evening*
das Abenteuer (-) *adventure*
aber *but, however*
ab|fahren* *to depart*
ab|holen *to pick up, fetch*
das Abitur (-e) *leaving exam at Gymnasium, roughly A-levels*
die Adresse (-n) *address*
alles *everything*
der Alptraum (¨e) *nightmare*
alt *old*
altmodisch *old-fashioned*
anders *different/ly*
der Anfang (¨e) *beginning*
an|fangen* *to begin, start*
ab|kommen* *to arrive*
an|rufen* *to telephone, call up*
anschließend *afterwards*
anstrengend *tiring, strenuous*

die Antwort (-en) *answer*
an|ziehen* *to put on*
der Anzug (¨e) *suit*
der Apfel (¨) *apple*
der Apparat (-e) *apparatus, phone*
die Arbeit (-en) *work*
arbeiten *to work*
arbeitslos *unemployed*
arm *poor*
der Arm (-e) *arm*
der Arzt (¨e) /die Ärztin (-nen) *doctor*
auch *also*
Auf Wiedersehen! *Goodbye!*
der Aufenthalt (-e) *stay*
aufregend *exciting*
auf|stehen* *to get up*
das Auge (-n) *eye*
der Augenblick (-e) *moment*

der Ausdruck ("e) *expression*
der Ausflug ("e) *excursion, outing*
ausgezeichnet *excellent*
die Auskunft ("e) *information, directory enquiries*
der Ausländer (-) / die -in *foreigner*
aus|probieren *to try out*
jemandem etwas aus|richten *to pass on a message to someone*
die Aussage (-n) *statement*
aus|sehen* *to look, appear*
außerhalb *outside*
die Aussicht (-en) *prospect, outlook*
das Auto (-s) *car*
der Automechaniker/ die -in *mechanic*

das Baby (-s) *baby*
die Bäckerei (-en) *bakery*
das Bad ("er) *bath*
das Badezimmer (-) *bathroom*
die Bahn *rail, railway*
der Bahnhof ("e) *railway station*
bald *soon*
der Balkon (-s/-e) *balcony*
die Bank (-en) *bank*
der Bankkaufmann ("er)/ -frau (-en) *qualified bank clerk*
der Bauch ("e) *stomach, belly*
bauen *to build*
der Baum ("e) *tree*
beantworten *to answer*
der Becher (-) *beaker, cup; sundae dish*
bedeckt *overcast*
bedeuten *to mean*

beenden *to finish*
das Bein (-e) *leg*
das Beispiel (-e) *example*
bekannt *famous, well known*
bekommen* *to get*
beliebt *popular*
bequem *comfortable*
der Berg (-e) *mountain*
der Beruf (-e) *profession, occupation*
berufstätig *working, employed*
berühmt *famous*
besetzt *busy, engaged*
besonders *especially*
die Besprechung (-en) *meeting*
bestellen *to order*
besuchen *to visit*
betragen* *to amount to*
das Bett (-en) *bed*
die Bewerbung (-en) *application*
bezahlen *to pay*
die Bibliothek (-en) *library*
das Bier (-e) *beer*
der Biergarten (") *beer garden*
das Bild (-er) *picture*
billig *cheap*
bis *until, by*
bisschen – ein bisschen *a bit (of)*
bitte *please*
blau *blue*
bleiben* *to stay*
die Blume (-n) *flower*
der Blumenkohl (-e) *cauliflower*
die Bluse (-n) *blouse*
der Bonbon (-s) *sweets*
brauchen *to need*
braun *brown*
bringen* *to bring*

das Brot (-e) *bread*
das Brötchen (-) *bread roll*
der Bruder (¨) *brother*
der Brunnen (-) *well, fountain*
die Brust (¨e) *chest, breast*
das Buch (¨er) *book*
buchen *to book, reserve*
buchstabieren *to spell*
die Bundesrepublik Deutschland
 the Federal Republic of
 Germany
bunt *colourful*
das Büro (-s) *office*
der Bus (-se) *bus*
der Busen (-) *bosom, breast, bust*
die Bushaltestelle (-n) *bus stop*
die Butter *butter*

das Café (-s) *café*
die CD (-s) *CD*
der Chef (-s) / die Chefin *head,*
 boss
der Computer (-) *computer*

da *there; also: here*
damals *then, at that time*
die Dame (-n) *lady*
danach *after that, afterwards*
daneben *next to*
der Dank – Vielen Dank *thanks –*
 Many thanks
danke – Danke schön *thank you*
 – Thank you very much
dann *then*
dauern *to last*
denken* *to think*
Deutsch *German (language)*
Deutscher / Deutsche *German*
 (person)

dick *fat*
die Disco / Disko (-s) *disco*
das Dorf (¨er) *village*
dort *there*
die Dose (-n) *can*
dunkel *dark*
durstig *thirsty*
die Dusche (-n) *shower*

die Ecke (-n) *corner*
die Ehe (-n) *marriage*
ehemalig *former*
das Ei (-er) *egg*
eigentlich *actually*
einfach *single (journey); simple*
das Einfamilienhaus (¨er)
 detached family house
ein|führen *to introduce*
ein|kaufen *to shop*
ein|laden* *to invite*
die Einladung (-en) *invitation*
einmal *once*
der Eintritt (-e) *entrance, start*
der Einwohner (-) *inhabitant*
das Eis *ice cream*
die Eltern (pl.) *parents*
empfehlen* *to recommend*
das Ende (-n) *end*
der Engländer (-) /die -in
 Englishman, -woman
der Enkelsohn (¨e) /-tochter (¨)
 grandson/ -daughter
entdecken *to discover*
entlassen* *to release*
entschuldigen *to excuse*
die Erfahrung (-en) *experience*
erfolgreich *successful*
erhalten* *to receive*
erreichbar *reachable*

erscheinen* *to appear*
erzählen *to tell, narrate*
essen* *to eat*
etwa *around, approximately*
das Examen (-) *examination*

das Fach (¨er) *subject*
fahren* *to go (in a vehicle), drive*
die Fahrkarte (-n) *ticket*
der Fahrplan (¨e) *timetable (for transport)*
das Fahrrad (¨er) *bicycle*
die Familie (-n) *family*
die Farbe (-n) *colour*
das Fax (-e) *fax*
fehlen *to be missing, lacking*
die Feier (-n) *celebration*
feiern *to celebrate*
der Feiertag (-e) *public holiday*
die Ferien (pl) *holidays*
fern|sehen* *to watch TV*
der Fernseher (-) *TV set*
die Ferse (-n) *heel*
das Fett *fat*
der Film (-e) *film*
finden* *to find, to think*
der Finger (-) *finger*
die Flasche (-n) *bottle*
das Fleisch *meat*
fliegen* *to fly*
fließend *fluent(ly)*
der Flohmarkt (¨e) *flea market*
der Flug (¨e) *flight*
der Flur (-e) *corridor, hall*
fotografieren *to take photos*
die Frage (-n) *question*
fragen *to ask*
der Franzose (-n)/ die Französin *Frenchman/ -woman*

Französisch *French (language)*
die Frau (-en) *woman; Mrs*
frei *free, vacant*
der Freund (-e)/ die Freundin *boyfriend/girlfriend; friend*
frisch *fresh*
der Friseur /die -in *hairdresser*
die Frisur (-en) *hairstyle*
früh *early*
der Frühling (-e) *spring*
das Frühstück (-e) *breakfast*
fühlen *to feel*
der Führerschein (-e) *driving licence*
der Fuß (¨e) *foot*
der Fußball (¨e) *football*
die Fußgängerzone (-n) *pedestrian precinct*

der Garten (¨) *garden*
der Gast (¨e) *guest*
das Gebäude (-) *building*
geben* *to give*
das Gebiet (-e) *area, region*
der Geburtstag (-e) *birthday*
gefährlich *dangerous*
gefallen (+ dative) *to be pleasing*
gegen *around (of time); against*
das Gegenteil (-e) *opposite*
gehen* *to go*
gelb *yellow*
das Geld (-er) *money*
gemischt *mixed*
das Gemüse *vegetables*
genau *exactly, precisely*
genug *enough*
geradeaus *straight ahead*
gern – Ich trinke gern Tee. *I like drinking tea.*

das Geschäft (-e) *business, shop*
geschäftlich *on business*
das Geschenk (-e) *present*
die Geschichte (-n) *history, story*
geschieden *divorced*
der Geschmack (¨er) *taste*
das Gesicht (-er) *face*
gesund *healthy*
die Gesundheit *health*
das Getränk (-e) *drink*
das Gewicht (-e) *weight*
gewinnen* *to win*
das Gewitter (-) *thunderstorm*
das Glas (¨er) *glass*
glauben *to believe*
gleich *straight away; also: equal, same*
das Gleis (-e) *track*
das Glück *fortune, luck, happiness*
glücklich *happy*
der Grafiker (-)/ die -in *illustrator; graphic designer*
das Gramm *gram*
grau *grey*
die Grenze (-n) *border*
die Grippe (-n) *flu*
groß *large, big*
grün *green*
gründen *to establish, found*
die Grundschule (-n) *primary school*
ins Grüne *into the countryside*
günstig *favourable, reasonable (of price)*
gut *good, fine*
das Gymnasium (…ien) *grammar school*

das Haar (-e) *hair*
haben* *to have*
die Hähnchenbrust (¨e) *chicken breast*
der Hals (¨e) *neck, throat*
die Hand (¨e) *hand*
das Handy (-s) *mobile phone, cell phone*
der Hang (¨e) *slope*
hängen *to hang*
hassen *to hate*
hässlich *ugly*
häufig *frequently*
das Hauptgericht (-e) *main course*
die Hauptstadt (¨e) *capital city*
das Haus (¨er) *house*
die Hauseinweihungsfeier (-n) *house-warming party*
die Haut (¨e) *skin*
heiraten *to marry*
heiß *hot*
heißen* *to be called*
heiter *bright, fine*
hektisch *hectic*
helfen* (+ dative) *to help*
hell *light, bright*
das Hemd (-en) *shirt*
der Herbst (-e) *autumn*
der Herr (-en) *gentleman; Mr*
das Herz (-en) *heart*
heute *today*
hier *here*
hin und zurück *return (journey); there and back*
hinterlassen *to leave (a message)*
das Hobby (-s) *hobby*

das **Hochhaus** (¨er) *tower block*
die **Hochzeit** (-en) *wedding*
hoffen *to hope*
hoffentlich *hopefully*
der **Höhepunkt** (-e) *highlight*
holen *to fetch, to get*
hören *to hear*
die **Hose** (-n) *(a pair of) trousers*
das **Hotel** (-s) *hotel*
der **Hut** (¨e) *hat*
die **Hypothek** (-en) *the mortgage*

die **Idee** (-n) *idea*
der **Imbissstand** (¨e) *hot-dog stand*
immer *always*
die **Insel** (-n) *island*
insgesamt *all together*
interessant *interesting*

die **Jacke** (-n) *jacket*
das **Jahr** (-e) *year*
　– **vor einem Jahr** *a year ago*
die **Jahreszeit** (-en) *season*
jeder / jede / jedes *every, each*
jeden Tag *every day*
jetzt *now*
der **Job** (-s) *job*
der / das **Joghurt** (-s) *yoghurt*
die **Jugendherberge** (-n) *youth hostel*
jung *young*
der **Junge** (-n) *boy*

der **Kaffee** (-s) *coffee*
kalt *cold*
das **Kännchen** (-) *pot*
die **Kartoffel** (-n) *potato*

der **Käse** *cheese*
die **Kasse** (-n) *cash desk, checkout*
kaufen *to buy*
das **Kaufhaus** (¨er) *department store*
kein *no, not a*
der **Keller** (-) *cellar*
der **Kellner** (-) / die **-in** *waiter/ waitress*
kennen* *to know, be acquainted with*
die **Kenntnis** (-se) *(often pl.) knowledge*
das **Kilo** (-[s]) *kilo*
das **Kind** (-er) *child*
das **Kino** (-s) *cinema*
die **Kirche** (-n) *church*
die **Kirsche** (-n) *cherry*
das **Klassentreffen** (-) *class reunion*
sich kleiden *to dress (oneself)*
die **Kleidung** *clothing*
klein *small*
das **Klima** (-s) *climate*
die **Kneipe** (-n) *pub*
das **Knie** (-) *knee*
der **Knoblauch** *garlic*
kochen *to cook*
der **Kollege** (-n) / die **Kollegin** (-nen) *colleague*
komfortabel *comfortable*
kommen* *to come*
das **Königshaus** (¨er) *monarchy*
können *to be able to, can*
das **Konzert** (-e) *concert*
der **Kopf** (¨e) *head*
der **Körper** (-) *body*

der Körperteil (-e) *part of the body*

der Kosmetiker (-) / die -in *beautician, cosmetician*

kosmopolitisch *cosmopolitan*

kosten *cost*

krank *ill, sick*

das Krankenhaus (¨er) *hospital*

die Krankenkasse (-n) *health insurance fund*

der Krankenpfleger (-) *male nurse*

die Krankenschwester (-n) *female nurse*

die Krankenversicherung (-en) *health insurance*

die Krawatte (-n) *tie*

der Krimi (-s) *crime novel*

die Küche (-n) *kitchen*

der Kuchen (-) *cake*

kühl *cool*

der Kühlschrank (¨e) *refrigerator*

der Kunde (-n) / die Kundin (-nen) *customer, client*

der Kurs (-e) *course*

kurz *short, shortly*

die Küste (-n) *coast*

der Laden (¨) *shop*

die Lampe (-n) *lamp*

das Land (¨er) *country*
   – aufs Land fahren *to go the country*

lang *long*

langweilig *boring*

laufen* *to walk, run*

laut *loud, noisy*

leben *to live*

das Leben (-) *life*

der Lebenslauf (¨e) *CV*

die Lebensmittel (pl.) *food, groceries*

lecker *delicious, tasty*

ledig *single, unmarried*

legen *to lay, put*

die Lehre (-n) *apprenticeship*

der Lehrer (-) / die -in *teacher*

leid – Das tut mir leid *I am sorry*

die Leitung (-en) *line*

lernen *to learn*

lesen* *to read*

die Leute (pl.) *people*

lieben *to like very much, to love*

lieber – Ich trinke lieber Kaffee. *I prefer drinking coffee.*

die Lieblingsfarbe (-n) *favourite colour*

das Lied (-er) *song*

liegen* *to lie (in the sun etc.)*

die Limonade (-n) / die Limo (-s) *lemonade*

links *(on the) left*

die Lippe (-n) *lip*

das Lotto *national lottery*

die Luft (¨e) *air*

der Luftballon (-s) *balloon*

Lust haben *to feel like*

machen *to do, to make*

das Mädchen (-) *girl*

der Mais *sweetcorn*

malen *to paint*

man *one*

manchmal *sometimes*

der Mann (¨er) *man*

der Mantel (¨) *coat*

das Märchen (-) *fairy tale*

die Mark (-) *mark*

der Markt (¨e) *market*
das Maß (-e) *measure*
die Mauer (-n) *wall*
der Maurer (-) /die -in *bricklayer*
der Mechaniker (-) /die -in *mechanic*
das Meer (-e) *sea*
meinen *to think, to mean*
die Meinung (-en) *opinion*
meistens *mostly*
die Mensa (…sen) *refectory*
der Mensch (-en) *person, human being*
die Messe (-n) *(trade) fair*
die Miete (-n) *rent*
mieten *to rent*
die Milch *milk*
die Minderheit (-en) *minority*
mindestens *at least*
das Mineralwasser (-) *mineral water*
die Minute (-n) *minute*
mit|kommen* *to come (along, as well)*
das Mittagessen (-) *lunch*
mittags *at midday*
die Mitte (-n) *middle*
das Möbel (-) *furniture*
möchten – Was möchten Sie? *What would you like?*
die Mode (-n) *fashion*
modisch *fashionable*
möglich *possible*
die Möglichkeit (-en) *possibility*
der Moment (-e) *moment*
der Monat (-e) *month*
der Morgen (-) *morning*
morgen *tomorrow*

morgens *in the morning*
das Motorrad (¨er) *motor bike*
müde *tired*
der Mund (¨er) *mouth*
die Musik *music*
der Musiker (-) /die -in *musician*
das Müsli (-s) *muesli*
müssen *to have to, must*
die Mutter (¨) *mother*
die Muttersprache (-n) *mother tongue*
die Mütze (-n) *cap*

der Nachbar (-n) *neighbour*
nachher *afterwards*
nachmittags *in the afternoon*
die Nachricht (-en) *message*
die Nachspeise (-n) *dessert*
die Nacht (¨e) *night*
nachts *at night*
die Nähe – in der Nähe von *near*
der Name (-n) *name*
die Nase (-n) *nose*
natürlich *of course*
der Nebel (-) *fog*
nehmen* *to take*
nett *nice*
neu *new*
nicht *not*
nie *never*
noch *still*
noch (ein)mal *again, once more*
die Nordsee *North Sea*
nötig *necessary*
die Nudel (-n) *pasta*
die Nummer (-n) *number*
nun *now*
nützlich *useful*

das **Obst** *fruit*
obwohl *although*
oder *or*
offen *open*
öffnen *to open*
oft *often*
das **Ohr (-en)** *ear*
die **Ökologie** *ecology*
das **Omelett (-e or -s)** *omelette*
der **Onkel (-s)** *uncle*
der **Orangensaft (¨e)** *orange juice*
der **Österreicher (-) / die -in** *Austrian*
die **Ostsee** *the Baltic*

die **Packung (-en)** *packet*
das **Parfüm (-s)** *perfume*
der **Park (-s)** *park*
der **Parkplatz (¨e)** *parking lot*
die **Party (-s)** *party*
der **Pazifik** *the Pacific*
pensioniert *retired*
die **Person (-en)** *person*
das **Pfund (-e)** *pound*
der **Pilz (-e)** *mushroom*
die **Pizza (Pizzen)** *pizza*
die **Platte (-n)** *record*
der **Platz (¨e)** *square, place, seat*
plötzlich *suddenly*
die **Polizei** *police*
die **Pommes frites (pl.)** *French fries*
die **Postkarte (-n)** *postcard*
das **Praktikum (…ka)** *work experience*
der **Preis (-e)** *price*

prima (inform.) *brilliant, great*
das **Problem (-e)** *problem*
der **Produzent (-en) / -in** *producer*
die **Prüfung (-en)** *examination*
der **Pullover (-), Pulli (-s)** *pullover*

das **Rad (¨er)** *wheel, cycle*
Rad fahren *to cycle*
das **Radio (-s)** *radio*
die **Radiosendung (-en)** *radio broadcast*
raten* (+ dative) *to advise*
das **Rathaus (¨er)** *town hall*
rauchen *to smoke*
der **Raum (¨e)** *room, space*
der **Realschulabschluss (¨e)** *school exams, roughly equivalent to GCSE in the UK*
rechts *(on the) right*
der **Redakteur (-e) / die -in** *editor*
reden *to talk*
das **Regal (-e)** *shelves*
der **Regen** *rain*
der **Regenschirm (-e)** *umbrella*
regnen *to rain*
reich *rich*
das **Reihenhaus (¨er)** *terraced house*
die **Reinigung (-en)** *dry cleaner's*
der **Reis** *rice*
die **Reise (-n)** *journey, trip*
reisen *to travel*
reservieren *to reserve*
die **Richtung (-en)** *direction*
das **Rindfleisch** *beef*
der **Rock (¨e)** *skirt*
der **Roman (-e)** *novel*

die Romantik *the Romantic Period*
rot *red*
der Rücken (-) *back*
ruhig *quiet*

die Sache (-n) *thing*
der Saft (¨e) *juice*
sagen *to say*
die Sahne *cream*
die Salami (-s) *salami*
der Salat (-e) *salad*
sammeln *to collect*
der Sänger (-) / die -in *singer*
der Satz (¨e) *sentence*
die Schallplatte (-n) *record*
scheinen* *to shine*
schenken *to give (as a present)*
der Schinken (-) *ham*
schlafen* *to sleep*
das Schlafzimmer (-) *bedroom*
schlecht *bad*
schlimm *bad*
das Schloss (¨er) *castle*
der Schlüssel (-) *key*
schmecken *to taste*
  – Hat es geschmeckt? *Did it taste good?*
der Schmerz (-en) *pain*
der Schnaps (¨e) *spirit; schnapps*
der Schnee *snow*
schneiden *to cut; to edit*
schneien *to snow*
schon *already*
schön *beautiful, nice*
der Schrank (¨e) *cupboard*
schrecklich *terrible*
schreiben *to write*
der Schreibtisch (-e) *desk*

schreien* *to yell, scream*
der Schriftsteller (-) / die -in *author*
der Schuh (-e) *shoe*
die Schule (-n) *school*
schwarz *black*
die Schwester (-n) *sister*
schwimmen* *to swim*
das Segeln *sailing*
sehen* *to see*
die Sehenswürdigkeit (-en) *sight (worth seeing)*
sehr *very*
die Seide *silk*
sein* *to be*
der Sekretär (-e) / die -in *secretary*
der Sekt *German bubbly wine*
selten *seldom, rarely*
der Sessel (-) *armchair*
sicher *sure, certain(ly)*
singen* *to sing*
sitzen* *to sit*
Ski laufen* / fahren* *to ski*
die Socke (-n) *sock*
das Sofa (-s) *sofa*
sogar *even*
der Sohn (¨e) *son*
der Soldat (-en) *soldier*
der Sommer (-) *summer*
die Sonne (-n) *sun*
die Sonnenbrille (-n) *(pair of) sunglasses*
sonnig *sunny*
sonst *otherwise*
  – Sonst noch etwas? *Anything else?*
sowieso *in any case*
der Spaß *fun*

– Es macht Spaß *It's fun*
spät *late*
　– Wie spät ist es? *What's the time?*
spazieren gehen* *to go for a walk*
der Spaziergang (¨e) *walk*
　– einen Spaziergang machen *to go for a walk*
die Speisekarte (-n) *menu*
das Spiel (-e) *game*
spielen *to play*
der Sport *sport*
die Sprache (-n) *language*
sprechen* *to speak*
das Stadion (Stadien) *stadium*
die Stadt (¨e) *town, city*
die Stadtführung (-en) *guided tour (of a town)*
stark *strong*
stehen* *to stand*
stellen *to put, to place*
das Stellenangebot (-e) *job advert*
sterben* *to die*
die Stimme (-n) *voice*
das Stipendium (-ien) *grant*
der Strand (¨e) *beach*
die Straße (-n) *street*
die Straßenbahn (-en) *tram, street-car*
der Strom *electricity*
der Strumpf (¨e) *stocking*
die Strumpfhose (-n) *pair of tights*
das Stück (-e/ -) *piece*
der Student (-en) / -in (-nen) *student*
das Studentenwohnheim (-e) *student residence*
studieren *to study*
das Studium (-ien) *study*
die Stunde (-n) *hour (60 minutes)*
suchen *to look for, to seek*
der Supermarkt (¨e) *supermarket*
die Suppe (-n) *soup*
das Surfen *surfing*
süß *sweet*
die Süßigkeit (-en) *sweet, confectionery*

die Tablette (-n) *tablet*
der Tag (-e) *day*
die Tante (-n) *aunt*
tanzen *to dance*
die Tasse (-n) *cup*
das Tauchen *diving*
das Taxi (-s) *taxi*
der Tee (-s) *tea*
teilen *to share, divide*
das Telefon (-e) *telephone*
telefonieren *to telephone*
die Temperatur (-en) *temperature*
das Tennis *tennis*
der Termin (-e) *date, appointment*
der Terminkalender (-) *appointments diary*
teuer *dear, expensive*
der Teufel (-) *devil*
der Texter (-)/ -in (-nen) *copywriter*
das Theater (-) *theatre*
das Theaterstück (-e) *play*
das Thema (…men) *topic, theme*

der Tisch (-e) *table*
der Tischler (-) / -in (-nen) *carpenter*
die Tochter (¨) *daughter*
toll *great, terrific*
die Tomate (-n) *tomato*
total *total(ly)*
die Touristeninformation (-en) *tourist information*
die Tournee (-n) *tour*
tragen* *to wear*
trainieren *to train, work out*
der Traum (¨e) *dream*
treffen* *to meet*
der Treffpunkt (-e) *meeting place*
trennbar *separable*
treten* – in den Ruhestand treten *to retire (go into reitrement)*
trinken* *to drink*
der Tropfen (-) *drop (liquid)*
trotzdem *nevertheless*
Tschüs!/ Tschüss! *bye!*
tun* *to do*
der Türke (-n) / die Türkin *Turk*
der Turnschuh (-e) *trainer*
die Tüte (-n) *bag*
der Typ (-en) *type*
typisch *typical*

die U-Bahn (-en) *underground, subway*
über *over, above, about*
überhaupt nicht *not at all*
übersetzen *to translate*
die Übung (-en) *exercise*
die Uhr (-en) *clock*
 – neun Uhr *nine o'clock*

die Umfrage (-n) *survey*
der Umgang *contact, dealings*
um|steigen* *to change (a train, bus etc.)*
die Umwelt *environment*
und *and*
ungefähr *approximately, about*
die Universität (-en) *university*
das Unterhemd (-en) *vest*
unterzeichnen *to sign*
der Urlaub (-e) *holiday*

der Vater (¨) *father*
die Verabredung (-en) *arrangement, appointment*
die Verantwortung *responsibility*
das Verb (-en) *verb*
verbinden* *to connect, put through*
die Verbindung (-en) *connection, link*
verboten *forbidden*
verbringen *to spend (time)*
verdienen *to earn*
die Vergangenheit (-en) *past*
verheiratet *married*
verkaufen *to sell*
der Verkäufer (-) / -in (-nen) *shop assistant*
der Verkehr *traffic*
die Verkehrsmittel (pl.) *means of transport*
die Verkehrsverbindungen (pl.) *transport (links)*
verlassen* *to leave*
veröffentlichen *to publish*
verschieden *different, various*
verschreiben* *to prescribe*
verstehen* *to understand*

versuchen to try
der Vertrag (¨e) treaty
verwitwet widowed
viel much, a lot
vielleicht perhaps
das Viertel (-) quarter
  -Viertel nach acht quarter past
  eight
vor|bereiten to prepare
die Vorlesung (-en) lecture
der Vormittag (-e) morning
die Vorspeise (-n) starter

wach awake
wahr true
wahrscheinlich probably
die Währung (-en) currency
wandern to hike, to ramble
wann? when?
war/waren was/were (simple past
  tense of **sein**: to be)
warm warm
warten to wait
warum? why?
was? what?
das Wasser water
wechseln to change
der Wecker (-) alarm clock
weh|tun to hurt, ache
weil because
der Wein (-e) wine
weiß white
weit far
die Welt (-en) world
der Weltkrieg (-e) World War
wem whom (dative of who)
wen whom (accusative of who)
wenig – nur ein wenig only a
  little

wenn when, whenever
wer who
der Werdegang (¨e)
  development, career
werden* to become
das Werk (-e) work
das Wetter weather
der Wetterbericht (-e) weather
  report
die Wettervorhersage (-n)
  weather forecast
wichtig important
wie? how?
wie viel? how much? how many?
Wie viel Uhr ist es? What time
  is it?
wieder again
Wiederhören – Auf
  Wiederhören! Goodbye! (on
  radio or phone)
wieder|kommen* to come again,
  come back
Wiedersehen – Auf
  Wiedersehen! Goodbye!
die Wiedervereinigung
  reunification
der Wind (-e) wind
windig windy
der Winter (-) winter
wirklich really
die Wirtschaftswissenschaften
  (pl.) economics
wissen* to know (a fact)
der Witz (-e) joke
wo where
wohin where (to)
die Woche (-n) week
das Wochenende (-n) weekend
der Wodka vodka

woher? *where … from?*
wohnen *to live*
die Wohngemeinschaft (-en) *flat-share*
die Wohnung (-en) *flat*
das Wohnzimmer (-) *living room*
wolkig *cloudy*
die Wurst ("e) *sausage*
das Würstchen (-) *(small) sausage*

die Zahl (-en) *number, figures*
der Zahn ("e) *tooth*
der Zahnarzt ("e) / die Zahnärztin (-nen) *dentist*
die Zehe (-n) *toe*

zeigen *to show*
die Zeit (-en) *time*
die Zeitschrift (-en) *journal*
die Zeitung (-en) *newspaper*
zentral *central(ly)*
zerstören *to destroy*
ziehen* *to move*
ziemlich *quite, fairly*
das Zimmer (-) *room*
der Zucker *sugar*
der Zug ("e) *train*
die Zunge (-n) *tongue*
zurück|rufen* *to call back*
zusammen *together*
der Zuschlag ("e) *supplement*

English-German vocabulary

This reference vocabulary is intended to help you recall and use some of the most important words that you have met during the course. It is not intended to be comprehensive.

* indicates this verb or its root form is in the verb list preceding the German–English vocabulary, and is irregular.

| indicates that a verb is separable (e.g. an|rufen).

about **ungefähr**
actually **eigentlich**
address **die Adresse (-n)**
adventure **das Abenteuer (-)**
to advise **raten* (+ dative)**
afternoon **der Nachmittag (e)**
afterwards **anschließend, nachher**
again **wieder**
against **gegen**
ago **vor (+ dative)**; *a year ago* **vor einem Jahr**
air **die Luft ("e)**
alarm clock **der Wecker (-)**
already **schon**
also **auch**
although **obwohl**
always **immer**
and **und**
to answer **beantworten**
answer **die Antwort (-en)**
apartment **die Wohnung (-en)**
apparatus **der Apparat (-e)**
to appear (seem) **aus|sehen***

to appear **erscheinen***
apple **der Apfel (")**
application **die Bewerbung (-en)**
appointment **der Termin (-e)**
apprenticeship **die Lehre (-n)**
approximately **ungefähr**
area **das Gebiet (-e)**
arm **der Arm (-e)**
armchair **der Sessel (-)**
to arrive **an|kommen***
to ask **fragen**
aunt **die Tante (-n)**
Austrian (person) **der Österreicher (-) / die -in (-nen)**
autumn **der Herbst (-e)**
awake **wach**

baby **das Baby (-s)**
back **der Rücken (-)**
bad **schlecht; schlimm**
bag **die Tüte (-n)**
bakery **die Bäckerei (-en)**
balcony **der Balkon (-s/-e)**

balloon **der Luftballon (-s)**
Baltic **die Ostsee**
bank **die Bank (-en)**
bath **das Bad (¨er)**
bathroom **das Badezimmer (-)**
to be **sein***
be able to **können**
to be called **heißen***
beach **der Strand (¨e)**
beautician **der Kosmetiker (-) /
   -in**
beautiful **schön**
because **weil**
to become **werden***
bed **das Bett (-en)**
bedroom **das Schlafzimmer (-)**
beef **das Rindfleisch**
beer **das Bier (-e)**
to begin **an|fangen*; beginnen***
beginning **der Anfang (¨e)**
to believe **glauben**
belly **der Bauch (¨e)**
bicycle **das Fahrrad (¨er); das
   Rad (¨er)**
big **groß**
birthday **der Geburtstag (-e)**
bit: a bit (of) **bisschen: ein
   bisschen**
black **schwarz**
blouse **die Bluse (-n)**
blue **blau**
body **der Körper (-)**
to boil **kochen**
book **das Buch (¨er)**
to book **buchen**
border **die Grenze (-n)**
boring **langweilig**
boss **der Chef (-s) / die Chefin**

(-nen)
bottle **die Flasche (-n)**
boy **der Junge (-n)**
boyfriend **der Freund (-e)**
bread roll **das Brötchen (-)**
bread **das Brot (-e)**
breakfast **das Frühstück (-e)**
bricklayer **der Maurer (-) /die -in**
bridge **die Brücke (-n)**
bright **hell**
to bring **bringen***
brother **der Bruder (¨)**
brown **braun**
to build **bauen**
building **das Gebäude (-)**
bus stop **die Bushaltestelle (-n)**
bus **der Bus (-se)**
business **das Geschäft (-e)**
but **aber**
butter **die Butter**
to buy **kaufen**

café **das Café (-s)**
cake **der Kuchen (-)**
to call **rufen***
to call (on the phone) **an|rufen***
to call back **zurück|rufen***
can **die Dose (-n)**
cap **die Mütze (-n)**
capital city **die Hauptstadt (¨e)**
car **das Auto (-s)**
carpenter **der Tischler (-) / die -in
   (-nen)**
to carry **tragen***
cash desk **die Kasse (-n)**
castle **das Schloss (¨er)**
cauliflower **der Blumenkohl (-e)**
CD **die CD (-s)**

to celebrate **feiern**
celebration **die Feier (-n)**
cellar **der Keller (-)**
central heating **die Zentralheizung (-en)**
central(ly) **zentral**
certain(ly) **sicher**
to change **wechseln**
to change (a train, bus, etc.) **um|steigen***
to chat **schwatzen**
cheap **billig**
cheese **der Käse**
cherry **die Kirsche (-n)**
chest **die Brust (¨e)**
child **das Kind (-er)**
church **die Kirche (-n)**
cinema **das Kino (-s)**
climate **das Klima (-s)**
clock **die Uhr (-en)**
clothing **die Kleidung**
cloudy **wolkig**
coast **die Küste (-n)**
coat **der Mantel (¨)**
coffee **der Kaffee (-s)**
cold **kalt**
colleague **der Kollege (-n) / die Kollegin (-nen)**
to collect **sammeln**
colour **die Farbe (-n)**
to come **kommen***
comfortable **bequem**
computer **der Computer (-)**
concert **das Konzert (-e)**
to connect **verbinden***
connection **die Verbindung (-en)**
to cook **kochen**
cool **kühl**

corner **die Ecke (-n)**
corridor **der Flur (-e)**
to cost **kosten**
country **das Land (¨er)**
course **der Kurs (-e)**
cream **die Sahne**
cup **die Tasse (-n)**
cupboard **der Schrank (¨e)**
currency **die Währung (-en)**
customer **der Kunde (-n) / die Kundin (-nen)**
to cut **schneiden***
CV **der Lebenslauf (¨e)**
cycle **Rad fahren***

to dance **tanzen**
dangerous **gefährlich**
dark **dunkel**
date **der Termin (-e)**
daughter **die Tochter (¨)**
day **der Tag (-e)**
dear **teuer**
delicious **lecker**
dentist **der Zahnarzt (¨e) / die Zahnärztin (-nen)**
to depart **ab|fahren***
department store **das Kaufhaus (¨er)**
desk **der Schreibtisch (-e)**
dessert **die Nachspeise (-n)**
devil **der Teufel (-)**
to die **sterben***
different **verschieden**
direction **die Richtung (-en)**
directory enquiries **die Auskunft (¨e)**
disco **die Disco / Disko (-s)**
to discover **entdecken**

to divide **teilen**
diving **das Tauchen**
divorced **geschieden**
to do **machen; tun***
doctor **der Arzt (¨e) / die Ärztin (-nen)**
dreadful **scheußlich**
dream **der Traum (¨e)**
to dress (oneself) **sich kleiden**
to drink **trinken***
drink **das Getränk (-e)**
to drive **fahren***
driving licence **der Führerschein (-e)**
drop **der Tropfen (-)**
dry cleaner's **die Reinigung (-en)**

ear **das Ohr (-en)**
early **früh**
to earn **verdienen**
Earth **die Erde**
to eat **essen***
ecology **die Ökologie**
economics **die Wirtschaftswissenschaften (pl.)**
editor **der Redakteur (-e) / die -in (-nen)**
egg **das Ei (-er)**
end **das Ende (-n)**
engaged (phone line etc.) **besetzt**
Englishman, -woman **der Engländer (-) / die -in (-nen)**
enough **genug**
environment **die Umwelt**
especially **besonders**

euro **der Euro (-)**
even **sogar**
evening; in the evening **der Abend (-e); abends**
every **jeder / jede / jedes**
everything **alles**
exact(ly) **genau**
examination **die Prüfung (-en); das Examen (-)**
example **das Beispiel (-e)**
excellent **ausgezeichnet**
exciting **aufregend**
excursion **der Ausflug (¨e)**
to excuse **entschuldigen**
exercise **die Übung (-en)**
expensive **teuer**
experience **die Erfahrung (-en)**
expression **der Ausdruck (¨e)**
eye **das Auge (-n)**

face **das Gesicht (-er)**
fair (trade) **die Messe (-n)**
fairly **ziemlich**
fairy tale **das Märchen (-)**
family **die Familie (-n)**
famous **berühmt**
far **weit**
fashion **die Mode (-n)**
fashionable **modisch**
fat **das Fett; dick**
father **der Vater (¨)**
favourite colour **die Lieblingsfarbe (-n)**
to feel **fühlen**
to fetch **holen; ab|holen**
figure **die Zahl (-en)**
film **der Film (-e)**
to find **finden***

finger **der Finger (-)**
to finish **beenden**
flat **die Wohnung (-en)**
flea market **der Flohmarkt (¨e)**
flight **der Flug (¨e)**
flower **die Blume (-n)**
flu **die Grippe (-n)**
fluent(ly) **fließend**
to fly **fliegen***
fog **der Nebel**
food **die Lebensmittel (pl.)**
foot **der Fuß (¨e)**
football **der Fußball (¨e)**
forbidden **verboten**
foreigner **der Ausländer (-) / die -in (-nen)**
to forget **vergessen***
former **ehemalig**
fortune **das Glück**
to found **gründen**
free **frei**
French (language) **Französisch**
French fries **die Pommes frites (pl.)**
Frenchman/ -woman **der Franzose (-n) / die Französin (-nen)**
frequently **häufig**
fresh **frisch**
friend **der Freund (-e) / die Freundin (-nen)**
fruit **das Obst**
fun **der Spaß**
furniture **das Möbel (-)**

game **das Spiel (-e)**
garden **der Garten (¨)**
garlic **der Knoblauch**

gentleman **der Herr (-en)**
German (language) **Deutsch**
German (person) **ein Deutscher / eine Deutsche**
to get up **auf|stehen***
to get **bekommen***
girl **das Mädchen (-)**
girlfriend **die Freundin (-nen)**
to give **geben***
to give (as a present) **schenken**
glass **das Glas (¨er)**
to go **gehen***
to go for a walk **spazieren gehen*; einen Spaziergang machen**
good **gut**
Goodbye! **Auf Wiedersehen!; Auf Wiederhören! (on radio or phone)**
gram **das Gramm (-)**
grammar school **das Gymnasium (Gymnasien)**
grandson / -daughter **Enkelsohn (¨e) /-tochter (¨)**
grant **das Stipendium (-ien)**
graphic designer **der Grafiker (-) / die -in (-nen)**
green **grün**
grey **grau**
to grow **wachsen**
guest **der Gast (¨e)**
gym **das Fitnesscenter (-)**
hair **das Haar (-e)**
hairdresser **der Friseur (-e) / die Friseurin (-nen)**
hairstyle **die Frisur (-en)**
ham **der Schinken (-)**
hand **die Hand (¨e)**

to hang **hängen**
happiness **das Glück**
happy **glücklich**
hat **der Hut (¨e)**
to hate **hassen**
to have **haben***
to have to **müssen**
head **der Kopf (¨e)**
health **die Gesundheit**
health insurance **die Krankenversicherung (-en)**
healthy **gesund**
to hear **hören**
heart **das Herz (-en)**
hectic **hektisch**
heel **die Ferse (-n)**
to help **helfen* (+ dative)**
here **hier**
to hike **wandern**
history **die Geschichte (-n)**
hobby **das Hobby (-s)**
to hold **halten***
holiday **der Urlaub (-e)**
holiday (public) **der Feiertag (-e)**
holidays **die Ferien (pl.)**
to hope **hoffen**
hopefully **hoffentlich**
hospital **das Krankenhaus (¨er)**
hot **heiß**
hotel **das Hotel (-s)**
hour **die Stunde (-n)**
house **das Haus (¨-er)**
how? **wie?**
how many? **wie viele?**
how much? **wie viel?**
however **aber**
human being **der Mensch (-en)**
to hurt **weh|tun**

ice cream **das Eis**
idea **die Idee (-n)**
ill, sick **krank**
important **wichtig**
information **die Auskunft (¨e)**
inhabitant **der Einwohner (-)**
interesting **interessant**
to introduce **ein|führen**
invitation **die Einladung (-en)**
to invite **ein|laden***
island **die Insel (-n)**

jacket **die Jacke (-n)**
job **der Job (-s)**
joke **der Witz (-e)**
journal **die Zeitschrift (-en)**
journey **die Reise (-n)**
juice **der Saft (¨e)**

key **der Schlüssel (-)**
kilo **das Kilo (-[s])**
kitchen **die Küche (-n)**
knee **das Knie (-)**
to know (a fact) **wissen***
to know (be acquainted with) **kennen***
knowledge **die Kenntnis (-se) (often pl.)**

lady **die Dame (-n)**
lamp **die Lampe (-n)**
language **die Sprache (-n)**
large **groß**
to last **dauern**
late **spät**
to lay **legen**
to learn **lernen**
least, at least **mindestens**

to leave **verlassen***
to leave (a message)
   hinterlassen
lecture **die Vorlesung (-en)**
left **links**
leg **das Bein (-e)**
lemonade **die Limonade (-n) /**
   die Limo (-s)
library **die Bibliothek (-en)**
to lie (in the sun, etc.) **liegen***
life **das Leben (-)**
lip **die Lippe (-n)**
to live **leben; (dwell) wohnen**
living room **das**
   Wohnzimmer (-)
long **lang**
to look **aus|sehen***
to look for **suchen**
to lose **verlieren***
loud **laut**
to love **lieben**
lunch **das Mittagessen (-)**

magazine **die Zeitschrift (-en)**
main course **das**
   Hauptgericht (-e)
to make **machen**
man **der Mann (¨er)**
market **der Markt (¨e)**
married **verheiratet**
to marry **heiraten**
to mean **bedeuten**
meat **das Fleisch**
mechanic **der Mechaniker / die**
   -in (-nen)
to meet **treffen***
menu **die Speisekarte (-n)**
message **die Nachricht (-en)**

message: pass on a message to
   someone **jemandem etwas**
   aus|richten
middle **die Mitte**
milk **die Milch**
mineral water **das**
   Mineralwasser
minority **die Minderheit (-en)**
minute **die Minute (-n)**
mixed **gemischt**
moment **der Augenblick (-e); der**
   Moment (-e)
money **das Geld (-er)**
month **der Monat (-e)**
morning **der Morgen (-)**
mostly **meistens**
mother **die Mutter (¨)**
mother tongue **die**
   Muttersprache (-n)
motor bike **das Motorrad (¨er)**
mountain **der Berg (-e)**
mouth **der Mund (¨er)**
much **viel**
mushroom **der Pilz (-e)**
music **die Musik**
musician **der Musiker (-) /die -in**

name **der Name (-n)**
near **die Nähe; in der Nähe von**
necessary **nötig**
neck **der Hals (¨e)**
to need **brauchen**
neighbour **der Nachbar (-n)**
never **nie**
nevertheless **trotzdem**
new **neu**
newspaper **die Zeitung (-en)**
nice **nett; schön**

night **die Nacht ("e)**
nightmare **der Alptraum ("e)**
noisy **laut**
North Sea **die Nordsee**
nose **die Nase (-n)**
not **nicht**
not a **kein**
novel **der Roman (-e)**
now **nun**
now **jetzt**
number **die Nummer (-n); die Zahl (-en)**
nurse (female) **die Krankenschwester (-n)**
nurse (male) **der Krankenpfleger (-)**

occupation **der Beruf (-e)**
of course **natürlich**
office **das Büro (-s)**
often **oft**
old **alt**
old-fashioned **altmodisch**
omelette **das Omelett (-e or -s)**
once **einmal**
open **offen**
to open **öffnen**
opinion **die Meinung (-en)**
opposite **das Gegenteil (-e)**
or **oder**
orange juice **der Orangensaft ("e)**
to order **bestellen**
otherwise **sonst**
outing **der Ausflug ("e)**
outside **außerhalb**

packet **die Packung (-en)**

pain **der Schmerz (-en)**
to paint **malen**
parents **Eltern (pl.)**
park **der Park (-s)**
to park **parken**
party **die Party (-s)**
past **die Vergangenheit (-en)**
pasta **die Nudeln (pl.)**
to pay **bezahlen**
pedestrian **der Fußgänger (-)**
people **die Leute (pl.)**
perfume **das Parfüm (-s)**
perhaps **vielleicht**
person **der Mensch (-en); die Person (-en)**
to pick up **ab|holen**
picture **das Bild (-er)**
piece **das Stück (-e)**
to play **spielen**
play **das Theaterstück (-e)**
please **bitte**
police **die Polizei**
poor **arm**
popular **beliebt**
possibility **die Möglichkeit (-en)**
possible **möglich**
postcard **die Postkarte (-n)**
pot **das Kännchen (-)**
potato **die Kartoffel (-n)**
pound **das Pfund**
to prefer: I prefer drinking coffee. **Ich trinke lieber Kaffee.**
to prepare **vor|bereiten**
to prescribe **verschreiben***
present **das Geschenk (-e)**
price **der Preis (-e)**
probably **wahrscheinlich**

problem **das Problem (-e)**
producer **der Produzent (-en) /
   die -in (-nen)**
prospect **die Aussicht (-en)**
pub **die Kneipe (-n)**
to publish
   veröffentlichen
to pull **ziehen***
pullover **der Pullover (-), Pulli (-s)**
to put **stellen**
to put on (clothes)
   an|ziehen*

quarter **das Viertel (-)**
question **die Frage (-n)**
quiet **ruhig**

radio **das Radio (-s)**
railway **die Bahn**
railway station **der Bahnhof (¨e)**
rain **der Regen**
to rain **regnen**
ramble **wandern**
rare(ly) **selten**
to read **lesen***
really **wirklich**
to receive **erhalten***
recommend **empfehlen***
record **die Schallplatte (-n)**
red **rot**
refrigerator **der Kühlschrank (¨e)**
rent **die Miete (-n)**
to rent **mieten**
to reserve **reservieren**
responsibility **die Verantwortung**
responsible
   verantwortlich
retire **in den Ruhestand treten***

retired **pensioniert**
return (ticket) **hin und zurück**
reunification **die
   Wiedervereinigung**
rice **der Reis**
rich **reich**
right **rechts**
room **das Zimmer (-)**
to run **laufen***

sailing **das Segeln**
salad **der Salat (-e)**
salami **die Salami (-s)**
salesperson **der Verkäufer (-) /
   die -in (-nen)**
same **gleich**
sausage **die Wurst (¨e)**; small ~
   das Würstchen (-)
to say **sagen**
school **die Schule (-n)**
to scream **schreien***
sea **das Meer (-e)**
season **die Jahreszeit (-en)**
seat **der Platz (¨e)**
secretary **der Sekretär (-e) / die
   -in (-nen)**
to see **sehen***
to seek **suchen**
seldom **selten**
to sell **verkaufen**
sentence **der Satz (¨e)**
to share **teilen**
shelves **das Regal (-e)**
to shine **scheinen***
shirt **das Hemd (-en)**
shoe **der Schuh (-e)**
shop assistant **der Verkäufer (-) /
   die -in (-nen)**

shop **das Geschäft (-e); der Laden (¨)**
to shop **ein|kaufen**
short **kurz**
to shout **schreien***
to show **zeigen**
shower **die Dusche (-n)**
sight (worth seeing) **die Sehenswürdigkeit (-en)**
sign **unterschreiben*; unterzeichnen**
silk **die Seide**
simple **einfach**
to sing **singen***
singer **der Sänger (-) / die -in (-nen)**
single **ledig**
sister **die Schwester (-n)**
to sit **sitzen***
ski **Ski laufen* / fahren***
skin **die Haut (¨e)**
skirt **der Rock (¨e)**
to sleep **schlafen***
slope **der Hang (¨e)**
small **klein**
to smoke **rauchen**
snack **der Imbiss (-e)**
snow **der Schnee**
to snow **schneien**
sock **die Socke (-n)**
sofa **das Sofa (-s)**
soldier **der Soldat (-en)**
sometimes **manchmal**
son **der Sohn (¨e)**
song **das Lied (-er)**
soon **bald**
sorry **leid**; *I am sorry* **Das tut mir leid**

soup **die Suppe (-n)**
space **der Raum (¨e)**
to speak **sprechen***
to spell **buchstabieren**
to spend (money) **aus|geben**
to spend (time) **verbringen**
sport **der Sport**
spring **der Frühling (-e)**
square (in a town) **der Platz (¨e)**
stadium **das Stadion (Stadien)**
to stand **stehen***
to start **an|fangen***
starter **die Vorspeise (-n)**
to stay **bleiben***
stay **der Aufenthalt (-e)**
still **noch**
stocking **der Strumpf (¨e)**
stomach **der Magen (¨)**
story **die Geschichte (-n)**
straight ahead **geradeaus**
straight away **gleich; sofort**
street **die Straße (-n)**
streetcar **die Straßenbahn (-en)**
strenuous **anstrengend**
strong **stark**
student **der Student (-en) / -in (-nen)**
study **das Studium (Studien)**
to study **studieren**
subject **das Fach (¨er)**
subway (train) **die U-Bahn (-en)**
successful **erfolgreich**
sugar **der Zucker**
suit **der Anzug (¨e)**
summer **der Sommer (-)**
sun **die Sonne (-n)**
sunglasses **die Sonnenbrille (-n)**

sunny **sonnig**

supermarket **der Supermarkt (¨e)**

sure **sicher**

surfing **das Surfen**

survey **die Umfrage (-n)**

sweet **der Bonbon (-s); süß**

sweetcorn **der Mais**

to swim **schwimmen***

table **der Tisch (-e)**

tablet **die Tablette (-n)**

to take **nehmen***

to talk **reden**

to taste **schmecken**

taste **der Geschmack (¨er)**

taxi **das Taxi (-s)**

tea **der Tee (-s)**

teacher **der Lehrer (-) / die -in (-nen)**

telephone **das Telefon (-e)**

to telephone **telefonieren; an|rufen***

to tell **erzählen**

temperature **die Temperatur (-en)**

tennis **das Tennis**

terraced house **das Reihenhaus (¨er)**

terrible **schrecklich**

thank you; thank you very much **danke; danke schön**

theatre **das Theater (-)**

then **damals; dann**

there **dort; da**

therefore **deshalb**

thing **die Sache (-n)**

to think **denken***

thirsty **durstig**

throat **der Hals (¨e)**

thunderstorm **das Gewitter (-)**

ticket **die Fahrkarte (-n)**

tie **die Krawatte (-n)**

tights **die Strumpfhose (-n)**

time **die Zeit (-en)**

timetable **der Fahrplan (¨e)**

tired **müde**

tiring **anstrengend**

today **heute**

toe **die Zehe (-n)**

together **zusammen**

tomato **die Tomate (-n)**

tomorrow **morgen**

tongue **die Zunge (-n)**

tooth **der Zahn (¨e)**

topic **das Thema (Themen)**

tour **die Tournee (-n)**

tower block **das Hochhaus (¨er)**

town **die Stadt (¨e)**

town/city hall **das Rathaus (¨er)**

track **das Gleis (-e)**

traffic **der Verkehr**

train **der Zug (¨e)**

trainer **der Turnschuh (-e)**

tram **die Straßenbahn (-en)**

to translate **übersetzen**

to travel **reisen**

treaty **der Vertrag (¨e)**

tree **der Baum (¨e)**

trip **die Reise (-n)**

trousers (a pair of) **die Hose (-n)**

true **wahr**

to try **versuchen**

to try out **aus|probieren**

tube (train) **die U-Bahn (-en)**

Turk **der Türke (-n) / die Türkin (-nen)**

TV set **der Fernseher (-)**
type **der Typ (-en)**
typical **typisch**

ugly **hässlich**
umbrella **der Regenschirm (-e)**
uncle **der Onkel (-s)**
understand **verstehen***
unemployed **arbeitslos**
university **die Universität (-en)**
until **bis**
useful **nützlich**

vacation **der Urlaub (-e)**
various **verschieden**
vegetable(s) **das Gemüse**
verb **das Verb (-en)**
very **sehr**
vest **das Unterhemd (-en)**
village **das Dorf (¨er)**
to visit **besuchen**
voice **die Stimme (-n)**

to wait **warten**
waiter/waitress **der Kellner (-) /
die -in (-nen)**
walk **der Spaziergang (¨e)**
to walk **(spazieren) gehen**
wall **die Mauer (-n)**
warm **warm**
to wash **waschen***
to watch TV **fern|sehen***
water **das Wasser**
to wear **tragen***
weather **das Wetter**
weather forecast **die**

Wettervorhersage (-n)
weather report **der
Wetterbericht (-e)**
wedding **die Hochzeit (-en)**
week **die Woche (-n)**
weekend **das Wochenende (-n)**
weight **das Gewicht (-e)**
well-known **bekannt**
what? **was?**
wheel **das Rad (¨er)**
when? **wann?**
whenever **wenn**
where … from? **woher?**
where? **wo?**
white **weiß**
why? **warum?**
widowed **verwitwet**
to win **gewinnen***
wind **der Wind (-e)**
windy **windig**
wine **der Wein (-e)**
winter **der Winter (-)**
woman **die Frau (-en)**
work **die Arbeit (-en)**
to work **arbeiten**
world **die Welt (-en)**
World War **der Weltkrieg (-e)**
to write **schreiben***

year **das Jahr (-e)**
yellow **gelb**
yoghurt **der / das Joghurt (-s)**
young **jung**
youth hostel **die
Jugendherberge (-n)**

Taking it further

If you have enjoyed working your way through *Complete German* and want to take your German further, why not try *Perfect your German?* You should find it ideal for building on your existing knowledge and improving your listening, reading and writing skills.

Here are just three examples of websites that you might find helpful:

http://www.goethe.de The *Goethe Institut* is represented in most countries and staff may be able to inform you about German language courses in your area. They will also have information on short intensive courses based in Germany.

http://www.austria.org for information about Austrian life and culture.

http://www.swissinfo.org for information about Swiss life and culture.

TRY SOME REAL GERMAN!

Have a go at listening to German-speaking radio and TV stations and reading German newspapers and magazines.

Whatever you try, it's best to concentrate on small extracts at first – either a video or audio clip or a short article. See how much you can work out, going over the material several times. Then look up any key words that you have not understood, and go on till you are satisfied that you have grasped the main ideas. If you do this on a regular basis, you'll find that your command of German increases steadily.

Sources of real German

- ▶ *Newspapers, magazines (e.g. Bild-Zeitung, Stern, Focus).*
- ▶ *Satellite and cable TV channels (e.g. ARD, RTL, SAT1, ZDF).*
- ▶ *Radio stations via satellite and, within Europe, on Medium Wave after dark.*
- ▶ *Internet – most German newspapers have websites where you can browse for short articles that interest you. TV and radio stations, too, have websites where you can often find audio and video clips of the latest newscasts. In some cases you will also find transcripts of the newscasts to help you if you run into difficulties with the spoken language.*
- ▶ *You can use our homepage or a German-language search engine or portal such as http://www.google.de or http://de.yahoo.com to find any of the above and lots more besides.*
- ▶ *Last but not least, we would highly recommend that you try speaking German with native-speakers, whether in your home country or in a German-speaking country. Explore Berlin, Vienna or Zürich (or any other German-speaking city) and make contact with the locals!*

Viel Spaß beim Weiterlernen!

Index to grammar

The numbers after each entry refer to the units. For a summary of grammatical terminology used in this book, see the Glossary of grammatical terms.

adjectives: *endings 13, 17, 18, 21; possessive 4, 15*

articles: *definite 5; indefinite 5*

cases: *nominative 7; accusative 7, 9; dative case 12, 15, 18; genitive case 21*

comparisons *15*

conjunctions *10, 19, 23*

direct object *18*

gender *5, 6*

indirect object *18*

infinitive *1, 9*

negation *2*

numbers *3, 5*

participles, past *13, 14*

passive voice *23*

plural of nouns *8*

possessive adjectives *4, 15*

prepositions: *+ accusative 9, 16; + accusative/dative 11, 16; + dative 12; + genitive 21; + places 20*

pronouns, personal *1, 3*

questions *yes–no 3*

subject–verb inversion *8*

superlative *16*

tenses: *present tense 1, 2, 3, 4; imperfect/simple past 20, 22; present perfect 13, 14, 20*

verbs: *endings 1, 2, 3, 4; modal verbs 11, 19, 20; position of verb 1, 8,*

10, 19, 23; separable verbs 10; with vowel change 9

word order: *position of verb 1, 8; initial items in the German sentence 10; with conjunctions 10, 19, 23*

Photo credits